THE LIMITS OF THE LAND

PERSPECTIVES ON ISRAEL STUDIES
S. Ilan Troen, Natan Aridan, Donna Divine,
David Ellenson, and Arieh Saposnik, editors

*Sponsored by the Ben-Gurion Research Institute for the Study of Israel and Zionism
of the Ben-Gurion University of the Negev and the Schusterman Center for
Israel Studies of Brandeis University*

THE LIMITS OF THE LAND

HOW THE STRUGGLE FOR THE WEST BANK
SHAPED THE ARAB-ISRAELI CONFLICT

Avshalom Rubin

INDIANA UNIVERSITY PRESS

This book is a publication of

INDIANA UNIVERSITY PRESS
Office of Scholarly Publishing
Herman B Wells Library 350
1320 East 10th Street
Bloomington, Indiana 47405 USA

iupress.indiana.edu

© 2017 by Avshalom Rubin
All rights reserved

No part of this book may be reproduced or utilized in any form or by any means, electronic or mechanical, including photocopying and recording, or by any information storage and retrieval system, without permission in writing from the publisher.

The paper used in this publication meets the minimum requirements of the American National Standard for Information Sciences—Permanence of Paper for Printed Library Materials, ANSI Z39.48-1992.

Manufactured in the
United States of America

Cataloging information is available from the Library of Congress.

ISBN 978-0-253-02888-4 (cloth)
ISBN 978-0-253-02897-6 (paperback)
ISBN 978-0-253-02910-2 (ebook)

1 2 3 4 5   22 21 20 19 18 17

TO RACHEL

CONTENTS

Abbreviations   *ix*
Note on Transliteration   *xi*
Note on Sources   *xiii*
Acknowledgments   *xvii*

Introduction   *1*

CHAPTER 1   Partition's Inheritance: The Making of the Israeli-Jordanian Entente, 1949–1962   *9*

CHAPTER 2   The Jordanian Crisis of 1963 and Its Consequences   *49*

CHAPTER 3   A Status Quo Settlement? 1964–1965   *74*

CHAPTER 4   Louder than a Bomb: Israel, Jordan, and the Palestinians, 1964–1966   *105*

CHAPTER 5   Partition's Undoing: The End of the Israeli-Jordanian Entente, 1967   *140*

CHAPTER 6   The Harvest of War, June–November 1967   *177*

CHAPTER 7   A Chance for Peace? 1968   *211*

CHAPTER 8   The Jordanian Civil War and the Seeds of Disengagement, 1969–1970   *248*

Conclusion   *289*

Sources   *293*
Index   *306*

ABBREVIATIONS

AECID	Abba Eban Centre for Israeli Diplomacy
AMAN	Intelligence Branch, Israel Defense Forces
BGA	Ben-Gurion Archives
BNA	British National Archives
CAB	Cabinet Office
CIA	Central Intelligence Agency
DDRS	Declassified Documents Reference System (electronic version)
DFPI	Israel State Archives, *Documents on the Foreign Policy of Israel*
DNSA	Digital National Security Archive
DOD	Department of Defense
DOS	Department of State
DOSCF	Department of State Central Files
FCO	Foreign and Commonwealth Office
FM	Foreign Ministry
FO	Foreign Office
FRUS	Department of State, *Foreign Relations of the United States*
GRFL	Gerald R. Ford Presidential Library
IDF	Israel Defense Forces
IDFA	Israel Defense Forces Archives
IIL	Israel Intelligence Library
INR	Department of State, Bureau of Intelligence and Research
ISA	Israel State Archives
JAA	Jordan Arab Army
JCS	Joint Chiefs of Staff

JFKL	John F. Kennedy Presidential Library
KFADC	Knesset Foreign Affairs and Defense Committee
LBJL	Lyndon B. Johnson Presidential Library
LPA	Labor Party Archives
MAC	Mixed Armistice Commission
MAP	Military Assistance Program
Memcon	Memorandum of conversation
MOD	Ministry of Defense
NA	United States National Archives and Records Administration
NIE	National Intelligence Estimate
NPT	Non-Proliferation Treaty
NSAM	National Security Action Memorandum
NSC	National Security Council
NSF	National Security Files
PDFLP	Popular Democratic Front for the Liberation of Palestine
PFLP	Popular Front for the Liberation of Palestine
PLA	Palestine Liberation Army
PLO	Palestine Liberation Organization
PREM	Prime Minister's Office
RG	Record Group
RMNPM	Richard M. Nixon Presidential Materials
Telcon	Telephone conversation
UAC	Unified Arab Command
UAR	United Arab Republic
UN	United Nations
UNEF	United Nations Emergency Force
UNRWA	United Nations Relief and Work Agency
UNTSO	United Nations Truce Supervisory Organization
WSAG	Washington Special Actions Group
YHP	Ya'akov Herzog Papers
YLE	Yad Levi Eshkol

NOTE ON TRANSLITERATION

WHEN TRANSLITERATING HEBREW AND ARABIC NAMES, TERMS, and phrases, I have relied on a simplified version of the generally accepted rules of transliteration, omitting diacritical marks and accents except for the ʻ sign to indicate the Arabic letter *ʻayn* and the Hebrew letter *ʻayin*, and the ʼ sign to indicate the Arabic *hamza*. In some cases, I have chosen to use spellings of names and places that are more familiar to English-speaking readers—for instance, Gamal Abdul Nasser rather than Jamal ʻAbd al-Nasir, King Hussein rather than Husayn, and so on.

NOTE ON SOURCES

LIKE MOST WORKS OF DIPLOMATIC HISTORY, THIS BOOK IS based primarily on declassified government documents. The opening of thousands of documents in Israel, the United States, the United Kingdom, and to a lesser extent the former Soviet Union has made it possible for historians to gain unprecedented insight into the dynamics of Arab-Israeli relations in the 1960s. Most of the relevant American and British sources have been opened to the public. Most of the relevant Israeli Foreign Ministry files, some of which contain Mossad or IDF Intelligence Branch (AMAN) documents in addition to diplomatic cables and memoranda, have also been opened for research. Nearly all of Levi Eshkol's papers and many of Golda Meir's papers have also been declassified, along with the minutes of the Knesset Foreign Affairs and Defense Committee from the 1960s. David Ben-Gurion's papers, including his diary, are available at his archive in Sedeh Boker.

Still, many important Israeli documents remain unavailable. The Israel State Archives has released cabinet minutes through the first half of 1967, but the minutes of the cabinet defense subcommittee, which made most of the important decisions on foreign policy, remained closed to the public when this manuscript was completed. Documents produced by the Mossad and the General Security Service (Shabak) are generally withheld, as are most documents dealing with Israel's nuclear history. Documents dealing with Israel's nuclear history are generally withheld. Many important discussions of the subject were probably never recorded. Nevertheless, archival material dealing with the Israeli nuclear program is not impossible to find, and more of it has been released in recent years. The IDF Archives has opened the General Staff minutes from 1967, along with many files containing intelligence and operational planning documents from the 1960s. Yet important military records, including General Staff minutes from earlier in the 1960s, were unavailable to researchers when I completed the research for this book. Some of these documents have nevertheless been published in abridged form or provided to well-connected scholars, whose findings have made their way into the public domain.[1]

In addition to publicly available Israeli archival materials, I benefited from access to private papers held by former officials. In 2008, while still a graduate student, I was granted access to papers held by Miriam Eshkol, Prime Minister Levi Eshkol's widow, as well as the private papers of Ya'akov Herzog, Eshkol's confidante and Hussein's principal Israeli contact.[2] I am grateful to both Mrs. Eshkol and Ms. Shira Herzog for permitting me to use these papers, which vastly enriched my understanding of my subject.

The greatest obstacle faced by scholars of Arab-Israeli relations is a lack of access to Arab government archives. With the exception of Nigel Ashton, no scholar that I am aware of has received access to King Hussein's papers.[3] At one time, the ISA allowed researchers to examine Jordanian intelligence documents captured in 1967, but access to these files was later severely restricted. The Israel Intelligence Library in Glilot offers scholars access to a limited number of Egyptian, Jordanian, and Syrian papers captured by the IDF in 1967, mainly operational orders and plans. I have tried to shed light on the Jordanian, Egyptian, Syrian, and Palestinian sides of this story by utilizing relevant Arabic-language memoirs, newspapers, and official publications. American and British archival materials also offered me crucial insight into Jordanian decision-making. King Hussein and other members of the Jordanian elite spoke fluent English, met frequently with Western diplomats and intelligence officers, and generally felt comfortable sharing sensitive information with them. These sources are no substitute for Jordanian documents, but they still offer a valuable window onto Jordanian domestic politics and foreign policy.

Future researchers with access to additional sources may tell a richer version of the story than I present here. Yet I am nevertheless confident that this narrative offers a full and accurate account of the events in question.

Finally, while this book began its life as a doctoral dissertation, it was completed after I began working for the US Department of State. The views expressed here are my own, and do not necessarily reflect those of the Department of State or the United States government. All US documents cited here are declassified and available to any researcher.

ACKNOWLEDGMENTS

WHEN WRITING A BOOK, ONE INEVITABLY INCURS MANY debts, financial and otherwise. Most of the research for this book was carried out while I was a graduate student at the University of Chicago. During that time, I was privileged to receive funding from a Fulbright-IIE fellowship, a Mellon first-year fellowship in the humanities, a David L. Boren National Security Education Program fellowship, and numerous grants from the University of Chicago, most importantly the Phoenix fellowship and the Mellon Dissertation Year write-up fellowship in the social sciences. I am very grateful to all of these funding sources for making it possible for me to study Middle Eastern history, polish my Arabic and Hebrew, travel to archives, and spend extended periods of time abroad.

I would like to acknowledge the assistance that I received from archivists, whose work makes research of this kind possible in the first place. I owe a particularly large debt of gratitude to Helena Vilensky and Michal Saft of the Israel State Archives, as well as Yehoshua Freundlich, the ISA's former director. Helena deserves special thanks for graciously putting up with all of my requests for documents long after I returned to the United States from Israel. I would also like to thank Regina Greenwell of the Lyndon B. Johnson Archives, Doron Aviad of the IDF Archives, Haim Gal of the Moshe Dayan Center's Arabic press library, and all the other archivists who offered me their time and knowledge. I would have found it equally impossible to conduct serious research without the language teachers who helped me whip my Hebrew and Arabic into shape over the years. In particular, I'd like to acknowledge Noha Forster, Annie Higgins and Farouk Mustafa of the University of Chicago, Hebatalla Salem and Abbas al-Tonsi of the American University in Cairo, and Irit Matmor of Ben-Gurion University. And I'd also like to thank the Freedenbergs, the Edelmans, the Hendins, the Arbels, *lishkat* Rubinstein, Ben Adler, Max Kardon, and Jordan Taylor for opening their doors to Rachel and myself during research trips to Washington, Jerusalem, Boston, and Austin. In addition to the archival and published sources used in this book, I benefited from access to two key collections of private papers: the papers of Prime Minister Levi Eshkol and the papers of Ya'akov Herzog, director-general of the Israeli prime minister's office under Eshkol and Golda Meir. I would like to thank Shira Herzog, Dr. Herzog's daughter, for granting me permission to view her father's papers, and Miriam Eshkol, Prime Minister Eshkol's widow, for sharing documents, memories, and tea with me in her Jerusalem home. I would also like to thank Maj. Gen. Shlomo Gazit (ret.) for sharing his recollections of the 1960s with me.

Along the way, I have been helped by many other historians. I would like to thank Yoav Alon, Abigail Jacobson, Guy Laron, Craig Daigle, Moshe Maoz, Benny Morris, Michael Oren, and Avi Shlaim for their input and assistance at various points. While at the University of Chicago, I benefited from the support of Ralph Austen, Orit Bashkin, and Holly Shissler. My dissertation chair, Bernard Wasserstein, deserves special acknowledgment for all of his help and good counsel. Eve Mayer and Ariel Ahram, in addition to being good friends, helped me navigate the murky process of finding a publisher.

I am exceptionally grateful to Ilan Troen for recommending this book for publication in Indiana University Press's series in Israel studies. It is an honor and privilege for me to have my book included. At IUP, I would like to thank Dee Mortensen, Paige Rasmussen, Darja Malcolm-Clarke, and Eric Levy for shepherding this book through the publication process. I would also like to thank IUP's two anonymous reviewers for their constructive criticism. I am indebted to Erin Greb for preparing the wonderful maps, and to Yvette Chin for the index.

Most importantly, I would like to thank all of my friends and my family on both the Rubin/Weistrop and Fleischer/Singer sides. For fear of leaving somebody out, I will not try to thank them all here. But I should make special mention of Gabe Chasnoff, Dan Freeman, and Benji Feldheim for their friendship over the course of many years. The Levines, Hermans, and Gurwitz-Kazhdans also deserve special thanks for all of the support they have given our family since we relocated to Maryland in 2011. So do my aunt and uncle, Penina and Sam Freedenberg, who, in addition to hosting me on several research trips to Washington, provided me with a quiet place to work on the manuscript in its final stages. I thank my grandmother, Francine Weistrop, for inspiring all her grandchildren to be curious people, and Jerome Weistrop, Sidney Rubin, and Frances Rubin, z"l. My siblings, Gabe, Judah, and Tamar, deserve much credit for keeping me amused and for being great intellectual sparring partners. I am grateful to my parents, Aviva and David Rubin, for all the love and sustenance they've given me, and for always encouraging me to learn more about the world. My wonderful children, Kobi and Amira, make sure that life is always exciting and put my intellectual obsessions into proper perspective. It is a pleasure to watch them grow. As for Rachel, I cannot imagine a better partner or friend. Her love, insight, and humor have kept me grounded and sustained me the whole way. I cannot thank her enough.

For the past six years, I have been privileged to work for the US Department of State, first as a historian and currently as an analyst. I would like to thank Nathaniel Smith, James Wilson, David Nickles, David Zierler, Laura Kolar, Paul Pitman, Seth Center, and Kathy Rasmussen for their support during my time at the Office of the Historian, and all of my current colleagues for their camaraderie and for continually enriching my understanding of the Middle East.

NOTES

1. For abridged versions of many of these documents, see Rosenthal, *Yitzhak Rabin*. For books whose writers benefited from exclusive access to certain IDF materials, see Gluska, *Eshkol*; Golan, *Milhamah be-shalosh hazitot*; and Drory, *Esh ba-kavim*. Golan wrote his book in an official capacity for the IDF's History Department. Gluska and Drory are both former IDF colonels who have gone on to become academics.

2. For other books that make use of Herzog's records, see Segev, *1967*; Raz, *Bride and the Dowry*; Zak, *Hussein 'oseh shalom*; Shlaim, *Lion of Jordan*; and Bar-Zohar, *Yaacov Herzog*.

3. See Ashton, *King Hussein*. Indeed, the material made available to Ashton apparently revealed little about the years examined here. The chapters of his book that cover the years 1952–1970 include 614 citations. Only 16 of them refer to documents from the Royal Hashemite Archives, some of which are cited two or three separate times.

THE LIMITS OF THE LAND

INTRODUCTION

WHY DID ISRAEL GO TO WAR ON JUNE 5, 1967? FOR MOST Israelis, particularly those old enough to remember the tense and frightening weeks before the war, the answer is simple: they had no other choice. Egyptian president Gamal Abdul Nasser had massed his forces in the Sinai Peninsula, ordered United Nations peacekeepers to leave, and closed the Straits of Tiran, Israel's gateway to the Red Sea. Syria, Iraq, and Jordan had all prepared for war as well. Israel struck first in order to escape destruction, and nothing more. "We have no aim of conquest," Defense Minister Moshe Dayan informed Israel's soldiers as they readied themselves for battle. "Our sole objectives are to put an end to the Arab attempt to conquer our land and to suppress the blockade and the belligerence mounted against us.... We are a small but brave people. We want peace, but we are ready to fight for our land and our lives."[1]

Few Arabs believe that the Israelis acted in self-defense. They argue that the speed and magnitude of Israel's victory in 1967 proves that the Israelis could not have feared defeat. Israel's choice to go to war must have been rooted in something more sinister—a long-standing desire to seize all of former Mandatory Palestine. When Nasser's advisor Mahmud Fawzi addressed the United Nations that June, he described Israel's campaign as "carefully planned aggression," the culmination of "the tarnished history of Israel in Arab lands, a history saturated and overflowing with aggression even—strangely enough—since before Israel was born."[2] Over the subsequent decades, arguments like Fawzi's have gained almost universal acceptance in the Arab world.

Nearly fifty years have elapsed since the 1967 war. The participants have written their memoirs, and governments have declassified millions of documents. We can finally learn why the Arabs, Israelis, and their superpower patrons behaved as they did. And indeed, over the past fifteen years or so, historians have shed much light on many of the mysteries surrounding the 1967 war, its origins, and its aftermath.[3] Yet no historian has really tried to answer two fundamental questions about Israel's strategy both before and after 1967. First, did Israel's leaders intend to widen their borders before they went to war?[4] And, if the Israelis did not plan to enlarge their territory, why did they change their minds once the guns fell silent?[5] The answers to these questions matter not only to historians, but also to anyone trying to make sense of the Arab-Israeli conflict today. On many occasions, Israeli leaders have argued that since they acted in self-defense in 1967, they should be allowed to keep territory that they conquered. "In the wake of such a war, it is not only the law, but also the practice, that territorial changes do take place, as agreed upon by the parties," declared Prime Minister Menachem Begin in 1978.[6] Those who view the 1967 war as an act of premeditated Israeli aggression, on the other hand, have argued that Israel should simply withdraw from the occupied territories without demanding anything in return.

In reality, though, wars rarely result from simple aggression by one side, whether Arab, Israeli, or otherwise. While an international lawyer or a political theorist studying the 1967 war might focus on whether Israel's decision to strike Egypt was truly an act of "anticipatory self-defense," most diplomatic historians would probably agree that such an approach does not explain the deeper causes of the conflict. Scholars of international relations tend to look for the origins of wars not in their immediate antecedents, but in the long-term shifts in balances of power between states.

When I started to write this book, I wanted to step back from the immediate prewar crisis and look at how the strategic landscape in the Middle East evolved during the two decades that preceded it. I thought that by taking a longer view, I could better understand the Israelis' goals on the eve of the 1967 war and the extent to which they hoped to acquire more territory. Understanding the Israelis' prewar aims, I thought, would also allow me to determine whether their postwar policies reflected a radical change in their outlook or simply revealed what they had wanted to do all along.

What I concluded was that contrary to the Israeli narrative, Israel's leaders *did* want wider borders. Yet contrary to the Arab narrative, the Israelis were *not* determined to expand at any cost. For Israel's leaders, the allure of territorial expansion waxed and waned depending on how they thought the great powers would respond and whether they believed there were other ways to preserve their military edge. By 1957, the Israelis believed that they could not acquire more territory without fatally compromising their ability to absorb immigrants, generate economic growth, and obtain capital, advanced arms, and diplomatic support from the West. Over the following decade, they sought a way to live within their existing boundaries by preserving Jordan's independence, building strategic ties to the United States, and building a nuclear program. In 1967, however, Israel's strategy failed to prevent war, and its leaders determined that they needed to keep some, if not all, of the Arab territory they had conquered.

To understand how the Israelis thought about the strategic importance of territory in general, I chose to examine how they felt about the West Bank in particular. Why the West Bank? Because the West Bank was, in the words of William Macomber, John F. Kennedy's ambassador to Jordan, "comparable in minuscule to Berlin."[7] Like Berlin in Cold War Europe, the West Bank was the most strategically sensitive place where two sides of a great conflict confronted each other.[8] Year after year, Israel's leaders asked themselves whether they could allow the West Bank to stay in Arab hands and how long they could go on living within their narrow boundaries while surrounded by numerous adversaries. To study the West Bank issue is to study what the Arab-Israeli conflict in the 1950s and 1960s was really all about: whether the de facto partition of Palestine that occurred in 1948 could survive changes to the Middle Eastern balance of power.

The years that followed the rise of Israel and the incorporation of the West Bank into Jordan witnessed the end of empire in the Middle East. Though the United States and the USSR rapidly moved into the vacuum left by European colonial powers, newly independent Middle Eastern states nonetheless enjoyed an unprecedented opportunity to chart their own destinies. For Nasser, this postcolonial, Cold War context offered Egypt a chance to dominate the region. Like Indonesian president Sukarno and Ghanaian president Kwame Nkrumah, his fellow postcolonial neutralists, Nasser believed that he could maneuver between the superpowers and reshape his country's strategic environment. Nasser's ambitions were not limited to the Middle East; he also sought a leadership role in the nonaligned movement and backed national liberation movements in sub-Saharan Africa. Yet the eastern Arab world was always the focus of Nasser's quest for power. Iraq, Syria, and Jordan had not been separate countries before World War I. The illegitimacy of these states in the eyes of many of their citizens made them natural breeding grounds for Pan-Arabist ideas, and provided Egypt with a chance to extend its influence into the Levant and establish itself as the dominant power in the Middle East.

Nasser's ambitions inevitably placed Egypt in conflict with Israel. For the Egyptian president and his compatriots, Israel was not only an alien colony built on usurped Arab territory, but a physical barrier between Egypt and its Arab hinterland. The essential conflict of interests between the two countries was just as apparent to Israeli policymakers and military men. For Israel, a small, regionally isolated state, it was fundamentally important that no other regional power should dominate the Middle East. "We will absolutely not agree to let Egypt have the upper hand in the Middle East," summed up one important Mossad memorandum early in 1967. "This would effectively place our fate in Egyptian hands."[9]

Though inter-Arab and Arab-Israeli relations are often treated as separate subjects, anyone who studies the Arab-Israeli conflict during the age of Nasserism is struck by how intertwined they were. The Arab-Israeli balance of power was never determined solely by the number of tanks and planes that either side had in its arsenals. From 1954 until 1967, the Arab-Israeli conflict was shaped by Egypt's efforts to achieve hegemony within the eastern Arab world, which played out in a series of contests over the political orientation of the weaker Arab states.

Jordan was one such bellwether state, and since it contained the West Bank, its inter-Arab orientation was incredibly important to the dynamics of Arab-Israeli relations. As one British analyst put it, the West

Bank was "the only starting point from which an invading army could hope to overrun Israel's principal centers of population, administration, and communication and to do lasting damage to her physical assets, before outside intervention . . . could become effective."[10] If a stronger Arab state could deploy its army on the West Bank, Israel could become intolerably vulnerable to surprise attack. In the late 1950s and early 1960s, the heyday of Pan-Arabism and Arab unification schemes, the possibility that the West Bank would become a staging area for Egypt or Iraq seemed real.

In the early 1950s, Israel's leaders hoped to eventually conquer the West Bank. After the Soviet Union and the United States forced them out of the Gaza Strip and the Sinai Peninsula in 1957, however, the Israelis concluded that they had no chance of expanding their territory through war. To live with their existing boundaries, they needed a Jordanian partner who would keep the West Bank a buffer zone until Egypt no longer threatened the Middle Eastern balance of power. They found one in King Hussein, who desperately needed allies willing to help protect his regime against its numerous opponents and preserve Jordan as an independent state.

And so, beginning in 1958, Israeli policymakers set aside their doubts about the staying power of the Hashemite monarchy and their dreams of conquering the West Bank. They lobbied for Hussein in Washington, kept a watchful eye on his domestic enemies, and made it clear that they would go to war to prevent another Arab state from taking over Jordan. For his part, Hussein worked to absorb Jordan's Palestinians into their surrounding society, suppressed cross-border infiltration, and kept non-Jordanian troops out of his kingdom. By 1965, this Israeli-Jordanian entente gained staunch support from the United States, whose leaders had come to appreciate its importance for regional stability. It now seemed less likely than ever that Jordan would merge with another Arab state, especially following Egypt's failed union with Syria and its disastrous intervention in Yemen. It appeared unlikely that Arabs and Israelis would go to war over the West Bank before Israel acquired nuclear weapons, which its leaders believed would shift the regional balance of power decisively in its favor and render its lack of strategic depth irrelevant.

So why did Israel still end up conquering the West Bank? I argue that the Israeli-Jordanian entente was ultimately destroyed by two formidable forces: resurgent Palestinian nationalism and the superpowers' commitment to nuclear nonproliferation. By 1967, Fatah and other Palestinian guerrilla organizations had almost wrecked King Hussein's effort to merge Jordan's East and West Banks. Fear of popular unrest forced Hussein to place his army under Egyptian command and allow non-Jordanian troops into his kingdom. When this critical moment arrived, Israel chose to launch a preemptive strike rather than rely on its nascent atomic capability. Not wanting to alienate the United States or provoke Soviet intervention on the Arabs' behalf, the Israelis chose war over deterrence.

The 1967 crisis thus led to preemptive war, territorial conquest, and the beginning of a protracted Israeli-Jordanian diplomatic struggle over the West Bank. For Israeli policymakers, the 1967 war illustrated that a nuclear capability was no substitute for strategic depth. It was no coincidence that Yigal Allon, perhaps the most prominent prewar critic of the Israeli nuclear program, also authored the most important Israeli plan for the future of the West Bank. Though the fate of the West Bank was never put to a vote, Israel's leaders generally agreed with Allon's argument that Israel needed to detach the area from its "great Arab hinterland" by keeping the Jordan Valley.[11] The problem was that Hussein envisioned a return to the prewar boundaries, or something close to them. And the United States, the patron of both parties, was unwilling to break the stalemate.

The longer that stalemate continued, the less support Hussein could expect from both West Bank Palestinians and other Arab leaders. By 1970, Palestinian guerrilla organizations nearly succeeded in toppling the king. Hussein managed to reestablish his control over Jordan's East Bank, but at the price of his claim to represent the Palestinians living under Israeli occupation. The stage was set for Jordan's eventual disengagement from the West Bank, and the reemergence of the basic problem that preceded the birth of Israel: how Palestine should be divided between Arabs and Jews.

NOTES

1. Dayan's message was quoted by Israeli permanent representative Gideon Rafael in his remarks at a meeting of the UN Security Council on June 5, 1967. For the verbatim record of this meeting, see the United Nations Information System on the Question of Palestine (UNISPAL), https://unispal.un.org/DPA/DPR/unispal.nsf/9a798adbf322af f38525617b006d88d7/cd0beba6a1e28eff0525672800567b2c?OpenDocument.
2. See Fawzi's remarks to the UN General Assembly on June 21, 1967. The verbatim record of this session of the General Assembly can be found at UNISPAL, https://unispal.un.org/DPA/DPR/unispal.nsf/9a798adbf322aff38525617b006d88d7/e5704ad6 5dd33b11052565fc0055fd3d?OpenDocument.
3. For recent scholarship on the 1967 war, see Oren, *Six Days of War*; Gluska, *Eshkol*; Shemesh, *Meha-nakbah la-naksa*; Shalom, *Diplomatiyah be-tsel milhamah*; Ro'i and Morozov, *Soviet Union*; Golan, *Milhamah be-shalosh hazitot*; Segev, *1967: Israel*; Ginor and Remez, *Foxbats over Dimona*; Louis and Shlaim, *1967 Arab-Israeli War*.
4. To the extent that scholars have addressed the question of Israel's war aims, they have done so in short academic articles narrowly focused on the immediate prewar crisis. Avi Shlaim and Michael Oren have both argued that Israel's behavior during the May–June 1967 crisis demonstrates that its leaders wanted to avoid war and had no plans for territorial conquest. See Oren, "Did Israel Want the Six Day War"; and Shlaim, "Israel: Poor Little Samson." Roland Popp, who makes no use of Israeli archival material, has argued that the Israelis did not feel threatened and sought to take advantage of a strategic "window of opportunity" while they could. See Popp, "Stumbling Decidedly."
5. Avi Raz and Gershom Gorenberg have written illuminating accounts of the early years of Israeli rule over the occupied territories. Still, they say little about how Israel's leaders thought about their state's borders before 1967 or how the war transformed their strategic thinking. See Raz, *Bride and the Dowry*, esp. 266–270; Gorenberg, *Accidental Empire*, esp. 7–53.
6. "Statement by Prime Minister Begin at the National Press Club—Washington—23 March 1978," in Medzini, *Israel's Foreign Relations*, 377.
7. Gilpatrick-Macomber memcon, August 27, 1963, JFKL/NSF/Robert Komer Papers, box 429.
8. On the Cold War in Europe through the early 1960s, see especially Trachtenberg, *Constructed Peace*.
9. "Appendix C: Topics for Dialogue with Egypt," unsigned, undated (early 1967), ISA /FM/4091/19.
10. G. Maclean, "War between Israel and Jordan," September 27, 1965, BNA/FO/180653.
11. Labor Party political committee minutes, June 3, 1968, ISA/A/7921/13.

Israel, 1949–1967

ONE

PARTITION'S INHERITANCE

The Making of the Israeli-Jordanian Entente, 1949–1962

FROM 1949 ONWARD, ISRAEL'S LEADERS WERE ALL TOO AWARE of how easily an Arab army could reach Israel's largest cities, roads, and military bases from Jordan's West Bank. No matter what, the Israelis would have worried about their neighbor to the east, but the fact that Jordan seemed to have no future gave them particular cause for alarm. The Hashemite kingdom was a British imperial creation in an age of decolonization, a weak state in a time of Pan-Arab unity schemes, a monarchy in an era of populist coups. It seemed like only a matter of time before Jordan merged with a stronger Arab state, leaving Israel to face a powerful adversary along its narrowest frontier.

Until 1956, Israel's leaders hoped to conquer the West Bank before it became part of a much larger Arab state. The Suez War, however, forced Israeli prime minister David Ben-Gurion to accept the territorial status quo and to see Jordan's King Hussein as the one man who could keep the West Bank a buffer zone between Israel and its stronger Arab enemies. Hussein recognized the shift in the Israelis' outlook, and the two sides reached a tacit deal. Hussein would keep his border quiet and keep other Arab armies out of the West Bank. In exchange, Israel would advocate for Jordan in Washington and deter Hussein's Arab rivals from toppling him.

But this Israeli-Jordanian entente was still shaky. Hussein was unpopular at home and regarded ambivalently by the Americans, now his principal patrons. The Israelis still had to assume that the king might not survive, and that Jordan would merge with Syria, Egypt, or Iraq if he fell. Until Hussein's regime grew stronger or the regional balance of power shifted decisively in Israel's favor, Ben-Gurion and his colleagues would continue to wonder whether they should allow the West Bank to remain in Arab hands.

FROM PARTITION TO PEACE?

Late in 1953, the Jerusalem correspondent for the London *Times* vividly described how Israelis and Jordanians viewed the long, winding armistice line that separated Israel's coastal plain from the hill country of Jordan's West Bank. "Most Arabs," the reporter wrote, "find it hard to understand the sense or purpose of frontiers. . . . Even less can they understand the purpose of a frontier that cuts off a village from its cultivable land or its water source." For Palestinian refugees who had fled to the West Bank in 1948, "the whole idea of the frontier" was "more than the ill-nourished flesh and hot blood of most of them can stand." The Israelis, on the other hand, had "become more frontier conscious than most other peoples have the misfortune to be." In West Jerusalem, Israel's government met daily in offices that could be shelled from the east side of the city, which the Jordanians controlled. The highway from Tel Aviv to Haifa lay "for more than half its way through a thin strip of coastal plain where the distance from frontier to sea is in places less than 10 miles wide, and where large coastal centers of trade and industry, such as [Netanyah], are within easy gunshot of the border." Passengers on Israel's only railway line could "look straight from their compartment windows into Jordan, and come so close to the Jordan towns of Qalqiliya and Tulkarm that they can throw a cherry stone through the window into the street below."[1]

Simply put, the Israeli-Jordanian armistice line was not the sort of fence that made good neighbors. It separated Israelis from the Jewish holy sites of the Old City of Jerusalem and offered them little strategic depth. It cut the fields and villages of West Bank Palestinians in half and barred others from their former homes and family members. It was a recipe for irredentism.

But the tense scenes that defined life along the Israeli-Jordanian frontier in 1953 had not seemed inevitable six years earlier. In November 1947, Jordan's King Abdullah and the leaders of the Zionist movement had secretly agreed to peacefully divide Palestine between themselves. While David Ben-Gurion and his compatriots publicly supported the UN plan to partition Palestine into Jewish and Arab countries, they privately shuddered at the thought of a state ruled by Palestinian nationalist leader Haj Amin al-Husayni. The wily, ambitious Abdullah offered the Zionists a solution. The son of a venerated Arabian family that traced its lineage to the prophet Muhammad, Abdullah had been the architect of his father Husayn's alliance with Britain against the Ottoman Empire during World War I. Afterward, the British had installed him as the ruler of the newly created Transjordan, an arid backwater with no major cities and a population that was still half-nomadic in 1922. For Abdullah, as Mary Wilson has written, "Transjordan was but the threshold to greater power." He dreamed of ruling Syria, where his brother Faysal briefly reigned, and Palestine, where he courted both al-Husayni's Arab opponents and the Zionists.[2] In the fall of 1947, as the UN debate on Palestine drew to a close, Abdullah met with Zionist officials and struck a bargain. Jordanian troops would take over the area that the United Nations allotted to the Palestinian Arabs, but would not enter the territory designated for a Jewish state.

The Palestinian Arabs' rejection of partition, followed by Arab-Jewish civil war and Pan-Arab invasion in May 1948, allowed the Israelis to regard the UN plan as a dead letter. Thereafter, they extended the boundaries of their state as far as they could push the invading Arab armies. Still, the fundamentals of Abdullah's prewar understandings with the Zionists were upheld.[3] Fighting on the Israeli-Jordanian front was confined mainly to the Jerusalem area and the Latrun salient. Jordan's Arab Legion, commanded by the British general John Bagot Glubb and accompanied by Iraqi forces, took most of the Jordan Valley and the mountain ridge overlooking it without bloodshed.

Of course, if postwar outcomes reflected prewar understandings, it was partly because outside forces prevented both sides from advancing any further. When ammunition shortages forced the Arab Legion to halt, Abdullah's British patrons made no effort to help him gain more territory.[4] In the fall of 1948, when the Israel Defense Forces (IDF) reached the peak of their power, Prime Minister Ben-Gurion considered pushing the Arab Legion across the Jordan. Fear of British intervention, however, held Israel back, and the IDF aimed its last thrusts at the Egyptian army instead.⁵ Nevertheless, both Israel and Jordan still acquired large amounts of land at the Palestinians' expense. Even after Abdullah relinquished the Wadi 'Ara area to Israel in their April 1949 armistice agreement, he held onto 5,440 square kilometers of newly conquered territory.⁶ The Israelis now controlled nearly 6,000 square kilometers more than the partition plan had granted them.⁷ Given the scope of their conquests and the war-weariness of their societies, both the Israeli leadership and Abdullah had good reason to favor a settlement based on the status quo.

Yet after signing the armistice agreement, both Ben-Gurion and Abdullah hesitated to talk peace. Abdullah hoped that the British and American governments would force Israel to give him a corridor of land that would connect Jordan to the Mediterranean Sea and Egypt. And Ben-Gurion could not decide whether to accept the Israeli-Jordanian armistice line as a permanent border.⁸

"Uncertain" was not a word often used to describe "the Old Man," as Ben-Gurion's supporters reverently called their white-haired, sharp-tongued leader. Domineering, visionary, and decisive, Israel's prime minister was at the height of his powers in 1949. He had come a long way from his humble beginnings in Plonsk, Poland, where he and his siblings had survived on the meager wages that their father earned writing legal documents on behalf of Polish peasants.⁹ Though Ben-Gurion was often gruff and awkward, his tremendous intelligence and single-minded devotion to the cause of Jewish statehood allowed him to rise above his modest background and propelled him to the forefront of the socialist-Zionist camp in Palestine. A committed Jewish nationalist who studied the Bible obsessively, he was also ruthlessly pragmatic, and had long viewed partition as a necessary evil in order to bring a Jewish state into being. His realism had led him to accept both the 1947 UN partition plan and the 1949 armistice with Jordan. Publicly, Ben-Gurion ridiculed Menachem Begin's right-wing, revanchist Herut party, which called for a Jewish state on both banks of the Jordan, and the left-wing, socialist Mapam, which called for conquering the remainder of Palestine and establishing an Arab state ruled by "progressive elements."¹⁰

But while Ben-Gurion scorned his political rivals' high-flown rhetoric about Israel's "historic borders," he shared his military commanders' doubts about the defensibility of the armistice lines. Many of the IDF's best officers wanted to keep fighting, especially veterans of the Palmah, an elite Zionist commando force that had been disbanded in 1948. The Palmahniks' desire to seize all of Mandatory Palestine was motivated by both strategic and ideological considerations. Many were followers of Mapam, most prominently IDF Southern Command chief Yigal Allon. Unlike Ben-Gurion and his generation, who grew up in Eastern Europe, Allon had been born in a small village in the Galilee. All the qualities that the prime minister and his contemporaries worked hard to attain—mastery of Hebrew, intimacy with the land, physical toughness—belonged to Allon from birth. He had never known a time when he was not fighting Arabs over territory. Upon celebrating his bar mitzvah, Allon had been handed a Browning semiautomatic by his father and sent out to guard their fields that night.[11]

On the eve of the armistice with Jordan, Allon made it clear that he was not done fighting yet. He personally implored Ben-Gurion to seize the West Bank. "There is no need for a perfect military education to understand the permanent danger to the peace of Israel from the presence of large hostile forces in the western land of Israel—in the [Jenin-Nablus-Tulkarm] Triangle and the Hebron Hills," Allon wrote to the prime minister.[12] Not one to be ordered around, Ben-Gurion sharply rebuked the young commander. At the same time, he shared Allon's fear that what remained of Arab Palestine would become part of a much larger Arab state. "An Arab state in the western part of the land of Israel is less dangerous than a state connected with Transjordan, and perhaps tomorrow Iraq," he had written in his diary in December 1948.[13] The fact that Iraq was ruled by a branch of Abdullah's Hashemite dynasty added to Ben-Gurion's worries.

But Ben-Gurion had not yet lost hope of peace with Jordan. Abdullah was more willing to negotiate than any other Arab leader, and the British and the Americans also supported a Jordan-first approach to peacemaking.[14] And so, on November 26, 1949, Ben-Gurion met with a small group of Israeli diplomats and described his conditions for talks with Abdullah. The prime minister did not intend to demand major changes to the armistice lines, but he still wanted to guarantee that the West Bank would not become a staging area for more powerful forces.

Ben-Gurion wanted assurances that Britain would build no bases west of the Jordan River, and that the Anglo-Jordanian Treaty of 1948 would not apply to the West Bank. He also wanted the Jordanians to know that Israel would regard any agreement as null and void if Jordan merged with another Arab state.[15] By making such demands, the prime minister intended to guarantee that Israel could seize the West Bank without provoking Britain's wrath if a stronger Arab army moved into Jordan.

In the end, the Israelis and Abdullah never discussed the fundamental strategic questions bound up with the West Bank's future. Though Israeli and Jordanian representatives initialed a draft nonaggression pact in February 1950, Abdullah's cabinet refused to accept it.[16] Officially, the Jordanian ministers rejected the pact because it called for renewing trade with Israel, but the real sources of their opposition ran deeper. Before 1948, Jordan, generally regarded as the Middle East's most artificial country, actually had many characteristics of a strong state. Though the kingdom depended on a British budgetary subsidy and military assistance, it still had a strong army and a functioning central government, and its powerful tribes were well-integrated into state institutions.[17] By 1950, however, it was clear that Abdullah's foray into Palestine had, in the words of British ambassador Alec Kirkbride, transformed "the tribal patriarchy of Transjordan into the pseudo-democracy of Jordan complete with the nationalistic ideologies of a modern Arab state."[18] The king now ruled over approximately 950,000 Palestinians, about half of them refugees. Many resented the idea of being ruled by a British-backed monarch from the Arabian Peninsula, and fervently opposed peace with Israel.[19] The Jordanian ministers feared that by approving a nonaggression pact with Israel, they would hand their Arab foes an opportunity to stir up Palestinian opposition to the annexation of the West Bank, which they had planned for that April.[20]

The events of the spring of 1950 affirmed Ben-Gurion's skepticism about negotiating with Abdullah. "Transjordan," Ben-Gurion told Reuven Shiloah, one of his advisors on Arab affairs, "is not a natural and stable entity but a single person—totally dependent on Britain, who could die at any moment." Given Jordan's cloudy future, why should Israel permanently confine itself to the armistice boundaries, even for a peace agreement? "Do we really have an interest in these ridiculous borders?" Ben-Gurion asked.[21] On July 20, 1951, a Palestinian assassin shot and killed Abdullah in Jerusalem. It seemed like only a matter of time before Israel's "ridiculous borders" were redrawn.[22]

TOWARD A SECOND ROUND

Miraculously, Jordan did not disintegrate after Abdullah's death. During his long reign, the king had assembled a talented coterie of advisors, many of them transplanted Palestinians or Circassians who had no independent power base and were totally devoted to the Hashemite house. Led by Prime Minister Tawfiq Abu al-Huda, a dour, cautious Palestinian who had worked for Abdullah since the 1920s, these "king's men" managed to form a new government, hold parliamentary elections, and install Abdullah's son Talal on the throne without bloodshed. The following year, Abdullah's inner circle shepherded Jordan through another succession crisis when Talal, long prone to depression and bouts of violent and erratic behavior, proved unfit to rule. The Hashemite crown now passed to Talal's son Hussein, who was crowned king on his eighteenth birthday in May 1953.[23]

The young King Hussein had endured great hardship in the years leading up to his coronation. He had stood at his beloved grandfather's side when he was shot, witnessed his father's mental collapse, and bounced to and from six different schools in Amman and Alexandria before completing his education at Harrow and Sandhurst Military Academy in Britain. The one real source of stability in his life was his mother, Queen Zayn, a brilliant, powerful woman whose deft handling of court politics led one observer to dub her "the Metternich of the Arab world."[24] In retrospect, one can see that Hussein's early experiences left him with qualities that served him well as a monarch: resilience, cosmopolitanism, a sense of dynastic duty, and physical courage. Yet at the time, outsiders looked at Hussein, with his squiggle of a mustache and boyish frame, and concluded that Jordan was doomed. In Israel, skepticism about the Hashemite monarchy's future naturally led to talk about whether and when the IDF should seize the West Bank.

The failure of peace talks, the Arab economic boycott of Israel, persistent border warfare, and a constant barrage of anti-Semitic and anti-

Zionist rhetoric from Arab leaders and the Arab press led Israel's leaders to wonder when the next war would come and whether they should fight while they still had the upper hand. During the early 1950s, the Israeli national security establishment oscillated between positions staked out by Foreign Minister Moshe Sharett and future IDF chief of staff Moshe Dayan. A careful, compromising man, Sharett was far more sensitive than Ben-Gurion about how Israel was perceived by the outside world. Privately, he decried "the glaring inconsistency between our complete objective dependence on the support and sympathy of the world [on the one hand] and our subjective mental isolation from the world [on the other]."[25] Like most of Israel's political elite, Sharett hailed from Eastern Europe, but he had more empathy for Arabs than many of his peers did, having spent his initial years in Palestine living in an Arab village. Sharett was skeptical about territorial expansion. Israel, he believed, "should avoid any military adventure explicitly aimed at conquering additional area and at expansion." By initiating wars of conquest, Sharett thought, Israel would isolate itself internationally, destroy its chances for peace, and bring large numbers of Arabs under its rule, jeopardizing the country's Jewish majority.[26]

Dayan felt otherwise. Unlike his fellow Palmahnik and rival Yigal Allon, who was extroverted and popular, Dayan was a solitary, unknowable man, whose mystique was enhanced by the black eye patch he had worn since losing an eye while battling Vichy French forces in Lebanon. Like Allon, however, Dayan's worldview was shaped by the rough-and-tumble environment of the lower Galilee, where he was born in 1915. By the time he was ten years old, he could milk cows, drive mules, and, most importantly, handle a gun. As a teenager, Dayan both befriended and fought Bedouin boys who lived near Nahalal, his family's settlement. As an adult, he empathized with the Palestinian Arabs' connection to the land while maintaining a fierce resolve to defeat them.[27] Dayan often accused Sharett and other dovish Israelis of misunderstanding the intensity of Arab nationalism. He was convinced that the Arabs' desire for revenge made renewed conflict certain and that the military balance would shift against Israel as time passed. Israel, Dayan argued, should conquer additional territory, particularly the West Bank, while it still could.[28]

For the most part, Dayan's fellow officers also believed that Israel needed more land. Otherwise, they thought, there was no way that the country could continue to protect itself from numerically superior Arab foes. As Arab armies grew, they would eventually be able to easily overrun Israel's small standing army and reach the country's heartland before Israel could mobilize its reserves for a counterattack. LAVI, the IDF Operations Branch's 1953 war plan, assumed that Arab forces could conquer Israel's coastal plain in forty-eight hours if they caught the IDF unprepared.[29] Perhaps Israel could prevail if it mobilized its reserves in time, but an early call-up carried other risks. If the IDF stayed mobilized too long, the Israeli economy could grind to a halt. By 1952, full mobilization would require 19 percent of Israel's Jewish citizens to leave their farms, factories, and shops.[30] No matter how good the IDF's early warning capabilities were, Israel was bound to mobilize either too early or too late.

Increasingly, Israel's senior military commanders thought that Israel needed to choose when the next war took place. Operations Branch planners prepared for preemptive and even preventive war. War plans from 1951 called for attacking the Arab states five to seven days before an anticipated assault. By 1952, Operations Branch planners thought Israel should prepare for war if the Arab states demonstrated *any* readiness to fight, even if there were no signs of an imminent attack. By striking first, the IDF's strategists wanted to deny the initiative to the enemy, safeguard the home front, and allow reserves to mobilize. But they also clearly hoped that by quickly taking the fight to enemy territory, Israel could redraw its borders. One June 1951 war plan defined Israel's war aim as "removing the Arab states from the battlefield before they can initiate hostilities, with the goal of defending the existence of the state and rectifying its borders." Another 1951 plan called for "straightening the borders" by conquering Gaza, the West Bank, and southern Lebanon.[31]

And it was not only Israel's generals who felt squeezed by the armistice lines. Certainly, Sharett and senior Foreign Ministry officials tended to worry more that an aggressive foreign policy might taint Israel's international image. As professional diplomats, they were also more inclined to believe that negotiations could mitigate, if not actually resolve, Israel's conflicts with its Arab neighbors. Still, they too recognized that renewed war was likely and that the West Bank posed unique security problems. Even before Abdullah's death, Sharett worried that Jordan might unite with Iraq, creating an "Arab empire" on Israel's narrowest frontier.[32] By 1953, the foreign minister believed that Jordan was "disintegrating," a view shared by his staff.[33]

Though Sharett and his colleagues did not advocate preventive war, they did toy with resolving Israel's border problems through covert action. Among those who considered gaining strategic depth through subterfuge was Abba Eban, who served simultaneously as Israel's ambassador to the United States and to the United Nations until 1959. South Africa–born and Cambridge-educated, the tall, portly Eban had already acquired a reputation as a gifted diplomat and a spellbinding orator. Celebrated abroad, in Israel he was often regarded as pompous and out of touch. His bookish Zionism, acquired through years of studying Hebrew literature and Jewish history with his grandfather, sat poorly with Israelis who preferred tough farmer-soldiers like Allon and Dayan.[34] Yet when it came to the West Bank, Eban wanted to redraw the border just as much as his contemporaries from the Palmah did. "There is no chance of fixing the situation by military means," he wrote to Ben-Gurion and Sharett, but perhaps Israel could court Palestinian separatists on the West Bank and convince them to federate with Israel. Doing so, Eban argued, would "effectively annex the Triangle to Israel, thereby releasing Israel from the suffocation of the existing border."[35] Eventually a Foreign Ministry committee concluded that a Palestinian separatist movement would likely align itself with Egypt, Syria, or Haj Amin al-Husayni, and decided not to sponsor one.[36] But the fact that Eban wanted to do so illustrates the extent of Israeli discontent with the status quo.

In any case, the final say on Israel's national security policy lay with the cabinet, particularly the Mapai party and Ben-Gurion, who served as prime minister and defense minister until briefly retiring from government at the end of 1953. Like his generals, Ben-Gurion was deeply pessimistic about the prospects for peace. Israel's remaining Arab interlocutors, he thought, were "interchangeable gangs who murder each other ... dynasties that are rotten to the core."[37] He too worried that time was working against Israel. "We won [in 1948] not because our army always conducted itself gallantly, but because the Arab armies were rotten," he wrote. "Will this always be the case?"[38] Though Ben-Gurion thought the Arab world would remain hampered by poverty and authoritarianism, he was frightened by its tremendous advantages in population and natural resources. He viewed the Arab world as a single sociopolitical unit that could be unified and mobilized by a powerful and charismatic leader.[39] Like his generals, Ben-Gurion also worried about Israel's lack of strategic depth.[40] And the Israeli-Jordanian armistice line, in Ben-Gurion's view, was especially problematic because there was "always a danger that [Jordan] will unite with Iraq or Syria or both."[41]

But Ben-Gurion also understood that every action that Israel took to improve its security could involve trade-offs and countereffects. Wider borders might be desirable, but they were not an absolute good. Unlike the territorial maximalists in Mapam (most of whom, including Allon, left to form the Ahdut ha-'Avodah party in 1955) and Herut, Ben-Gurion had no fixed vision of Israel's historic borders. Israel's boundaries, he thought, would be dictated by the circumstances of the moment, not by rigid ideological precepts.[42] And the great powers did not seem willing to allow Israel to expand. In 1950, the United States, Britain, and France had issued a Tripartite Declaration guaranteeing the armistice lines. The Anglo-Jordanian Treaty also remained in force. Ben-Gurion knew that by initiating a war for territory, he would risk alienating the Western powers, derailing Israel's efforts to absorb Jewish immigrants, and exposing Israel to pressure to make territorial concessions. He would also risk losing the support of more dovish Mapainiks and the liberal General Zionists, who by 1952 had assumed a key role in his governing coalition.[43]

Hence, although Ben-Gurion contemplated seizing the West Bank on a few occasions, each time he fell short of gaining the domestic support and the international mandate that he knew he needed to do so. After Abdullah's death in 1951, Ben-Gurion told the cabinet that he would order the IDF "to go to the Jordan" if Iraq and Jordan united.[44] To ensure the support of great powers, he hoped to convince Winston Churchill that Israel's "need to reach the Jordan, and possibly Suez too" could serve British interests.[45] Yet stability returned to Jordan, and the Western powers remained reluctant to strengthen Israel at the Arabs' expense. In 1953, Ben-Gurion tried again, suggesting that the IDF capture part of the West

Bank in response to acts of violence and sabotage perpetrated by Arab infiltrators.[46] Staunch opposition from his cabinet, however, forced him to abandon the idea.[47] When Ben-Gurion retired to his kibbutz at Sedeh Boqer later that year, Israel still seemed unprepared to try to expand its borders by force.

THE OTHER SIDE OF SUEZ

In 1954, Israel's strategic environment dramatically changed. In Egypt, Col. Gamal Abdul Nasser emerged as the undisputed leader of the Free Officers regime that had toppled the Egyptian monarchy in 1952. The son of a postal clerk and a veteran of the 1948 war, the dashing, eloquent Nasser inspired millions of Arabs who had made the hard journey from countryside to city and yearned to eradicate what remained of European colonialism in the Middle East. By July 1954, Nasser had fulfilled the long-standing Egyptian dream of getting the British to agree to withdraw from their massive base in the Suez Canal zone. The strategic fulcrum of the Middle East now shifted to Iraq, which joined Britain, Turkey, Iran, and Pakistan in the so-called "Baghdad Pact" alliance in the winter of 1955. To mollify Nasser, who castigated the Baghdad Pact as an anti-Egyptian conspiracy, the Eisenhower administration agreed to provide Egypt with $40 million in economic aid, and tried to bribe him to take US military assistance.[48] Fearing Soviet encroachment, the Western powers appeared determined to court increasingly independent Arab states, regardless of the consequences for Israel.

Not surprisingly, the Anglo-Egyptian Treaty and the Baghdad Pact transformed the Israeli debate about preventive war. During 1954, Sharett, who became prime minister following Ben-Gurion's retirement, fought an uphill battle against Defense Minister Pinhas Lavon and Dayan, whom Ben-Gurion had appointed IDF chief of staff before his departure. Lavon and Dayan argued that the status quo was intolerable and that Israel needed to act, while Sharett opposed a "war of choice."[49] In hope of avoiding conflict, Sharett sent out peace feelers to Nasser and pleaded with the United States and Britain to admit Israel into a regional defense pact. Both of Sharett's efforts failed.[50] Israel remained a regional pariah without external backing, while the military balance seemed to be tilting against it. In February 1955, Ben-Gurion returned to the defense ministry, and joined Dayan in pushing for retaliatory operations in response to violence along the Egyptian border. Both men hoped that border clashes would eventually spiral into war.

But there were two important brakes on Israel's slide toward war. The first was Sharett, who remained prime minister until November 1955, and often mobilized the cabinet against Ben-Gurion and Dayan. The intra-Israeli dynamic only shifted after Nasser signed a major arms deal with Czechoslovakia in September 1955, turning Israel's remaining doves into activists.[51] The great powers provided the second brake. Nasser's opposition to the Baghdad Pact, advocacy of nonalignment, and decision to purchase weapons from the Soviet bloc irked the Americans and the British, but neither abandoned hope of winning him over. To entice the Egyptian president, US president Dwight Eisenhower and British prime minister Anthony Eden promoted peace plans that would have obliged Israel to relinquish parts of the Negev. Wary of provoking more Anglo-American pressure, Ben-Gurion overruled the General Staff's calls for preventive war.[52] Only after Nasser nationalized the Suez Canal Company in July 1956 did Ben-Gurion think that Israel could secure great power support for an assault on Egypt. By October, the French were willing to back an Israeli attack, but Ben-Gurion wanted the British on board as well. Otherwise, the prime minister worried, Israel might end up fighting Britain over Jordan.

By this point, it looked as though the Hashemite kingdom would almost certainly be devoured by its neighbors. During 1954 and 1955, parties like the Ba'th, the Jordanian Communist Party, the Arab Nationalists Movement, the Muslim Brotherhood, and the Liberation Party, which drew heavily on Palestinian support and opposed Jordan's ties to Britain, all gained ground.[53] In December 1955, tensions between the monarchy and its opponents exploded in massive riots over whether Jordan would join the Baghdad Pact. For Hussein, the pull of British patronage could no longer counter the push of domestic anti-imperialism, backed by a rising Egypt. Not only did Jordan not join the Baghdad Pact, but the king unceremoniously expelled John Glubb from Jordan on March 1, 1956. The

Arab Legion was renamed the Jordan Arab Army (JAA), and Jordanian officers replaced Glubb and his British colleagues.[54] By dispensing with Glubb, Hussein made it clear to Queen Zayn and his grandfather's old cronies that he would have the final say on matters of policy, and gained more respect from his subjects. Yet at the same time, the king's gamble badly damaged his ties to the power that had preserved his dynasty and state for decades.

In Israel, Glubb's ouster was seen as yet another attempt by Nasser to attain regional hegemony. The Egyptian leader, Sharett wrote shortly after Glubb's removal, wanted to "pave the way to West Asia and further the encirclement of Israel."[55] For the most part, however, the Israelis worried about what Britain, not Egypt, would do with Jordan. From London, Israeli ambassador Eliyahu Elath reported that the British wanted Iraq to take over Jordan, thereby empowering their major regional client and preventing Hussein's fall.[56] Since the Anglo-Jordanian Treaty was still in force, any Israeli attempt to prevent an Iraqi-Jordanian merger could lead to Israeli-British war. By September 1956, the possibility of such a conflict seemed very real. With border violence rising and pro-Nasserist forces predicted to do well in Jordan's upcoming parliamentary elections, Britain began encouraging Iraq to send troops to Hussein's aid.[57]

Ben-Gurion nevertheless believed that a solution could be found that would satisfy both Israel and Britain. For him, the obvious answer was to partition Jordan between Iraq and Israel. That way, Israel could redraw its eastern border *and* Britain could build a strong Hashemite counterweight to Egypt. Israeli diplomats had suggested dividing Jordan to their British counterparts as early as May 1956.[58] With war on the horizon, the idea moved to the top of Ben-Gurion's agenda. During the British-French-Israeli talks at Sevres that preceded the Suez War, Ben-Gurion described his plan for remapping the Middle East to French premier Guy Mollet. Nasser, Ben-Gurion proposed, should be toppled. Part of Lebanon would become a Christian state, while Israel and Syria would swallow the rest. And Jordan would be partitioned between Israel and Iraq, where large numbers of Palestinian refugees would be resettled.[59]

Though the French, British, and Israelis never discussed Ben-Gurion's ideas at length, Israel's prime minister returned from Sevres confident that his allies would allow the IDF to take the West Bank if properly provoked. The Protocol of Sevres, which finalized the terms for the assault on Egypt, obliged Israel not to attack Jordan, but also obligated Britain not to intervene if Jordan attacked Israel.[60] Ben-Gurion believed that the British would allow Israel to "do whatever we want to do" so long as the JAA moved first.[61] "If [Jordan] attacks, it is not a problem, but quite the opposite," he told one colleague.[62] The Israeli prime minister's hopes were well founded. Jordan was moving rapidly toward war. On October 21, the kingdom held the freest parliamentary elections in its history. Opposition politicians, including Communists, Ba'thists, and members of the Liberation Party and the National Socialist Party, won eighteen out of forty seats in Jordan's Chamber of Deputies. Hussein formed a government headed by the National Socialist Party's Sulayman al-Nabulsi, and signed a mutual defense pact with Egypt, Syria, and Saudi Arabia. Jordan now seemed certain to fight if Israel struck Egypt.[63]

Indeed, when the IDF invaded the Sinai, Hussein immediately phoned Nasser and told him that he was ready to attack Israel. Only a last-minute change to the JAA's battle plans prevented Jordan from entering the war. Chief of Staff 'Ali Abu Nuwar feared that Israel's air force would decimate his troops if they advanced across the coastal plain, and ordered an assault on the hills southwest of Jerusalem instead. The new plan, however, required Syrian and Saudi troops to take part, and they had not yet arrived in Jordan. While the JAA waited, the Egyptians contacted Hussein and asked him to cancel his attack. According to Abu Nuwar, Hussein could not contain his disappointment. Was there any possibility that the offensive could proceed? he asked. The chief of staff gently dissuaded the young, excitable monarch, and the JAA stayed on the sidelines.[64]

Suez ended without Israel conquering the West Bank, but that outcome was largely a matter of circumstance and chance. France and Britain had freed the Israelis to move against Jordan, and Hussein nearly gave them a pretext to do so. But the years that followed saw Israeli-Jordanian relations take a different turn. Conscious of their rapidly changing regional environment, the leaders of both countries sought a modus vivendi.

THE POST-SUEZ INTERREGNUM

Contrary to Ben-Gurion's hopes, Israel failed to remap the Middle East in 1956. Though Egypt's army faltered on the battlefield, Nasser managed to turn his military defeat into a diplomatic triumph. The UN General Assembly voted overwhelmingly for Britain, France, and Israel to withdraw their forces from Egypt. Eisenhower threatened to punish the invaders economically, while Soviet leader Nikita Khrushchev blustered about using nuclear weapons. Over the next few months, the invading armies drew back. Ben-Gurion believed that he had no alternative. If Eisenhower sanctioned Israel, he thought, "we'll be finished."[65] The Israeli prime minister thought that in the coming years, Israel would need the United States to provide it with arms and counter the pressure that the USSR had exerted so brutally on Egypt's behalf.[66] "Without weapons, especially in the air, we will be lost," he wrote in his diary. "... I cannot be responsible for forcing the IDF to fight when it can be defeated. ... I am not prepared to take on this grave danger for the sake of Gaza."[67]

The crowded refugee camps of the Gaza Strip provided Ben-Gurion with another reason to withdraw. Prior to Suez, Israel's leaders had no clear plan for what to do with the West Bank and the Gaza Strip if the IDF conquered them. Some influential figures, like Shiloah and Eban, spoke of establishing a Palestinian state or autonomous regime. Others, like Yitzhak Rabin, head of IDF Northern Command, hoped that "it would be possible to remove" most of the West Bank's Palestinians, allowing Israel to secure a "geographic area that would be easy to defend in the event of a third round."[68] Israel's occupation of the Gaza Strip, though brief, allowed its leaders to see that the events of 1948 would not repeat themselves. Gaza's refugees did not flee, and tentative Israeli proposals to resettle them aroused scant interest from US and UN officials.[69] By March 1957, Ben-Gurion thought that prolonged occupation would saddle Israel with the same problems that plagued colonial powers all over the world. "How can we provide for 200,000 refugees and 60,000 settled inhabitants?" he wondered. "And the political danger is even greater. There is no doubt that the refugees will commit acts of terror. Can we repress them, the way that the British are doing in Cyprus and the French

David Ben-Gurion and Golda Meir discuss the situation on Israel's borders with UNTSO chief of staff E. L. M. Burns, 1956. Israel Government Press Office/Teddy Brauner.

in Algeria? Without a solution to the refugee problem—meaning, their resettlement in an Arab country—the Gaza Strip is a curse and a danger under any condition."[70]

But if Israel could not widen its borders, how would it meet its long-term strategic needs? For the moment, Ben-Gurion thought that his country could rely on conventional deterrence. "Our physical security is more or less safe for the next few years, so long as Russia doesn't want to destroy us by force," he remarked.[71] Still, how long could the IDF's conventional military edge last—especially if the USSR continued to sell arms to the Arab states? Even if Israel could buy advanced weapons abroad, the Arabs' vast manpower reserves would eventually allow them to prevail in the arms race if they acquired similar equipment. If Israel could not expand its boundaries, then it had only two long-term strategic options: either it could attain weapons that rendered the conventional military balance irrelevant, or it could convince one or both superpowers to guarantee its safety.

Thus, in 1957, Israel began to pursue both atomic weapons and clearer commitments of American support. Just before Suez, Ben-Gurion had authorized Shimon Peres, the youthful director-general of the Defense Ministry, to seek French help in establishing a nuclear program. Prone to intellectual flights of fancy and grandiose schemes, Peres was nevertheless a natural political operator who easily found friends within France's disorganized and divided bureaucracy. In October 1957, Peres's efforts paid off when the French agreed to construct a nuclear reactor outside Dimona in the Negev desert.[72] But the nuclear project would take years to complete. In the meantime, Israel could not allow the conventional balance to shift in the Arabs' favor. Its leaders needed to acquire arms and convince the superpowers to help prevent war, and in practice that meant convincing the United States. (Ben-Gurion believed that a US-Soviet agreement to guarantee the security of Middle Eastern states was "95 percent impossible" at the time.[73]) Jordan would soon become the testing ground of the compatibility of Israel's quest for security with America's search for a new Middle Eastern order.

THE CRISES OF 1957 AND 1958

Suez intensified the struggle over the future of Jordan's political system and diplomatic orientation. The war emboldened the Jordanian Left, which now pushed the government to abrogate the Anglo-Jordanian Treaty. Publicly, Hussein endorsed Prime Minister Sulayman al-Nabulsi's efforts to pursue a subsidy offered by Egypt, Saudi Arabia, and Syria, but he secretly pressed US officials to take up Britain's burden.[74] Yet the king failed to persuade the Americans that aid to Jordan would be money well spent. Secretary of State John Foster Dulles, a former Wall Street lawyer famed for both his brilliance and his self-righteousness, spoke for most US policymakers when he described Jordan as "an artificial country," a British "trick device."[75] Despite his reputation as an arch anti-Communist, the aloof, brusque Dulles claimed to be "not much alarmed" about the possibility of Jordan becoming a Soviet satellite.[76] Hussein therefore had no alternative to Arab aid. On January 19, 1957, he signed an Arab Solidarity Agreement with Egypt, Saudi Arabia, and Syria, which promised Jordan an infusion of 12 million Egyptian pounds annually for ten years.[77]

Privately, however, Hussein had no intention of either moving into Nasser's orbit or allowing his opponents to take control of Jordan. The king worked to force a confrontation with al-Nabulsi and attain American backing before it was too late. The long-anticipated showdown between the monarch and his enemies occurred that April, when al-Nabulsi demanded that Hussein fire several veteran royalist officials. The king ordered the prime minister to resign, while crushing a coup plot supposedly masterminded by 'Ali Abu Nuwar. By May, Hussein emerged victorious, having imposed martial law, banned political parties, arrested al-Nabulsi and several hundred others, and exiled Abu Nuwar and his purported co-plotters to Syria. The king's triumph impressed the Americans, who decided that he deserved at least temporary support. The Eisenhower administration sent the US Sixth Fleet into the eastern Mediterranean and declared "the independence and integrity of Jordan" to be "vital." Afterward, the United States gave Jordan $10 million in budgetary aid, followed by two additional aid packages that summer.[78]

Initially, Ben-Gurion and his colleagues were pleased with the outcomes of the April 1957 crisis. Relieved that Jordan had not fallen under Nasser's sway, Israeli officials began discussing how they could help preserve Hussein's regime. That summer, a Foreign Ministry committee recommended that Israel secretly supply Hussein with intelligence and assure him that the IDF would not try to take the West Bank while he remained in power.[79] More broadly, the Israelis thought the crisis proved that the United States wanted to block Egypt's regional ambitions. They now hoped that Eisenhower would throw his support behind a non-Arab bloc consisting of Israel, Turkey, Iran, and Ethiopia, pitting the Americans against Nasser without building up Egypt's Arab rivals.[80]

Yet it soon became clear that American and Israeli interests diverged. Eisenhower and his advisors did not oppose Pan-Arabism per se. Many senior American officials were prepared to endorse mergers between Arab countries so long as they respected Western interests and opposed Communism.[81] For the Americans, support for Arab unity carried an added bonus: it would allow the United States to pass on the costs of supporting Jordan to other Arab countries. As Dulles said, the United States did not want Jordan to fall "into the clutches of Egypt," but also did not want to finance a country that "had never been a viable state."[82] The Eisenhower administration thus sought to build an anti-Nasser Arab bloc. The National Security Council's January 1958 Middle East policy guidelines called for the administration to support "the union of two or more Arab states" and to "discreetly encourage a strengthening of ties among Saudi Arabia, Jordan, and Iraq, with a view to the ultimate federation of two or all of these states." Israel was expected to express "continuing acquiescence" in such schemes.[83]

By 1958, Israel's leaders feared that Jordan would inevitably be absorbed by a Soviet-backed Egyptian-Syrian bloc or a Western-backed Iraq. That winter, when Egypt and Syria merged into a single country, the United Arab Republic (UAR), Foreign Minister Golda Meir feared that Jordan might be next to join. Even more than Ben-Gurion, Meir tended to see the Arab world as an undifferentiated mass. A salty, plain-spoken woman from a poor family that had fled Russia for Milwaukee, Meir ran away from home at fifteen after her parents tried to marry her off to a much older man. She eventually found a refuge in Zionism, where her formidable work ethic and organizing abilities catapulted her to the top of the movement's largely male leadership. None of her talents, however, allowed her to overcome her childhood fears of anti-Semitic violence. "Being frightened," she later wrote, "is the clearest of all my memories."[84] Deeply worried that Jordan might join the UAR if Hussein were overthrown, she proved equally anxious when Iraq and Jordan formed a conservative "counterfederation," the Arab Union. Secretly, Meir ordered her diplomats to try to convince the Iraqis to adhere to the Israeli-Jordanian armistice; the idea of demilitarizing the West Bank was also first discussed in Israeli diplomatic circles at this time.[85] But there was really no way that Israel could back Hussein wholeheartedly so long as he could unite Jordan with a neighboring state.

The fall of the Iraqi monarchy solved that problem. On July 14, 1958, a clique of Iraqi army officers led by Brigadier 'Abd al-Karim Qasim staged a coup d'état in Baghdad. The entire Arab world appeared to be falling into Nasser's grasp. In Washington and London, Eisenhower and British prime minister Harold Macmillan scrambled to answer pleas for help from Lebanese president Camille Chamoun and King Hussein. On July 15, British chargé d'affaires Barbara Salt asked Ben-Gurion to let RAF planes overfly Israel to save the Hashemite monarchy.[86]

This time, Ben-Gurion did not look for an excuse to conquer the West Bank. Partly he was reluctant to take responsibility for more Palestinians. Hours after the Iraqi coup, the prime minister had rejected IDF chief of staff Chaim Laskov's proposal to seize the Hebron hills and the West Bank's central mountain ridge. "This time, [the Palestinians] won't run away!" he wrote in his diary, perhaps thinking of Israel's recent experience in Gaza.[87] He later told his cabinet that he did not want to "have to confront [the West Bank Palestinians] with bayonets." Israel, Ben-Gurion proclaimed, could not "keep tabs on a million Arabs, among them 400,000 mortal enemies [e.g., refugees], whose houses and fields we took."[88]

With Suez in mind, Ben-Gurion also had little faith that the superpowers would allow Israel to hold the West Bank. If Israel seized the West Bank, he warned his cabinet, the United States and the Soviet Union could "pull an Algeria on us," alluding to France's quarrels with the superpowers over its refusal to relinquish its North African colony.[89] "Everything depends on the international situation," he remarked a week later. "If America and Russia are opposed, then we have no chance of taking anything by force." Ben-Gurion did not rule out military action if a pro-Nasser government seized power in Jordan. He planned to order the IDF to seize Jerusalem's Mount Scopus, "secure access to the [Old City of Jerusalem's] Jewish Quarter," and possibly take the sparsely populated Hebron Hills as well. But the prime minister ruled out preemption until "Nasser or the men from Baghdad stand outside Netanyah."[90] "The best thing for us is if the status quo persists [in Jordan]," he argued that October. "Then, we have no issue with Egypt, Syria, or Iraq, only with a weak state that's not to be feared."[91]

Thus, Ben-Gurion convinced his government to allow the Western powers to prop up Hussein. The key debate took place on July 17, when the prime minister told his cabinet that he planned to let Britain fly 1,500 soldiers through Israeli airspace into Amman. Ministers from Mapam and Ahdut ha-'Avodah protested. They thought that Israel should not take sides in inter-Arab disputes, lest it alienate African and Asian states or provoke the USSR. But Ben-Gurion and Meir were adamant. For Meir, there was just one question that mattered: "Can we allow ourselves to be surrounded on all sides by Nasser or not?" Ben-Gurion felt the same. Though he feared the USSR, he was more afraid of angering the United States and allowing a pro-Nasserist government to take over Jordan. "The greatest question facing us," he said, "is the question of time, if we have enough time to *retrench, retrench, retrench.*" Israel required years of quiet to absorb immigrants, grow economically, and gain "more military power." To do so, the country would need to avoid war and stem the tide of Nasserism for as long as it could. "It's possible that the process of unification in the Arab world is inevitable," Ben-Gurion argued. "But if it takes years, that has great value for us. If it had happened fifteen years ago, there would be no Jewish state." Israel had an interest in having "weak neighbors around us," rather than an Arab world unified under Nasser's leadership. "I am not afraid of Lebanon..." Ben-Gurion said, "and I do not see any danger in Hussein, even if I don't love him." The cabinet voted to allow the overflights, which continued into the fall of 1958.[92]

The Israelis did not think that Britain's rescue of Hussein solved their long-term problems. Once American and British forces departed the Middle East, Eban told Dulles, "Israel would be left alone amidst augmented xenophobia."[93] During the fall of 1958, Ben-Gurion and his diplomats lobbied the Americans for security guarantees, arms, and promises to neutralize the West Bank if Hussein were overthrown.[94] At first, the Israelis tried one last time to get the Americans to consider partitioning Jordan. If Hussein fell, Eban suggested to one State Department official, the East Bank could unite with Iraq, while the West Bank could become "some kind of autonomous political unit" linked with Israel.[95] When the Americans responded coolly, Ben-Gurion adopted what would become Israel's default position regarding Hussein's overthrow. On October 26, he told the London *Times* that if the status quo in Jordan changed, he would insist on the "complete demilitarization of the West Bank," international guarantees of Israel's frontiers, and the "implementation" of the armistice agreement's Article 8, which promised Israel access to Mount Scopus and the Jewish Quarter of Jerusalem's Old City.[96] Behind Ben-Gurion's conditions lurked an implicit threat: if the Western powers wanted to keep Israel from seizing the West Bank, they would have to continue propping up Hussein or find some other way to neutralize the area.

But in the end, Israel did not reap major benefits from the Jordan crisis of 1958. Despite Ben-Gurion's decision to permit British overflights, Eisenhower and Dulles refused to offer Israel security guarantees. "Sometimes an undefined relationship was somewhat more dependable," Dulles disingenuously told Eban.[97] Even after Khrushchev sent Ben-Gurion a note blasting Israel's role in the airlift, Dulles would not pledge to defend Israel from a Soviet or Arab attack.[98] The Americans proved no more forthcoming with arms, rejecting Ben-Gurion's requests for heavy weapons such as tanks, submarines, and Hawk antiaircraft missiles.[99] And they declined to discuss the demilitarization of the West Bank, lest doing so encourage Israel to conquer it. "All parties involved," Dulles told Meir, should "refrain from taking action that might disturb the situation."[100]

For the foreseeable future, Israel's basic security problems, especially those posed by the West Bank, would persist. Not only did Nasser enjoy unprecedented popularity in the Arab world and Soviet backing, but the United States now began courting him too. For many American officials, the 1958 crisis demonstrated the futility of confronting Nasser, while subsequent events seemed to show that he was not a Communist stooge after all. After the Iraqi strongman Qasim purged his pro-Egyptian colleagues and drew closer to the Iraq Communist Party, Nasser jailed Egyptian Communists and publicly attacked the USSR.[101] By December 1958, the State Department agreed to provide Egypt with wheat, marking the beginning of US efforts to draw Nasser away from the Soviets. The Americans "see only the communist danger," Ben-Gurion grumbled. "We see the Nasser danger."[102] From the Israeli perspective, America's tilt toward Egypt did not bode well for Jordan, either. As US relations with Nasser warmed, would the Americans continue to back Hussein and preserve Jordan's independence?

Israel's leaders now had more compelling reasons than ever to back Hussein. The king's survival now offered the best guarantee that the West Bank would not become a staging area for more powerful Arab armies. With the Iraqi monarchy gone, Hashemite Jordan could not conceivably unify with any of its Arab neighbors. The Israelis now wanted to bolster Hussein and convince the Americans to do the same. And the king and his supporters understood this perfectly.

JORDAN'S ISRAEL OPTION

When news of the Iraqi coup reached Jordan, Hussein begged British and American officials to help him invade Iraq and put the Hashemites back in power. "If Iraq and the Gulf went," he asked, "what would be Jordan's place in the Arab world?"[103] Britain's intervention only temporarily cooled the Jordanian leadership's anxieties. They knew that British troops would not stay in Jordan and that they would have to find a way to survive in a vastly different Middle East. They also did not feel that they could depend on their Western benefactors. Perhaps, speculated Prime Minister Samir al-Rifa'i, the Americans and the British had already decided that "Hussein must eventually go as [the] price [of] Jordan['s] accommodation with its surrounding neighbors."[104]

And in fact, the Jordanians were right to fear that the Americans wanted to give them up. A desire to disengage from Jordan pervaded the highest levels of the Eisenhower administration. Even as Dulles backed Britain's intervention in the summer of 1958, he griped about the pointlessness of preserving Jordan as a separate state. To "maintain this citadel is not profitable," he said, since Jordan would not survive "even if we spent all this money."[105] Many, if not most, American officials felt the same. "Over the long-run," argued one interagency intelligence estimate, "we have little confidence in Hussein's ability to hold his throne, or, indeed, in the viability of Jordan as a state."[106] By November 1958, the National Security Council defined US support for Hussein as an "obstacle to our establishing a working relationship with Arab nationalism." The United States, argued one key policy paper, should encourage Jordan's "peaceful political adjustment" to a postcolonial, Nasserist age, which could involve Jordan's "partition, absorption, or internal political realignment."[107]

The thrust of American thinking was no mystery to the Jordanian elite. Dulles and his subordinates could be quite blunt. In October 1958, for example, the secretary told 'Abd al-Mun'im al-Rifa'i, Jordan's UN ambassador, that Jordan was "essentially an artificial state carved out of the old Palestine Mandate by the British to serve as a strategic base in the area" and that a "long-range solution" to the country's problems depended on an "honorable understanding with its neighbors."[108] But the Jordanians did not reject such prognoses outright. Prime Minister al-Rifa'i himself admitted that Jordan was "a nonviable state, created originally by [the] British in their own national interest."[109] Rather than try to prove the Americans wrong, the king and his advisors tried to convince them to revive the monarchy in Iraq or remove Syria from Egypt's grip. The UAR, 'Abd al-Mun'im al-Rifa'i told Dulles, would "not ... necessarily prove permanent," and Hussein's "special qualifications" might allow Jordan to unify with Syria and Iraq.[110] The old Hashemite dream of Greater Syria, Prime Minister al-Rifa'i told State Department officials, might still be attainable, since Syria was an "unhappy colony of Egypt." "The only solution to the long-term problem of Jordan's viability," he argued, "is the unity of Jordan and Syria."[111]

But the Americans and their British junior partners were not interested in a Hashemite restoration in Iraq, nor in Hussein's dreams of Greater Syria. In October 1959, when Iraqi Ba'thists nearly assassinated Qasim, Hussein readied the JAA to invade Iraq. Convinced that a Jordanian invasion would be a fiasco, the Americans and the British implored Hussein to stand down, and the king had no choice but to hold back his troops.[112] Hussein's plans for Syria got a similarly unenthusiastic reception in Washington. The United States would oppose Jordanian military action against Syria, Assistant Secretary of State William Rountree told al-Rifa'i, even though "the outlook for Jordan as a separate and independent state is not bright."[113] In August 1960, when a bomb planted by UAR agents killed Jordanian prime minister Hazza' al-Majali and eleven others, the Americans warned Hussein not to invade Syria in response. A Jordanian attack, Eisenhower informed Hussein, "could easily be disastrous, not only for Jordan, but for the area as a whole and indeed for the world."[114]

Presumably, Jordan's leaders had to ask why the United States helped them at all. If the Americans wanted to disengage from Jordan and align with Egypt, then why were they prolonging the inevitable, at the cost of large sums of money and Nasser's potential goodwill? The answer, of course, was that the Americans feared that the "disintegration of Jordan" could lead to Arab-Israeli war and a "very dangerous chain reaction in the international field," as Dulles put it.[115]

Though Jordan's leaders did not know what the Americans said about their country in private, they understood that Israel's threats to take the West Bank deterred Nasser and prevented the Western powers from withdrawing their support from Jordan. During the 1958 crisis, when Israeli radio broadcasts declared that the IDF would not take the West Bank if a coup occurred, Queen Zayn called on British ambassador Charles Johnston and demanded that such transmissions stop.[116] When UN secretary-general Dag Hammarskjold suggested that UN peacekeepers deploy on the West Bank, Hussein and his government turned the idea down. A UN force, they told Hammarskjold, would eliminate the threat of Israeli invasion and untie Nasser's hands.[117]

The Jordanian leadership clearly believed that radical Arab nationalism, not Israeli expansionism, was now the main threat to Jordan's survival. "Syria and Iraq," al-Rifaʻi remarked in December 1958, "[are] much more of [a] problem in this country than Israel."[118] Jordan's leaders, noted Johnston, "understand fully that Israel is on their side, wishes them well, and . . . is prepared to help them within practicable limits."[119] And Hussein was determined to keep it that way.

THE DEAL

By the early 1960s, an Israeli-Jordanian entente was taking shape. At its core lay a shared commitment to keeping the West Bank a buffer zone. This commitment was never formally articulated by Hussein or the Israeli government, but it was clearly understood by both sides.

The Israelis fulfilled their part of the bargain by promising Hussein that they did not covet the West Bank and by deterring Nasser and his Syrian allies from bringing him down. In October 1959, when Hussein prepared to invade Iraq, the Israelis informed him through Iranian channels that they "would not move against Jordan if the Jordanian army became involved in Iraq."[120] When UAR agents assassinated Jordanian prime minister al-Majali in 1960, Ben-Gurion sent Hussein a secret message promising that Israel would pose no threat if Jordan attacked Syria.[121] When Hussein sent back an emissary asking whether the IDF would help Jordan repulse a Syrian counterattack, Ben-Gurion ordered Chaim Herzog, the head of AMAN (the IDF's intelligence branch), to reply that Israel "would do all that it could to safeguard their security."[122] Months later, when the Israeli intelligence community concluded that Egyptian troops were preparing to invade Jordan via Syria, Ben-Gurion warned American diplomats that Israel would attack the UAR if Nasser were not reined in.[123] The Israelis also quietly shared intelligence with Hussein about the many coup and assassination plots that his enemies devised against him. The full extent of these exchanges will probably never be revealed, but they clearly continued into the early 1960s.[124]

At the same time, the Israelis sought to make Jordan a stronger, more viable country. Israeli officials were all too aware of how pessimistically many US officials felt about Jordan's economy. They believed that the Americans were more likely to continue helping Jordan if they thought they were making a lasting contribution to regional stability, not just providing life support for a terminally ill patient.[125] Golda Meir and her diplomats therefore did everything they could to persuade the Americans that Jordan could be made viable, offering pointers from Israel's experience with forestry, land management, and mining.[126] Meir wanted so badly for these efforts to succeed that she even allowed her diplomats to promote US aid for Jordanian industries that competed directly with Israeli economic interests.[127] Such was the depth of the Israelis' desire to strengthen the Jordanian state.

In return, Israel could rely on Hussein to avoid unity with Jordan's "republican" neighbors, keep other Arab armies out of the kingdom, refuse Soviet weapons, and invest foreign aid in East Bank infrastructure and industry, thus speeding up the dispersion and resettlement of the kingdom's Palestinian refugees.[128] Since inter-Arab rivalries were fierce and most ordinary Jordanians despised Israel, Hussein could only go so far. In public, the king remained just as anti-Israel as his radical counterparts. But privately, the king made a point of telling Western diplomats that he rejected the idea of solving the Arab-Israeli conflict militarily and regarded the UAR as his principal enemy, knowing that such messages would reach Israeli ears.[129] Following al-Majali's assassination, the king responded warmly to Israeli messages of support conveyed by Emmanuel Herbert, a British-Jewish doctor who both was a friend of Israeli ambassador Elath and treated several members of the Jordanian royal family. "It was very important that during difficult times we had nothing to fear from this side," Hussein instructed Herbert to tell his Israeli contacts. "Over the years, a growing confidence has been established, which has quieted the border. One day it will be possible through the UN to reach an honorable agreement. Now that contact has been established, we can look forward with increasing confidence to the future."[130]

While the Israelis found Hussein's message heartening, they never assumed that their tacit understandings or clandestine contacts with the king pointed toward a diplomatic breakthrough. "If Egypt does not make peace, no one will dare. . . . It's enough that the Jordanians are keeping the border quiet," Ben-Gurion told his cabinet in 1959.[131] The "deal" with Jordan was just a part of Israel's larger effort to keep the conventional military balance in its favor until its strategic circumstances dramatically improved. And it was still not clear whether the regional balance of power was shifting in Israel's favor or not. By the early 1960s, the Israelis had good reason to feel more hopeful, but in many respects their future still looked dark.

On the positive side, it no longer seemed like Arab unity was inevitable, or that Jordan could never survive as an independent state. For Nasser, the heady days of July 1958 soon gave way to setbacks: first his feud with Qasim, then the collapse of the UAR in September 1961. "Today, Hussein's fall does not mean a pro-UAR government in Jordan the way it did two months ago," IDF chief of staff Tsvi Tsur told the cabinet. "Before, we faced a unified force on two sides, but today, we face a divided force which has never managed to unify. It seems doubtful that they will now try to establish a framework which will include Jordan and Iraq."[132]

No longer threatened from the north, Hussein could attend to festering domestic problems that had long hindered Jordanian economic development. In the fall of 1961, the king permitted Jordan's first parliamentary elections since 1957, and appointed a new cabinet of young technocrats led by Prime Minister Wasfi al-Tal, an aggressive and energetic alumnus of the American University in Beirut. Raised in Irbid, where anti-Hashemite feelings were much more widespread than in southern Transjordan, al-Tal had been a devout Pan-Arabist as a youth. As a teenager, he once tossed an old mortar shell packed with explosives into a district governor's office to protest Abdullah's moderation on the Palestine issue. After fighting in the 1948 war, however, al-Tal developed a sober appreciation of Israel's power and a deeply critical view of Arab societies. Arabs, al-Tal thought, should align themselves with the West and devote their energies to internal reform, not futile wars or premature unity schemes. As prime minister, al-Tal worked energetically to root out bureaucratic corruption and accelerate economic growth, with impressive results.[133] For the first time since Suez, it seemed like Jordan might survive the age of Nasserism intact, a possibility of enormous consequence for Israel's security.

Yet as one American assessment put it, neither political nor economic independence were "within immediate sight" for Jordan.[134] It would take several years for al-Tal's reforms to yield definitive results, and who knew what would happen in the meantime? The Israelis still questioned America's commitment to the Hashemite monarchy, and had no illusions that Nasser had gained more respect for the sovereignty of his rivals. Stung by the collapse of the UAR, Nasser would now "try to undermine every state in the Arab League," predicted Tsur. Ben-Gurion warned, "He will now try to take over Jordan, since the whole West Bank is pro-Nasserist.... All that's necessary is for one bullet to hit Hussein."[135]

And if Nasser wanted to undermine his Arab enemies, the Israelis thought, the superpowers would not stand in his way. From 1958 through 1962, Israel's leaders worried that the United States and its allies were losing ground to the USSR and the nonaligned nations. As early as 1959, IDF chief of staff Laskov predicted that the coming of nuclear parity between the superpowers would encourage Egypt to act more aggressively.[136] By the time the Berlin Wall went up in 1961, many other Israelis shared his pessimism. The international scene, Rabin thought, was "more dire than any time since the second world war"; the West was in the process of "protracted withdrawal."[137] Ben-Gurion spoke of "American weakness despite Russian aggressiveness." "The whole West," he said, "has no courage."[138] By 1962, AMAN concluded that Nasser no longer feared that the IDF would attack if Egypt intervened elsewhere in the Arab world. Israel's intelligence analysts believed that the Egyptian president was confident that his "network of diplomatic connections with both East and West" would hold Israel back.[139]

From the Israeli perspective, the international context also had grave implications for the Arab-Israeli arms race. After eight years of arm's-length dealings with the Eisenhower administration, the Israelis had welcomed the youthful, ebullient John F. Kennedy into the White House in 1961. Ben-Gurion and his advisors believed that Kennedy, a Democrat who had campaigned hard for Jewish votes, could only be an improvement. They would later conclude that they had only been partly correct. Though pleased that Kennedy agreed to sell them Hawk antiaircraft missiles, the Israelis disliked Kennedy's attempts to court nonaligned countries, including Nasser's Egypt. During the first two years of Kennedy's presidency, the United States vastly expanded its economic assistance to Egypt.[140] Though the Israeli intelligence community acknowledged that economic aid might give the Americans some leverage over Nasser, they believed that this hardly compensated for the fact that it freed up resources for Egypt to buy more Soviet weapons.[141] Between 1960 and 1962, Egypt received an estimated $570 million worth of Soviet military assistance, including MiG-21 fighters, Tu-16 bombers, T-54 tanks, and surface-to-air missiles.[142] The Israelis were convinced that if both superpowers continued to aid their enemies in this way, they would lose the arms race. Israel could not compete indefinitely against "states who are getting their equipment at cheaper prices and have unlimited opportunities to equip themselves," Rabin argued in 1959.[143] Eventually, Ben-Gurion predicted, the qualitative gap between Israeli and Arab armed forces would disappear and "quantity would decide."[144] By early 1963, AMAN believed that Israel could soon begin to "collapse beneath the burden" imposed by the arms race; it could not "carry it alone forever."[145]

The more weapons the Arabs acquired, the more Israel's lack of strategic depth mattered. The so-called "Rotem" episode of February 1960, when Nasser suddenly moved six infantry and three armored brigades into Sinai following an IDF raid on Syria, demonstrated how easily Israel might be caught off guard.[146] At one time, the IDF could have absorbed a surprise attack and mobilized for a counteroffensive, but could it still pull off such a feat? The outcome of the next war would depend heavily on air power, and Israel's narrow borders and small number of military airfields meant that most of its warplanes could be wiped out if Egypt struck first. Within three years, Ben-Gurion told his cabinet in March 1961, the Arabs might be able to destroy Israel in a surprise attack.[147] Presumably, Israel would be even harder pressed if the IDF had to fend off Iraqi, Syrian, or Egyptian troops advancing from the West Bank. "The principal threat," argued Gen. Meir Zorea of the Operations Branch in 1959, "is likely to come from Jordan."[148] Four years later, Chief of Staff Tsvi Tsur made a similar argument. "The problem will be if a Nasserist force sits in Jordan, alongside the center of the country," he told the cabinet. "If the Syrians launch a war from the Golan Heights—I know exactly what the answer is ... but if Nasserist forces sit in Qalqiliya, Tul Karm, and Jerusalem—it's not so simple."[149]

Before Suez, the trajectory of the arms race and Israel's lack of strategic depth inspired Ben-Gurion and his generals to consider preventive war and territorial conquest. But by the early 1960s, expansionist ideas had fallen out of favor with Israel's leaders. Ben-Gurion, who dominated the government's national security discussions, remained skeptical about territorial expansion. "We will not seize the West Bank," he told his cabinet in September 1960. "In my opinion, the state of Israel will cease to exist if it has another million Arabs."[150] In Ben-Gurion's view, Israel could not expect to gain much through war. The next Arab-Israeli clash, he told the Knesset Foreign Affairs and Defense Committee in 1963, would be far more bloody and destructive than its predecessors. Even if Israel won, the cost might be more than its populace, most of them newly settled immigrants, could bear. "We would undoubtedly win," Ben-Gurion said, "but I don't wish for such a victory. We would pay a high price."[151]

"What we need," Ben-Gurion wrote in his diary in 1962, is "deterrence, not victory in war."[152] In 1959, he told the General Staff that the IDF should avoid initiating war at all costs, unless Nasser blockaded the Straits of Tiran, Israel's gateway to the Red Sea.[153] During the Rotem crisis of 1960, Ben-Gurion chose to mobilize only some of Israel's reserves, fearing that a full call-up would provoke Nasser to attack.[154] Better, he thought, for Israel to avoid war and solve its basic security problems in other ways.

Despite Ben-Gurion's pessimism about the West's ability to resist Soviet pressure, he hoped that the Berlin Crisis might end in a superpower settlement that would have positive spillover effects on the Middle East. From 1960 through 1962, Ben-Gurion pressed Eisenhower, Macmillan, and Kennedy to join Khrushchev in calling for a "mutually acceptable" Arab-Israeli settlement, based on the territorial status quo.[155] If the United States and the USSR both called for Arab-Israeli rapprochement, he told Kennedy, "there is no doubt that it will be done, for Egypt will not be able to stand up against the two powers which it needs so badly in its most vital affairs."[156] Yet unwilling to trust Israel's fate to the vicissitudes of the international system, Ben-Gurion also pressed on with the nuclear project. For the prime minister and his protégé, Deputy Defense Minister Peres, the Dimona reactor offered Israel its best chance to maintain a credible deterrent and become a force to be reckoned with on the global stage.[157]

It is possible that Israel's generals might have advocated more aggressive policies had they been left to their own devices. While no evidence suggests that the General Staff seriously considered preventive war during this period, the IDF brass was clearly more willing than Ben-Gurion to risk conflict. According to Rabin, the General Staff launched the retaliatory raid that preceded the Rotem crisis to "test the intentions of the UAR" in light of its "increasing, ceaseless provocations" on the Syrian border and against Israel-bound ships in the Suez Canal. The General Staff presumed that Nasser would back off, but if he chose to fight, "better now than in three years, or any time determined by the UAR."[158] This was not the thinking of men who desperately wanted war, but Israel's generals were certainly not blind to the benefits of fighting before Egypt became stronger.

Moreover, even if the General Staff no longer entertained the idea of *preventive* war as seriously, they definitely favored *preemption* if faced with an imminent threat. In January 1959, the General Staff unanimously agreed that Israel should strike the first blow if an Arab attack seemed certain, and at no time before 1967 did they change their minds.[159] Chief of Staff Tsur spoke for most of his compatriots when he argued that the difference between landing and not landing the first blow was "like night and day." If the IDF could "begin a few hours early and put the air force into action, we could gain command of the air and our victory would be practically guaranteed," he told the cabinet in 1963. "If someone attacks us, it's another story altogether."[160]

But did the IDF's offensive ethos indicate that its commanders still hungered for more land? Certainly there remained some powerful irredentist voices in the Israeli armed forces, most notably Ezer Weizman, who headed the Israeli air force from 1958 until 1966. As a pilot, Weizman was particularly sensitive to the armistice lines' proximity to Israel's cities and bases. Each time an Israeli plane flew to Jerusalem or the Ramat David airbase outside Haifa, he later recalled, it nearly strayed into enemy airspace.[161] Israel, he told the General Staff, needed to find a "more historical solution" to its strategic problems by conquering the West Bank and the Sinai.[162] But Weizman's expansionist views made him something of an oddball. Later he recalled how his lectures about "a unified Jerusalem and Hebron and Nablus and the Land of Israel within its natural borders" inspired bewilderment and unease among his fellow officers. "It was taboo," he wrote. "It was forbidden to talk about the borders of the Land of Israel, forbidden to speak of Jerusalem."[163]

Indeed, by the early 1960s, most of the IDF brass seem to have regarded the armistice lines with grudging acceptance. Many Israeli officers drew the same conclusions as Ben-Gurion did in 1956. "We all lived in the shadow of [Suez]," recalled Israel Tal, who led the Armored Corps for much of the post-Suez period. "We didn't think we could hold the territories."[164] The IDF's 1961 war plan, MATTITYAHU, acknowledged that Israel could live comfortably with a Jordanian-controlled West Bank so long as Hussein stayed in power.[165]

While the General Staff often complained that they had insufficient influence over nuclear matters, its top two commanders apparently shared Ben-Gurion's view that atomic weapons, rather than territorial expansion, would ensure Israel's survival.[166] Tsur was close to Shimon

Peres and a vocal proponent of the Dimona project.[167] Deputy Chief of Staff Rabin has often been regarded as a nuclear skeptic because of his close relationship with Yigal Allon and personal rivalry with Peres, but recently declassified documents indicate otherwise. Rabin, a former Palmahnik with a keen strategic mind and a shy, awkward personality, did not want nuclear research and development to come at the expense of the IDF's near-term conventional needs. Nevertheless, he too thought that nuclear weapons would ultimately ensure Israel's security. As early as 1959, Rabin thought that the arms race would change direction once Israel acquired "modern weapons"—"things that might provide us with a basic solution in five years or more."[168] In a 1961 letter to his friend Uzi Narkiss, he argued that Israel could solve its problems by "developing military capabilities" that would satisfy "long-term needs"—meaning nuclear arms.[169]

But after Dimona became public knowledge in December 1960, the future of the Israeli nuclear program was suddenly threatened. At home, Ben-Gurion's atomic ambitions came under fire from both dovish intellectuals and hawks like Meir and Ahdut ha-'Avodah's Allon and Yisrael Galili. Dimona's insider critics did not oppose an Israeli nuclear deterrent in principle—"I support the idea of deterrent weapons wholeheartedly!" Allon would later tell the cabinet.[170] Yet while Allon and Galili believed Israel should develop the *capacity* to produce nuclear weapons, they cautioned against using the bomb as a substitute for a firm conventional deterrent. A policy of overt nuclear deterrence, they argued, would compel the Arabs to develop their own atomic weapons. Once Israel lost its nuclear monopoly, its small size, coupled with the instability of Arab regimes, would make a "balance of terror" impossible to achieve.

Meir, on the other hand, worried about how Dimona would affect relations between Jerusalem and Washington.[171] After the reactor's existence became publicly known, the Americans began to press Ben-Gurion to pledge that Dimona would serve "peaceful purposes" and to open it to international inspections.[172] Early in Kennedy's term, the Americans' efforts remained relatively low-key, since they were not yet linked to a larger nonproliferation agenda. But there was no telling how long the United States would stay so restrained.[173]

By the early 1960s, Ben-Gurion had carved out a path for Israel to grow and even flourish within the narrow confines of the 1949 armistice lines. His strategy, which enjoyed broad support among Israel's political elite and military leadership, involved preserving the Jordanian status quo and a conventional military edge until Israel obtained nuclear weapons or an alliance with a superpower—or until the Cold War in the Middle East came to an end. It was a bold and innovative vision for overcoming Israel's basic deficiencies in size, manpower, and resources. Its success, however, depended on the survival of the embattled King Hussein and global trends that Israel had no power to influence. In 1963, it would face its toughest tests yet.

NOTES

1. *Times* (London), November 16, 1953.
2. Wilson, *King Abdullah*, 55, 85–150.
3. The literature on the Israeli-Jordanian dimension of the 1948 war is vast. See Shlaim, *Collusion across the Jordan*; Bar-Joseph, *Best of Enemies*; Sela, "Transjordan, Israel and the 1948 War"; Abu-Nuwar, *Jordanian-Israeli War*; Schueftan, *Optsiyah yardenit*; and Gelber, *Israeli-Jordanian Dialogue*.
4. Morris, *Road to Jerusalem*, 142–172.
5. Ben-Gurion diary, October 31 and November 10, 1948, in Oren and Rivlin, *David Ben-Gurion*, 790, 807–808.
6. Gubser, *Jordan*, 5.
7. Golan, *Gevul ham*, 22.
8. Shlaim, *Collusion across the Jordan*, 483–512.
9. Teveth, *Ben-Gurion*, 1–13.
10. Segev, *1949*, 19–20.
11. Shapira, *Yigal Allon, Native Son*, 1–2.
12. Morris, *1948*, 385–386.
13. Ben-Gurion diary, December 18, 1948, in Oren and Rivlin, *David Ben-Gurion*, 885.
14. Louis, *British Empire*, 579–581.
15. Shlaim, *Collusion across the Jordan*, 520.
16. Amman to Foreign Office, March 1, 1950, BNA/FO 371/82178.
17. Alon, "Tribal System."
18. Kirkbride, "Annual Report on the Hashemite Kingdom of Jordan for 1951," BNA/FO 371/98856.
19. Wilson, *King Abdullah*, 190–199.
20. Maddy-Weizmann, *Crystallization*, 105–137.
21. Ben-Gurion diary, February 13, 1951, BGA.

22. Gelber, *Israeli-Jordanian Dialogue*, 195–205; Shlaim, *Collusion across the Jordan*, 582–605.
23. Satloff, *From Abdullah to Hussein*, 13–72.
24. Ashton, *King Hussein of Jordan*, 20.
25. Quoted in Caplan, "Oom Shmoom Revisited," 177.
26. Sheffer, *Moshe Sharett*, 547–548.
27. See Bar-On, *Moshe Dayan*, 1–15.
28. See Shlaim, *Collusion across the Jordan*, 571–573; Golan, *Gevul ham*, 83.
29. Sheffy, *Hatra'ah be-mivhan*, 21–23.
30. Oren, "Seder ha-kohot," 125.
31. Golan, *Gevul ham*, 213–243.
32. Shalom, "'Emdot,'" 148.
33. Cabinet minutes, February 4, 1953, ISA; meeting of senior Foreign Ministry staff, February 2, 1953, *DFPI*, 8:95.
34. On Eban, see Siniver, *Abba Eban*.
35. Eban to Ben-Gurion and Sharett, December 26, 1952, *DFPI*, 7:730. See also Shalom, "'Emdot,'" 140–141.
36. Gelber, *Israeli-Jordanian Dialogue*, 235–237.
37. Cabinet minutes, October 17, 1951, ISA.
38. Shalom, *David Ben-Gurion*, 110.
39. Ibid., 13–30.
40. Shalom, "'Emdot,'" 126.
41. Cabinet minutes, October 17, 1951, ISA.
42. Shalom, *David Ben-Gurion*, 170–171.
43. On the influence of domestic politics on Ben-Gurion's strategy, see especially Laron, "Domestic Sources," 206–208.
44. Cabinet minutes, August 29, 1951, ISA.
45. Shlaim, *Collusion across the Jordan*, 611–612. Churchill was standing for election at the time.
46. Cabinet minutes, February 4, 1953, ISA.
47. Laron, "Domestic Sources," 208; Kuperman, "Impact of Internal Politics," 5–6.
48. Hahn, *United States*, 180–186.
49. Sheffer, *Moshe Sharett*, 720–734.
50. Oren, *Origins of the Second Arab-Israeli War*, 66, 104–105.
51. Golani, *Tihiyeh milhamah ba-kayits*, 27–61, 93–109.
52. Summary of a discussion in the war room, December 22, 1955, and editorial note, in Rosenthal, *Yitzhak Rabin*, 169–171. See also Laron, "'Logic dictates,'" 82–83.
53. J. Richmond, "Jordan: Annual Review for 1954," BNA/FO 371/115635; Glubb, *Soldier with the Arabs*, 347–357. On the Jordanian political opposition in this period, see Cohen, *Political Parties*; Anderson, *Nationalist Voices in Jordan*.
54. Oren, "Winter of Discontent," 174–179; Dann, *King Hussein*, 25–34.
55. Sharett to missions abroad, March 4, 1956, *DFPI*, 11:208–209.
56. Elath to British Commonwealth division, March 7, 1956, *DFPI*, 11:228–229.
57. Bar-On, *Gates of Gaza*, 201–247; Golani, *Tihiyeh milhamah ba-kayits*, 323–328. See also Lucas, "Redefining the Suez 'Collusion.'"
58. Oren, *Origins of the Second Arab-Israeli War*, 179n37.
59. Ben-Gurion diary, October 22, 1956, BGA.

60. For French and Hebrew versions of the Protocol of Sevres, see *DFPI*, 11:819–821.
61. Lahav, "Small Nation Goes to War," 68.
62. Quoted in Laron, "'Logic dictates,'" 83.
63. Robins, *History of Jordan*, 95–96. Robins also defines the Muslim Brotherhood, which won four seats, as an opposition party. In light of the Brotherhood's subsequent support for Hussein, I am not certain this designation is justified.
64. Abu Nuwar, *Hina talashat al-'arab*, 254–259.
65. Heller, *Yisrael veha-milhamah ha-karah*, 202.
66. Ben-Gurion speech to Mapai Knesset members, May 19, 1957, in Shaltiel, *David Ben-Gurion*, 400–401.
67. Ben-Gurion diary, March 10, 1957, BGA.
68. Remarks at a meeting in the war room, April 12, 1956, in Rosenthal, *Yitzhak Rabin*, 179–180.
69. Kafkafi, *Milhemet brerah*, 126–153.
70. Ben-Gurion diary, March 10, 1957, BGA.
71. Ben-Gurion speech to Mapai Knesset members, May 19, 1957, in Shaltiel, *Ben-Gurion*, 401.
72. Cohen, *Israel and the Bomb*, 10–12, 52–59; Pinkus, "Atomic Power to Israel's Rescue."
73. Govrin, *Israeli-Soviet Relations*, 51.
74. Satloff, *From Abdullah to Hussein*, 144–159; Dann, *King Hussein*, 42–48.
75. Eisenhower-Dulles telcon, October 15, 1956, DDRS/CK3100177817.
76. Dulles-Lloyd memcon, December 10, 1956, *FRUS*, 1955–1957, 13:74; editorial note, *FRUS*, 1955–1957, 13:76.
77. Satloff, "Jekyll and Hyde Origins," 120–122.
78. For accounts of the April 1957 crisis, see Dann, *King Hussein*, 45–67; Satloff, *From Abdullah to Hussein*, 160–176; Yaqub, *Containing Arab Nationalism*, 129–140; Tal, *Politics*, 38–53.
79. Shalom, *Superpowers*, 97.
80. Podeh, "Demonizatsiyah shel ha-oyev," 173.
81. See, for example, Rountree to Dulles, January 21, 1958, *FRUS*, 1958–1960, 12:4.
82. DOS memcon, July 12, 1957, *FRUS*, 1955–1957, 560.
83. NSC 5801/1, January 24, 1958, *FRUS*, 1958–1960, 12:25, 29–30.
84. Meir, *My Life*, 1.
85. Levey, *Israel and the Western Powers*, 107; DOS memcon, February 27, 1958, *FRUS*, 1958–1960, 13:25–26; "Political Considerations regarding Jordan," unsigned [Mordechai Gazit], October 13, 1966, ISA/FM/4092/9.
86. Ben-Gurion diary, July 15, 1958, BGA.
87. Ben-Gurion diary, July 14, 1958, BGA.
88. Cabinet minutes, July 28 and August 3, 1958, ISA.
89. Cabinet minutes, July 28, 1958, ISA.
90. Cabinet minutes, August 3, 1958, ISA.
91. Bar-On, *Gevulot 'ashenim*, 332–333.
92. Cabinet minutes, July 17, 1958, ISA.
93. Dulles-Eban memcon, July 20, 1958, *FRUS*, 1958–1960, 13:70–72.
94. On the US-Israeli exchanges during the 1958 crisis, see Oren, "Test of Suez"; Tal, "Seizing Opportunities"; Shlaim, "Israel, the Great Powers."

95. Rountree-Shiloah-Eban memcon, July 27, 1958, *FRUS*, 1958–1960, 13:74–77.
96. Enclosed in Tel Aviv to FO, October 28, 1958, BNA/FO 371/134294.
97. Dulles-Eban memcon, July 20, 1958, *FRUS*, 1958–1960, 13:70–72.
98. Dulles-Eban memcon, August 3, 1958, *FRUS*, 1958–1960, 13:82–83.
99. Oren, "Test of Suez," 78–83; Little, "Making of a Special Relationship," 566–567.
100. Dulles to Meir, October 31, 1958, *FRUS*, 1958–1960, 13:106
101. Yaqub, *Containing Arab Nationalism*, 254–265.
102. Quoted in Hahn, *Caught in the Middle East*, 270.
103. Amman to FO, July 15, 1958, BNA/PREM 11/2380.
104. Amman to State, August 22, 1958, *FRUS*, 1958–1960, 11:514.
105. Dulles-Herter telcon, August 23, 1958, *FRUS*, 1958–1960, 11:519. For similar remarks by Dulles, see New York to FO, August 15, 1958, BNA/PREM 11/2381; Dulles-Lloyd memcon, August 12, 1958, *FRUS*, 1958–1960, 11:458; Dulles-Gromyko memcon, August 12, 1958, *FRUS*, 1958–1960, 11:462.
106. "The Outlook for Jordan," NIE 36.3-59, March 10, 1959, DDRS/CK100330734.
107. NSC 5820/1, November 4, 1958, *FRUS*, 1958–1960, 12:196.
108. Dulles–al-Rifa'i memcon, October 15, 1958, *FRUS*, 1958–1960, 11:610.
109. Amman to State, August 22, 1958, *FRUS*, 1958–1960, 11:514.
110. Dulles–al-Rifa'i memcon, October 15, 1958, *FRUS*, 1958–1960, 11:610.
111. al-Rifa'i–Rountree memcon, December 10, 1958, *FRUS*, 1958–1960, 11:668–669.
112. Amman to FO, October 8, 1959; Amman to FO, October 12, 1959; Amman to FO, October 16, 1959, BNA/FO 371/142122.
113. al-Rifa'i–Rountree memcon, December 10, 1958, *FRUS*, 1958–1960, 11:668–669.
114. Eisenhower to Hussein, September 10, 1960, DDRS/CK3100024386.
115. Dulles-Macmillam memcon, July 27, 1958, BNA/PREM 11/2380; Dulles-Lloyd memcon, August 12, 1958, *FRUS*, 1958–1960, 11:458.
116. Almog, *Britain, Israel, and the United States*, 184.
117. Oren, "Test of Suez," 79–80.
118. Amman to State, December 29, 1958, *FRUS*, 1958–1960, 11:678.
119. Johnston to Lloyd, December 4, 1958, BNA/FO 371/134011.
120. Tehran to FO, October 26, 1959, BNA/FO 371/142123.
121. Ben-Gurion to Hussein, August 30, 1960, *DFPI*, 14:36–37.
122. Herzog, *Derekh hayim*, 197–198.
123. Jerusalem to Washington, May 13, 1961, ISA/RG130.15/3759/7. Israeli intelligence sources indicated that the JAA leadership opposed Hussein's impending marriage to Toni Gardiner, a British woman. Ben-Gurion believed that Nasser hoped to exploit these intramilitary divisions and topple Hussein's regime.
124. See, for example, the references to Israeli-Jordanian intelligence exchanges in Ya'akov Herzog, "Meeting with Charles," September 24, 1963, YHP.
125. Embassy advisor to US division, October 26, 1960; Bern to Cohen, May 30, 1961; Bar-Hayim to Bern, June 8, 1961, ISA/RG130.15/3759/7. See also Chaim Herzog's remarks to the General Staff, April 3, 1961, in Lammfromm, *Chaim Herzog*, 203.
126. Washington to London, October 27, 1960; Washington to Meroz, October 27, 1960, ISA/RG130.15/3759/7.
127. Gazit to Ya'ari, June 19, 1961, ISA/RG130.15/3759/7.
128. On the Jordanian government's favoritism toward the East Bank, see Robins, *History of Jordan*, 85–87. The Israelis applauded such policies. See, for example, Ya'ari to Yahil, May 10, 1961, ISA/RG130.15/3759/7.

129. M. Fisher to M. Sasson, February 2, 1960, ISA/RG130.15/3759/7.
130. Shomron to Cohen, October 20, 1960; "Dr. Herbert-King Hussein meeting," October 30, 1960; Cohen to E. Sasson, October 31, 1960, ISA/RG130.15/3782/21.
131. Cabinet minutes, May 3, 1959, ISA.
132. Cabinet minutes, October 8, 1961, ISA.
133. Susser, *On Both Banks*, 9–41.
134. "Country Assistance Strategy for Jordan," USAID memo, February 10, 1963, JFKL/NSF/Robert Komer papers, box 429.
135. Cabinet minutes, October 8, 1961, ISA.
136. Sheffy, *Hatra'ah be-mivhan*, 37–38. See also editorial note, in Lammfromm, *Chaim Herzog*, 168.
137. Rabin to Narkiss, September 19, 1961, in Rosenthal, *Yitzhak Rabin*, 294.
138. Cabinet minutes, October 8, 1961, ISA.
139. "The Arab Military Buildup, 1962/1963," unsigned, undated (Fall 1963), ISA/FM/4327/7.
140. See Bass, *Support Any Friend*, 47–91.
141. US Division to Bar-Hayim, February 13, 1963, ISA/FM/3378/14.
142. "The Soviet Program of Military Aid to Less Developed Countries, 1955–1965" CIA report, September 1965, http://www.foia.cia.gov/sites/default/files/document_conversions/89801/DOC_0000232637.pdf; "Soviet Military Aid to the United Arab Republic, 1955–1966" CIA report, March 1, 1967, http://www.foia.cia.gov/sites/default/files/document_conversions/89801/DOC_0000496350.pdf.
143. Remarks to the General Staff, June 25, 1959, in Rosenthal, *Yitzhak Rabin*, 232.
144. Editorial note, in Rosenthal, *Yitzhak Rabin*, 245.
145. US Division to Bar-Hayim, February 13, 1963, ISA/FM/3378/14.
146. On "Rotem," see Sheffy, *Hatra'ah be-mivhan*.
147. Heller, *Yisrael veha-milhamah ha-karah*, 291.
148. Remarks at a meeting of the IDF General Staff, January 8, 1959, in Rosenthal, *Yitzhak Rabin*, 218; editorial note, in Rosenthal, *Yitzhak Rabin*, 220.
149. Cabinet minutes, April 25, 1963, ISA.
150. Cabinet minutes, September 4, 1960, ISA.
151. KFADC minutes, March 27, 1963, ISA/A/7568/9.
152. Quoted in Heller, *Yisrael veha-milhamah ha-karah*, 306.
153. Editorial note, in Rosenthal, *Yitzhak Rabin*, 219.
154. Bar-Joseph, "Rotem," 559–560.
155. Harman to Foreign Ministry, March 11, 1960, *DFPI*, 14:209–210; Ben-Gurion–Macmillan memcon, March 17, 1960, *DFPI*, 14:422–424; Ben-Gurion–Kennedy memcon, May 30, 1961, *FRUS*, 1961–1963, 17: doc. 57.
156. Ben-Gurion to Kennedy, August 20, 1962, JFKL/POF/Israel-Security, 1961–1963, box 119.
157. Cohen, *Israel and the Bomb*, 148–149.
158. Rabin to Narkiss, February 5, 1960, in Rosenthal, *Yitzhak Rabin*, 250.
159. Editorial note, in Rosenthal, *Yitzhak Rabin*, 218.
160. Cabinet minutes, April 25, 1963, ISA.
161. Weizman, *Lekha shama'im, lekha arets*, 199–200.
162. Editorial note, in Rosenthal, *Yitzhak Rabin*, 272.
163. Weizman, *Lekha shama'im, lekha arets*, 208.

164. Quoted in Gluska, *Eshkol*, 443.

165. Rosenthal, *Yitzhak Rabin*, 275n2.

166. Rabin, for example, complained that while he and Tsur were allowed to participate in discussions of "the two key subjects"—i.e., Israel's nuclear and ballistic missile programs—most IDF officers were sidelined. See Rabin to Alrom, August 30, 1962, in Rosenthal, *Yitzhak Rabin*, 306.

167. Cohen, *Israel and the Bomb*, 144.

168. Remarks to the General Staff, June 25, 1959, in Rosenthal, *Yitzhak Rabin*, 232; remarks to the General Staff, December 31, 1959, in Rosenthal, *Yitzhak Rabin*, 248.

169. Rabin to Narkiss, September 19, 1961, in Rosenthal, *Yitzhak Rabin*, 295.

170. Cabinet minutes, May 5, 1963, ISA.

171. Cohen, *Israel and the Bomb*, 137–151.

172. Gerlini, "Waiting for Dimona."

173. Cohen, *Israel and the Bomb*, 99–113. See also Shalom, *Israel's Nuclear Option*, 11–31.

TWO

THE JORDANIAN CRISIS OF 1963 AND ITS CONSEQUENCES

BY THE EARLY 1960S, ISRAEL'S LEADERS HAD FOUND A WAY TO live with their narrow West Bank border. For the time being, Israel would try to keep King Hussein in power in order to prevent Jordan from being absorbed by another Arab state. Israel could thereby preserve the West Bank's buffer status and buy time to develop a nuclear deterrent. There were, to be sure, some figures within the Israeli establishment who disagreed with aspects of this approach. But this was the strategy that Ben-Gurion had designed and that was driving Israeli policy.

In 1963, however, Ben-Gurion's strategy fell into disarray. Following a popular uprising in April of that year, Hussein sought rapprochement with Nasser, leading the Israelis to fear that he would be co-opted by the Arab radical camp. And while Ben-Gurion's policy of bolstering Hussein became the subject of doubt, so did the prime minister's hope that atomic weapons could compensate for Israel's lack of strategic depth. The Kennedy administration now threatened to cut off support for Israel if it developed a nuclear capability.

For Ben-Gurion's strategy to succeed, the United States and Israel would have to resolve their differences on the nuclear question. And Hussein and the Israelis would have to prevent Jordan's return to the Arab fold from wrecking their delicate entente.

THE PATH TO CRISIS

From 1961 to 1963, King Hussein and his advisors never stopped worrying that Egypt and Syria would reunite. If the two countries ever merged again, Prime Minister Wasfi al-Tal argued, "moderate progressive capitalist governments such as in Jordan" would have to sacrifice internal development in order to maintain "iron fist totalitarian control."[1] He and Hussein worked hard to roll back Egypt's influence throughout the Middle East. Together with the Saudis, Hussein allegedly paid Syrian prime minister Ma'amun al-Kuzbari "hundreds of thousands of liras" to stay outside Nasser's orbit. The Jordanian government was also widely rumored to have backed a coup attempt by Lebanon's Syrian National Party.[2] Nor were Hussein's anti-Egyptian moves limited to the Levant. Increasingly he sought alliances with the Arabian oil monarchies, sending troops to help protect Kuwait from Iraq in 1961, and signing a military and economic cooperation agreement with King Sa'ud in August 1962.[3] When the Yemeni civil war began in the fall of 1962, Hussein joined the Saudis in supporting the deposed Imam al-Badr against the Yemeni republicans and their Egyptian backers. The Hashemite monarchy supplied twelve thousand rifles to Yemeni royalist fighters, and sent military advisors and Hawker Hunter jets to Saudi Arabia. Hussein also implored President Kennedy not to recognize Col. 'Abdallah al-Sallal's new government.[4] If the Saudis "went down," he proclaimed, he was "prepared to go down with them."[5]

But Hussein and al-Tal's Yemen policy backfired. The Americans did not rally behind Jordan and Saudi Arabia. Kennedy believed that the Yemeni republicans would win, and hoped to "persuade Jordan and Saudi Arabia that it [was] not in their interest to keep fighting."[6] On December 19, the United States recognized the Yemeni republican regime. And while Hussein's meddling accomplished little in Yemen, it did hurt him at home. By the winter of 1963, US diplomats in Amman found themselves "unable to find one person" besides high-ranking Jordanian officials who supported Hussein's Yemen policy.[7]

Hussein now confronted an increasingly vocal and angry opposition in parliament and on the street. The Jordanian parliamentary elections of November 1962 produced a crop of deputies who were far less willing to kowtow to the monarchy. Nearly half had university degrees and many had identified with the nationalist opposition during the mid-1950s. In January 1963, eighteen of these new deputies cast votes of no confidence against al-Tal's government. Later that month, protests erupted in Jerusalem after al-Tal fired Anwar Nusayba, the district governor and an outspoken critic of the government's Yemen policy.

Hussein visited Jerusalem and managed to pacify the city, but the calm that followed did not last.[8] During the winter of 1963, upheaval rocked Jordan's neighbors. In February, a coalition of Ba'thist and Nasserist army officers staged a bloody coup d'état in Iraq. Ba'thist officers seized power in Syria that March. From March 14 to April 14, the new rulers of Syria and Iraq met with Nasser in Cairo to discuss how they might unify their countries.[9]

Not since 1958 had Hussein felt so encircled by Arab enemies. Hoping to placate Nasser, the king dismissed al-Tal and formed a new cabinet headed by King Abdullah's old crony Samir al-Rifa'i. Though elderly and illiberal, al-Rifa'i was also restrained and pragmatic in his approach to Egypt.[10] "Even if a wall could be built around Jordan and a paradise created within it," the new prime minister privately admitted, "this would not satisfy the Jordanian people, who feel themselves to be an integral part of the larger Arab world."[11] Al-Rifa'i and Hussein made several overtures to Egypt. The king fired Salah Abu Zayd, Jordan's fiercely anti-Nasserist director-general of information and broadcasting, and reinstated a number of army officers whom he had previously forced to retire on political grounds. On April 17, when the leaders of Egypt, Syria, and Iraq announced that they would form a tripartite federation, the Jordanian press hailed the news. The speaker of the Jordanian parliament praised the federation as a "blessed step toward Arab unity."[12]

Hussein and al-Rifa'i's attempts to appease Nasser fell flat. The Cairo newspaper *al-Gumhurriya* depicted Hussein and al-Rifa'i as puppets manipulated by a giant, grinning Uncle Sam.[13] Nasser even refused to accept the king's congratulations when the tripartite talks successfully ended.[14] It was also all too clear that many Jordanians shared the Egyptian president's hostility toward Hussein. On April 17 and 18, demonstrators took to the streets in Nablus, Hebron, and Jerusalem, calling for Jordan to join the federation and for Hussein's overthrow. On the morning of April 20, a crowd of 2,500 marched up Salah al-Din Road in the Old City of Jerusalem, chanting anti-Hashemite slogans, waving pictures of Nasser, and tearing down Jordanian flags on public buildings. In the Chamber of Deputies, thirty-one out of sixty deputies announced that they would oppose al-Rifaʿi in a vote of confidence, forcing him to resign.[15]

It was time, Hussein grimly commented, for a "display of toughness reminiscent of the 1950s." Against US and British advice, the king accepted al-Rifaʿi's resignation and dissolved parliament, hoping that its deputies could later be "prosecuted for subversive activities."[16] The monarchy moved to crush the protests in the West Bank. In Jerusalem, policemen and JAA troops fired live ammunition into crowds and sprayed demonstrators with fire hoses.[17] The government imposed curfews upon the West Bank's largest cities—Jerusalem, Hebron, Nablus, Ramallah, Tulkarm, Jericho, and Jenin.[18] According to official figures, 13 people were killed and 106 injured before the protests subsided, though the real numbers may have been higher.[19]

Toughness at home, however, could not shield the Hashemite monarchy from its Arab enemies. To survive the crisis, Hussein also had to counter the viciously anti-Hashemite propaganda broadcast by Egyptian, Syrian, and Iraqi media outlets, and restrain Nasser from encouraging his Jordanian supporters to attempt a coup or an assassination. And so the king and his advisors began to invoke the Israeli threat. On April 25, ʿAbd al-Munʿim al-Rifaʿi, Jordan's ambassador to the United Nations, pleaded with Secretary-General U Thant to ask Nasser to stop attacking Hussein on the radio and supplying arms to his opponents. If Hussein were overthrown, al-Rifaʿi cautioned, the IDF would "march to the Jordan River."[20] Similar hints were dropped to US ambassador William Macomber in Amman. If Israel intervened in Jordan, "things would really be in a mess," warned Hussein.[21] As in 1958, the king hoped that the threat of an aggressive Israel would be enough to deter Nasser and rally the United States behind his regime.

ISRAEL, THE WESTERN POWERS, AND THE QUESTION OF "INTERNAL OVERTHROW"

As Nasser's rivals toppled in Yemen, Iraq, and Syria, Israel's leaders had watched Jordan with growing anxiety. "The Jordanian regime is now more isolated than ever, it is an exceptional case within the inter-Arab system," lamented IDF chief of staff Tsur.[22] "There are elements in Jordan who wish to deal with Hussein in a similar fashion," Golda Meir remarked, "and if it's possible in Yemen and Iraq, why wouldn't it be possible with Hussein?"[23]

To the Israelis, the ascent of Nasser's ideological bedfellows seemed all the more ominous because the Americans appeared to support it. The Israeli intelligence community was convinced that the Kennedy administration had engineered the Iraqi coup and rescued Nasser from defeat in Yemen.[24] Tsur spoke for many when he later described US policy as "decisively pro-Nasserist, a policy of supporting any process of unification."[25] While Israeli officials did not think the Americans were actively conspiring against Hussein, they did not think the United States would do much to keep the king afloat, either. The United States would not use force to save the Hashemite monarchy, Ben-Gurion glumly concluded.[26] By March, Meir and new Mossad chief Meir Amit resolved to launch an all-out diplomatic offensive to convince the Americans to "strengthen Hussein's self-confidence" and restrain Nasser.[27] When Deputy Defense Minister Shimon Peres visited Washington soon afterward, he warned Kennedy that Israel would not "stand aside" if Egypt invaded Jordan or intervened in a civil war there. Even if a purely local rebellion erupted, Israel might have to intervene. Kennedy smiled wryly. "You certainly never thought the day would come that you would pray for the welfare of Hussein and Faysal!" he joked.[28]

Yet when the Jordanian crisis erupted, Ben-Gurion wanted to avoid sending his army into the West Bank. Though the General Staff believed that the IDF enjoyed a "serious advantage" over any Arab coalition, Ben-Gurion did not try to use the turmoil in Jordan as a pretext for war. When the prime minister addressed his cabinet on April 25, he refused to discuss any military plans until Hussein was overthrown or assassinated. Once again, Ben-Gurion pointed out that the West Bank was home to nearly a million Palestinians, whom Israel could not rule. Once again, he warned that the next war, unlike Suez, would involve all the Arab states, and that Israel would "confront the entire world" if the IDF struck first.

Ben-Gurion's caution did not go entirely unchallenged. Yigal Allon and Moshe Dayan, now ministers in the cabinet, hoped to exploit the crisis in Jordan to widen Israel's borders. If Hussein fell, Allon argued, the IDF had to move immediately—"Everything west of the Jordan must be Israel." Allon believed that if Israel seized the West Bank, many of its Palestinian residents would flee. "Even if a large percentage of Arabs remain, better that they be under our rule than Nasser's," he added. Not to be outdone, Dayan demanded that the government discuss "the fate of Israel's borders, not just the borders in east and west Jordan, but also the Gaza Strip and the demilitarized zones with Syria." He argued that the IDF should use rioting in Jerusalem as an excuse to seize the route to Mount Scopus, where the old Hebrew University campus stood, maintained by small groups of Israelis who were periodically trucked through the surrounding Arab neighborhoods by UN escorts. Though Dayan did not explicitly state that seizing the road to Mount Scopus could spark a war that would allow Israel to conquer more territory, his remarks about "the fate of Israel's borders" suggest that this was exactly what he had in mind.[29]

Yet when Ben-Gurion challenged Dayan to put his proposal to a vote, the former general backed down. The cabinet voted only to hold an emergency meeting "if serious disturbances break out in Jordan."[30] At this point, it looked as if such a meeting would never be held. The Israeli intelligence community believed Hussein had withstood the worst of the rioting, and that Nasser was too afraid of war to order a Jordanian coup. If Egypt, Syria, and Iraq failed to actually unite, the king would survive.[31]

But on April 27, the crisis suddenly intensified. At 8:50 AM in Washington, Undersecretary of State George Ball phoned Secretary of Defense Robert McNamara. "We had some information last night indicating there may be coups in Jordan today," Ball announced. Intelligence reporting warned of "an army or military coup done with the complete knowledge of the UAR."[32] Less than two hours later, Ball, McNamara, and a handful of other top officials sat down with a worried John F. Kennedy in the White House. The president seemed resigned about the Hashemite monarchy's fate. He did not ask what the United States could do to keep Hussein or his family in power. Instead, Kennedy wanted to know how to prevent a regional war after a coup had already occurred. While clearly annoyed with Egypt, the president saw Ben-Gurion, not Nasser, as the key to containing the crisis. "The real problem now," Kennedy said, "was that the Israelis might move, not the Arabs.... Israel is really the danger, since it wants to move first if there is a coup in Jordan."[33]

And so that afternoon, Ball summoned Israeli ambassador Avraham Harman and minister Mordechai Gazit to inform them of the plot against Hussein. While the United States would "try to keep the Hussein government in control," Ball said, Israel "should not act precipitously" if the king fell. Ball and his colleagues tried to convince the Israelis that a post-Hussein regime might well remain independent, and that the regional balance of power would not change if he were overthrown. Their arguments went nowhere. "Any successor regime in Jordan which held out against union after an uprising," Harman scoffed, "would have the April 17 agreement cited against it." What happened in Jordan went "to the heart of Israel's security," the Israeli ambassador proclaimed. "It would be gratifying to be able to report to Jerusalem that the US will take very definite action to protect the situation." The Americans offered no such reassurance. "It would be, at minimum, many months before Israel's considerable deterrent advantage could be jeopardized. Therefore, Israel can afford to see what emerges," Ball responded.[34]

Whatever their worries about US policy, Israel's diplomats had not thought the Kennedy administration would be quite so blasé about Hussein's fate. As late as April 21, Harman had predicted that the Americans would back the king until the end, for fear that his "ouster [would] lead, sooner or later, to the disintegration of Jordan."[35] Ball's comments forced the ambassador to realize he was wrong. Kennedy and his advisors clearly did not think Hussein's fall would lead to the disintegration of Jordan or to regional war, Harman now reported. Nor did the president and his advisors want to alienate the Arab world's "forces of tomorrow" in order to prop up the king for a few more months. "They will object to any military intervention by us as a matter of principle," the Israeli ambassador concluded.[36] The moment that Ben-Gurion had long dreaded had arrived. At any instant, Israel might have to choose between allowing a pro-Nasserist regime to take over Jordan and wrecking its ties with the United States.

To judge by Ben-Gurion's next moves, he believed that a pro-Nasserist takeover would leave him with no choice but to seize the West Bank, no matter the cost to the US-Israeli relationship. On April 28, Ben-Gurion sent Harman back to Ball with a message. "Any change" in Jordan, the Israeli ambassador said, "would make it imperative to have the West Bank completely demilitarized. It would be impossible to ask

Israel to acquiesce in the presence there of Egyptian, Syrian, or Iraqi troops, or Jordanian troops should there be a change in Jordan." "Since April 17," Harman added, "not a day has passed without some measure taken to consolidate Nasser's triumph. . . . Any change in Jordan would have to be viewed in this context."[37] Essentially, Ben-Gurion was arguing that Israel could not consider any Jordanian coup a purely local phenomenon. Israel had to assume that *any* new regime in Jordan would unify the kingdom with its neighbors.

Though Ben-Gurion still refrained from discussing military moves with his cabinet, the evidence shows that he was ready to back up his warnings with force. Foreign Ministry contingency plans, probably prepared at the prime minister's direction, assumed that Israel would "seize strategic positions in the West Bank" if the monarchy were violently overthrown in a coup organized and encouraged from the outside.[38] The IDF's operational orders also indicate that Ben-Gurion abandoned his earlier restraint. Prior to the April 27 coup scare, Central Command had gone on twelve-hour alert, but no reservists were called up, and the IDF's operational planning focused on limited forays into East Jerusalem.[39] After April 27, the IDF prepared for much larger moves. By May 2, the Operations Branch and Central Command had prepared plans for the military administration of occupied territory in case they were ordered to implement Plan SHAHAM ("Granite"), which called for taking the entire West Bank.[40]

Still, Ben-Gurion assumed that Israel would not be able to keep any territory that it conquered. In his April 28 message to Kennedy, he made no claims on the West Bank, but instead demanded its demilitarization, as he had done in 1958. "Pay attention to the fact that the prime minister has, for the first time, defined our political and security goals in the event that Jordan's regime and status changes," wrote Hayim Yahil, director-general of Israel's Foreign Ministry, in a top-secret cable to Israel's most important embassies. "Our goal is not a change in Israel's territorial status, but a guarantee of her security. We have no interest in annexing Arab-populated areas, but rather, in distancing ourselves from enemy forces upon our borders that endanger our security and existence."[41] The prime minister's limited goals reflected the long-standing Israeli assumption that the superpowers would not allow the IDF to hold the West Bank. The Foreign Ministry's contingency plans even speculated that the British and the Americans might send troops to stop the IDF. The best Israel could hope for was that the United States would "agree to a compromise involving the demilitarization of the West Bank by deploying UN forces there."[42]

In reality, the Israelis' fears that they could end up facing off against American soldiers were quite overblown. "I don't see the president going to war with Israel to recover the West Bank," predicted National Security Advisor McGeorge Bundy.[43] But a Suez-like outcome was probably the best that Israel could have achieved. The NSC's contingency plans, for example, assumed that if Israel seized the West Bank, the Kennedy administration would suspend economic and military aid until the IDF withdrew. At most, the United States would help put together a peacekeeping force that would deploy on the West Bank after the Israelis left.[44]

In any event, Hussein survived the coup scare, thanks perhaps to John Badeau, the US ambassador in Cairo. After learning of the plot against Hussein on the morning of April 27, Badeau immediately tracked down Sami Sharaf, Nasser's aide-de-camp. Speaking without instruction, the ambassador warned that US-Egyptian ties could be "irreparably ruptured" if an "armed coup" occurred in Jordan. He speculated that the international community might not be able to force Israel to withdraw from the West Bank, and demanded to know how cash-strapped Egypt could financially support Jordan.[45] The following day, Nasser summoned Badeau to his office. Visibly exhausted, the Egyptian president admitted that the ambassador's warnings had kept him up "most of [the] previous evening." Though he claimed not to know of any plot against Hussein, Nasser acknowledged that a coup in Jordan would be blamed on him anyway. It was "quite possible," he said, that "Hussein would last through [the] current crisis."[46] However far the plot against Hussein may have advanced, and whatever Egypt's role in supporting it, no further alarms went off in Amman. By the beginning of May, a tense calm took hold in Jordan.

Yet for the Israelis, the April 1963 crisis served as an unpleasant reminder that they had not solved their West Bank problem. And the consequences of the Jordanian crisis were doubly severe because it coincided with a long-brewing showdown between Kennedy and Ben-Gurion over Israel's nuclear program.

THE JORDANIAN CRISIS AND THE
US-ISRAELI NUCLEAR DIALOGUE

For Israel's leaders, the Jordanian crisis of 1963 seemed to confirm that they could not take and hold on to the West Bank. Yet there still seemed to be no good alternative to Hashemite rule. Ben-Gurion and his colleagues probably did not have high hopes for a West Bank peacekeeping force; after all, the United Nations Emergency Force (UNEF) had already failed to prevent Nasser from moving large numbers of troops into the Sinai during the 1960 Rotem crisis.[47] With or without peacekeepers, a post-Hussein West Bank could still serve as a staging ground for an Arab attack, which would become more likely as the conventional military balance shifted.

And the military balance was indeed shifting. Just a few weeks after the Jordan crisis, Chief of Staff Tsur painted a frightening picture of the Middle Eastern arms race for the cabinet. The armed forces of Egypt, Lebanon, Jordan, Syria, Saudi Arabia, Iraq, and Yemen could already field twice as many troops as the IDF, he said. Combined, the Arab states had 700 more tanks, 350 more jets, and many more naval vessels than Israel. To judge by Egypt's performance in Yemen, Tsur concluded, the individual Arab soldier remained a poor fighter, but he would continue to improve. Ben-Gurion agreed. "In another five years," the prime minister said, "the balance of forces will change."[48]

Israel could not remedy its insecurity through preemptive or preventive war, Ben-Gurion argued. "Victory over the Arabs will cost us dearly," he said. "We are interested in having a deterrent that will make an attack on us inconceivable to them."[49] The prime minister doubted that the Soviets and the Americans would cooperate to resolve the Arab-Israeli conflict, or that Israel could obtain a military alliance with the United States or France.[50] Israel, he stressed, needed to rely on its own strength: "We need to see if we can get concrete help from deterrent weapons," he told his cabinet.[51] Though Ben-Gurion did not dwell on the subject of "deterrent weapons," it is clear that he regarded them as the key to Israel's survival. Nuclear weapons, in his view, would free Israel from having to fight preventive wars or depend on external forces that would not help in times of crisis.

And it was not only Shimon Peres who shared Ben-Gurion's enthusiasm for nuclear weapons. A variety of Israeli hawks *and* doves viewed the nuclear project as Israel's one real alternative to preventive war and territorial expansion. On the nuclear issue, there was little difference between Minister of Religious Affairs Zerah Warhaftig, the cabinet's leading dove, who believed that "from a military standpoint, only nonconventional weaponry will give us a chance," and Generals Tsur and Rabin, the top two men in the IDF.[52] When the General Staff briefed Ben-Gurion's successor Levi Eshkol in July 1963, Rabin eloquently argued that territorial expansion was politically unfeasible and would soon become militarily unnecessary. In theory, Rabin remarked, Israel's ideal borders might include the Litani River in Lebanon, the Jordan River, and the Suez Canal. But in practice, it did not behoove the IDF to "philosophize" about revising the armistice lines. The IDF could defend Israel within its existing borders, and outside powers would respond harshly if Israel started a war.[53] Rabin acknowledged that in the conventional arms race, Israel was at a long-term disadvantage. But Israel's developing nuclear capability meant this would not necessarily matter. "There is no need," he said, "to force the end because of the assumption that time is working against us."[54] In a meeting with Eshkol a few months later, Tsur also argued quite explicitly that only a nuclear deterrent could solve Israel's security problems. "The IDF today is strong," he said, "but I don't know if we'll manage to prevail in this competition by the 1970s. By the 1970s, we will need something nonconventional."[55]

But by the time Rabin and Tsur offered their opinions to Eshkol, the future of Israel's nuclear project was uncertain. Kennedy administration officials had long worried that the Israeli nuclear program could drive Arab governments to launch a preventive war, develop atomic weapons of their own, or seek a Soviet nuclear umbrella.[56] By 1963, however, the president and his advisors had broader geopolitical reasons to get tough with Israel. Following the Berlin and Cuban missile crises, the Kennedy administration hoped to work toward a European settlement with the USSR, and doing so depended on keeping West Germany nonnuclear. To prevent tension within the Western alliance, the Americans had to make it seem as if they opposed nuclear nonproliferation in general, rather than just a German bomb. Aspiring nuclear powers like Israel had to be checked.[57]

Thus, on March 26, Kennedy approved National Security Action Memorandum 231, a top-secret directive that called for ramping up US efforts to keep the Middle East free of nuclear weapons.[58] On April 2, just a few weeks before the Jordan crisis erupted, US ambassador Walworth Barbour asked Ben-Gurion to open the Dimona reactor to semiannual inspections.[59] Ben-Gurion responded by again demanding a joint US-Soviet guarantee of Middle Eastern borders.[60] When Kennedy replied that there was no way that the Soviets would go along with Ben-Gurion's plan, the Israeli prime minister sent the president an even more forceful message.[61] Arguing that Arab leaders and their peoples were "capable of following the Nazi example," Ben-Gurion outlined how the United States could help solve the Arab-Israeli dispute without involving the Soviets. First, if Hussein fell, the West Bank should be demilitarized and placed under international supervision. Second, the United States could call for regional disarmament. If the Arabs refused to stop enlarging their forces, the United States could sign a mutual defense treaty with Israel instead. If Kennedy expected the Israelis to live with their narrow West Bank border, Ben-Gurion was saying, he needed to help preserve the strategic balance in Israel's favor. And if the president could not offer Israel what it needed, then Israel would have to develop nuclear weapons.[62]

Yet Kennedy did not relent. Rather than answer Ben-Gurion's second request for a security guarantee, he shot back a tough message stressing that Israel's nuclear ambitions could "seriously jeopardize" the US-Israeli relationship and demanded that Israel allow US inspectors to make "periodic visits" to Dimona.[63] At the same time, US officials began discussing a far-reaching Middle East arms control initiative, the brainchild of NSC staffer Robert Komer. Komer, a bespectacled, owlish former CIA analyst, had a knack for getting what he wanted. One contemporary compared arguing with him to having a flamethrower aimed at the seat of one's pants.[64] Komer had already played a key role in convincing Kennedy to court Nasser, and now he wanted to remake the US-Israeli relationship as well. The United States, Komer argued, *should* offer Israel a security guarantee, and it should be tied "not only to Jordan but also Israeli agreement not to develop nuclear weapons."[65]

Komer's idea won over his boss, McGeorge Bundy, who thought a security guarantee for Israel was "something which is going to have to be done eventually and had better be done sooner rather than later."[66] By mid-May, even the State Department, which usually opposed closer ties to the Jewish state, was on board. Secretary of State Dean Rusk proposed that Kennedy send an emissary to Israel and Egypt to negotiate an arms control agreement. If the Egyptians balked, the United States could negotiate an agreement with Israel alone. In either case, the Israelis would be expected to forswear nuclear weapons and "offensive missiles" and open Dimona to inspections. They would also have to agree to "no territorial expansion" and "no cross-border military action," and to help resolve the Palestinian refugee problem and the Jordan waters issue.[67] In exchange, the United States would not offer Israel a "treaty" but an "executive instrument," perhaps a presidential statement in support of Israel's security.[68]

In June, Kennedy decided to send long-time Washington insider John McCloy to Egypt and Israel to launch Komer's plan. "We should give Israel reasonable assurances in return for their agreement not to move into Jordan or to develop nuclear weapons," the president told a small group of senior officials. If American diplomacy failed, Kennedy warned, "we're likely to have both sides developing nuclear weapons and the Israelis moving into Jordan on the earliest excuse they can find, in order to get it over with while they are still ahead."[69] The president and his advisors clearly understood how Israel's deteriorating conventional position and lack of great power support drove its leaders to consider nuclear weapons and territorial expansion. It remained to be seen if Kennedy could offer the Israelis enough to assuage their fears.

By the time McCloy arrived in the Middle East, Ben-Gurion had resigned. His faith in the redemptive power of nuclear weapons had not weakened. "I am confident that science is able to provide us with the weapon that will secure the peace, and deter our enemies," he told a group of Israeli weapons scientists a few weeks after stepping down. Yet "the Old Man" had left the US-Israeli nuclear impasse for his successor Levi Eshkol to resolve.[70]

A good-humored, laid-back man with a penchant for Yiddish jokes, Eshkol had served ably as the head of the Jewish Agency's settlement department, minister of agriculture, and minister of finance. Ben-Gurion, who had little patience for budgetary matters, had relied heavily upon Eshkol to find the money Israel needed to absorb Jewish immigrants, build infrastructure, and procure weapons. However, the new prime minister had little experience dealing with foreign leaders, and lacked the decisiveness that Ben-Gurion possessed in spades. Unlike his predecessor, Eshkol liked to govern by consensus and compromise, and was given to long, rambling conversations in which he wandered through all sides of an issue. While Eshkol's personality endeared him to colleagues who had grown tired of the humorless, dictatorial Ben-Gurion, he frequently proved incapable of making firm decisions on important questions.[71] Now Eshkol had to decide whether to listen to his generals or to Kennedy, who warned him on July 4 that US support for Israel could "seriously be jeopardized" over Dimona.[72]

Typically, Eshkol had mixed feelings about what to do. Like his close ally Golda Meir, he did not want to confront the Americans over the nuclear issue. "I doubt if a rift with the United States strengthens us. I won't hesitate to say that it weakens us," he told his generals.[73] At a meeting with a small group of senior officials that September, Eshkol waxed skeptical when Moshe Dayan proclaimed that there was "no substitute" for Dimona's "finished product." Would it really be so easy to deflect US pressure? he asked. Eshkol suggested using Dimona as a bargaining chip: "Maybe we should start by saying that we've got a [plutonium] separation plant. We're prepared to do nothing for half a year, two years, three years, but you—Kennedy—should provide us with other forms of deterrence," he proposed.[74] Eshkol also wondered if the beginning of détente in Europe might transform the Arab-Israeli conflict as well.[75] As US-Soviet tensions waned, he told Meir, both powers might finally decide to support the status quo in the Middle East. Perhaps "a visionary like Herzl" could convene an international conference where the great powers would recognize Israel as the official sanctuary of the Jewish people and guarantee its borders once and for all. Afterward, Israel would become a neutral state—"like Switzerland"—and withdraw from the United Nations.[76]

In more guarded moments, though, Eshkol voiced doubt about the value of great power guarantees. Kennedy, he thought, needed to know that he was "dealing with the existence of a state and a people." Like Ben-Gurion, Eshkol did not want to trade Israel's nuclear potential for promises that future US presidents or Congress might disregard.[77] In the end, the legendarily indecisive prime minister opted to stall. On July 17, Eshkol informed Kennedy that he was still acquainting himself with "all the details of the Dimona project" and would send him "a substantive reply" later.[78]

Had Nasser shown any interest in Kennedy's arms control initiative, Eshkol's delaying tactics might not have bought Israel much time. But when John McCloy raised the idea of an Arab-Israeli arms control regime with Nasser late that June, the Egyptian president balked. The UAR, Nasser told McCloy, could not agree to any kind of inspections regime. Egypt could not look like a "protectorate" or a "satellite."[79] Without any significant concessions from Nasser, the Americans doubted that they could get the Israelis to compromise on Dimona at a price the United States could actually pay.[80] On July 23, Kennedy told his advisors that "we should not do anything for the time being."[81] By fall, the Americans no longer felt the same sense of urgency to reconsider their role in the Arab-Israeli conflict. With Eshkol striking a less truculent pose on Dimona and the Jordan crisis now a fading memory, Rusk argued, "we can look at the arms limitation problem in slightly longer perspective today than seemed feasible last spring."[82] On October 2, five months after Ben-Gurion submitted his second request for a security guarantee, Kennedy finally turned the Israelis down.[83]

The Americans had temporarily suspended their efforts to halt Israel's nuclear program, but Dimona's future remained in question. Eshkol and his colleagues had good reason to believe that the United States would try to get them to forswear atomic weapons and territorial conquest without offering much in return.

THE ISRAELI-JORDANIAN ENTENTE ENDANGERED

Nuclear deterrence no longer seemed like a safe bet for Israel. What about Ben-Gurion's more immediate objective of keeping Jordan from joining a unified Arab bloc? Eshkol, if anything, was even more optimistic than his predecessor about quietly reaching out to Arab leaders. "We have to figure that as time goes by, their recognition of our existence strengthens," he told Meir. Eshkol mused aloud about contacting Algerian president Ahmad Ben Bella and even the leaders of the Syrian Ba'th.

After all, he reasoned, the Ba'th, like Mapai, was a socialist party.[84] Again, this sort of whimsical talk hid Eshkol's tougher side. Like Ben-Gurion, he believed in approaching the Arab world from a position of strength. His efforts to seek partners in the Arab world were also designed first and foremost to prevent Israel's neighbors from uniting against it. Almost immediately upon becoming prime minister, Eshkol launched major covert operations in support of Kurdish rebels in Iraq and the Yemeni royalists battling Nasser's forces.[85] A similar desire to divide and weaken the Arab world led him to build upon Ben-Gurion's tacit deal with Hussein.

The summer of 1963 seemed like a good time for Israel to reinforce its ties to the Hashemite monarchy. Hussein's distrust of the Kennedy administration had reached new heights, but so had his need for US aid and reassurance, which he did not get. When American, British, and Jordanian officers held talks that June, the American and British representatives recommended that Hussein dismiss his entire National Guard, reduce the JAA's ammunition stockpiles, and cut Jordan's standing army by 1,250 men.[86] Frustrated, the king took to scolding US officials. He was "sick and tired" of being thought of as a "young hothead" by them, he told Ambassador Macomber. The United States clearly had "reservations about him personally" as well as a "somewhat defeatist attitude regarding the possibilities for ultimate success of moderate regimes in this part of the Arab world."[87]

To remind the Americans not to take him for granted, Hussein visited French president Charles de Gaulle and flirted with Communist and nonaligned countries, allowing Poland and Czechoslovakia to open trade offices in Amman, signing a trade pact with India, and establishing diplomatic relations with the USSR.[88] And he again sought to have Israel plead his case in Washington. When Ya'akov Herzog, deputy director-general of the Israeli Foreign Ministry, contacted Queen Zayn through Emmanuel Herbert and asked for a meeting, the king offered to meet Herzog himself.[89] To bolster his connection with the United States, Hussein was willing to give the Israelis what they so desperately wanted: face-to-face contact with an Arab head of state.

On September 24, 1963, Hussein and Herzog met at Herbert's house in St. John's Wood, a leafy, affluent enclave in northwest London. On the surface, Herzog seemed to be an unlikely candidate for a secret liaison with an Arab king. The Irish-born son of Israel's first chief rabbi, Herzog was a quiet, scholarly man who had translated the Mishna into English while in his twenties. Yet as a young man, Herzog had accompanied his father on numerous missions to help rescue European Jews from the Nazis, and later to aid Holocaust survivors. In the process, he acquired a taste for high-stakes clandestine diplomacy, and learned to be discreet and keep his personal ambitions in check. These qualities, along with his intelligence and his eloquence in English, made Herzog an outstanding diplomat and a natural choice for sensitive meetings with Arab leaders.[90]

While the simple fact of Herzog's meeting with Hussein was momentous, it marked continuity in Israeli-Jordanian relations rather than change. Their conversation revealed that the basis of the Israeli-Jordanian entente was still the same: shared hostility toward Nasser and frustration with America's flirtation with him. At present, Hussein complained, his trouble "was with his friends more than with his enemies." The Americans supported Nasser "without any reservation" and were backing the Baʻth as well. When Herzog suggested that Israel, Jordan, Turkey, Iran, and "perhaps Lebanon" adopt a "clear line of policy . . . a new concept for the Middle East which might provide a counterbalance to Nasser's diplomatic and propaganda activities in the US," the king wholeheartedly agreed. Much of Hussein and Herzog's discussion, however, involved the two men promising that their governments would stick with policies that they had already adopted. Hussein pledged to keep border incidents to a minimum, while Herzog offered to help Jordan procure US aid and to burnish Jordan's reputation in the US media and in Congress. Essentially, the Herzog-Hussein meeting provided a chance for Israel's and Jordan's leaders to reaffirm established understandings after a period of crisis and uncertainty.[91]

Still, by the fall of 1963, the foundations of Israeli-Jordanian rapprochement already looked less solid. For the first time since 1958, it seemed like the Egyptian threat might not suffice to keep Hussein and the Israelis together. As Nasser struggled to escape the Yemeni quagmire and reverted to bickering with the Syrians and the Iraqis, Hussein sensed that he could reconcile with the Egyptian president and strengthen his position at home.[92] The king's tilt toward Nasser began that August, when the Jordanian intelligence services arrested twenty-seven Baʻthists

Levi Eshkol and Ya'akov Herzog. Israel Government Press Office/Moshe Pridan.

on flimsy charges of plotting against the monarchy.[93] Simultaneously, Hussein employed Hikmat al-Masri, a Nablus notable and a veteran of Sulayman al-Nabulsi's National Socialist Party, as an emissary to the Egyptian government.[94] At the end of September, Hussein granted an interview to Muhammad Hasanayn Haykal, the editor of *al-Ahram* and one of Nasser's closest confidantes. Seizing the opportunity, the king blamed the Ba'thist takeovers in Iraq and Syria on the CIA, an accusation guaranteed to annoy the Kennedy administration and please Nasser at the same time.[95]

By the end of 1963, it looked as if Hussein had calculated correctly. In November, a group of pro-Nasserist officers led by 'Abd al-Salam 'Arif pushed aside the Ba'th-dominated regime in Iraq.[96] Domestically embattled and regionally isolated, Syria's leaders sought to improve their position by calling for the Arabs to unite against Israel's nearly completed National Water Carrier, designed to divert the headwaters of the Jordan to the Negev.[97] Nasser, still entangled in Yemen, did not want the Syrians to bait him into a war that he was sure to lose. And so, on December 23, he invited all Arab leaders to a summit in Cairo to plan for a decisive showdown with Israel.[98]

Unsurprisingly, Hussein was the first Arab leader to respond to Nasser's call.[99] Like the Egyptian president, he wanted to defuse Syria's calls for war.[100] Mainly, however, Nasser's call for Arab solidarity attracted Hussein because of what it offered him at home. By going to Cairo, he explained to British ambassador Roderick Parkes, he hoped to snag badly needed money from the Gulf states to build up his army. Most of all, he wanted to force Nasser to recognize the legitimacy of his regime.[101]

When the summit ended on January 17, the king had good reason to feel pleased. Syria's calls for an immediate attack on Israel went unheeded. The Arab leaders instead decided to prepare for war by 1968, before Israel could build nuclear weapons.[102] To counter Israel's diversion plans, Lebanon, Jordan, and Syria would divert the headwaters of the Jordan away from the Jewish state. To blunt an Israeli military response to Arab diversion activities and prepare for war, a Unified Arab Command (UAC) would be created, headed by Egyptian general 'Ali 'Ali 'Amir and paid for by the Arab League. The Arab oil producers would bear the costs of the Arab water diversion efforts.[103]

Hussein would now have far more money to build up Jordan's water infrastructure and strengthen his army, the pillar of his regime. The king was less ecstatic that the Arab League authorized Ahmad al-Shuqayri, who represented the Palestinians on the Arab League Council, to create a "Palestinian entity," but he disregarded the threat of Palestinian nationalism for the sake of mending fences with Nasser. During the summit, the two men agreed to restore diplomatic ties and end propaganda warfare. Their reconciliation did not please the royal family or many of Hussein's traditional supporters on the East Bank, but for the most part it was "enthusiastically greeted" in the kingdom.[104]

A series of goodwill gestures toward Egypt followed. Jordanians were allowed to legally buy Egyptian newspapers and periodicals again. The Jordanian pilots who had defected to the UAR in 1962 were permitted to return home. Jordan recognized the republican government in Yemen.[105] Most importantly, in July, Hussein appointed Bahjat al-Talhuni prime minister. Al-Talhuni, who had headed another Jordanian cabinet from 1960 to 1962, was notoriously corrupt; one British diplomat described him as "summing up the worst features of the Hashemite regime."[106] As prime minister, al-Talhuni had granted monopolies to well-connected businessmen and allowed other cronies to enrich themselves by bending the terms of military procurement contracts.[107] Nevertheless, as an advocate of good relations with Egypt, al-Talhuni was Hussein's first choice. The king clearly intended to extend his honeymoon with Nasser for as long as it would last.

The Israelis watched Hussein's moves with unease. They understood why the king felt compelled to go to Cairo. Even Golda Meir, not known for her empathy toward Arab leaders, recognized "the complex which he bears, the complex of his grandfather who cooperated with the Zionists." Hussein, she thought, clearly relished the fact that "big brother has let him into the club, and suddenly he's been made the mediator between Nasser and Faysal and so forth."[108] The danger, as the Israelis saw it, was that the king's conciliatory gestures would create a permissive political environment that his opponents could easily exploit.[109] "King Hussein has thus far controlled internal developments," admitted Mossad head Amit in August 1964, "but the point could be reached before long where some of the developments will begin to control the king."[110] "Hussein has gone too far into Nasser's arms. Are we doing something about this?" grumbled Eshkol.[111]

The trouble was that Israel could not really do anything about Jordan's tilt toward Egypt so long as Hussein stayed in power. For years the Israelis had prepared for a clear, sharp breach of the status quo in Jordan—an externally sponsored coup, perhaps even an Egyptian invasion. As the crisis of April 1963 had shown, it would be far trickier for Israel to justify military action if Hussein were undermined from within. Golda Meir thought that the subject of "indirect change" was so sensitive that the Israeli government should not even raise it with outsiders. If Israeli officials began arguing that they might act in the event of "indirect change" in Jordan, she warned, "they will begin to ask questions. For example: There are elections in Jordan ... there's a pro-Nasserist parliament, Hussein remains in his place, and everything's fine. And let's suppose that if there's a pro-Nasserist parliament, Hussein will maybe have a pro-Nasserist prime minister, maybe a pro-Nasserist foreign minister. It's happened before. And then they'll ask us: 'Would you attack Jordan in such an instance?' Why should I set myself up to have to answer that? It is impossible to simply answer such a question."[112] Perhaps a slow, incremental process of regime change was what Nasser preferred, speculated Ze'ev Bar-Lavi, who headed AMAN's Jordan desk. The Egyptians might want "a situation where they can at will overthrow the Hashemite regime but to hold back from actually bringing about Hussein's downfall till it suits them."[113] Jordan would be slowly drawn into Egypt's sphere of influence, but in the meantime it would be impossible for Israel to act.

It seemed that the Israelis were going to have to rethink their whole West Bank strategy. Ben-Gurion's policy of backing Hussein's regime while seeking a nuclear deterrent had been called into question. To defuse the West Bank issue, Israel, Jordan, and the United States would have to reconcile their other competing priorities.

NOTES

1. Amman to State, April 2, 1962, *FRUS, 1961–1963*, 17: doc. 232.
2. Haykal, *Sanawat al-ghalayan*, 582. For Egyptian allegations of Jordanian involvement in the SNP coup attempt, see Cairo to State, January 11, 1962, *FRUS, 1961–1963*, 17: doc. 161; Haykal, *Sanawat al-ghalayan*, 597. Though al-Tal denied direct Jordanian involvement in the coup attempt, he did not deny that Jordan provided aid to the SNP. See "Rad 'ala ittihamat," in Tal, *Kitabat fi al-qadaya al-'arabiyya*, 182.
3. Podeh, "'Suez in Reverse,'" 118–119. The text of the Saudi-Jordanian agreement can be found in BNA/FO 371/164090.
4. Tal, *Politics*, 91–93; Amman to State, November 20, 1962, JFKL/NSF/Country Files/Jordan, box 125A.
5. Amman to State, November 8, 1962, JFKL/NSF/Country Files/Jordan, box 125A.
6. Memo for the record, November 15, 1962, DDRS/CK3100114165.
7. Amman to State, January 8, 1963, JFKL/NSF/Country Files/Jordan, box 125A.
8. Ottawa to FM, January 17, 1963, ISA/FM/3418/17; Research Branch to FM, January 14, 1963, ISA/FM/3418/20; Jerusalem to FO, January 31, 1963, BNA/FO 371/170264.
9. For the classic account of the Cairo talks, see Kerr, *Arab Cold War*, 44–76.
10. Amman to State, March 27, 1963, NA/RG59/DOSCF 1963/POL 2-1 JORDAN; Roderick Parkes, "Jordan: Annual Review for 1963," January 9, 1964, BNA/FO 371/175645; CIA cable, "Intention of King Hussein to Form a New Government," March 20, 1963, JFKL/NSF/Country Files/Jordan, box 125A.
11. Amman to State, March 31, 1963, NA/RG59/DOSCF 1963/POL 15 JORDAN.
12. Roderick Parkes, "Jordan: Annual Review for 1963," January 9, 1964, BNA/FO 371/175645. See also Musa, *Tarikh al-urdun*, 56.
13. *al-Gumhurriya*, April 2, 1963.
14. *al-Ahram*, April 19, 1963.
15. Tel Aviv to FO, April 20, 1963, BNA/FO 371/170529; Roderick Parkes, "Jordan: Annual Review for 1963," January 9, 1964, BNA/FO 371/175645; Jerusalem to State, April 18, 1963, NA/RG59/DOSCF 1963/POL 25 JORDAN.
16. Amman to State, April 22, 1963, NA/RG59/DOSCF 1963/POL 25 JORDAN.
17. Musa, *Tarikh al-urdun*, 57; Jerusalem to State, April 20, 1963, NA/RG59/DOSCF 1963/POL 25 JORDAN.
18. Amman to State, April 24, 1963, NA/RG59/DOSCF 1963/POL 2-1 JORDAN.
19. Amman to State, May 1, 1963, NA/RG59/DOSCF 1963/POL 2-1 JORDAN. British estimates indicated that the number of people killed in the riots could have been anywhere between ten and forty. See "Developments in the Middle East," April 24, 1963, BNA/FO 371/170154.
20. New York to State, April 25, 1963, NA/RG59/DOSCF 1963/POL 25 JORDAN.
21. Amman to State, April 22, 1963, NA/RG59/DOSCF 1963/POL 25 JORDAN.
22. KFADC minutes, March 13, 1963, ISA/A/7568/9.
23. KFADC minutes, February 12, 1963, ISA/A/7568/9.
24. On Yemen, see Rabin to Braun, December 27, 1962, in Rosenthal, *Yitzhak Rabin*, 313. On Iraq, see Gazit to Kidron, February 12, 1963, ISA/FM/3378/14. See also cabinet minutes, April 25, 1963, ISA.
25. Cabinet minutes, April 25, 1963, ISA.

26. KFADC minutes, March 27, 1963, ISA/A/7568/9.
27. Arad to Washington and London, March 31, 1963, ISA/FM/3378/14.
28. Cabinet minutes, April 30, 1963, ISA.
29. Cabinet minutes, April 25, 1963, ISA.
30. Ibid.
31. See Aharon Yariv's briefing to British officials, April 26, 1963, BNA/FO 371/170155. Tsur gave a similar assessment to the Israeli cabinet the previous day.
32. Ball-McNamara telcon, April 27, 1963, *FRUS*, 1961–1963, 18: doc. 221.
33. Memo for the record, April 27, 1963, *FRUS*, 1961–1963, 18: doc. 222.
34. DOS memcon, April 27, 1963, *FRUS*, 1961–1963, 18: doc. 225.
35. Washington to FM, April 21, 1963, ISA/FM/3378/10.
36. Washington to FM, April 27, 1963, ISA/FM/3377/13.
37. DOS memcon, April 28, 1963, *FRUS*, 1961–1963, 18: doc. 227.
38. "Analysis of Possibilities Developing in Jordan's Situation," unsigned, May 9, 1963, ISA/FM/3377/13.
39. IDF Operations Branch, "Twelve-Hour Alert for the Implementation of NEVOT," April 21, 1963, IDFA/337/65/106. This document does not reveal the specific objectives of the plan, but these can be inferred from documents pertaining to its implementation. All intelligence-gathering efforts pertaining to the plan, for example, focused on parts of Jordanian Jerusalem abutting the route to Mount Scopus and Government House Ridge. See Appendix 7, "Plan for Organizing Reconnaissance—NEVOT," IDFA/394/64/52.
40. Operations Branch to Central Command, May 2, 1963, IDFA/337/65/106.
41. FM to Paris, Rome, New York, Washington, London, and Ottawa, May 1, 1963, ISA/FM/3378/10.
42. "Analysis of Possibilities Developing in Jordan's Situation," unsigned, May 9, 1963, ISA/FM/3377/13.
43. Ball-Bundy telcon, April 29, 1963, *FRUS*, 1961–1963, 18: doc. 228.
44. "Contingency Plan—Jordan (Second Draft)," May 4, 1963, JFKL/NSF/Country Files/Jordan, box 125A.
45. Cairo to State, April 27, 1963, DDRS/CK3100263033.
46. Cairo to State, April 29, 1963, DDRS/CK3100263037.
47. Barak, "Caught in the Middle."
48. Cabinet minutes, May 12, 1963, ISA.
49. Cabinet minutes, May 12, 1963, ISA.
50. Cabinet minutes, April 30 and May 5, 1963, ISA. However, Ben-Gurion believed that the Cold War would end within ten to fifteen years. See Heller, *Yisrael vehamilhamah ha-karah*, 343.
51. Cabinet minutes, May 5, 1963, ISA.
52. Cabinet minutes, April 25, 1963, ISA.
53. Remarks at a meeting of the General Staff, July 8, 1963, in Rosenthal, *Yitzhak Rabin*, 320–321.
54. Quoted in Gluska, *Eshkol*, 51.
55. "Consultation on the Exchange of Letters with the President of the United States," September 6, 1963, George Washington University, National Security Archive, Miscellaneous Hebrew Documents, http://www.gwu.edu/~nsarchiv/israel/documents/hebrew/index.html.
56. Cohen, *Israel and the Bomb*, 115–117.

57. Trachtenberg, *Constructed Peace*, 379–398.
58. NSAM 231, March 26, 1963, John F. Kennedy Presidential Library and Museum, http://www.jfklibrary.org/Asset-Viewer/o9tKrOeAAoCRn-2Az_yETw.aspx.
59. Cohen, *Israel and the Bomb*, 118.
60. Ben-Gurion to Kennedy, April 26, 1963, JFKL/POF/Israel—Security, 1961–1963, box 119.
61. State to Tel Aviv, May 4, 1964, *FRUS*, 1961–1963, 18: doc. 236.
62. Ben-Gurion to Kennedy, May 12, 1963, ISA/FM/3377/9.
63. State to Tel Aviv, May 18, 1963, *FRUS*, 1961–1963, 18: doc. 252.
64. Tim Weiner, "Robert Komer, 78, Figure in Vietnam, Dies," *New York Times*, April 12, 2000.
65. Memo for the record, April 27, 1963, *FRUS*, 1961–1963, 18: doc. 222.
66. Memo for the record, May 1, 1963, *FRUS*, 1961–1963, 18: doc. 231.
67. "Framework and Tactics for Negotiations," undated, JFKL/POF/Israel: Security: Arms Control, 1963, box 119A. This paper was given to Kennedy under a May 16 covering memorandum from Komer. See Komer to Kennedy, May 16, 1963, *FRUS*, 1961–1963, 18: doc. 250.
68. "Possible United States-Israel Security Assurance," undated, JFKL/POF/Israel: Security: Arms Control, 1963, box 119A. This paper was also given to Kennedy by Komer on May 16.
69. Memo for the record, June 15, 1963, *FRUS*, 1961–1963, 18: doc. 273.
70. Cohen, *Israel and the Bomb*, 12, 134–136.
71. For recent biographical studies of Eshkol, see Goldstein, *Eshkol*; and Oren, "Levi Eshkol." A recent volume of documents dealing with Eshkol's life and career published by the Israel State Archives (Lammfromm and Tsoref, *Levi Eshkol*) also contains useful biographical data.
72. Kennedy to Eshkol, July 4, 1963, JFKL/POF/Israel—Security, 1961–1963, box 119.
73. Quoted in Gluska, *Eshkol*, 63.
74. "Consultation on the Exchange of Letters with the President of the United States," September 6, 1963, George Washington University, National Security Archive, Miscellaneous Hebrew Documents, http://www.gwu.edu/~nsarchiv/israel/documents/hebrew/index.html.
75. That spring, Eshkol had been among the most enthusiastic supporters of Ben-Gurion's request for a joint US-Soviet guarantee of the borders of Middle Eastern states. See cabinet minutes, May 5, 1963, ISA.
76. Eshkol-Meir memcon, July 9, 1963, ISA/A/7921/1.
77. Shalom, *Bein dimona le-washington*, 109–110.
78. "Excerpts from Presidential Correspondence (JFK, Ben-Gurion, and Eshkol) on Arms Limitation Control (e.g. Dimona) in the Middle East," July 30, 1963, DDRS/CK3100550720.
79. Cairo to State, June 28, 1963, *FRUS*, 1961–1963, 18: doc. 283; Cairo to State, June 30, 1963, *FRUS*, 1961–1963, 18: doc. 285.
80. Komer to Kennedy, July 19, 1963, *FRUS*, 1961–1963, 18: doc. 298. See also Komer to Kennedy, July 23, 1963, *FRUS*, 1961–1963, 18: doc. 300.
81. Kennedy-McCloy et al. memcon, July 23, 1963, *FRUS*, 1961–1963, 18: doc. 303.
82. Rusk to Kennedy, September 10, 1963, *FRUS*, 1961–1963, 18: doc. 323.

83. State to Tel Aviv, October 2, 1963, *FRUS*, 1961–1963, 18: doc. 332.
84. Eshkol-Meir memcon, July 9, 1963, ISA/A/7921/1.
85. On Israeli aid to the Kurds, see Nakdimon, *Tikvah she-karsah*. On Israeli involvement in Yemen, see Jones, *Britain and the Yemen Civil War*, 146–150.
86. Amman to FO and enclosure, June 12, 1963, BNA/FO 371/170312.
87. Amman to State, July 24, 1963, NA/RG59/DOSCF 1963/POL 1 JORDAN-US.
88. Roderick Parkes, "Jordan: Annual Review for 1963," January 9, 1964, BNA/FO 371/175645.
89. Herzog to Lurie, September 8, 1963, ISA/RG130.15/3782/16; Zak, *Hussein 'oseh shalom*, 63.
90. See Bar-Zohar, *Yaacov Herzog*.
91. Ya'akov Herzog, "Meeting with Charles," September 24, 1963, YHP.
92. On the collapse of the Tripartite Federation, see Podeh, "To Unite or Not to Unite," 166–176.
93. Amman to State, January 21, 1964, LBJL/NSF/Country Files/Jordan, box 146.
94. London to State, August 16, 1963, NA/RG59/DOSCF 1963/POL JORDAN-UAR.
95. *al-Ahram*, September 27, 1963.
96. *al-Ahram*, November 19, 1963; *al-Ahram*, November 20, 1963.
97. Shemesh, "Prelude to the Six-Day War," 5–14.
98. *al-Ahram*, December 24, 1963.
99. Musa, *Tarikh al-urdun*, 72.
100. See, for example, Amman to State, October 7, 1963, NA/RG59/DOSCF 1963/POL 15–1 JORDAN.
101. Amman to FO, January 2, 1964, BNA/FO 371/175556.
102. Ya'akov Herzog, "Meeting with Charles on Sunday, July 2nd, from 8:10 P.M. to 9:45 P.M.," July 2, 1967, YHP. Other sources also confirm 1968 as the Arab governments' target date for war, although without specific reference to the Israeli nuclear program. See, for example, Jum'a, *al-Mu'amara wa-ma'arakat al-masir*, 120.
103. Shuqayri, *Min al-qima ila al-hazima*, 48–49; Riyadh, *Mudhakirrat Mahmud Riyadh, al-joz al-thani*, 285; Harold Beeley, "The Arab Summit Conference," January 28, 1964, BNA/FO 371/175557.
104. Parkes to Morris, September 16, 1964, BNA/FO 371/175647.
105. Harold Beeley, "The Arab Summit Conference," January 28, 1964, BNA/FO 371/175557; J. F. S. Phillips, "Jordan 1964: Arma Virumque," January 7, 1965, BNA/FO 371/180728.
106. W. Morris, "The New Jordan Government," July 7, 1964, BNA/FO 371/175646.
107. Tell, *Social and Economic Origins*, 123.
108. KFADC minutes, September 22, 1964, ISA/A/8160/8.
109. "The Arab Summit Conference: Summary and Implications," AMAN special estimate 9/64, February 3, 1964, ISA/FM/4327/19.
110. Tel Aviv to State, August 15, 1964, NA/RG59/DOSCF 1964–1966/POL ISR-JORDAN.
111. Eshkol-Yahil memcon, August 10, 1964, ISA/A/7933/7.
112. KFADC minutes, September 22, 1964, ISA/A/8160/8.
113. "Israeli Appreciation of Pro-Nasser Trends in Jordan," undated, BNA/FO 371/175650.

THREE

A STATUS QUO SETTLEMENT?

1964–1965

BY THE SPRING OF 1965, THE ISRAELI-JORDANIAN ENTENTE gained a new lease on life, thanks to the Johnson administration's decision to radically enlarge the US role in the Arab-Israeli arena. For the first time, the United States agreed to sell tanks to both Israel and Jordan, while asking Hussein to keep his new armor off the West Bank. For the foreseeable future, Israel would preserve its conventional military superiority over the Arab states and the West Bank would remain effectively demilitarized.

In exchange, the Americans demanded a price: the Israeli government pledged not to "introduce" nuclear weapons into the Middle East. Even if Israel moved forward with its nuclear program, it would have to maintain a conventional edge over the Arab states, and it would still need Hussein to keep other Arab armies out of the West Bank. If Hussein, for domestic political reasons, could not remain neutral, Israel would likely have to go to war.

In 1965, when Nasser was bogged down in Yemen and Hussein's regime seemed relatively stable, the Israelis did not have to worry too much about a possible confrontation over the West Bank. Yet as they would soon discover, the risk of such a conflict would not easily disappear.

THE JORDAN WATERS ISSUE, 1964–1965

No matter what, Israel, Jordan, Lebanon, and Syria would have found it hard to share the waters of the Jordan River basin. A context of regional conflict, however, had made this difficult problem impossible to solve. In 1955, Eric Johnston, the US special ambassador for water in the Middle East, had devised a water-sharing plan for the Jordan River riparian states, but the Arab League refused to endorse it.[1]

Nevertheless, as on so many other issues, Ben-Gurion and Hussein reached a tacit compromise on the Jordan waters problem. In 1958 and 1959, both leaders separately promised the Eisenhower administration that they would adhere to the so-called Johnston Plan in exchange for American help with their irrigation projects. Over the following five years, the Americans financed the building of Israel's National Water Carrier and Jordan's East Ghor Canal, which channeled water from the Yarmuk River to the arid lower Jordan Valley.

In 1964, however, Arab summitry suddenly threatened to wreck Israel and Jordan's quiet modus vivendi. At the Arab League summit in Alexandria in September 1964, Hussein agreed to build a dam at Mukhayba on the Yarmuk River, which would catch water that Syria and Lebanon had already diverted away from the Jewish state.[2] On the surface, it appeared that Jordan had completely abandoned the Johnston Plan.

Yet while Hussein publicly embraced the Arab diversion agenda, Jordan did not actually consume any more water than it had before. Jordan would stay "within [the] limits" of the Johnston Plan, the king told Adlai Stevenson, the American ambassador to the UN.[3] The Jordanians began planning to build the Mukhayba Dam, but they knew that the dam would not affect Israel's water supply until Syria and Lebanon began to divert the Jordan's headwaters. And Hussein clearly expected the Syrians and Lebanese to fail. Any Arab diversion plan, Hussein told US ambassador Robert Barnes, "was perhaps too late, since Israel [was] so far advanced in its diversion plan that [the] Arab position before world opinion would be weak."[4] After the Alexandria summit, the king speculated that the Lebanese would not divert any water until their armed forces were built up, which could take "virtually unlimited time." Hussein thought that the Syrians would need two or three years to build their diversion works, which would give the Israelis ample time to destroy them.[5]

The Israelis, for their part, never really saw Hussein as a player in the struggle over the Jordan waters. From the Cairo summit onward, AMAN assumed that the Jordanians would merely pay lip service to the Arab League's plans.[6] Such assessments were soon affirmed by messages from Hussein himself. In May 1964, Ya'akov Herzog, now director-general of the prime minister's office, met the king again in London, where Hussein assured him that he aimed "at keeping Arab plans within the Johnston framework."[7] "As of right now, Hussein is working with us on the water issue," Golda Meir told the Knesset Foreign Affairs and Defense Committee in September. "Our [water] professionals are not worked up about the Mukhayba Dam at all."[8] In the spring of 1965, the IDF attacked Syria's diversion works, effectively putting the water issue to rest. So long as the Syrians and Lebanese could not divert the Jordan's headwaters, the Israelis did not have to worry about Hussein trapping and storing them.

Thus, the Jordan waters issue never seriously threatened the Israeli-Jordanian entente. The Unified Arab Command, another product of the Cairo summit, would force Eshkol and Hussein to confront far more difficult dilemmas.

ISRAEL, JORDAN, AND THE
UNIFIED ARAB COMMAND

Unlike the Arab diversion plans, the Unified Arab Command never sparked any Arab-Israeli clashes, yet it was in some ways more worrisome to the Israelis. At the start of 1964, the Israeli intelligence community overwhelmingly believed that Egypt would not actually go to war over the Jordan waters issue.[9] Nasser, Rabin predicted, would not fight while the conventional military balance remained in Israel's favor and Egypt had "between twenty thousand and thirty thousand troops in Yemen."[10] Yet AMAN still regarded the UAC as the "outstanding manifestation" of a new and threatening Arab strategy. The basic premise of that strategy, as AMAN understood it, was that Egypt could not defeat Israel alone. Syria, Jordan, and Lebanon needed to contribute more to an Arab war effort, and the UAC would help them do so.[11] United under one command, the Arab frontline states could plan jointly for war, move troops from one country to another, and share money collected by the Arab League. And indeed, following the last of the pre-1967 Arab summits at Casablanca in September 1965, the Israeli intelligence community concluded that the UAC was the one product of the Cairo conference that still mattered.[12] By that point, the Israelis estimated that Jordan, Syria, and Lebanon had received £24.5 million in cash for weapons. The Arab League had authorized the confrontation states to spend another £125.5 million by the end of 1968, Nasser's target date for war with Israel.[13]

Neither the Jordanian nor the Israeli government wanted non-Jordanian troops deployed in Jordan under the UAC's auspices. At the Alexandria summit, the Jordanians joined Lebanon and Syria in rejecting UAC chief 'Ali 'Ali 'Amir's demand that they allow other Arab troops into their countries.[14] Privately, the king assured Herzog that "no foreign forces will come into Jordan," and the Israeli intelligence community assumed that he would keep his word.[15]

But the UAC was also meant to finance the enlargement and modernization of the Syrian, Lebanese, and Jordanian armies. The Israelis, of course, did not want the Jordanians to substantially expand their army, which would force the IDF to divert forces from the Egyptian front. Hussein, however, had long hoped to enlarge the JAA. Since the late 1950s, the Americans had rejected Jordanian requests for new weapons, arguing that they could not allow their budgetary aid to be wasted on arms that the JAA did not really need. Now, with the UAC footing the bill, Hussein could reasonably argue that he could revamp his armed forces without compromising Jordan's economic development.

When the king visited Washington in April 1964, he begged President Lyndon Johnson and his advisors to sell Jordan state-of-the-art weapons, promising that the UAC would pay the costs.[16] Unmoved, Johnson and Undersecretary of State George Ball warned Hussein that the Arab military buildup could force them to sell heavy weapons to Israel. They offered him nothing, urging him to rely on the United States for protection.[17]

Had the Soviet Union not jumped into the fray, Hussein might not have gotten any further with the Americans. In May 1964, however, Soviet leader Nikita Khrushchev visited Cairo and urged Nasser to push Jordan to acquire Soviet arms. That June and July, three UAC delegations, comprising mainly Egyptian officers, visited the Hashemite kingdom and advised Hussein to integrate Jordan's largely Palestinian National Guard into the JAA, expand the number of brigades on the West Bank, and purchase Soviet missiles, planes, and tanks. Since the UAC could provide the funds, Hussein could not refuse to expand his army. When veteran JAA officers, most of them East Bankers, tried to oppose the UAC plans, the king abruptly dismissed ninety-three of them.[18]

Yet Hussein stayed firm on one point: his new weapons had to come from the United States. The king was determined not to let the Soviets or Egyptians penetrate his army and subvert his regime.[19] At the end of July he sent 'Amir Khammash, the JAA's director of planning and operations, to Washington with a shopping list including twenty F-104 supersonic jets and M-48A3 tanks.[20] Khammash, who became JAA chief of staff a year later, was the most prominent representative of a younger group of Jordanian officers who wanted the JAA to recruit more Palestinians, cooperate more closely with Egypt, and adopt American military doctrine.[21] Hussein's choice to send Khammash, rather than a more conservative figure, signaled his determination to remain on good terms with both the Arab radicals and the West.

In Washington, American policymakers were split over what to tell Khammash. Keen to stay out of the Arab-Israeli arms race, Secretary of State Dean Rusk and other top State Department officials wanted to sell only a small amount of ground equipment to Jordan. They feared that Jordan would go bankrupt buying aircraft, and that if the Israelis found out about the sale, they would demand American warplanes of their own. Secretary of Defense Robert McNamara and the Joint Chiefs of Staff, on the other hand, wanted to consider selling Jordan aircraft. They argued that doing so would not upset the Arab-Israeli military balance, and that American planes in Jordan would scare the Israelis less than Egyptian and Soviet trainers.[22]

In the end, the Johnson administration adopted a compromise formula proposed by Robert Komer of the NSC staff, who recommended that the United States offer Jordan tanks but withhold aircraft until Hussein received "ironclad Arab guarantees of all the dough involved."

When Khammash angrily rejected this offer, President Johnson chose to personally intervene. On August 4, the president sent Hussein a letter warning that if Jordan sought Soviet arms, the United States would be forced to cut off its budgetary aid.[23] By September, Hussein backed down and accepted the American proposal.[24] At the Alexandria summit, when UAC Chief 'Amir called for all of Israel's neighbors to purchase Soviet arms, the Jordanians refused, and Nasser, unwilling to strangle Arab summitry in its cradle, did not press the subject any further.[25]

But the Americans had more trouble fulfilling their part of the bargain. At the end of 1964, the US government still had not sold any arms to Jordan for fear of how the Israelis might react. Once again, the question of Jordan's role within the regional configuration of power had become intertwined with the US-Israeli nuclear dialogue. The three governments still needed to find a way to satisfy Hussein's need for arms, resolve Israel's security dilemmas, and address the Americans' concerns about their regional position all at once.

WALKING BETWEEN THE RAINDROPS

By 1964, the Americans still had not gotten the Israelis to promise not to build nuclear weapons or take over the West Bank. Ben-Gurion had made it clear that Israel would not compromise its freedom of action for anything less than a full-fledged US-Israeli alliance or a US-Soviet guarantee of the status quo. Indeed, the Israelis seemed more determined than ever to rely on their own strength. In November 1963, during joint staff talks in Washington, Komer and other US officials had tried to convince the Israelis that their nuclear and missile programs would speed up the arms race and allow the Soviets to further penetrate the Middle East. Israel, they argued, should rely on US protection instead. The Israelis were not persuaded. Without a formal US-Israeli alliance, Rabin argued, Israel would seek to protect itself by any means necessary.[26] Eshkol made similar arguments. If Israel were attacked, he told Mike Feldman, Johnson's deputy special counsel and unofficial ambassador to the American Jewish community, "Washington's tendency would be to take [the] matter to [the] UN, wait [a] few days, [and] ascertain Moscow's reaction" while many Israelis died. Israel's "basic philosophy," according to Eshkol, was "autoemancipation of surviving Jews; self-labor and self-defense." The United States could "say its protective umbrella covers Israel," but Israel needed to "stand on [its] own feet and be able to touch the umbrella."[27]

Yet while Eshkol and Rabin believed that Israel should stand up for itself, they also knew that doing so required American arms, at least for the near future. "If nuclear weapons appear," Rabin told the General Staff in July 1963, "it's only the start of the show, and it's doubtful that they will have any practical implications for the IDF's force structure."[28] Eshkol likewise believed that in the short run, the IDF had to stay ready to fight "regular wars."[29] And so, in January 1964, Ambassador Harman approached Rusk and told him that the IDF's armored corps was "completely outclassed by the UAR." Israel wanted to buy three hundred American M-48A3 and M-60 tanks. The Israelis also wanted US Military Assistance Program (MAP) funds to help cover the cost, since they were already spending 40 percent of their budget and 15 percent of their GNP on defense.[30]

The Israelis had good reason to believe that they would get what they wanted. From the beginning, they regarded Lyndon Johnson as their friend. A coarse, physically imposing former schoolteacher from Texas's impoverished Hill Country, Johnson generally liked the familiar, nitty-gritty world of domestic politics much more than the rarefied world of diplomacy. "Foreigners," he once joked, "are not like the folks I am used to."[31] Still, the president tended to feel more at home with Israelis than with most other foreigners. Though Johnson did not encounter many Jews while growing up in rural Texas, most of his relatives were evangelical Protestants who believed that the establishment of a Jewish state would precede the Second Coming. While Johnson was not particularly religious, his family's staunch Christian Zionism almost certainly contributed to his positive feelings toward Israel. Like Kennedy before him, Johnson also valued the support of liberal Jewish voters and prominent Jewish Democrats.[32] Eshkol and his colleagues fondly remembered how, as Senate majority leader, Johnson had decried Eisenhower's threats to impose sanctions on Israel.[33] They hoped that he would approach arms sales in the same spirit.

Yet despite the fact that 1964 was an election year, Johnson and his advisors initially treated Israel's requests for weapons with a familiar reticence. When Eshkol visited the United States that June, he returned home full of warmth toward Johnson but without the arms deals he had wanted. Talking with Johnson, Eshkol told the cabinet, felt "like a friend is walking with you on a dark night and neither of you are afraid." Still, the Americans were not quite ready to supply Israel with offensive weapons. Instead, they sought, as Eshkol put it, to "walk between the raindrops" by offering to secretly help Israel buy surplus American tanks from West Germany.[34] And even US officials who wanted to help the Israelis get new tanks did not want to do so for nothing. The United States, Komer argued, should "tie tanks to missiles," and by extension to the nuclear issue.[35] The president's other advisors agreed.[36] As they arranged for West Germany to sell Israel the tanks, they crafted yet another Middle East arms control initiative. By August, Johnson sent John McCloy back to Cairo to present this new proposal to Nasser.[37]

But at this point, Hussein's requests for arms began to undermine the Johnson administration's strategy. In August, the Israelis learned that Hussein wanted to buy American tanks. Eshkol, Rabin, Meir, and a number of senior Foreign Ministry officials decided that Israel should unconditionally oppose an American tank sale to Jordan.[38] One tank in the West Bank, Eshkol told the Foreign Ministry's Mordechai Gazit, "was worth three or four in the Sinai." It made no difference whether Jordan received tanks "from [the United States] or from Nasser."[39]

In theory, the Americans might have prevented Jordan's requests for arms from complicating their dialogue with Israel by convincing Nasser and the Soviets to sign on to a regional arms control regime. Eshkol might have soured on the idea of security guarantees from the United States alone, but he still thought that a guarantee from *both* superpowers could have real value. The Israeli prime minister had not abandoned the hope that the beginnings of US-Soviet détente in Europe could have ripple effects in the Middle East.[40] Indeed, he had cautiously reached out to Khrushchev, emphasizing Israel's and the USSR's shared interests as status quo powers. When the Soviet leader issued a call for the peaceful resolution of territorial disputes in December 1963, Eshkol urged him to also call for Middle East peace, based on the "obligation of all states in the region to respect the territorial integrity of all other states as they are today."[41] Privately, the Israeli prime minister considered sending Golda Meir to the USSR or one of its satellites to start a dialogue with the Soviet leadership, and repeatedly tried to get the Americans to intercede with the Soviets on Israel's behalf.[42] As of September 1964, Eshkol still thought that his outreach to the USSR could eventually succeed. "After the [US presidential] elections, Johnson and Khrushchev will discuss an end to competition and the consolidation of their relations, and the consolidation of our situation, and then maybe it will be possible to discuss an end to the [arms] race," he told Gazit.[43]

But American and Israeli efforts to get the Soviets out of the Middle Eastern arms race went nowhere. There was no real chance for a Middle Eastern arms control agreement, Rusk told Harman. US officials encountered "colossal indifference" when they raised the idea with Soviet diplomats in Geneva.[44] In December 1964, Abba Eban met with Soviet foreign minister Andrei Gromyko and discussed a possible global "ban on solving border conflicts by force."[45] Yet at the start of 1965, it was clear that the Soviets were not ready to help broker an end to the Arab-Israeli arms race. By this time, it was quite apparent that Nasser also had no interest in a regional arms control deal. The "problem in [the] Middle East," the Egyptian president had told John McCloy, "was not [the] problem of missiles, but [the] problem of Palestine."[46]

While Nasser and his Soviet patrons balked at arms control, the secrecy of the Israeli–West German tank deal eroded. By October 1964, news of the sale leaked to the West German and American press.[47] Arab leaders, particularly Nasser, blasted West German chancellor Ludwig Erhard and demanded that he withhold the tanks.[48] Fearing that the Arab world would align with Communist East Germany, Erhard suspended military aid to Israel on February 10.[49] By then, only forty tanks had reached the Jewish state.[50]

The Johnson administration's strategy was in tatters. The Americans had failed to get West Germany to satisfy Israel's tank requests, and US efforts to get Nasser to compromise on his missile program had accomplished nothing. They had lost their main sources of leverage in their nuclear dialogue with Israel. And in the background, Hussein's requests for arms were growing louder.

"THE EXCUSE FOR SELLING TO ISRAEL TOO"

At the beginning of 1965, senior US policymakers felt they could not make Hussein wait to buy arms any longer. Even State Department officials thought the United States should sell tanks to Jordan, while encouraging Hussein to purchase aircraft in Europe.[51] The Americans had to persuade Hussein to accept this arms package and then reconcile the Israelis to that deal.

The Jordanian side of the problem proved easier to solve. On February 7, Assistant Secretary of State Phillips Talbot met with Hussein and Khammash in Amman. He warned Hussein of dire consequences if he bought Soviet arms, and urged him to accept a $42 million arms package for the JAA's ground forces. The United States could not sell Jordan supersonic aircraft, Talbot added, because that would force them to sell planes to Israel as well.[52]

Hussein and Khammash put up a token show of resistance, but they clearly understood that they could not push the Americans very far. The king freely admitted that he needed more weapons for political, not military, reasons. Jordan's requests for weapons, said Hussein, "while somewhat relevant to Jordanian defense problems along [the] Israeli border, became necessary chiefly to help Jordan stand up to UAC pressures."[53] After Talbot left Amman, the king flew to Cairo to persuade Nasser to approve the American proposals. He warned Nasser that if Jordan bought Soviet weapons, the main Arab "confrontation states" would all be aligned with the USSR, allowing Israel to gain unlimited US backing. Though Nasser was not easily convinced, he grudgingly conceded that the Arabs had no interest in forcing the United States to sell Israel warplanes. When Hussein returned to Amman, he promised Ambassador Barnes that he would buy weapons from "free world sources" alone.[54]

But the Americans did not want to sell tanks to Jordan without getting a nod from the Israelis first. A few days earlier, Johnson had narrowly kept the Senate from slashing all food aid to Egypt.[55] The president did not want another battle with pro-Israeli congressmen over a tank sale to Jordan. "We can never get anything in the Congress again unless we are careful," he told George Ball.[56] And unsurprisingly, when Ambassador Barbour presented the details of the US-Jordanian deal to Israel's leaders, they put up a fierce fight. Meir conceded that Hussein did not want war. "But can he stand up to Nasser?" she asked. There was no guaranteeing that at a "critical moment" Hussein would not use his "dangerous toys" against Israel.[57] In a letter to Johnson, Eshkol warned that a US-Jordanian tank deal would place a "large aggressive force only [a] few kilometers from Tel Aviv."[58]

It was time, Komer thought, for US policymakers to face "the fact of life that we were going to have to change our policy." Johnson needed Israel's "active support if we were to get away with the Jordan arms sale," and the only way to get that support "was to tell them we'd sell to them too."[59] For Johnson's influential staffer, however, there was much more than domestic politics at stake. More than any other US official, Komer saw the debate about arming Jordan as part of "the major new Arab-Israeli crisis" that had begun with the Cairo summit. In light of Soviet arms sales to the Arab states, "if we want to prevent Israeli nuclear proliferation yet protect Israel and forestall another conflict," Komer argued, "we'll have to provide Israel with its own arms." He thought that an arms sale to Jordan "could give us the excuse for selling to Israel too."[60] Ultimately, according to Komer, US arms sales to Israel could help solve the Arab-Israeli conflict. If the Arab regimes knew they could not win the arms race, "a damping down of the Arab-Israeli dispute" would eventually result.[61] At the same time, the United States could dissuade Israel from openly going nuclear or resorting to preventive war.

As in 1963, Komer won over the president. On February 9, Johnson decided to send the NSC staffer to Israel, to be joined later by Undersecretary of State Averell Harriman, a former ambassador to Moscow and a pillar of the Democratic foreign policy establishment.[62] Komer was instructed to warn the Israelis that by obstructing US arms sales to Jordan, they risked "ultimate UAR domination" of the country. If the Israelis refused to budge, perhaps the United States would mollify them by selling them tanks as well. But this would require "certain undertakings from Israel."[63] The Johnson administration would expect the Israelis to "actively" support US aid to Jordan, "assist in abetting the stir over aid to the UAR," and "forgo nuclear weapons and accept full IAEA safeguards" for the Dimona reactor. The Americans would also ask the Israelis not to deploy surface-to-surface missiles and not to take "premature preemptive action" against the Arab diversion works."[64] Would Eshkol's government actually agree?

THE HARRIMAN-KOMER MISSION

When Komer arrived in Israel, he was stunned by how vehemently Eshkol and his advisors opposed a US tank sale to Jordan. "Everything I've heard here," Komer reported, "tends to fortify my conviction that to sell arms to Jordan without at least doing the same for Israel will generate a major crisis in our relations."[65] The Israelis simply could not accept the idea that "the US should arm an Arab member of a new unified command aimed at Israel." More specifically, there was the "geographic fact" that the "bulge of Arab Palestine on the West Bank of the Jordan almost cuts Israel in two," and a stronger army there "would require Israel to redeploy a substantial part of the forces it now has in the north and south against the main Arab threats." A US arms sale to Jordan, Komer argued, could provoke the Israelis to go to war or go nuclear unless the United States did "certain things that we would probably have to do sooner or later anyway if Arab-Israeli tensions heat up."[66] Komer briefly returned to Washington and came back to Israel with Harriman a few days later. By this point, Johnson had given them permission to offer the Israelis tanks if they compromised on the nuclear and Jordan waters issues.[67]

Yet no amount of tough talk by Komer and Harriman could convince the Israelis to concede anything. It would be "awful for us to have a head-on like Suez" over the Jordan waters, Harriman warned Eshkol.[68] Nuclear proliferation, Komer told Rabin, was "one issue on which [the] vital interests of 190 million Americans would simply have to override those of 2.5 million Israelis."[69] Eshkol and his advisors nevertheless held firm. The Israelis knew that the Americans would not sell Hussein arms without their support, and doubted that they would simply refuse to sell arms to anyone if Israel did not accept their proposals. As Rabin later put it, the Israelis did not believe that the United States "had invested $500 million in Jordan and were prepared to leave it all."[70] The Israelis, Komer noted, believed that the United States would ultimately offer them more favorable terms "because of the Jordanian sword of Damocles hanging over our heads.... [I am] forced to admit they [are] right."[71]

Eshkol also understood that Johnson would not force him to renounce Israel's nuclear potential if that meant helping Ben-Gurion return to power. The former prime minister's relationship with Eshkol and the rest of Mapai's veteran leaders had badly deteriorated since his resignation; the "Old Man" would eventually leave the party to found the Israel Workers' List (Rafi) later that year.[72] With Israeli elections approaching in November 1965, Johnson and his advisors had to choose whether to lean on Eshkol at the risk of later confronting Ben-Gurion, whose intransigence on the nuclear issue was well known. According to one close Johnson associate, the president vastly preferred Eshkol to Ben-Gurion, who "talked too much."[73] Eshkol knew that the Americans would rather deal with him, and accordingly played up his domestic political problems. On March 2, the prime minister told Harriman that any nuclear concessions would require the approval of the whole Israeli cabinet and Israel's Atomic Energy Commission, which was headed by a "political opponent." "I recommend that we not attempt to force Israelis beyond what Eshkol can do at this time," Harriman told Johnson.[74] On March 7, Bundy informed Komer that he had spoken with the "highest authority"—Johnson—who thought the United States "cannot now get a guarantee on the nuclear matter or even on Jordan waters." Still, the president wanted to offer tanks to Israel and Jordan.[75]

While the Israelis battered away at Komer's conditions, they worked hard to get the Americans to accept a linkage of their own. Ever since Eshkol learned of the impending US-Jordanian arms deal, he had hoped to tie it to the demilitarization of the West Bank. The idea first came up when Eshkol discussed Hussein's interest in American arms with Mordechai Gazit that September. Gazit, who had argued about the West Bank at length with US officials during the 1963 crisis, thought the Johnson administration might support the idea of demilitarization. The Americans understood that "the West Bank is an existential issue for Israel," he told Eshkol.[76] In December, the prime minister had Ya'akov Herzog raise the idea of demilitarization with Hussein during their third meeting in London. Could Hussein promise to keep the JAA on the East Bank? Herzog asked. "What have you to fear?" Hussein responded, smiling. "You know how strong you are." Nevertheless, he promised Herzog that he would consider the idea.[77]

Eshkol apparently took Hussein's response as an encouraging sign. He instructed Shimon Peres to suggest a "private trilateral understanding" to Komer: if the United States sold tanks to Hussein, the king could secretly promise not to deploy them on the West Bank. The "maintenance of the de facto neutralization of the West Bank," Peres told the NSC staffer on February 12, "is [a] national imperative for Israel."[78] When Komer met with Eshkol and his advisors a few days later, the prime minister raised the issue himself. "You can make up this guarantee—a tripartite guarantee—Jordan-Israel—you in the middle?" he asked. Komer replied, "I think [demilitarization] would be a great idea, except it would be suicide for Hussein to accept it." But the Israelis refused to drop the subject. Later in the same meeting, Rabin argued that a US-Jordanian arms deal would allow the JAA to easily launch a surprise attack from the West Bank. The threat, Rabin warned, would justify preemptive Israeli action, "and once there is a border along the Jordan, I don't care who is on the eastern bank."[79]

In reality, Rabin's warning was mostly bluster. "To go to war is not child's play," Peres admitted to Eshkol, Rabin, Meir, and a few other top officials on February 21. "We cannot just go and conquer the West Bank, and we know this in our hearts." The best outcome of the talks with the Americans, he stressed, would be if the West Bank became "like Sharm al-Shaykh," another strategically sensitive piece of territory that had quietly been neutralized.[80] But Rabin's tough talk paid off. By the time the second round of negotiations started, Johnson ordered Komer and Harriman to tell Eshkol that the United States would ask Hussein for a "firm private understanding" to keep Jordan's armor off the West Bank.[81]

TOWARD A SETTLEMENT?

On March 10 and March 11, 1965, US-Israeli and US-Jordanian Memoranda of Understanding (MOUs) were signed. On the surface, the MOUs were two separate bilateral agreements between two small Middle Eastern states and their great power patron. In reality, they amounted to much more. Together they provided Israel and Jordan with the support they needed in order to avoid going to war over the West Bank.

The MOUs were not the sort of arrangements that Kennedy had envisioned in the summer of 1963. He had hoped for a formal settlement: in exchange for American security guarantees, Israel would promise not to develop nuclear weapons or seize the West Bank. The MOUs committed both the United States and Israel to much less. The Americans declared their "concern" for Israel's security and opposition to "aggression in the Near East," but did not pledge to defend Israel in any way. In turn, the Israelis did not promise to shut down their nuclear program, conceding only that they would "not be the first to introduce nuclear weapons into the Arab-Israel area."[82] Nor did the Israelis forswear conventional preemption. Since the Soviets and the Egyptians refused to seriously discuss regional arms control, the Americans set the idea of a formal settlement aside. Instead, they decided to give Israel and Jordan what they needed in order to preserve the status quo themselves.

How was this to be done? First, the Americans promised to supply Israel with tanks if the West Germans did not, and to "ensure an opportunity" for Israel to buy American warplanes later.[83] For the first time, the United States had offered to play an ongoing role in keeping the conventional military balance in Israel's favor. It was, as Golda Meir had told her colleagues, a "historic turning point" in the US-Israeli relationship. While Israel would doubtless have to bargain with the United States over future arms requests, the Johnson administration had finally dispensed with the long-standing US policy of not supplying Israel or its neighbors with offensive heavy weapons.[84] Additionally, Israel could now preserve its conventional superiority until it could produce nuclear weapons. "Our situation with regard to the purchase of weapons is, for practical purposes, better than ever," Rabin summed up later that year. Israel's ability to keep up in the arms race would no longer be restricted "by diplomatic constraints or the problem of what to acquire," but now would be limited by budget alone. Despite the Arab military buildup, Rabin predicted, Israel would retain conventional superiority over the Arab states for approximately eight years.[85]

The Memoranda of Understanding were also designed to preserve the West Bank as a buffer zone. The US-Jordanian MOU declared that the United States would immediately stop shipping arms to Jordan if Hussein also bought weapons from the Eastern bloc. No matter how much money Hussein received from the UAC, he could not buy American and Soviet arms at once. The United States would control the quantity and quality of arms that reached Jordan, ensuring that the JAA would not become more powerful than Israel could tolerate.[86] Even more importantly, the US-Israeli MOU stated that Hussein had promised to "keep his armor on the East Bank of the Jordan."[87] The sale of American tanks to Jordan, in other words, had been tied to the de facto demilitarization of the West Bank.

The MOUs satisfied the basic needs of Israel, Jordan, and the United States all at once. The Americans had damped down the Israelis' nuclear aspirations and preemptive inclinations without having to offer them a security guarantee. Hussein could rest assured that the United States wanted to preserve his regime. And the Israelis could maintain their conventional military superiority without radically compromising their freedom of action. The question, however, was how well these agreements would hold up when threatened by enemies of the status quo, most importantly Nasser's Egypt. Would the MOUs prove to be mere stopgap solutions to problems of a more fundamental nature? Or could they provide a foundation for a future Arab-Israeli settlement?

The great flaw in the system constructed by the MOUs was that if Egypt or another revisionist power challenged that system, it was unlikely to be preserved by anything other than an Israeli resort to force. Without external guarantees, the West Bank's buffer status depended on Hussein's desire to avoid conflict, and the king clearly remained vulnerable to domestic and inter-Arab pressures. Notably, the clause that called for Hussein to keep his tanks off the West Bank appeared in the *US-Israeli* MOU; the US-Jordanian agreement did not even mention it. Instead, Hussein promised Ambassador Barnes that under "normal conditions" he would "keep tanks on [the] East Bank," but added that "obviously under wartime conditions this assurance would not apply."[88] If Hussein did move forces into the West Bank, they would in fact pose a much greater threat to Israel than they would have in the past. Thanks to the US-Jordanian arms deal, AMAN concluded, the JAA would be strong enough to launch attacks on Israeli targets unaided and achieve the element of surprise.[89]

Of course, the MOUs built upon previous Israeli-Jordanian understandings, and the Israeli leadership had never assumed that those were inviolate either. But the Israelis had also believed that their modus vivendi with Jordan would allow them to buy time to attain a nuclear option. Now Eshkol had formally promised not to "introduce" nuclear weapons into the Middle East. The following year, when the Americans offered to sell Israel forty-eight A-4 Skyhawk bombers, the Israelis had to make similar pledges, promising not to "manufacture" nuclear weapons or "use any US-supplied aircraft as a nuclear weapons carrier."[90]

The Johnson administration had clearly begun to give up on denying Israel the *potential* to develop nuclear weapons. Yet the Americans were still not going to allow Israel to become a declared nuclear power, and that raised major questions about what purpose an Israeli nuclear capability would actually serve. By 1966, senior IDF and Defense Ministry officials had compiled a list of scenarios in which Israel might use nuclear weapons, including the penetration of an Israeli population center by an Arab army, the destruction of the Israeli air force, the threat of a chemical, biological, or massive air attack against an Israeli city, and the use of nuclear weapons against Israel.[91] In these situations, Israel's survival would be immediately at stake, and its leaders might have to shelve their concerns about the political and moral implications of using nuclear weapons. But could Israel also use a nuclear capability to deter the Arab states from provocations that did not pose immediate existential threats? And if not, then how could Israel deal with such challenges, except through territorial conquest or an endless series of preemptive wars? After all, even the most advanced conventional weapons could not eradicate the manpower gap between Israel and the Arab world or the possibility of an Arab surprise attack. They could only guarantee that Israel could strike quickly and decisively before its enemies deployed all of their forces along its borders.

There is no evidence that Israel's political leadership seriously considered conquering more land at this stage. Neither Eshkol nor any senior figure in Mapai advocated territorial expansion, and with outsiders, they took pains to state that they accepted the armistice lines as de facto borders. The Israeli government accepted its "present frontiers as inviolate," Abba Eban, who replaced Meir as foreign minister in December 1965, told Rusk.[92] Within the labor Zionist camp, there were certainly important politicians, particularly Yigal Allon and Moshe Dayan, who still dreamed of widening Israel's borders, but their lingering irredentism had no real effect on how their parties actually behaved. Allon's Ahdut ha-'Avodah quietly accepted its role as junior partner to Mapai. When the two parties competed as a unified list in the 1965 elections, Ahdut ha-'Avodah did not demand that Mapai adopt any specific position on territorial issues. Dayan, who followed Ben-Gurion into the Rafi party, remained in the shadow of the former prime minister, who firmly accepted the territorial status quo. Even in Menachem Begin's Herut, the great stronghold of Israeli irredentism, calls for territorial expansion had lost much of their cachet. When Herut and the centrist Liberal Party merged into the Gahal bloc in 1965, Begin quietly agreed not to include Herut's usual pledge to uphold the nation's right to a Greater Israel in their joint program.[93]

As for the IDF's commanders, they too remained mindful of the lessons of Suez, despite their preoccupation with strategic depth. On many occasions, Chief of Staff Rabin made it clear that he thought territorial expansion through war was politically impossible. "As time passes, the fact of Israel's existence becomes something unshakable, but the passage of time likewise makes any straying beyond Israel's present borders increasingly difficult," he told the IDF's top officers in January 1964. Territorial expansion, in Rabin's view, was not immoral, but it was also not a realistic war aim. The superpowers, he reminded his comrades, had already forced Israel to withdraw from captured territory twice: in 1949, after the IDF had crossed into the Sinai Peninsula, and in 1957, from Sinai and the Gaza Strip.[94] "I don't believe in the political possibility of holding territory acquired as the result of a military initiative," he remarked at one General Staff meeting in 1965.[95] In 1966, when the General Staff debated whether to strike Syria, Rabin scoffed at the idea that Israel could seize and keep the Golan Heights. "If we were forced to withdraw from Gaza," he said, "we will certainly be forced out of Qunaytra."[96] And these were not just the chief of staff's personal views, but the basic underlying assumptions of Israeli strategic planning. The Operations Branch's Planning Division, responsible for numerous expansionist plans in the early 1950s, defined the IDF's basic goals for 1965–1966 as "1) deterring the Arab states from a military confrontation at their initiative, and 2) securing the sovereignty of the state *within its existing borders* and protecting its sovereign rights beyond its borders."[97] Unlike in the pre-Suez era, Israel's strategic planners assumed that their mission was to defend Israel from inside the armistice lines.

Yet Israeli military doctrine remained essentially preemptive. Israel's generals still believed that the IDF needed to take the fight to enemy territory as quickly as possible. "Our principal problem," Rabin summed

Yitzhak Rabin (far right) and Levi Eshkol (second from right) observing East Jerusalem, 1965. Israel Government Press Office/Moshe Milner.

up, "is to ensure a time span that allows us to ensure that if we're attacked our forces will be mobilized and deployed in the best possible way."[98] The government never predelegated the authority to go to war to the General Staff, and the IDF's final pre-1967 war plan, SADAN, assumed that Israel would not be able to strike first.[99] In practice, though, the fact that the IDF's plans were designed to rapidly carry the battle to enemy territory meant that they could easily be adapted to a preemptive strike. And the General Staff clearly hoped that if war seemed imminent, the political leadership would allow them to make the first move. "Whoever delivers the first blow acquires enormous advantages for himself," Rabin remarked in January 1964. If Arab armies appeared ready to strike, "the IDF will definitely try to secure permission to open fire with an air, land, and sea attack, in order to be the first."[100] Israel's 1965 Memorandum of Understanding with the United States did not represent a break with this sort of thinking. On the contrary, the agreement made preemption seem *more* attractive, since the Americans had quite conspicuously not tied their arms sales to Israeli pledges not to initiate war. Rabin, for one, thought the way that the Americans had dealt with the preemption issue was "a historic reform," Israel's "greatest achievement" in the negotiations.[101]

There was nothing about Israel's military doctrine that was expansionist per se. But its underlying logic held that Israel could only cope with the possibility of surprise attack in two ways: to always strike first, or to find ways to better predict and prepare for an Arab offensive. There were many ways that Israel could gain more warning time, including collecting better intelligence on its enemies. But the most obvious way that the Israelis could expand their margin of warning was to lengthen the distance that Arab armies needed to travel in order to reach Israel's population centers. Expansionist arguments might have carried little political weight in Israel by the mid-1960s, but the basic military rationale for acquiring more territory lived on. And now, it was no longer clear that Israel's nuclear program would render its lack of strategic depth irrelevant.

In 1965, however, the Israelis could afford to overlook the less stable aspects of the system that they, the Americans, and the Jordanians had constructed. After all, the Arab states seemed unlikely to actually go to war. During the winter of 1965, the General Staff did briefly worry that Nasser might overplay his hand on the Jordan waters issue, but they soon discovered that their worries were unfounded.[102] The Egyptians indeed feared premature confrontation with Israel. Field Marshal 'Abd al-Hakim 'Amir, the head of the Egyptian armed forces, told Soviet officials that 1965 would be an optimal year for Israel to go to war, since Egypt was tied down in Yemen, Iraq was preoccupied with a Kurdish rebellion, and the Syrian, Jordanian, and Lebanese armies were weak and ineffectual.[103] Not only did Nasser not respond when the IDF struck the diversion works in Syria, but he openly bemoaned his lack of military options. "How can I attack Israel while fifty thousand of our soldiers are stuck in Yemen?" he complained in a May 1965 speech.[104] At the Casablanca summit in September, Nasser declared that efforts to divert the Jordan should be left to individual Arab states, effectively ending the "war over water."[105] "For all practical purposes," Rabin observed, "I would say that the principal outcome of Arab summitry has been dealt a death blow."[106] With the war over water won and American arms on the way, Israel seemed well positioned to avoid war until it reached the nuclear threshold. The question now was how Israel's leaders could use their nascent atomic capability to get Arab governments to come to terms with them.

At the time, the Israelis had good reason to believe that rapprochement with the Arabs was within reach, and not only because of what was happening in the military sphere. The likelihood of the dreaded *mikreh ha-kol*—an all-Arab attack—also depended on how badly the superpowers wanted to prevent a regional conflict and how effectively the Arab states could cooperate with one another. By 1965, it seemed less likely than ever that Nasser would be able to unite the Arabs against Israel or that the superpowers would allow him to do so.

The international environment no longer favored Egypt's pursuit of regional hegemony. The Johnson administration had abandoned Kennedy's efforts to woo nonaligned leaders and was increasingly at loggerheads with Third World strongmen whose regional ambitions clashed with America's global aims.[107] By 1965, the Americans lost patience with Nasser, whose troops in Yemen threatened both Saudi Arabia and Britain's Aden protectorate. In January, the Johnson administration suspended previously negotiated sales of wheat to Egypt for six months. When the Americans finally signed a new aid deal with Egypt in January 1966, they agreed to provide only $55 million worth of food over six months—a far cry from the massive multiyear aid package they had offered Nasser in 1962. Without American help, the Egyptians found themselves short of foreign currency, making it hard for Nasser to pay his debts to the increasingly demanding Soviets. Khrushchev, the great champion of anticolonial liberation movements, had been ousted in October 1964. His successors, still smarting from the Cuban missile crisis, were less inclined to back Third World nations unconditionally, especially when they threatened to draw the USSR into conflict with the West.[108] A crisis in Egyptian-Soviet relations was narrowly avoided in September 1965, when the USSR agreed to forgive half of Egypt's $1 billion debt. Yet this generosity came with strings attached. The fall of 1965 marked the beginning of regular Soviet naval visits to Egypt and pressure for military bases on Egypt's Mediterranean coast. Egypt, formerly

Gamal Abdul Nasser. UN Photo.

one of the brightest stars of the nonaligned movement, was becoming an impoverished Soviet dependency.[109]

Egypt's stature in the Arab world was also in decline. For the first time since Nasser consolidated his power in 1954, the gap between his regime's domestic standing and that of his Arab rivals was narrowing. The years 1964 and 1965 witnessed demonstrations, strikes, and "grumbling about food shortages, black markets, and high prices" in Egypt.[110] In contrast, Egypt's conservative Arab opponents were doing better than they had in years. Arab summitry provided a welcome respite from the propaganda warfare and Egyptian-inspired subversion that defined Arab politics in the late 1950s and early 1960s, and allowed Arab monarchies to neutralize their domestic opponents and focus on internal development.

Nowhere was the ascendance of the conservative Arab states more evident than in Jordan, whose very existence had been denigrated by Nasser for so long. Between 1960 and 1965, Jordanian GNP grew at an average annual rate of 10 percent. Key industries like tourism and mineral extraction boomed. In 1965 alone, Jordanian phosphate production increased by 50 percent. Five hundred thousand foreigners visited the kingdom—two hundred thousand more than the number of visitors Israel received that year.[111] In contrast to Egypt, Jordan's currency reserves were in strikingly good shape, with a surplus balance of 7.3 million Jordanian dinars forecast for April 1966.[112] The kingdom's future prospects also looked good. In February 1965, Hussein felt confident enough to replace the pro-Egyptian prime minister Bahjat al-Talhuni with Wasfi al-Tal and his "brain trust" of young technocrats, whom he handed a sweeping mandate for bureaucratic and economic reforms.[113] Even if Jordanian economic independence remained "a while off," as one US official wrote, it no longer seemed that the kingdom could not survive.[114] Cuts in US aid to Jordan no longer inspired the same degree of trepidation in Amman, and with good reason. By 1966, the Hashemite kingdom ranked among only four countries in the world to receive direct US budgetary aid. The others, notably, were South Vietnam, Laos, and South Korea—all major Cold War battlegrounds.[115] Though the Jordanians and their American benefactors still quibbled over how much financial support the United States should provide, there was no question that US policymakers wanted to preserve Jordan's independence.[116] As the Jordanian economy grew, the Americans felt comfortable reducing their aid, but US policymakers no longer hoped that the kingdom would merge with its Arab neighbors.

Thus, by 1966, many within the Israeli national security establishment looked at the Arab world and concluded that Nasserism was in the process of irreversible decline. For the first time since the consolidation of the Free Officers' regime, Foreign Ministry officials noted early in 1966, there were signs of instability and discontent inside Egypt. The "decline of Abdul Nasser's standing" appeared to be the defining phenomenon in Arab politics.[117] Arab summitry had not allowed Egypt to regain the ground it had lost, concluded AMAN: "Over the long term, solidarity strengthens the regimes which always feared Egyptian hostility and propaganda."[118] From the Israeli perspective, the important thing about this trend in Arab politics was that there was little chance that new ventures in Arab unity would suddenly upset the regional balance of power. The possibility that Egypt would merge with another Arab state, Rabin noted, "was further away than ever before."[119] Abba Eban made similar arguments. "The goal of splitting up the Arab bloc," he told the Knesset Foreign Affairs and Defense Committee in the summer of 1966, "is now becoming real. . . . In Tunis, Baghdad, Damascus, Saudi Arabia, Jordan—there are varying but unmistakably clear degrees of national independence. I don't know if it makes a big difference if the Arab states are hostile to Israel separately or together, but there is nevertheless a difference in terms of the possibility of translating this enmity into action."[120]

Many Israeli officials nevertheless assumed, albeit cautiously, that it *did* make a difference whether the Arab states were "hostile to Israel separately or together." Perhaps, some Israeli diplomats and intelligence officials thought, Arab "pluralism" might lead to Arab "realism." As Egypt's influence over other Arab states declined, their leaders might feel freer to take different stances on the Arab-Israeli issue. They might conclude that it was futile and destructive to remain at war with Israel and seek reconciliation instead.

By the end of 1965, the Israelis saw many signs that realism was starting to take hold in the Arab world. There was, of course, the secret dialogue with Hussein, and there were also more public indications that Nasser no longer called the tune on Palestine. When Nasser implored his fellow Arab leaders to cut their ties to West Germany after Bonn established diplomatic relations with Israel, Saudi Arabia, Libya, Tunisia, and Morocco refused outright, while other countries, including Jordan, took only minor symbolic steps.[121] In April, Tunisian president Habib Bourguiba engaged in an even more brazen display of realism when he publicly called for the Arab states to negotiate with Israel on the basis of the UN partition plan of 1947. While Bourguiba's fellow Arab leaders rejected his idea, they also ignored Nasser's call for Tunisia to be expelled from the Arab League. The Israelis were ecstatic. AMAN viewed the Tunisian president's plan as a possible harbinger of "a practical turning point in the near future," and the Foreign Ministry tried to have him nominated for the Nobel Peace Prize.[122] Bourguiba's initiative, noted one Foreign Ministry analysis, grew from the same source as Nasser's response to the war over water: "the stabilizing and strengthening phenomenon of Israel, and the feeling that time is working in Israel's favor."[123]

The challenge now was to convince Nasser and his Soviet patrons that they should accept the status quo. By 1966, Eshkol's government was cautiously reaching out to both. The Soviets, as Eban told US officials, remained Israel's "number one problem," but the Israelis still hoped they would moderate their Middle East policy in the name of détente. After all, Eban noted, the USSR was trying to play a mediating role in the Cyprus dispute and had sponsored successful Indo-Pakistani peace talks at Tashkent. Perhaps the Soviets might also adopt a less one-sided approach to the Arab-Israeli issue.[124] Following the Tashkent summit, Eshkol wrote to Alexei Kosygin, chairman of the USSR's council of ministers, to ask the USSR to help end the Arab-Israeli arms race. Eban presented a similar proposal to Soviet ambassador Dmitri Chuvakhin, calling for an agreement between the United States, France, Britain, and the USSR to stem the flow of arms to the Middle East.[125] To remind the Soviets what was at stake, Eshkol apparently authorized former Mossad chief Isser Harel to tell Moshe Sneh, the leader of Maki, Israel's Communist party, that Israel was building nuclear weapons, correctly assuming that Sneh would pass this information along to the Soviets.[126] Eshkol's message was clear: if the Soviets did not stop selling arms to the Arabs, Israel would go nuclear, generating Arab pressure for the Soviets to intervene in the Middle East and risk conflict with the United States.

Eshkol also tried to use Israel's emerging military edge to bargain with Egypt. In the fall of 1965, a shadowy European businessman known only as "Steve" helped the Mossad establish contact with 'Azzam al-Din Mahmud Khalil, an Egyptian air force general and confidante of Nasser. Through Steve, Khalil informed the Israelis that Nasser might be willing to support the Johnston Plan if Israel helped Egypt secure economic aid from Europe. Intrigued, Eshkol authorized Mossad chief Meir Amit to meet Khalil in Paris and make him a far-reaching offer: Israel would help Egypt secure low-interest loans from European banks and stop undermining US-Egyptian ties if Nasser backed the Johnston Plan, allowed Israel-bound ships to pass through the Suez Canal, and clamped down on anti-Israeli incitement in the Egyptian media. The Egyptian and Israeli governments would also establish a "hotline" and maintain regular contact to reduce the risk of accidental war. Eventually, Israeli and Egyptian defense experts would meet and discuss ways to end the regional arms race. When Nasser received the Israeli proposal, he replied that he would be willing to discuss it, but only if Amit personally came to Cairo to do so. Eshkol wanted to consider the idea, but several of his advisors suspected that Nasser might try to capture Amit, and ultimately the prime minister did not let his frustrated Mossad chief go to Egypt.[127] The channel to Khalil, however, was not closed down, and Israeli officials continued to argue over the possibility of détente with Egypt—something that would have been unthinkable five years earlier.[128]

"We must look upon Jordan in a different context from Syria and Egypt," Ya'akov Herzog had written to Eshkol following his December 1964 meeting with Hussein. "The contact must be carefully nurtured. Its full possibilities will only emerge within a general Middle Eastern policy on our part, the lines of which can be discerned but have yet to be clearly defined and pursued."[129] By the end of 1965, the Israeli government was groping its way toward such a policy. The Israelis were coming to terms with the vast changes that were taking place in global politics and within the Arab state system. For the first time since Suez, it was possible to imagine that the very nature of the Arab-Israeli conflict might change.

The foundations of a possible Arab-Israeli settlement, based on the territorial status quo, had been laid by the mid-1960s. The principal elements of that settlement included US support for the status quo, Israeli military superiority, and the solidification of existing state structures in the Arab world. Yet a number of key questions remained unresolved. Without a parallel Soviet commitment, how far would the United States go to preserve the existing order in the Middle East? After Israel crossed the nuclear threshold, would it refrain from preemption if threatened? How much political pressure could Nasser's Arab rivals, especially Hussein, really withstand? By 1966, the Israelis found themselves wrestling with this last question as the Palestinian national movement, moribund since 1948, came roaring back to life.

NOTES

1. Wishart, "Breakdown of the Johnston Negotiations."
2. "The Jordan Waters Dispute: Review of Developments to May 1964," undated, BNA/FO 371/175578; "Special Report: The Jordan Waters Issue," CIA memo, December 4, 1964, LBJL/NSF/Country Files/Jordan, box 146.
3. New York to State, April 21, 1964, NA/RG59/DOSCF 1964–1966/POL 15-1 JORDAN.
4. Amman to State, August 11, 1964, LBJL/NSF/Country Files/Jordan, box 146
5. Parkes to Crawford, September 23, 1964, BNA/FO 371/1755561.
6. Central Command monthly intelligence report for January 1964, IDFA/1338/79/35.
7. Ya'akov Herzog, "Second Meeting with Charles, Part I," May 2, 1964, YHP.
8. KFADC minutes, September 22, 1964, ISA/A/8160/8.
9. Herzog to embassies, December 31, 1963; "The Arab Summit Conference: Summary and Implications," AMAN special estimate 9/64, February 3, 1964, ISA/FM/4327/19.
10. KFADC minutes, January 26, 1964, ISA/A/8160/5. See also Rabin's remarks to senior IDF officers, January 7, 1964, in Rosenthal, *Yitzhak Rabin*, 336–339.
11. Gazit to Harman, December 19, 1965, ISA/FM/3515/21.
12. KFADC minutes, November 10, 1964, ISA/A/8160/8; AMAN, "Special Intelligence Estimate No. 53/65: The Casablanca Summit—A Basic Summary," September 18, 1965, ISA/A/7936/6; FM Research Branch to Director-General, "Developments and Trends in the Middle East," January 25, 1966, ISA/A/7936/6.
13. "Liabilities Imposed by the Arab Summits," undated (December 1965), LBJL/NSF/Country Files/Israel, box 139 (2 of 2). This paper was provided to Dean Rusk by Harman on December 29, 1965. See *FRUS, 1964–1968*, 18: doc. 260.
14. Abu Gharbiyya, *Min mudhakirrat al-munadil Bahjat Abu-Gharbiyya*, 268–269. Abu Gharbiyya attended the summit as a member of the PLO delegation. See also Shuqayri, *'Ala tariq*, 19–21.
15. Ya'akov Herzog, "Third Meeting with Charles," December 19, 1964, YHP; Central Command monthly intelligence summary, October 1965, IDFA/1338/79/37. For a similar Israeli assessment, see Mordechai Gazit, "The Deployment of Arab Forces in Jordan," September 16, 1965, ISA/FM/7300/4.
16. Hussein-McNamara memcon, April 15, 1964, *FRUS, 1964–1968*, 18: doc. 40
17. Johnson-Hussein memcon, April 15, 1964, *FRUS, 1964–1968*, 18: doc. 41.
18. "King Husayn's Comments on Jordan's Current Arms Purchasing Mission to the United States," CIA cable, July 21, 1964, LBJL/NSF/Country Files/Jordan, box 146; Henderson to Stirling, July 14, 1964, BNA/FO 371/175646. See also Phillips to Butler, August 27, 1964, BNA/FO 371/175647.
19. "King Husayn's Comments on Jordan's Current Arms Purchasing Mission to the United States," CIA cable, July 21, 1964, LBJL/NSF/Country Files/Jordan, box 146.
20. Talbot to Rusk, July 22, 1964, *FRUS, 1964–1968*, 18: doc. 78.
21. See Tal, *Politics*, 107, 133.
22. Komer to Bundy, July 28, 1964, *FRUS, 1964–1968*, 18: doc. 80; JCS to McNamara, July 30, 1964, *FRUS, 1964–1968*, 18: doc. 81.

23. Komer to Bundy, July 28, 1964, *FRUS*, 1964–1968, 18: doc. 80; DOS to Amman, August 4, 1964, *FRUS*, 1964–1968, 18: doc. 82.

24. State to Amman, August 20, 1964, *FRUS*, 1964–1968, 18: doc. 92; State to Amman, August 23, 1964, *FRUS*, 1964–1968, 18: doc. 93.

25. Cairo to FO, September 13, 1964, BNA/FO 371/175559.

26. DOS circular, November 13, 1963, *FRUS*, 1961–1963, 18: doc. 359; memo for the record, November 14, 1963, *FRUS*, 1961–1963, 18: doc. 360.

27. Tel Aviv to State, April 7, 1964, *FRUS*, 1964–1968, 18: doc. 37. On Eshkol's apparent loss of interest in US security guarantees, see also Eshkol-Barbour memcon, LBJL/NSF/Country Files/Israel, box 138, 2 of 2; Tel Aviv to State, May 16, 1964, LBJL/NSF/Country Files/Israel—Eshkol Visit, box 143.

28. Remarks to the General Staff, July 20, 1963, in Rosenthal, *Yitzhak Rabin*, 320.

29. Gluska, *Eshkol*, 64.

30. Harman-Rusk memcon, January 3, 1964, *FRUS*, 1964–1968, 18: doc. 3.

31. Quoted in Logevall, *Choosing War*, 79.

32. Monte, "Fateful Alliance," 70–77.

33. Cabinet minutes, December 1, 1963, ISA.

34. Cabinet minutes, June 18, 1964, ISA.

35. Komer to Bundy, January 9, 1964, LBJL/NSF/Country Files/Israel-Tanks, box 145, 1 of 2.

36. Memo for the record, April 30, 1964, *FRUS*, 1964–1968, 18: doc. 49.

37. Rusk to Johnson, August 12, 1964, *FRUS*, 1964–1968, 18: doc. 89.

38. Jerusalem to Washington, August 26, 1964, ISA/FM/4301/4.

39. Eshkol-Gazit memcon, September 1, 1964, ISA/FM/4301/4. It should be noted, however, that Gazit disagreed with Eshkol on this point. The diplomat thought that an American arms sale to Jordan could help protect Hussein from Nasserist subversion. "Our point of departure has to be concern for the *yanuka* [infant, i.e., Hussein]," he said. Gazit's boss, Golda Meir, appears to have held similar views: see her remarks regarding why it would be better for Jordan to receive American arms, in cabinet minutes, February 28, 1965, ISA.

40. On Eshkol's hope to improve relations with the USSR, see especially Mapai political committee minutes, October 31, 1963, ISA/A/7921/9.

41. Eshkol to Krushchev, January 16, 1964, ISA/A/7936/1.

42. Eshkol-Peres memcon, July 27, 1964, ISA/A/7936/1. On the Israelis' efforts to get the Americans to make overtures to the Soviets on their behalf, see especially Gazit to Harman, December 28, 1964, ISA/FM/4301/4.

43. Eshkol-Gazit memcon, September 1, 1964, ISA/FM/4301/4.

44. Rusk-Harman memcon, September 23, 1964, *FRUS*, 1964–1968, 18: doc. 95. For a summary of how high-ranking State Department officials like Walt Rostow, Llewellyn Thompson, and Averell Harriman viewed Soviet policy toward the Middle East at the time, see Gazit to Harman, December 28, 1964, ISA/FM/4301/4.

45. Goldstein, *Eshkol*, 478.

46. Nasser-McCloy memcon, September 28, 1964, *FRUS*, 1964–1968, 18: doc. 96.

47. *New York Times*, October 31, 1964.

48. *New York Times*, January 26, 1965.

49. *New York Times*, February 11, 1965.

50. Editorial note, in Lammfromm and Tsoref, *Levi Eshkol*, 464.

51. DOS memcon, January 25, 1965, *FRUS, 1964–1968*, 18: doc. 126; NSC minutes, February 1, 1965, *FRUS, 1964–1968*, 18: doc. 130.
52. Amman to State, February 8, 1965, LBJL/NSF/Country Files/Jordan, box 146.
53. Amman to State, February 8, 1965, NA/RG59/DOSCF 1964–1966/DEF 12–5 JORDAN.
54. Amman to State, February 19, 1965, *FRUS, 1964–1968*, 18: doc. 154.
55. Editorial note, *FRUS, 1964–1968*, 18: doc. 127.
56. Editorial note, *FRUS, 1964–1968*, 18: doc. 133.
57. Tel Aviv to State, February 5, 1965, LBJL/NSF/Country Files/Israel, box 139, 1 of 2.
58. State to Tel Aviv, February 6, 1965, *FRUS, 1964–1968*, 18: doc. 137.
59. Komer to Bundy, February 7, 1965, *FRUS, 1964–1968*, 18: doc. 140.
60. Komer to Johnson, February 6, 1965, *FRUS, 1964–1968*, 18: doc. 138.
61. Ibid.
62. Memo for the record, February 9, 1965, *FRUS, 1964–1968*, 18: doc. 144.
63. Memo for Komer, February 10, 1965, *FRUS, 1964–1968*, 18: doc. 146.
64. Ball to Tel Aviv, February 10, 1965, LBJL/NSF/Country Files/Israel, box 139, 1 of 2.
65. Tel Aviv to State, February 15, 1965, *FRUS, 1964–1968*, 18: doc. 150.
66. Komer to Johnson, February 16, 1968, *FRUS, 1964–1968*, 18: doc. 152.
67. Johnson to Komer and Harriman, February 21, 1965, *FRUS, 1964–1968*, 18: doc. 157.
68. Tel Aviv to State, March 2, 1965, LBJL/NSF/Country Files/Israel-Tanks, box 145, 1 of 2.
69. Tel Aviv to State, March 5, 1965, LBJL/NSF/Country Files/Israel-Tanks, box 145, 1 of 2.
70. Remarks at a meeting of the General Staff, March 15, 1965, in Rosenthal, *Yitzhak Rabin*, 370.
71. Tel Aviv to State, March 5, 1965, LBJL/NSF/Country Files/Israel-Tanks, box 145, 1 of 2. For similar thoughts, see Komer to Bundy, March 6, 1965, *FRUS, 1964–1968*, 18: doc. 180.
72. On the deterioration of Ben-Gurion's relationship with Eshkol, see Shalom, *Ke-esh be-'atsmotav*, 22–61.
73. Washington to Bitan, June 28, 1965, ISA/FM/7331/9. Johnson apparently suspected Ben-Gurion of leaking news of the Israeli–West German arms deal to the press. Johnson's preference for Eshkol is also a key theme in Shalom, *Israel's Nuclear Option*.
74. Tel Aviv to State, March 2, 1965, *FRUS, 1964–1968*, 18: doc. 173.
75. State to Tel Aviv, March 7, 1965, *FRUS, 1964–1968*, 18: doc. 181.
76. Eshkol-Gazit memcon, September 1, 1964, ISA/FM/4301/4.
77. Ya'akov Herzog, "Third Meeting with Charles," December 19, 1964, YHP.
78. Tel Aviv to State, February 13, 1965, LBJL/NSF/Country Files/Israel, box 139.
79. Minutes of Eshkol and advisors' meeting with Komer, February 14, 1965, ISA/A/7939/1. See also Bitan to Harman and Gazit, February 16, 1965, ISA/FM/4328/6. This document was erroneously dated January 16.
80. Minutes of Eshkol's meeting with Rabin, Meir, Peres, et al., February 21, 1965, ISA/A/7936/6.

81. Johnson to Komer and Harriman, February 21, 1965, *FRUS*, 1964–1968, 18: doc. 157.

82. Tel Aviv to State, March 11, 1965, *FRUS*, 1964–1968, 18: doc. 185. During the negotiations, when Eshkol suggested this phrase, Harriman had responded, "Israel could 'introduce' weapons by insertion [of] one pin into [an] otherwise completed device." See Tel Aviv to State, March 2, 1965, LBJL/NSF/Country Files/Israel-Tanks, box 145, 1 of 2.

83. Tel Aviv to State, March 11, 1965, *FRUS*, 1964–1968, 18: doc. 185.

84. Cabinet minutes, February 28, 1965, ISA.

85. Lecture at the National Defense College, October 20, 1965, in Rosenthal, *Yitzhak Rabin*, 389. The idea that the conventional balance would remain in Israel's favor for about a decade appears to have been the consensus view of the General Staff by the summer of 1965. See Gluska, *Eshkol*, 132, 134–135.

86. State to Amman, March 10, 1965, DDRS/CK3100548oo.

87. Tel Aviv to State, March 11, 1965, *FRUS*, 1964–1968, 18: doc. 185.

88. Amman to State, March 12, 1965, *FRUS*, 1964–1968, 18: doc. 188.

89. Central Command monthly intelligence report, February 1965, IDFA/1338/79/35.

90. Eban-McNamara memcon, February 12, 1966, *FRUS*, 1964–1968, 18: doc. 271. On the Skyhawks sale, see Levey, "United States' Skyhawk Sale."

91. Cohen, *Israel and the Bomb*, 237.

92. Rusk-Eban memcon, October 12, 1966, *FRUS*, 1964–1968, 18: doc. 328.

93. Shilon, *Begin*, 197.

94. Remarks to senior IDF officers, January 6, 1964, in Rosenthal, *Yitzhak Rabin*, 338.

95. Quoted in Gluska, *Eshkol*, 132.

96. Remarks at a meeting of the General Staff, August 22, 1966, in Rosenthal, *Yitzhak Rabin*, 412.

97. Gluska, *Eshkol*, 443n30 (emphasis added). The reference to "sovereign rights beyond its borders" is apparently a reference to Israel's navigational rights in the Straits of Tiran and its usage of the Jordan waters, as well as the preservation of certain rights defined by the armistice agreements—e.g., access to Mount Scopus.

98. KFADC minutes, April 21, 1964, ISA/A/8160/6.

99. For documents pertaining to Plan SADAN, see IDFA/66/71/467.

100. Remarks to senior IDF officers, January 6, 1964, in Rosenthal, *Yitzhak Rabin*, 338.

101. Remarks at a meeting of the General Staff, March 15, 1965, in Rosenthal, *Yitzhak Rabin*, 372.

102. See, for example, Yariv's remarks to the General Staff on March 29, 1965, summarized in editorial note, in Rosenthal, *Yitzhak Rabin*, 372–373. See also Gluska, *Eshkol*, 97–111.

103. Erofeev-'Amir memcon, February 23, 1965, in Naumkin, *Blizhni vostochni konflikt*, doc. 206.

104. "Kalimat al-ra'is Jamal 'Abd al-Nasir fi al-mu'tamir al-watani al-Filastini min jami'at al-Qahira," May 31, 1965. The text of this speech, as well as the texts of all of Nasser's other speeches, can be found at Al-Ra'is Jamal 'Abd al-Nasir, http://nasser.bibalex.org. See also Nasser's comments in Shuqayri, *'Ala tariq*, 43–44.

105. Sela, *Decline of the Arab-Israeli Conflict*, 83–84.

106. Lecture at the National Defense College, October 20, 1965, in Rosenthal, *Yitzhak Rabin*, 390.

107. See Rakove, *Kennedy, Johnson*.

108. Westad, *Global Cold War*, 168–169.

109. This paragraph draws heavily on Ferris, *Nasser's Gamble*, 102–162.

110. "The Outlook for the United Arab Republic," NIE 36.1–66, May 19, 1966, Central Intelligence Agency Freedom of Information Act Electronic Reading Room, https://www.cia.gov/library/readingroom/docs/DOC_0000012090.pdf. See also Ferris, *Nasser's Gamble*, 174–215.

111. Siton to Gazit, "An American Report on the Jordanian Economy," May 31, 1966, ISA/FM/6554/20.

112. "Notes on Anglo-American Talks on Aid to Jordan, November 29 to December 1, 1965," BNA/FO 371/180742.

113. Central Command monthly intelligence summaries for January and February 1965, IDFA/1338/79/35; Amman to State, February 14, 1965, LBJL/NSF/Country Files/Jordan, box 146. For an overview of the second al-Tal government's economic reform efforts, see Kingston, "Rationalizing Patrimonialism," 128–142.

114. "Positive Developments in the Middle East, 1964–1966," unsigned, DDRS /CK3100301319.

115. Rostow to Johnson, June 16, 1966, *FRUS*, 1964–1968, 18: doc. 300.

116. On the second al-Tal government's dealings with the United States regarding budgetary support and development aid, see Kingston, "Rationalizing Patrimonialism," 139–142.

117. FM Research Branch to Director-General, January 25, 1966, ISA/A/7936/6.

118. AMAN, "Special Intelligence Estimate No. 53/65: The Casablanca Summit—A Basic Summary," September 18, 1965, ISA/A/7936/6.

119. Lecture at the National Defense College, October 20, 1965, in Rosenthal, *Yitzhak Rabin*, 388.

120. KFADC minutes, July 5, 1966, ISA/A/8161/1. See also his comments about Nasser's "failure to produce a Pan-Arab system" in Eban-Rusk memcon, October 7, 1966, ISA/FM/3977/20.

121. Sela, *Decline of the Arab-Israeli Conflict*, 79–80.

122. Laskier, *Israel and the Maghreb*, 192–212.

123. "Gleanings on Arab Realism," unsigned, ISA/A/7936/6.

124. DOS memcon, February 8, 1966, NA/RG59/DOSCF 1964–66/POL ARAB-ISR.

125. Heller, *Yisrael veha-milhamah ha-karah*, 490–492.

126. Laron, "Playing with Fire," 168. For a different interpretation of this episode, see Ginor and Remez, *Foxbats over Dimona*, 36–48.

127. Amit, *Rosh be-rosh*, 204–227.

128. See chapter 5 of this volume.

129. Ya'akov Herzog, "Third Meeting with Charles," December 19, 1964, YHP.

FOUR

LOUDER THAN A BOMB

Israel, Jordan, and the Palestinians, 1964–1966

IN DECEMBER 1966, ISRAELI FOREIGN MINISTER ABBA EBAN offered a handful of high-ranking US officials his thoughts on the state of the Arab-Israeli conflict. "Because of the balance of power in our area," he said, "Nasser was not interested in a war with Israel at this time." Yet now, Eban proclaimed, Israel faced a very different sort of challenge: "the new tactic of terrorism undertaken by the Palestinians." In the Middle East, as in other parts of the world, he remarked, "it was the gun and the hand grenade that had been making an impact on political realities, and not the atomic bomb."[1] Looming in the background was the shadow of recent events in Jordan. A month earlier, an Israeli retaliatory raid into the West Bank village of Samu' had provoked widespread rioting and demonstrations against King Hussein. Once again it seemed that an Arab-Israeli war might erupt as the result of the Jordanian monarchy's collapse.

The proximate cause of this new war scare was the Samu' raid itself, but the real reasons were deeper. By the mid-1960s, the same trends that inspired optimism among Israel's elites—the shift of the military balance in Israel's favor, the decline of Nasserism, the growing resilience of existing Arab states—led many Palestinians to believe that the Arab states might never unite against Israel. Among them were a small but determined minority who wanted to take the struggle against Israel into their own hands. These Palestinians, who joined Fatah and other guerrilla organizations, sought to drag the Arab world into war before it was too late. By 1967, they succeeded.

The Palestinian guerrillas, who referred to themselves as *fida'iyyun* (literally, "self-sacrificers"), achieved their goal of ensnaring the Arab states in a war with Israel by undermining the entente that Hussein and the Israelis had so painstakingly constructed. By attacking Israel from the West Bank, they provoked Eshkol's government to resort to force, thereby exposing Hussein's impotence and tapping into deeper wellsprings of Palestinian resentment. By the end of 1966, the Hashemite monarchy's survival was endangered once more, and Jordan's role in the regional configuration of power was once again in play.

"CONTRIBUTION TO THE TALKING MACHINE"

The idea of an "entity" that would give the Palestinians a political voice of their own did not originate with the Cairo summit. Nasser had been advocating a Palestinian entity since 1959. Until 1964, Hussein had staunchly opposed him, rightfully viewing the Egyptian president's scheme as a challenge to the legitimacy of Jordanian rule over the West Bank.[2] But at the Cairo summit, Hussein changed course and supported the decision to authorize Ahmad al-Shuqayri, the Palestinian representative on the Arab League Council, to organize a Palestinian entity. Though the king still feared that a resurrected Palestinian national movement could threaten his regime, he apparently believed that the benefits of reconciliation with Nasser outweighed any threat that a Palestinian entity might pose.

Hussein also probably felt that he had little to fear from al-Shuqayri himself. Despite his mandate, the man charged with creating a Palestinian entity lacked a real following among the Palestinian communities scattered throughout the Arab world. A lawyer from a distinguished family from Acre, al-Shuqayri had spent the 1950s and early 1960s as a roving diplomat, serving as a member of the Syrian UN delegation in New York, Arab League assistant secretary-general, and Saudi Arabia's minister for UN affairs before representing the Palestinians at the Arab League. Along the way, his bombastic, often abrasive personality gained him a number of enemies, including Wasfi al-Tal, who described al-Shuqayri as a "notorious political crook."[3] While Nasser's backing gave al-Shuqayri some badly needed clout, it also meant that he had to heed Egypt's desire for inter-Arab détente. Hussein thus enjoyed tremendous sway over the kind of entity al-Shuqayri could create. When the Palestinian politician visited Jordan in February 1964, Hussein bluntly told him that there was "great confusion in Amman" about a Palestinian entity's implications for Jordan, and popular fear of "sensitivity [*hassasiyya*] between Palestinian and Jordanian." The king demanded "clarification" that a Palestinian entity would not divide the West and East Banks, and al-Shuqayri dutifully broadcast a statement to that effect.[4]

Al-Shuqayri and Hussein's February encounter set the tone for the Palestine Liberation Organization's founding conference that May, which was just as tightly staged-managed. Hussein insisted that the conference take place at Jerusalem's Intercontinental Hotel atop the Mount of Olives, far from anywhere demonstrators could easily congregate. The site swarmed with JAA troops and security personnel.[5] Of the 391 delegates whom Hussein allowed to attend the conference, more than 100 served or had served in the Jordanian government.[6] Pressure from the king also shaped the National Charter adopted at the conference, which pledged that the PLO would not "exercise regional sovereignty over the West Bank of the Hashemite Kingdom of Jordan nor the Gaza Strip nor the Hama area." When al-Shuqayri addressed the delegates, one could hear Hussein's voice; the newly elected PLO chairman promised that he aimed not to divide Jordan but to "liberate our usurped patrimony west of the West Bank."[7]

No one knew how long al-Shuqayri and the PLO would abide by the National Charter's promises, but in the short term, they had no choice but to cooperate with the Hashemite monarchy. The PLO needed cordial relations with Hussein in order to operate in Jordan, and Nasser remained unwilling to let al-Shuqayri undermine Arab summitry. The Egyptian approach to PLO military activity was the obvious case in point. At the Alexandria summit, the Arab League had approved al-Shuqayri's call to establish a Palestine Liberation Army (PLA). Hussein, however, refused to allow any PLA recruitment or training in Jordan, arguing that with so many Palestinians in the JAA, there was no need for a separate Palestinian military organization.[8] Though al-Shuqayri protested, the Egyptians did not try to change Hussein's mind. Privately, Hassan Sabri al-Khuli, one of Nasser's advisors, assured US officials that "the UAR remained opposed to giving the Palestinians any military capability which they themselves would control." If Hussein "found it impossible" to allow the PLA to operate in Jordan, al-Khuli promised, "no pressure would be put on him by the UAR."[9]

By the fall of 1964, Hussein and his inner circle believed they had blunted whatever threat the PLO posed. In secret conversations with Israeli officials, they spoke dismissively of the organization. The PLO, a high-level Jordanian source told Foreign Ministry Arabist Yael Vered, "did not worry Hussein." Al-Shuqayri, the Jordanian added, frightened the West Bank elite, who believed that the PLO might try to establish a pro-Nasser regime in Jordan and force "Arab socialism" upon the kingdom's middle and upper classes.[10] Hussein struck a similar note in his third secret meeting with Ya'akov Herzog in December 1964. When Herzog remarked that al-Shuqayri and the PLO "presented a real danger to [Hussein] and the integrity of his country," the king was nonplussed. The PLO, he said, would not recruit followers in Jordan, and PLA units would not operate there. Hussein saw no harm in giving his Palestinian subjects an outlet for their frustration; they had "argued for years that they were not permitted self-expression." The Palestinians would ultimately tire of al-Shuqayri and accept their role as Jordanian citizens. "I withdraw and let them go their way," he remarked confidently. "They will return." Al-Shuqayri, Hussein added with contempt, "talks of having a government and a people. We are watching him."[11]

Hussein's disdain for the PLO was shared by Israeli policymakers and generals. Initially, the Israeli intelligence community worried that al-Shuqayri might incite Jordan's Palestinians to rise up against the Hashemite regime. In March 1964, AMAN warned that Hussein had "taken a grave danger upon himself" by allowing al-Shuqayri to visit Jordan.[12] But by the end of April, nearly a month before the founding of the PLO, the IDF's intelligence analysts believed that the small burst of Palestinian enthusiasm that followed al-Shuqayri's February visit had given way to "suspicion and doubt."[13] The Jerusalem congress seemed to offer definitive proof that the PLO would pose little immediate threat to Jordan's stability. AMAN reported that most Jordanian Palestinians "showed no interest" in the congress, and approvingly noted how Hussein had suppressed demonstrations and controlled the conference's deliberations.[14] AMAN chief Aharon Yariv acknowledged that the PLO might provide

Nasser with a means to "spoil Hussein's milk" in the future, but for the time being, Israel did not have to worry. "Has a serious organization with the capacity for action arisen?" he asked the General Staff. "The answer is—no!"[15] The Israeli Foreign Ministry shared his views. Veteran Arabist Ezra Danin scornfully described the PLO as a "contribution to the talking machine."[16] "No bona fide organization that represents the Palestinian people, if such a thing exists, has been established," summed up Yael Vered.[17]

Israeli officials apparently had only one significant concern regarding the PLO: that it would try to isolate Israel by linking the Arab-Israeli conflict to other postcolonial struggles. There was "a kind of terminology in the modern world, the 'liberated,' and if they [the PLO] have the intelligence to integrate themselves into it . . . I'm not saying that [the PLO] won't have some influence here and there," Golda Meir told the Knesset Foreign Affairs and Defense Committee (KFADC).[18] Abba Eban described the challenge posed by the organization in similar terms, describing the PLO as a "new ideological framework designed to persuade the world [that] the Palestine issue is still open and to equate Palestine with Algeria and Rhodesia."[19] Such concerns were prescient. Arab officials already hoped that the PLO would gain international recognition and gradually push Israel out of the United Nations; by the mid-1970s, it would go a long way toward realizing these goals.[20] But in 1964, threats to Israel's international image took a backseat to more imminent and tangible problems like the Unified Arab Command and Arab attempts to divert the Jordan. The PLO thus remained of marginal interest for Israel's leaders.

Yet Hussein and the Israeli government were not the only ones who regarded the PLO as a political nonentity. Al-Shuqayri had rivals among his own people, and unlike Hussein and the Israeli leadership, they did not regard his weaknesses with satisfaction. Initially, al-Shuqayri's fiercest Palestinian opponent was former grand mufti Haj Amin al-Husayni, who attacked the PLO as unrepresentative and a puppet of the Arab regimes.[21] While al-Husayni won few new followers, his critique of the PLO resonated with younger Palestinian nationalists. In 1965, some of them would begin to translate their frustrations into action, transforming the Arab-Israeli conflict forever.

THE GUERRILLA CHALLENGE

By the time the PLO was founded, Fatah, or the Palestinian National Liberation Movement (*harakat al-tahrir al-watani al-filastini*), was six years old, yet small and largely unknown on the Arab political scene. Its first cell had been established in Kuwait in 1958 by Palestinians who had gone there looking for work. Unlike the members of the Palestine National Congress, the men who founded Fatah were overwhelmingly young Palestinians from refugee families who had fled to the Gaza Strip and Syria in 1948. Several of the organization's founders, including Khalil al-Wazir, Salah Khalaf, and Yasir Arafat, had been active in the Gaza branch of the Muslim Brotherhood and took part in guerrilla raids on Israel before Nasser halted such attacks after Suez. Others, like Khalid and Hani al-Hasan and Mahmud Abbas, had been involved in the Muslim Brotherhood and various Palestinian student groups in Syria. In contrast to al-Shuqayri, Fatah's leaders did not believe in working through the Arab League. They were certain that Arab leaders would place their own national interests above the Palestinian cause unless their publics demanded that they do otherwise. Fatah's leaders believed they needed to wage guerrilla war against Israel from sanctuaries in neighboring Arab states. As Israel struck back, Arab publics would mobilize and force their governments to prepare for war.

Until 1964, Fatah's leaders had no clear plan to act, but Arab summitry forced their hand. The organization's publications argued that Nasser's strategy of controlled escalation would give Israel time to "acquire deterrent weapons, both human and material, by settling the Negev with millions of new immigrants and then by possessing nuclear weapons." Even if the Arab regimes followed through on their pledges to prepare for war, they would be too late to stop Israel from consolidating itself as a state. The PLO, thought Fatah's leaders, threatened to draw potential recruits away from Fatah while leaving the fight against Israel to the Arab regimes' discretion.[22] By the end of 1964, the die was cast. Fatah began attacking Israeli targets on New Year's Eve with a botched raid launched from Lebanon. In January 1965, its operatives made three more attempts at sabotage inside Israel.[23] In February, the Palestinian organization began specifically trying to kill or injure Israeli civilians.

At the end of May, Fatah agents planted bombs near houses in Ramat ha-Kovesh and ʿAfulah, leaving seven Israeli civilians injured.[24]

At first the Israelis believed that Fatah aimed solely to escalate the conflict over the Jordan waters, since the organization initially targeted water pumps, wells, and pipes.[25] But as the Palestinian militants moved on to civilian targets, the General Staff realized that their ambitions were much broader. "[Fatah] has a notion that since Israel will have an atomic bomb by the 1970s, the final trial must take place before then," Yariv told his fellow IDF commanders. "Since the Arab regimes can't be trusted, [Fatah] needs to create provocations and drag them into war." Nevertheless, Israel's military men believed that it would be dangerous not to react. Israel could not sit idle while Fatah staged increasingly deadly attacks, Rabin argued. Arab regimes must be forcefully reminded that they risked war if they did not police their borders.[26]

Though the Israelis knew that Hussein opposed Fatah and wanted to avoid war, they still saw Jordan as a more compelling target for retaliation than Syria, where the Palestinian guerrillas were headquartered. While Syria allowed Fatah to train on its soil and gave its exploits extensive press coverage, there was little evidence that the Baʿthist regime actually controlled the organization.[27] Moreover, targets in Syria were difficult to locate, and the mountainous topography of the Israeli-Syrian border required the IDF to penetrate deeply and utilize airpower. By striking Syria, Israel could pay a high price, without necessarily ending border violence.[28] On the other hand, the West Bank presented no such obstacles, and the perpetrators of nearly all of Fatah's attacks between January and May 1965 had come from there.[29]

Initially, AMAN believed that Hussein might stop Fatah on his own, as reports of stepped-up border patrolling, military alerts, heightened surveillance, and arrests flowed in from Jordan.[30] Yet over the following months, the IDF intelligence branch came to regard the king's efforts as halfhearted. Saboteurs who had been arrested that January were released after "giving a bribe, and following the general amnesty that was declared in Jordan to mark Prince Hassan's appointment as crown prince." At least some of those arrested in the Ramat ha-Kovesh and ʿAfulah attacks were let go after a "superficial investigation."[31] The problem, as the Israelis saw it, was that Hussein was not willing to confront the guerrillas.

Rabin thought the Jordanian government could prevent "maybe not 100 percent, but certainly 95 percent" of attacks launched from its territory.[32] Yet Israeli efforts to get the Jordanians to crack down on Fatah went nowhere. When the Israelis attempted to contact the king either directly or through British and American channels, Hussein responded evasively, even accusing Israel of staging Fatah's attacks.[33] Most likely, the king felt too politically vulnerable to act. The PLO was already protesting his refusal to allow the PLA to train or conscript soldiers in Jordan, and Hussein worried that such charges would strike a chord with his Palestinian subjects.[34] By May 1965, the Israeli government and military leadership had decided that Hussein would not repress Fatah unless compelled to do so by force.

"SOMEONE WHO REALLY DOESN'T WANT TO GET ENTANGLED WITH US"

On the night of May 27–28, 1965, the IDF launched its first reprisal raids into Jordan in nearly a decade. The General Staff selected nonresidential civilian targets—a Fatah base in Shuneh, two gas stations in Qalqilya, and a flour mill and a factory in Jenin—in order to minimize civilian casualties and avoid a clash with the JAA. The operation, which left two Israelis and five Jordanians dead, was regarded by the Israelis as a major success.[35] The raids took place just as Hussein, Nasser, and other Arab leaders were holding a "mini-summit" in Cairo, but drew little response from them. To the Israelis, the Arabs' silence showed that force, carefully applied, could compel the Arab states to suppress Fatah before the organization learned how to inflict significant damage. "They tried to do the diversion and they learned what we can do to them," Rabin boasted to the General Staff. "They've now gotten a hint with regard to Fatah." Israel's raids, he said, had forced Arab leaders "to face up to the truth—that they can't do anything."[36] The reprisals, according to Eban, were "shining examples of the utility of limited, measured use of force in order to achieve important goals, including avoiding the need to use greater force at a later time."[37]

The time appeared ripe to urge Hussein to act against Fatah again. On May 30, Eshkol sent Hussein a message calling for Israel and Jordan "to guard the border together."[38] This time, the king obliged. A series of Israeli-Jordanian intelligence exchanges on Fatah began a week later, first through UN and then through American channels. By the fall of 1965, the US embassies in Tel Aviv and Amman were regularly transmitting intelligence on Fatah back and forth between the Israeli and Jordanian governments.[39] At the same time, Wasfi al-Tal and Muhammad Rasul al-Kaylani, head of the Jordanian General Intelligence Directorate, launched a sweeping crackdown on the Palestinian organization. According to al-Tal, between June and September the Jordanian security services arrested twenty-four Fatah agents, captured two caches of explosives, and "more or less completely liquidated the organization south of Jerusalem." The Jordanian government, he told US officials, took the "Fatah problem more seriously than anybody else" and was "doing everything possible to control [Fatah's] tentacles within Jordan."[40]

Fatah nevertheless kept on attacking Israeli targets from the West Bank. From the beginning of June until the end of September 1965, Jordan accounted for thirty out of forty-seven "hostile incidents" along Israel's borders, fifteen of which occurred in September alone.[41] By the end of September, AMAN had concluded that "Hussein is still not ready to open a second front against Fatah" because of his feud with al-Shuqayri over the PLA.[42] The Israeli leadership had to decide whether to retaliate on a larger scale or give Hussein more time to act.

True to form, the General Staff called for more reprisal operations. By the summer of 1965, Rabin regarded Fatah as Israel's most pressing security concern. He no longer worried much about the trajectory of the arms race or the Arab diversion efforts, he told the General Staff, but he saw no way to solve the Fatah problem. Rabin worried that a major raid against Jordan might topple Hussein.[43] But the chief of staff and his colleagues were still skeptical about relying on static defense (increased patrolling and ambushes, improved border surveillance, lighting, fencing, etc.) to block Palestinian incursions. A defensive strategy could weaken Israel's strategic credibility, and was at odds with the IDF's policy of relying on large reserve forces and a small standing army. "Our entire concept of security," Rabin later stated, "is not to be strong at every point. The Arabs know that for every blow of theirs they'll get smacked in the head."[44] During two freewheeling General Staff discussions that

July, the IDF's top officers discussed all possible avenues for coping with Fatah, from assassinating its leaders to launching "counterterror" attacks against Jordanian civilians. Most of the IDF brass favored a large-scale retaliatory raid against Jordan or Syria that would force their governments to stamp out Fatah once and for all.[45]

Yet Israel's political leaders proved more cautious. Early in September, the cabinet authorized one small raid in which Israeli troops blew up eleven water pumps near Qalqiliya.[46] The operation's limited scope, which prompted grumbling from Rabin, reflected Eshkol's ambivalence about the value of reprisals. According to Aviad Yafeh, the prime minister's private secretary, Eshkol "was not convinced that Israeli punitive strikes such as . . . at Qalqilya are counterproductive, but neither is he convinced of the opposite. He just does not know if they will help or not."[47] Nor was Foreign Minister Golda Meir enthusiastic about retaliation. On September 12, she met with Foreign Ministry Special Advisor Mordechai Gazit, who informed her that nearly the entire Israeli intelligence community opposed further reprisals against Jordan. Unlike the General Staff, Israel's intelligence analysts believed that more raids would aggravate, not solve, the Fatah problem. They thought reprisals made it difficult for Hussein to recruit intelligence assets on the ground and were "raising Fatah's prestige in the eyes of the population (especially the border villagers)." If Israel hit Jordan too hard, the king might launch counterattacks, invite other Arab troops into Jordan, or simply let Fatah do as it pleased.[48] The conversation evidently made an impression on Meir. In testimony to the KFADC a few days later, she implicitly argued in favor of giving Hussein more time to act. "I have no doubt that Hussein and his loyal cabinet members oppose Fatah activity and are working against it, not with the vigor that we'd like, but they are doing a lot of things, and again, not for our sake," she said. Israel was "dealing with someone who really doesn't want to get entangled with us."[49] A few days later, Meir flew to Paris for a secret meeting with the king himself, in which she personally implored him to crack down on Fatah.[50]

As Israel's chief diplomat, Meir was keenly aware of America's enlarged role in Israeli-Jordanian border matters, which may also have swayed her against further retaliation. By mid-September, Hussein or al-Tal was meeting with US ambassador Robert Barnes daily to discuss the border situation, and reports of their meetings were immediately shared with the Israelis.[51] The American channel had become an invaluable way for Israel to maintain indirect dialogue with Hussein while "putting constant pressure" on him.[52] After meeting with Dean Rusk and Robert Komer at the end of September, Meir concluded that the Johnson administration understood the urgency of getting Hussein to act against Fatah.[53] Growing US involvement in Israeli-Jordanian border matters raised the political price of Israeli military action, and made it seem possible to cope with Fatah without resorting to violence.

The decisive moment in the intra-Israeli debate about reprisals came on October 3, 1965. Following a Fatah attack the night before, Rabin met with Yariv, Operations Branch chief Hayim Bar-Lev, and Southern and Central Command chiefs Tsvi Zamir and Yosef Geva. Rabin was convinced that "the time had come to do something more demonstrative, which will show Hussein that he cannot forever rest assured that we will not harm Jordan, lest we harm his prestige." Yet that afternoon, Rabin could not persuade Eshkol to retaliate. The prime minister could not understand why a large-scale reprisal, which could result in the fall of Hussein's regime "and maybe even war," was preferable to making an effort to improve Israel's border defenses. Rabin protested that it was not possible to "close" the Israeli-Jordanian border, but Eshkol had made up his mind. He did not authorize a retaliatory raid. Instead he met with the chiefs of Israel's regular and border police forces, and decided to allocate additional funds to improve Israel's static defenses. Israel did not launch another retaliatory attack against Jordan until the spring of 1966.[54]

Over the next several months, Eshkol's decision seemed to be vindicated. By holding back the IDF, Eshkol gave the Jordanian government the breathing space it needed to repress Fatah. Confronting the Palestinian organization remained difficult for Hussein, and not only for domestic political reasons. One basic problem was the Israeli-Jordanian armistice line itself. The "border was extensive," Hussein admitted, and despite the JAA's "best efforts at patrolling, there were always large gaps."[55] Fatah's diffuse command structure also made the organization difficult to confront. Even when the Jordanian security services managed to arrest West Bank villagers whom Fatah paid to carry out attacks, they rarely knew anything about other Fatah cells in Jordan. Most often, the raiders had been recruited on a one-time basis by Fatah agents who entered Jordan from Syria. Given the large volume of people who regularly traveled between Syria and Jordan, it was virtually impossible for the Jordanians to apprehend these operatives. Most of them had relatives or friends in Jordan and could easily stay a few days without being detected.[56]

Most importantly, like the Israelis, Hussein and al-Tal had to deal with the fact that Fatah's leadership and training facilities lay far beyond their borders. For a while, the Jordanians hoped to enlist the help of other Arab states where Fatah operated, particularly Lebanon, Syria, and Kuwait. As of August 1965, Wasfi al-Tal was still fairly optimistic about the prospects of a "regional attack on Fatah."[57] But by October, the prime minister's hopes had withered. Jordan, al-Tal complained, received "almost no support from other Arab states."[58] Realizing that the nerve center of the organization lay beyond their reach, the Jordanian security services concentrated on breaking Fatah's capacity to launch raids, targeting veteran infiltrators and smugglers in the West Bank. Such men, al-Tal thought, were "almost all working for money and not principle," and could easily be paid to work as government informants instead.[59]

By the beginning of 1966, the Jordanian government's efforts, combined with improved Israeli border patrolling, nearly crippled Fatah's capacity to attack Israel from Jordan. "Hostile incidents" on the Israeli-Jordanian front declined from their peak of fifteen in September 1965 to six in October, three in both November and December, and none at all in January 1966. Five such incidents occurred in February 1966, but all were random cross-border shooting episodes, not Fatah attacks.[60]

Fatah, Rabin had warned in October 1965, could be "the match that lights a giant flame," a catalyst for regional war.[61] Months later, the Palestinian organization appeared to be on the verge of oblivion. Fatah, Eshkol told the KFADC in February 1966, was "comatose, dying." The prime minister clearly believed that Israel's restraint had paid off. Though Eshkol credited Israel's initial raids with forcing the king's hand, he thought that future Israeli counterterrorism efforts would primarily involve the kind of defensive measures he had approved that fall. Both the IDF and the government, Eshkol stated, were trying to figure out how to deal with Fatah's brand of warfare over the long term. The IDF was studying how other states dealt with cross-border terrorism in hopes of finding better ways to secure the border than "positioning a man every ten meters." Dealing with guerrilla warfare, Eshkol concluded, was a problem that would require patience and creativity to solve. Israel did not always need to rush to use force.[62]

Just as Israeli-Jordanian rapprochement had survived the formation of the UAC and the Arab water diversion efforts, so it seemed destined to outlive the burst of Palestinian nationalism that followed the Arab summit conferences. With the Arab water diversion efforts in shambles, the regional military balance in Israel's favor, and Fatah in apparent decline, the chances of war seemed slim. But in February 1966, everything began to change.

THE SYRIAN COUP AND ITS CONSEQUENCES

On February 23, 1966, a small clique of Ba'thist officers staged a bloody intraparty coup, sending President Amin al-Hafiz and party founders Michel 'Aflaq and Salah al-Din al-Bitar into exile. Leftist intellectuals like Nur al-Din al-Atasi, Yusuf Zu'ayyin, and Ibrahim Makhus composed the public face of the new regime, holding the offices of president, prime minister, and foreign minister, respectively. But the backbone of the "neo-Ba'th" was what the CIA described as "a poorly cemented amalgam of military officers representing a variety of ideological and confessional interests."[63] Led by Salah Jadid, the assistant secretary of the Ba'th Regional Command, this small group of mainly Alawi and Druze officers lacked governing experience or significant support among Syria's Sunni majority. Driven by ideology, unfazed by Israel's power, and desperate to burnish their weak political credentials, the neo-Ba'thists enthusiastically embraced the idea of backing an Algerian- or Vietnamese-style "popular war" in the service of the Palestinian cause.

Syria's new leaders threw their weight behind Fatah, rejuvenating the "comatose" Palestinian organization. By the end of April 1966, Syrian assistance made it possible for Fatah to attack several Israeli targets via the West Bank. Israel responded as it had a year earlier, striking the country from which the Palestinian militants had come. On the night of April 29–30, Israeli troops attacked Khirbat Rafat in the Hebron hills and Tal al-Arba'in in the Jordan Valley, demolishing numerous houses. Eleven Jordanian civilians were killed and three were wounded.[64] Yet despite the efforts of the Jordanian security services afterward, Fatah could not be stopped. Between January and the end of June 1966, Fatah carried out forty-eight attacks on Israeli targets. Most of these attacks occurred from April onward, and forty of them were launched from Jordan.[65]

By the summer of 1966, the Israeli military leadership had concluded that the only way to stop Fatah was to hit Syria hard. The Israelis no longer had any doubt about the extent of Syrian support for Fatah. AMAN's reports indicated that Fatah had essentially been transformed into an instrument of Syrian policy. They described Fatah training camps administered directly by the Syrian government and army, and Fatah attacks carried out by Syrian intelligence operatives.[66] For the General Staff, the question was not whether to take on the Syrians, but how to convince the Israeli cabinet that doing so was a good idea.

But persuading Israel's politicians to strike Syria was not easy. Eshkol and his colleagues shared the generals' frustration with Syria, the main opponent of the "realism" they saw on the rise elsewhere in the Arab world.[67] They also feared they would damage Israel's relations with Hussein and the Johnson administration by launching more raids into the West Bank. "We don't want to hit Jordan anymore," Eshkol told Rabin after the April 29–30 raids. "It makes sense to leave the situation as it is, if possible, for two to three months. Otherwise it will seem to the world that the Jews are just lashing out."[68] Yet the Israeli cabinet's frustration with the neo-Ba'th and reluctance to strike Jordan did not automatically translate into a willingness to attack Syria. The topography of the border still gave them pause, and so did growing Soviet support for Syria. The Soviets, who had recently suffered setbacks in Algeria, Ghana, and Indonesia and watched helplessly as the United States intervened in Vietnam and the Dominican Republic, had embraced the neo-Ba'th regime, which they viewed as a Third World success story at an otherwise bleak time. When Syrian foreign minister Ibrahim Makhus demanded that the USSR warn Israel against massing its forces near the Syrian border, the Soviets readily complied.[69] The Soviets' warnings were likely intended to help Syria's leaders rally support for their beleaguered regime, but in Israel, they were interpreted as signs of a sudden, sinister turn in Soviet policy.[70]

By the end of the summer of 1966, the Israeli cabinet's anxiety about the possible fallout from a major clash with Syria rose considerably. When two Israeli soldiers and a civilian were killed by a mine near the Sea of Galilee on July 13, the cabinet approved retaliatory air strikes, accepting Rabin's arguments that Egypt would not intervene and that the Soviets would rein Syria in.[71] Nevertheless, the cabinet did not decide lightly to bomb what was left of Syria's diversion works, and Eshkol felt uneasy afterward. "We are not of a mind to always use airplanes," he told the KFADC. "The enemy knows how to prepare for it. And we understand that even in the days of the Vietnam War, that airplanes are something different. Israel is, in the end, only Israel. Certainly, there's reason to fear that in response to this, they'll bomb Tiberias."[72] Rabin continued to complain that the cabinet did not understand why Israel could and should strike Syria.[73] But on August 15, Eshkol's prediction that Israeli air strikes could prompt the Syrians to retaliate in kind was borne out. When an Israeli patrol boat ran aground on the Sea of Galilee, Syrian planes swooped out of the sky to attack it. The aircraft were eventually driven off, but for the Israelis, the implications of the incident were grave.[74] For the first time since 1956, an Arab state had the audacity to launch an aerial attack against an Israeli target.

On one hand, the August 15 incident only strengthened the General Staff's determination to stop Syria's provocations by force. Because of inter-Arab divisions and the state of the military balance, Rabin argued, the Syrians would eventually back down if dealt a "series of blows."[75] "There is no more appropriate time than the present," Rabin wrote to Tsvi Zamir, Israel's military attaché in London, "for a clash between Israel and Syria.... This is my opinion and the opinion of the majority of the General Staff."[76] For Eshkol and the cabinet, however, the Syrian air attack on the patrol boat indicated that the neo-Ba'thists might be acting out because they knew they could count on the Soviets in the event of war. The Israelis' worries about what the Soviets might do for Syria would fatefully shape how they responded to the Fatah attacks that escalated in tandem with intensifying tensions between Syria and Jordan.

HUSSEIN'S SYRIAN "ADVENTURE"

The Jordanian-Egyptian détente that followed the Cairo summit of 1964 never erased the basic ideological differences that separated Nasser and Hussein. Even during their brief honeymoon, the two leaders remained at odds, especially regarding Jordan's relationship to the UAC and the PLO. In October 1965, Hussein's dispute with al-Shuqayri over whether the PLO could conscript and arm Jordan's Palestinians burst into the open, forcing Nasser to personally restrain the PLO chairman. At the urging of Egypt and the Arab League, al-Shuqayri grudgingly agreed to negotiate with the Jordanians, and in March 1966, the two sides reached an agreement permitting the PLO to levy a "liberation tax" on Jordanian citizens and broadcast for an hour a week on Jordanian radio.[77] But by this point, the terms of the agreement hardly mattered. In the winter of 1966, Nasser abandoned his efforts to negotiate an end to the Yemen war and began attacking Saudi Arabia's calls for an "Islamic Conference" as an imperialist plot.[78] Inter-Arab détente, which had given Jordan two years of political stability, was coming to an end.

Hussein could clearly see what the future held for inter-Arab relations. In public, he still paid lip service to Arab unity.[79] Privately, he fully expected a "deterioration in relations" with Nasser and began preparing to "stabilize home base in anticipation [of] Nasser storms."[80] In April, the king moved to secure his domestic flank by ordering his security services to arrest 123 Ba'thists, Communists, and members of the Arab Nationalists Movement.[81] The following month, he convinced the Saudis to promise him a £5 million loan for development projects and pay for Jordan's military expenses if the UAC imploded.[82] Having braced himself, on June 14 Hussein delivered a scathing speech at a graduation ceremony in 'Ajlun, attacking the PLO and hinting that he had lost patience with the Arab radical camp as a whole.[83] Nasser soon replied in kind. At the end of July, he announced that he could no longer participate in the Arab summits, since they had been exploited by reactionary forces for nefarious ends. On July 26, Nasser directly attacked Hussein, accusing him of backing the Egyptian Muslim Brotherhood and its conspiracies against his regime.[84]

But while Hussein's quarrels with al-Shuqayri and Nasser generated a great deal of sound and fury, the feud that developed between him and Syria's new rulers would have more immediate and far-reaching consequences. From the very first moments following the neo-Ba'th putsch, Hussein, al-Tal, and other members of the Jordanian establishment saw Syria's government as both a threat and an opportunity. They feared that the new regime, unstable and left-leaning, might provide a gateway to a Communist takeover or be undermined by Nasserists who would seize power and reestablish the UAR. Even worse, Syria might descend into chaos. In any of these scenarios, Syria could become a haven for opponents of the Hashemite monarchy or for Palestinian guerrillas who would suck Jordan into conflict with Israel. Hussein and al-Tal, who remembered the 1958–1961 period all too well, vowed that they would go to war to prevent Syria from becoming a base for subversion again.[85] At the same time, Jordan's leaders believed that the coup in Syria offered them a chance to fundamentally transform Jordan's strategic position before the Arab cold war heated up once more. The Jordanian government and armed forces, US ambassador Robert Barnes reported, were abuzz with talk of how Jordan would invade Syria and establish a new regional order. A liberal parliamentary government would take control in Syria, and would align itself with Jordan and Saudi Arabia. Nasser's hegemonic ambitions would finally come to an end. Soviet penetration of the region would be curtailed. Peace with Israel would become possible.[86]

The Jordanians did not attempt to actually implement these grand designs in the immediate aftermath of the neo-Ba'th coup. The JAA had not done the operational planning or intelligence gathering necessary to invade Syria, and US diplomats warned Hussein against doing so.[87] In the meantime, the situation in Syria stabilized, and no Egyptian or Communist takeover took place, denying Hussein and al-Tal a reason to intervene. Still, into the spring and summer of 1966, the Jordanian leadership kept pondering the idea of overthrowing the new Syrian regime. In conversations with US officials, Hussein cautioned the Americans not to accept a reestablished UAR or a "possible Communist takeover in Syria." To test whether the Johnson administration would help him oust the neo-Ba'th, the king suggested that the United States share intelligence with Jordan and participate in "advance contingency planning directed toward preventing Communist takeover" in Syria.[88] The Americans politely rejected Hussein's overtures, but the king remained determined to topple the neo-Ba'th before they targeted him. As Fatah's raids from the West Bank multiplied, Hussein and his advisors grew particularly worried that Egypt and Syria were trying to entangle Jordan with Israel.

The Jordanians' fear that the Arab radicals sought to embroil them with Israel peaked in August, when the UAC informed them that Israeli troops had massed on the Syrian border. In accordance with Plan X, a UAC contingency plan, Jordan was expected to attack Israel if Israeli-Syrian hostilities broke out. Al-Tal and Crown Prince Hassan told Findley Burns, the new US ambassador in Amman, that the UAC order was "a trick of their enemies." If the JAA moved, the Israelis would "cut them to pieces." If the Jordanians held back, they would "be accused of cowardice and treason to the Arab cause."[89] Through American channels, the Jordanians' worries reached the Israelis, who sent back assurances that the UAC's reports were "a figment of somebody's imagination."[90] Nevertheless, the incident surely sharpened the Jordanian leadership's fears of Syrian-Egyptian collusion against them. To avoid entrapment, Hussein essentially had two options—lie low and hope for the best, or strike the neo-Ba'th before the Israelis did.

What happened next remains murky. The known facts are as follows: on September 8, 1966, Salim Hatum, a Syrian Druze colonel who had been relegated to a marginal post after playing a key role in the February coup, attempted to seize power in Damascus. The plot went awry, and Hatum fled to Jordan with a number of his supporters.[91] The Syrians and the Egyptians immediately pinned the blame for the abortive coup on Hussein.[92] There is no clear evidence linking the Jordanians to Hatum's failed putsch, but there is no question that they were plotting to overthrow the neo-Ba'th regime thereafter. In an October 5 conversation with US officials, al-Tal claimed to be in touch with eleven different Syrian dissident groups. He was "[no] longer thinking in terms of [Jordanian] military intervention in Syria," he said, but seemed "increasingly inclined [to] view [the] Syrians as capable of plotting their own coup," with the Jordanians "influencing post-coup cabinet formation and a redirection of Syrian policy."[93]

By early October, the Jordanians' machinations had become the subject of a fierce inter-Arab propaganda war, thanks to Col. Talal Abu 'Asali, a co-conspirator of Hatum's who had fled to Cairo. In a sensational interview with *al-Ahram*, Abu 'Asali claimed that he and Hatum had met with Hussein, al-Tal, and Muhammad Rasul al-Kaylani, who presented them with an elaborate plot to establish a "collaborator" regime in Syria. Backed by the CIA, MI6, and Saudi Arabia, the Jordanians would rally disaffected Syrian tribal and religious leaders, army officers, and wealthy capitalists, and organize them into a government in exile in Amman. In the meantime, the Jordanians and their allies would foment internal unrest in Syria. Once the situation neared civil war, they would intervene militarily and topple the neo-Ba'th regime, under the pretext of "sparing Arab blood."[94] The next day, an unnamed Egyptian source told *al-Ahram* that Egypt would intervene militarily in Syria in order to prevent the Jordanians from carrying out their plans.[95] The Jordanians responded with equal belligerence. If Egypt sent troops to Syria, al-Tal told reporters on October 4, he would "break Nasser's neck."[96] Hussein made similar statements. Jordan, he told the *Daily Telegraph*, "was capable of using force in Syria if there was any armed interference from outside. One Yemeni tragedy is enough for the Arab world. We are not going to tolerate another in Syria."[97]

Hussein and al-Tal's tough talk toward their enemies abroad belied their vulnerability at home. The king and his prime minister liked to claim that Jordan's economic growth had rendered its populace more resistant to radicalization. Despite al-Shuqayri's "attempt to split [the] Jordanian people," Hussein told British prime minister Harold Wilson, there was no reason for him to be "unhappy with the internal situation. Economic development was going well and there was a healthy realization of the benefits of stability."[98] The PLO, al-Tal boasted, was "finished in Jordan." According to the Jordanian prime minister, "99 percent of all Palestinians" would back Hussein against al-Shuqayri, and "the remaining one percent could be easily dealt with."[99] To show off its alleged popularity, the government trucked "delegations" of West Bankers to Amman, where they praised Hussein, denounced al-Shuqayri, and received elaborate press coverage.[100] At the same time, however, Hussein and al-Tal restricted the entry of Palestinians into Jordan, imposed new restrictions on gun ownership, and arrested another wave of PLO supporters, indicating that they did not feel entirely confident in their own bravado.[101]

For despite what Hussein and al-Tal said, the economic growth of the early 1960s had actually made Jordan *more* politically combustible, because of the baldly unequal way in which it was distributed between the East Bank and the West Bank. Though the United States had invested hundreds of millions of dollars in budgetary aid in the kingdom since the late 1950s, the United Nations Relief and Work Agency (UNRWA) remained the West Bank's only real source of foreign assistance. The Jordanian government spent virtually all foreign loans and project grants on the East Bank. While the West Bank generated approximately 35 percent of Jordan's GDP in 1966, it also contained 47 percent of its population, meaning that the region's economy punched well below its demographic weight. Though the West Bank was home to 65 percent of Jordan's industrial establishments, it employed only 45 percent of the country's industrial workforce, since most of the West Bank's "factories" were actually small workshops that employed only a few individuals and produced goods solely for the local market. Almost all of Jordan's large factories, including a cement plant, an oil refinery, and mines, had been built on the East Bank. Nor was West Bank agriculture particularly productive. The area accounted for only 40 percent of Jordan's total agricultural output, most of which was locally consumed. According to the US Agency for International Development, the region was a "food deficit area," producing surpluses of only olives, melons, and grapes. With the East Ghor Canal poised to dramatically boost the output of East Bank farmers, the West Bank agricultural sector appeared doomed to fall even further behind. To the extent that the region experienced economic growth during the early and mid-1960s, it was confined to the Jerusalem area, where tourism boomed. Otherwise, the West Bank's principal economic asset remained remittances sent home by Palestinians who had left the country.[102]

The glaring disparities in the distribution of growth within Jordan were not lost on the West Bank's residents, and the regime's hard line against the PLO and its backers brought their resentment bubbling to the surface. Many Jordanian Palestinians, US officials noted, did not like al-Shuqayri but feared that Hussein's anti-PLO turn foreshadowed intensified discrimination against them.[103] In Nablus, Senator Hikmat al-Masri, former foreign minister Qadri Tuqan, and Parliamentary deputy 'Abd al-Ra'uf al-Faris told US diplomats that they were not especially concerned about the PLO, but were bothered by a general lack of Palestinian influence on Hussein's decision-making and the government's "failure to pay adequate attention to the development needs of the West Bank."[104] Even in Jerusalem, US diplomats reported, many Palestinians felt that the central government profited more than they did from tourism. District governor Anwar al-Khatib had taken to portraying himself as a defender of West Bank interests against East Bank encroachment.[105]

"West Bankers are between two enemies: the Jews and the East Bankers," declared Justice 'Abd al-Maksud al-Khayri, a Palestinian notable and a Jordanian Supreme Court appointee.[106] The Palestinians' grievances were compounded by a general sense that Hussein was frivolous, self-absorbed, and insensitive to the plight of those he ruled. The young monarch's love of fast cars, sports, foreign travel, and "frequent Aqaba excursions, often with different female guests," the US embassy in Amman had reported that spring, "could lead a sizable number of Jordanians to the conclusion that the king isn't engaged in affairs of state on a 24 hour a day basis."[107] "He has never been popular," a CIA estimate noted later that year, "and even at his best probably commands the allegiance of not more than a quarter to a third of the population."[108]

The Syrian regime did not have to look hard for a way to counter Hussein and al-Tal's threats and plotting. The West Bank presented them with an Achilles heel that, if properly targeted, could bring down the Hashemite monarchy. And Fatah was the obvious weapon of choice.

THE SYRIAN COUNTERATTACK

Unlike the Israeli-Syrian frontier, the West Bank armistice line had been fairly quiet in August 1966. Not a single terrorist attack took place on Israeli soil during that month.[109] Following Hatum's failed coup in Syria, however, Fatah resumed its attacks via Jordan. On September 24 and 27, bombs went off near the Dead Sea. On October 4, an Israeli border police vehicle was fired on near the Latrun salient. On the night of October 8–9, bombs went off in Jerusalem's Romema neighborhood, damaging two houses and wounding four civilians. When Ya'akov Herzog arrived at Eshkol's office the following morning to discuss the attack, the prime minister angrily informed him that another one had already occurred, with deadlier results. Four Israeli border policemen had been killed when their jeep struck a mine at Sha'ar ha-Golan near the Syrian-Jordanian border.[110]

The question of whether and where to strike back loomed before Levi Eshkol once more. According to the logic of previous Israeli reprisals, since the attacks at Jerusalem and Sha'ar ha-Golan had been launched from the West Bank, Jordan should be held responsible, even if its government would rather have prevented them. Yet this time, Eshkol heeded those who counseled patience. Herzog, whose contacts with Hussein had sensitized him to the king's plight, and who had been thoroughly briefed on Hussein's anti-Ba'thist plots by US ambassador Walworth Barbour, proved instrumental in staying Eshkol's hand.[111] Herzog, military assistant Yisrael Lior, and veteran Foreign Ministry Arabist Moshe Sasson advised the prime minister to tell his cabinet that while Israel should hold Hussein responsible for attacks launched from his territory, it should nevertheless recognize his anti-Fatah efforts and not give Egypt and Syria a chance to undermine his regime. Eshkol accepted their counsel with visible relief.[112] Though the cabinet had considered retaliating against Jordan, he told the KFADC, they decided not to do so because Jordan "has been acting vigorously to prevent Fatah activity." There were forces in the Arab world, Eshkol warned, that were clearly interested in "entangling Israel in a clash with Jordan." Though the prime minister felt reluctant to give Hussein a free pass for attacks launched from his territory, he also did not want to "end up making life easy for Syria." An Israeli raid on Jordan, Eshkol added, could set back Jordanian efforts to overthrow the neo-Ba'th regime or force the Jordanians into the arms of the Arab radicals. "Better," he said, "to keep the fire between Syria and Jordan alive and burning." In the meantime, Israel would lay the diplomatic groundwork for an attack on Syria.[113]

The next three weeks witnessed an energetic Israeli diplomatic offensive to prepare international public opinion for the "frontal clash" with Syria that the General Staff had been clamoring for since that summer. The Operations Branch had in fact prepared orders for strikes against targets in Syria following the Jerusalem and Sha'ar ha-Golan attacks, but the cabinet rejected them.[114] With the UN General Assembly in session, Eshkol did not want to undermine Israel's case against Syria by striking too soon. Instead, he decided to use the occasion to air his country's grievances to the world.[115] On October 12, Michael Comay, Israel's permanent representative to the United Nations, submitted a complaint against Syria to the Security Council. On October 27, the United States and Britain presented a draft resolution calling on both Israel and Syria to work with the United Nations to stop the violence on their borders.[116] The Israelis expected that the Soviets would veto any resolution that held Syria responsible for border violence, but a victory in New York was never their real goal. Regardless of how the Security Council voted, Eban told the KFADC, Syrian-sponsored terrorism would continue. "Sooner or later—and I am speaking in terms of days and weeks, not months and years—there will be a serious clash between Syria and Israel," he said. The point of complaining to the Security Council was not to prevent such a clash, but to garner international sympathy before it occurred. With all of the UN's limitations, Eban joked, "it has one advantage: it is a giant loudspeaker."[117]

But by the time the Soviets vetoed a modified version of the US resolution on November 4, a "frontal clash" with Syria seemed much more risky.[118] Even as Eshkol's diplomats laid the diplomatic groundwork for an attack on Syria, he and his cabinet still felt uncomfortable about the idea. They had never totally accepted the Israeli intelligence community's view that the Syrians would back off if confronted, or that Egypt, Jordan, and the Soviet Union would not react if Israel struck Syria in a "vigorous and quick" way.[119] The prime minister and his colleagues remained mindful of the topographical advantages that the Syrians enjoyed, and worried that the Syrians would try to use warplanes against Israeli targets once again.[120] Their darkest fears, however, concerned the Soviet Union and Egypt. In the aftermath of the Jerusalem and Sha'ar ha-Golan attacks, Soviet ambassador Dmitri Chuvakhin met with Eshkol and accused Israel of preparing to invade Syria.[121] The Soviet ambassador's charges left the cabinet wary of how the USSR would respond to a major strike against Syria. Several ministers, Rabin told the General Staff, were unsure that any amount of Israeli diplomacy could neutralize Soviet hostility. As for Egypt, at least some members of the cabinet did not share AMAN's sanguine view that Nasser would not respond to an attack on Syria. They believed, Rabin reported, that "there is an object in the south of the country that is an ideal target for a 'limited response' which will have the support of the entire world. Dimona. [The ministers] say that Egypt will not move its forces, but will take out Dimona. It can be construed as a 'limited action,' rather than war."[122]

On November 4, Israel's advocates of a "frontal clash" with Syria suffered another setback when Egypt signed a mutual defense pact with Syria. AMAN analysts believed that the Egyptians had designed the pact to restrain the neo-Ba'th.[123] The Israeli government, however, was clearly not convinced. It would now be far more difficult to get the cabinet to authorize a strike against Syria, Rabin told the General Staff on November 6. "The Jews," he said, "are worried." But it was not only "the Jews," as Rabin and his fellow officers often called the mostly Diaspora-born, Yiddish-speaking cabinet ministers. Even Yariv, who was convinced that the Egyptians did not want war, feared that the Egyptian-Syrian pact might nevertheless pull Nasser in that direction. While the pact appeared to restrict the circumstances in which Egypt would have to defend Syria, it did not seem to impose any limits on Syrian sponsorship of the *fida'iyyun*. "I don't know if [the Egyptians] obligated the Syrians to stop supporting the guys operating through Jordan," the military intelligence chief admitted. "If there's a mine or two, and we pull our sword out of the scabbard, what will the Egyptians do?" he asked. Yariv repeated his conviction that Egypt would not respond to a short, limited Israeli attack, but added, "Truthfully, if there's something very strong, it will be much harder for the Egyptians not to intervene than beforehand."[124]

A brief lull followed the signing of the Egyptian-Syrian pact, but it did not last long. On the night of November 11–12, an Israeli vehicle rolled over a mine on a road near Arad. The ensuing blast wounded six soldiers and killed three, including one who was thrown almost forty meters by the explosion and died from the head wounds he received.[125]

SAMU'

Saturday, November 12, 1966, was a tense day for Wasfi al-Tal and King Hussein. "The hope that [the] UAR-Syrian defense pact would result in [the] UAR putting [a] damper on terrorist activities was not being realized, at least as far as [the] Jordan-Israel border is concerned," al-Tal told one US official. Both he and Hussein were terrified that Israel would retaliate against Jordan. A raid, al-Tal warned, could lead to "new and increased pressure . . . to accept PLO arming of Jordanian border residents or even stationing of other Arab forces in Jordan." The Jordanians had also begun to worry about *Israel's* ultimate intentions. Even before the Egyptian-Syrian pact was signed, Hussein began to wonder whether Israel might attack Jordan rather than Syria. What if the Israelis were not concerned with "teaching any one Arab state a lesson?" he asked. What if they simply wanted to force the international community to put an end to Fatah's attacks? If this was the case, Hussein speculated, Israel would not risk a costly assault on the Golan, but would instead seize parts of the West Bank and hold them "hostage." By doing so, Israel would "ensure [that the] major powers would be sufficiently exercised to pressure all Arab states against permitting anti-Israeli terrorist organizations on their territory."[126]

Still, Hussein did not think an Israeli attack was inevitable. While he had his suspicions about Israel's intentions, he had good reason to believe that the Israelis still valued the stability of his regime and recognized that he was doing his best to repress Palestinian guerrilla activity. Hoping to calm his Jewish neighbors, the king gave Burns an apologetic message for Eshkol. It was swiftly sent to State Department officials in Washington, but they did not deliver it to the Israeli embassy until Saturday evening, November 12, out of respect for the Jewish Sabbath. By the time Eshkol received it, it was already nine o'clock on Sunday morning, November 13, Israeli time. The IDF's retaliatory raid on Jordan was nearing its end.[127]

Would Eshkol have delayed Israel's response if he had received Hussein's message earlier? The prime minister's own reply to the question was characteristically indecisive: "I don't want to say yes and I don't want to say no."[128] However fascinating the episode of Hussein's message might be, it is best not to overstate its importance. Even if Eshkol had received the king's apology earlier, it would not have altered the basic choices available to his government, only the speed with which they were made. The Israelis had three options. The first, refraining from retaliation and resorting to diplomacy, was viewed as the least desirable, especially by Israel's military leaders. Restraint, Rabin argued later, would have been seen by the Arab world as an indication that "Israel's blood is free to shed."[129] Nor did going to the UN seem like a serious option, since the USSR had just vetoed a similar Israeli complaint.[130] Two choices remained—to strike Syria, which Israel had been preparing to do for months, or to strike Jordan, from where the saboteurs had come.

When the General Staff met on the morning of November 12, those present overwhelmingly favored retaliating against Jordan. Most of the IDF's senior commanders agreed that the Arad incident could not be reasonably attributed to Syria, since its perpetrators had come from the southernmost part of the West Bank. Israel had been patient with Hussein, they thought, but serious attacks from Jordan, particularly the Hebron area, had continued. The king should not be allowed to believe that Syrian sponsorship of terrorism absolved him of responsibility for keeping his border quiet.[131] Beneath this rationale lay deeper fears raised by the Egyptian-Syrian mutual defense pact. The General Staff clearly worried that a major Israeli attack on Syria so soon after the signing of the pact would test the limits of Egypt's restraint. In these circumstances, Rabin noted afterward, an Israeli attack on Syria could "lead to very undesirable developments."[132] Here, the IDF chief of staff was probably hinting at the same fear that had arisen in previous cabinet and General Staff discussions: that Nasser would use an Israeli attack on Syria as a pretext for an air strike on Dimona.

Eshkol was uneasy with the judgment of his senior commanders, but once again he allowed himself to be persuaded by them. The prime minister remained reluctant to strike Jordan. Just prior to the mining at Arad, he had sent Emmanuel Herbert a message for the king, expressing Israel's appreciation of his efforts to fight terrorism, and promising him that Israel would not attack Jordan. (Like Hussein's message, Eshkol's letter seems to have been delayed by the Sabbath. By the time it reached the king, the Samu' raid had already occurred).[133] A raid into Jordan could undermine Hussein's trust, destabilize his regime, and divert the international community's attention from Syria. Was there no way, Eshkol asked Rabin, that the mining near Arad could be linked to the neo-Ba'th? Impossible, Rabin replied.[134] That afternoon, the prime minister convened the cabinet defense subcommittee, which unanimously authorized a raid against Jordan. As Eshkol later recalled, however, the ministers agreed that Israel "had no interest in harming the prestige of the regime or the standing of the king." They intended for the IDF to target the civilian population of the Hebron area in order to deter them from supporting Fatah, but to do everything possible to avoid a clash with Jordanian troops.[135]

The details of the raid, however, were left to the IDF, and the operation that was launched the following morning far exceeded what Eshkol and his colleagues had envisioned. The Samu' raid would be Israel's largest military operation since Suez. Previous raids into the West Bank had been launched at night, and had not included armored vehicles. This time, the General Staff wanted to attack during the daytime and send tanks, believing that civilian casualties could be more easily prevented in daylight and that armor would deter the JAA from intervening.[136]

Initially the IDF planned only to destroy some buildings in Samu', a small village in the Hebron hills, in hope of deterring the locals from harboring guerrillas. Yet when the raiding party, consisting of four hundred troops, five Sherman tanks, eight Centurion tanks, fifty armored personnel carriers, and two Ouragon planes, crossed the border at six thirty in the morning on November 13, very little went as planned. Anticipating an Israeli raid, local JAA forces had shifted their positions during the night, bringing them into the IDF column's path. Undeterred by Israeli armor, the Jordanian troops engaged the enemy head-on, and were forced to summon air support. Four Jordanian Hawker Hunters flew to the scene, where Israeli Mirages shot down one of them. By the time the last of Israel's troops withdrew across the armistice lines at a quarter to ten, they left behind fifteen dead Jordanian soldiers and five dead civilians. Thirty-four soldiers and six civilians were also wounded, and ninety-three buildings were destroyed, including a police station and a school. The IDF lost one soldier; ten Israelis were wounded.[137]

The turmoil began the following day in the devastated village of Samu'. Government officials who arrived bearing food and medical supplies were angrily turned away. We don't want food, some of the villagers shouted. We want arms, to defend ourselves. Since the government could not protect the West Bank, others yelled, Hussein should allow the PLA to deploy there. Otherwise they would "prefer to let the Israelis take over their villages rather than continue to be at their mercy, and Amman be damned." On November 15, in nearby Hebron, two thousand students turned out to demonstrate against the government. They too condemned the JAA, and called upon the regime to bring the PLA to the area. When Hebron's chief of police attempted to address the crowd, they attacked him and nearly stoned him to death. The crowd then rampaged through the city, overturning UNRWA vehicles and the cars of government officials. They tore down any street sign that bore the name of the king or the Hashemite family. They chanted slogans in support of al-Shuqayri and the PLO, and called for the overthrow of the monarchy and for Hussein's execution.[138]

Over the following week and a half, similar demonstrations and riots erupted in every major city in the West Bank. By November 24, they spread to smaller villages and Palestinian refugee camps. The demonstrations eventually grew so violent that regular JAA troops, including armored units, were eventually called in. Rioters concentrated their fury on government offices and vehicles, and attacked the soldiers and police who came to disperse them. The worst clashes between soldiers and crowds occurred in Nablus on November 21 and in Jerusalem on November 24, where major riots broke out after Friday prayers. Of the eight demonstrators killed by the JAA, four were Nabulsis and four were Jerusalemites; an additional twenty-five were wounded.[139]

The riots of November 1966 dwarfed the protests of April 1963 in scale and intensity. It was the declared aims of the protesters, however, that made this outbreak of unrest so different from the ones that preceded it. The anti–Baghdad Pact protests of late 1955, the demonstrations in support of the al-Nabulsi government in 1957, and the April 1963 riots had all been most intense on the West Bank, and had all drawn upon Palestinian discontent with the monarchy and its policies. Yet in all of those protests, discontent with the Hashemite regime was expressed in terms of support for Arab unity. This time, specifically Palestinian concerns dominated. Petitions drawn up by "National Leadership" committees in Nablus, Jerusalem, Ramallah, and Hebron demanded that the government arm the West Bank's border villagers, give the *fida'iyyun* free rein, and allow other Arab troops into Jordan. The signatories included some opposition figures, including members of the PLO Executive Committee and the Arab Nationalists Movement, but also included members of the Jordanian parliament, prominent businessmen, and former government ministers.[140] From urban notables in Jerusalem and Nablus to herders and farmers in the border villages in the Hebron hills, West Bankers seemed united in their discontent with the monarchy and their support for Palestinian national self-expression and confrontation with Israel.

The countdown to the 1967 war had begun.

NOTES

1. Summary of Eban's discussions with Rostow, Komer, et al., December 12, 1966, ISA/FM/3977/20.
2. Shemesh, *Palestinian Entity*, 1–26.
3. Amman to State, September 15, 1962, JFKL/NSF/Country Files/Jordan, box 125A. The contempt was mutual. See Shuqayri, *'Ala tariq*, 109.
4. Shuqayri, *Min al-qima*, 59–64.
5. Ibid., 84–87.
6. Shemesh, *Arab Politics*, 71–74.
7. Hamid, *Muqararat al-majlis al-watani al-filastini*, 49–50; Shuqayri, *Min al-qima*, 90.
8. "The Palestine Liberation Organization," Joint Research Department memo, November 15, 1966, BNA/FO 370/2872.
9. Cairo to State, June 30, 1964, NA/RG59/DOSCF 1964–1966/POL 32-1 ISR-JORDAN.
10. Vered to Foreign Minister's office, September 9, 1964, ISA/FM/3552/11. Unfortunately, the Jordanian source quoted here is not identified by name.
11. Ya'akov Herzog, "Third Meeting with Charles," December 19, 1964, YHP.
12. Central Command monthly intelligence summary, March 1964, IDFA/1338/79/35.
13. Central Command monthly intelligence summary, April 1964, IDFA/1338/79/35.
14. Unit 154 to AMAN, June 14, 1964, ISA/FM/3552/11; Central Command monthly intelligence summary, June 1964, IDFA/1338/79/35.
15. Quoted in Gluska, *Eshkol*, 126–127.
16. Tel Aviv to State, June 18, 1964, NA/RG59/DOSCF 1964–1966/POL PAL.
17. KFADC minutes, June 30, 1964, ISA/A/8610/6.
18. KFADC minutes, September 22, 1964, ISA/A/8160/8.
19. DOS memcon, February 8, 1966, NA/RG59/DOSCF 1964–1966/POL ARAB-ISR.

20. See, for example, Sliusarenko-Khalil memcon, June 4, 1964, in Naumkin, *Blizhni vostochni konflikt*, doc. 191. The PLO's later efforts to achieve international recognition are covered in Chamberlin, *Global Offensive*.

21. Shuqayri, *Min al-qima*, 74.

22. Sayigh, *Armed Struggle*, 80–92, 100–108, 119–122; Abu Iyad, *My Home, My Land*, 27–43.

23. KFADC minutes, January 26, 1965, ISA/A/8160/10.

24. For an overview of Fatah's attacks between January and the end of May, see Harman's May 28 summary, State to Tel Aviv, May 29, 1965, NA/RG59/DOSCF 1964–1966/POL 32–1 ISR-JORDAN. On the Ramat ha-Kovesh and ʿAfulah attacks, see also monthly infiltration report for May 1965, ISA/A/7936/5.

25. See Rabin's remarks in KFADC minutes, January 26, 1965, ISA/A/8160/10.

26. Gluska, *Eshkol*, 130.

27. For early Syrian press coverage of Fatah's activities, see, for example, *al-Baʿth*, January 24 and 28, February 10, and March 11, 1965. On the Israelis' perception of Syria's relationship with Fatah during 1965, see Gluska, *Eshkol*, 132–134.

28. Regarding the problem of locating Fatah targets in Syria, see, for example, Yariv's remarks in Tel Aviv to State, December 17, 1965, LBJL/NSF/Country Files /Israel, box 139, 2 of 2, which indicate that it took until December 1965 for AMAN to learn the precise location of a Fatah training camp in Syria. On the general dilemmas inherent in an Israeli military operation against Syria, see Tel Aviv to State, June 7, 1965, NA/RG59/DOSCF 1964–1966/POL 32–1 ISR-JORDAN.

29. Tel Aviv to State, May 28, 1965, NA/RG59/DOSCF 1964–1966/POL 32–1 ISR-JORDAN.

30. Central Command monthly intelligence summary, February 1965, IDFA/1338/79/37.

31. Central Command monthly intelligence summary, May 1965, IDFA/1338/79/37.

32. KFADC minutes, June 1, 1965, ISA/A/8160/12.

33. Amman to State, March 2, 1965, and Amman to State, March 13, 1965, NA /RG59/DOSCF 1964–1966/POL 32–1 ISR-JORDAN. For secret Israeli messages to Hussein regarding Fatah's initial attacks, see Tel Aviv to State, May 30, 1965, NA /RG59/DOSCF 1964–1966/POL 32–1 ISR-JORDAN.

34. For remarks by Hussein to this effect, see Jerusalem to State, May 19, 1965, NA /RG59/DOSCF 1964–1966/POL 27–14 PAL/UN.

35. KFADC minutes, June 1, 1965, ISA/A/8160/12; editorial note, in Rosenthal, *Yitzhak Rabin*, 377.

36. Remarks at a meeting of the General Staff, May 30, 1965, in Rosenthal, *Yitzhak Rabin*, 377–379.

37. KFADC minutes, June 15, 1965, ISA/A/8160/13.

38. Aviad Yafeh diary, May 30, 1965, ISA/A/7933/6.

39. These intelligence exchanges are discussed in greater detail in Rubin, "Limits of the Land," 207–209.

40. Amman to State, August 21, 1965, NA/RG59/DOSCF 1964–1966/POL 32–1 ISR-JORDAN.

41. Monthly infiltration reports for July, August, and September 1965, ISA/A/7936/5. The report for June is missing from this file, but the relevant statistics can be found in the July report. It should be noted that most, but not all, of the "hos-

tile incidents" in question were Fatah raids (for which no precise numbers are given). Israeli criteria for "hostile" border incidents included spying, sabotage, murder, attempted murder, an attack with a firearm, the stealing of weapons or ammunition, the stealing of telephone or electric wires, and kidnapping. They did not include smuggling, petty theft, damaging armistice line markers, etc.

42. Central Command monthly intelligence report, September 1965, IDFA/1338/79/37.

43. Gluska, *Eshkol*, 132.

44. Lecture at Israel's National Security College, October 20, 1965, in Rosenthal, *Yitzhak Rabin*, 390.

45. Gluska, *Eshkol*, 131–136.

46. For further details on this raid, see cabinet minutes, September 5, 1965, ISA. For Rabin's view, see Gluska, *Eshkol*, 136.

47. Tel Aviv to State, October 1, 1965, NA/RG59/DOSCF 1964–1966/POL 32–1 ISR-JORDAN.

48. Gazit to Meir, September 13, 1965, ISA/FM/7300/4. This document is a memorandum summing up the points that Gazit had made to Meir the previous day.

49. KFADC minutes, September 16, 1965, ISA/A/8160/13.

50. Zak, *Hussein 'oseh shalom*, 79–80.

51. "Details of Activity," unsigned, undated (October 1965), ISA/A/7935/7.

52. "Our Activity regarding the al-Fatah Issue," unsigned, October 13, 1965, ISA/A/7935/7.

53. "Details of Activity," unsigned, undated (October 1965), ISA/A/7935/7.

54. Yisraeli to Yafeh, "Discussions with the Minister of Defense, October 3, 1965," April 15, 1966, ISA/A/7935/7. See also cabinet minutes, October 3, 1965, ISA.

55. Amman to State, October 5, 1965, NA/RG59/DOSCF 1964–1966/POL 32–1 ISR-JORDAN.

56. Amman to State, October 4, 1965, NA/RG59/DOSCF 1964–1966/POL 32–1 ISR-JORDAN.

57. Amman to State, August 4, 1965, NA/RG59/DOSCF 1964–1966/POL 32–1 ISR-JORDAN.

58. Amman to State, October 7 1965, NA/RG59/DOSCF 1964–1966/POL 32–1 ISR-JORDAN. For similar complaints about other Arab governments, see al-Tal's remarks in Amman to FO, October 23, 1965, BNA/FO 371/180658.

59. Amman to State, October 14, 1965, NA/RG59/DOSCF 1964–1966/POL 32–1 ISR-JORDAN. See also Central Command monthly intelligence summary, November 1965, IDFA/1338/79/37.

60. Monthly infiltration reports for September, October, November, and December 1965 and January and February 1966, ISA/A/7936/5.

61. Lecture at Israel's National Security College, October 20, 1965, in Rosenthal, *Yitzhak Rabin*, 391.

62. KFADC minutes, February 1, 1966, ISA/A/8160/14.

63. "Syria under the Ba'ath," CIA special report, May 20, 1966, NA/CIA-RDP79-00927A00530030004-9.

64. Central Command monthly intelligence summary, April 1966, IDFA/1338/79/37; Jerusalem to State, April 30, 1966, LBJL/NSF/Country Files/Israel, box 139, 2 of 2.

65. KFADC minutes, June 28, 1966, ISA/A/8160/16.
66. "Subject: Recent Activity and Possibilities for the Future—A Basic Guide from 245," August 16, 1966, ISA/FM/4096/13.
67. See, for example, Eban's description of Syria as an "exceptional area in the Arab family," in KFADC minutes, July 5, 1966, ISA/A/ISA/A/8161/1.
68. Quoted in Haber, *Ha-Yom tifrots milhamah*, 127–128.
69. Laron, "Playing with Fire," 168–169.
70. Ginor and Remez, *Foxbats over Dimona*, 64–67; Heller, *Yisrael veha-milhamah ha-karah*, 492–496.
71. Gluska, *Eshkol*, 122.
72. KFADC minutes, August 2, ISA/A/8161/2.
73. Gluska, *Eshkol*, 146.
74. The best description of the August 15 attack is Gluska, *Eshkol*, 148–150.
75. Remarks at a meeting of the General Staff, August 22, 1966, and editorial note, in Rosenthal, *Yitzhak Rabin*, 410–413.
76. Rabin to Zamir, August 27, 1966, in Rosenthal, *Yitzhak Rabin*, 415.
77. The breakdown of Jordanian-PLO relations during the fall of 1965 and the winter of 1966 is discussed at length in Dann, *King Hussein*; Susser, *On Both Banks*; Shemesh, *Meha-nakba la-naksa*; and Shuqayri, *'Ala tariq al-hazima*.
78. Ferris, *Nasser's Gamble*, 249–258.
79. For such pronouncements, see, for example, Hussein's interview in *al-Difa'*, March 30, 1966.
80. Beirut to State, April 27, 1966, FRUS, 1964–1968, 18: doc. 284.
81. Central Command monthly intelligence summary, April 1966, IDFA/1338/79/37.
82. Jidda to State, June 21, 1966, NA/RG59/DOSCF 1964–1966/POL 15–1 JORDAN. See also Philip Adams, "Jordan: Annual Review for 1966," January 15, 1967, BNA/FCO/17/208.
83. *Filastin*, June 15, 1966. The text of this speech is also reprinted in Shuqayri, *'Ala tariq al-hazima*, 162–171.
84. Dann, *King Hussein*, 152.
85. Amman to State, February 23, 1966; Amman to State, February 24, 1966, NA/RG59/DOSCF 1964–1966/POL 23–9 SYR.
86. Amman to State, February 28, 1966, NA/RG59/DOSCF 1964–1966/POL 23–9 SYR.
87. The State Department's recommendations for "discreet" advice against Jordanian intervention can be found in State to Amman, March 3, 1966, NA/RG59/DOSCF 1964–1966/POL 23–9 SYR.
88. Beirut to State, April 27, 1966, FRUS, 1964–1968, 18: doc. 284.
89. Amman to State, August 29, 1966, NA/RG59/DOSCF 1964–66/POL 32–1 ISR-SYR.
90. Tel Aviv to State, August 30, 1966, NA/RG59/DOSCF 1964–66/POL 32–1 ISR-SYR.
91. Seale, *Asad*, 109–113.
92. For Syrian claims of Jordanian responsibility, see *al-Ba'th*, September 11, 1966. For Egyptian claims, see *al-Ahram*, September 16, 1966.
93. Amman to State, October 5, 1966, NA/RG59/DOSCF 1964–66/POL 23–9 SYR.

94. *al-Ahram*, October 1, 1966.
95. *al-Ahram*, October 2, 1966.
96. Amman to State, October 4, 1966, NA/RG59/DOSCF 1964–66/POL 15–1 JORDAN.
97. Amman to State, October 10, 1966, NA/RG59/DOSCF 1964–66/POL 23–9 SYR.
98. Hussein-Wilson memcon, July 22, 1966, BNA/PREM/13/988.
99. Amman to State, June 20, 1966, NA/RG59/DOSCF 1964–1966/POL 15–1 JORDAN.
100. For coverage of these rallies, see *Filastin*, June 21–24, 1966.
101. Amman to State, July 11, 1966, NA/RG59/DOSCF 1964–1966/POL 23 JORDAN.
102. AID to Burns, July 13, 1967, NA/RG59/DOSCF 1967–1969/POL 28 JORDAN; "Economic Impact on Jordan of the Loss of Jerusalem or West Jordan," CIA memo, June 20, 1967, LBJL/NSF/Country Files/Middle East Crisis, box 109; "The Vitality of the West Bank to the Independent Existence of Jordan," FM Research Branch memo, August 7, 1967, ISA/FM/4296/7.
103. Washington to Gazit, June 28, 1966, ISA/FM/7300/4; Jerusalem to State, July 15, 1966, NA/RG59/DOSCF 1964–66/POL 3 PAL ENTITY.
104. Amman to State, July 11, 1966, NA/RG59/DOSCF 1964–1966/POL 23 JORDAN.
105. Washington to Gazit, June 28, 1966, ISA/FM/7300/4.
106. "Views of Hebron Officials," October 14, 1966, NA/RG59/DOSCF 1964–66 /POL 18 JORDAN.
107. Amman to State, May 20, 1966, NA/RG59/DOSCF 1964–66/POL 15–1 JORDAN.
108. "Current Problems for the Jordanian Regime," CIA special memo no. 19–66, November 18, 1966, LBJL/NSF/Country Files/Jordan, box 146. In the published version of this document, the words "has never been popular" are excised from the text. See *FRUS, 1964–1968*, 18: doc. 338.
109. Yitzhak Rabin, remarks to commanders at the Military Institute for Education, December 18, 1966, in Rosenthal, *Yitzhak Rabin*, 426.
110. KFADC minutes, October 12, 1966, ISA/A/8161/2; Ya'akov Herzog diary, October 9, 1966, ISA/4510/6; cabinet minutes, October 9, 1966, ISA.
111. Ya'akov Herzog diary, October 8, 1966, ISA/4510/6; Tel Aviv to State, October 9, 1966, NA/RG59/DOSCF 1964–1966/POL 32–1 ISR-SYR.
112. Ya'akov Herzog diary, October 9, 1966, ISA/4510/6.
113. KFADC minutes, October 12, 1966, ISA/A/8161/2.
114. Gluska, *Eshkol*, 154.
115. KFADC minutes, October 12, 1966, ISA/A/8161/2; cabinet minutes, October 16, 1966, ISA.
116. Minutes of the 1319th meeting of the United Nations Security Council, November 4, 1966, UNISPAL, https://unispal.un.org/DPA/DPR/unispal.nsf/9a798adb f322aff38525617b006d88d7/0300a576a050fa828525739a0067ff1f?OpenDocument.
117. KFADC minutes, November 1, 1966, ISA/A/8161/2.
118. Minutes of the 1319th meeting of the United Nations Security Council, November 4, 1966, UNISPAL, https://unispal.un.org/DPA/DPR/unispal.nsf/9a798adb f322aff38525617b006d88d7/0300a576a050fa828525739a0067ff1f?OpenDocument.

119. For the Israeli intelligence community's views, see Tel Aviv to State, October 20, 1966, NA/RG59/DOSCF 1964–1966/POL 32–1 ISR-SYR. Senior AMAN officers told US officials that Syria would have "effective military support from no one" in the event of a confrontation with Israel. Some Jordanian troops might take action locally, but the JAA would not commit soldiers at the brigade level. Noting that Nasser had sent no military equipment to Syria recently and that the Egyptian order of battle in Sinai had not changed, the Israelis also believed that Nasser still wanted to avoid any serious clash with Israel. As for the Soviets, when they warned the Israelis against attacking Syria, they were careful to speak of other Arab states coming to the neo-Ba'th's rescue—not themselves.

120. KFADC minutes, October 12, 1966, ISA/A/816.

121. Jerusalem to New York, October 12, 1966, ISA/A/7939/2.

122. Quoted in Gluska, *Eshkol*, 155.

123. Shalom, *Diplomatiyah be-tsel milhamah*, 151–152. See also Yariv's comments in Tel Aviv to State, November 8, 1966, NA/RG59/DOSCF 1964–66/POL 32–1 ISR-SYR.

124. Quoted in Gluska, *Eshkol*, 157–158.

125. KFADC minutes, November 22, 1966, ISA/A/8161/3. It is still not entirely clear which Palestinian organization planted the bomb, though it was probably not Fatah. The Jordanians suspected Ahmad Jibril's small Palestine Liberation Front; the Israelis would later blame the PLO-linked Heroes of the Return (Abtal al-'Awda).

126. Amman to State, November 3, 1966, NA/RG 59/DOSCF 1964–66/POL 32–1 ISR-SYR.

127. See KFADC minutes, December 13, 1966, ISA/A/8161/4, as well as Moshe Bitan's meeting with State Department officials, November 29, 1966, ISA/FM/3977/20. See also DOS memcon, November 29, 1966, NA/RG59/DOSCF 1964–66/POL 32–1 ISR-JORDAN.

128. KFADC minutes, December 13, 1966, ISA/A/8161/4.

129. Tel Aviv (Chief of Staff's Office) to FM, November 20, 1966, ISA/FM/4030/5.

130. Yitzhak Rabin, remarks to commanders at the Military Institute for Education, December 18, 1966, in Rosenthal, *Yitzhak Rabin*, 426.

131. Haber, *Ha-Yom tifrots milhamah*, 106–107.

132. Tel Aviv (Chief of Staff's Office) to FM, November 20, 1966, ISA/FM/4030/5.

133. Amman to State, December 11, 1966, LBJL/NSF/Country Files/Jordan, box 146. The message itself is missing from Ya'akov Herzog's personal papers, though Hussein discussed it during their first meeting following the 1967 war. See Ya'akov Herzog, "Meeting with Charles on Sunday, July 2nd, from 8:10 P.M. to 9:45 P.M.," July 2, 1967, YHP.

134. Haber, *Ha-Yom tifrots milhamah*, 107.

135. Cabinet minutes, November 13, 1966, ISA.

136. Tel Aviv (Chief of Staff's office) to FM, November 20, 1966, ISA/FM/4030/5.

137. For accounts of the Samu' raid, see Tel Aviv (Chief of Staff's Office) to FM, November 20, 1966, ISA/FM/4030/5; as well as Rabin's and Eshkol's testimonies in cabinet minutes, November 13, 1966, ISA; KFADC minutes, November 22, 1966, ISA/A/8161/3; and Rabin's remarks at a meeting of the General Staff, November 14, 1966, in Rosenthal, *Yitzhak Rabin*, 419–421. For the number of Israeli troops and tanks, I have relied on the internal Israeli reports cited above. Estimates of Jordanian

casualty figures, as well as of the number of demolished buildings, vary. I have relied on the figures in internal Jordanian reports cited in Shemesh, "IDF Raid on Samu'," 151. These are nearly identical to the figures cited in Central Command monthly intelligence summary no. 11, IDFA/1338/79/40.

138. See especially Judge Nihad Jarallah's eyewitness account in Jerusalem to State, November 17, 1966, NA/RG59/DOSCF 1964–66/POL 32–1 ISR-JORDAN.

139. The most vivid account, based on Jordanian intelligence documents, is Shemesh, "IDF Raid on Samu'," 153–156. For the casualty figures, see Central Command monthly intelligence summary no. 11, IDFA/1338/79/40.

140. On these petitions, see Amman to State, November 25, 1966, NA/RG59/DOCSF 1964–66/POL 32–1 ISR-JORDAN.

FIVE

PARTITION'S UNDOING

The End of the Israeli-Jordanian Entente, 1967

DESPITE THE TURMOIL THAT FOLLOWED THE SAMUʿ RAID, King Hussein and Israel's leaders did not change their policies toward each other afterward. Hussein lost confidence in Israel and severed direct contact with Eshkol's government, but he still believed there was no point in confronting his Jewish neighbors. Even when the king began to make overtures to Egypt in April 1967, he did not intend to join an Arab war coalition. If anything, the king hoped to exploit Nasser's apparent caution to break up the Egyptian-Syrian alliance. As for the Israelis, they still thought it would be politically impossible to conquer and hold the West Bank. They continued to hope that Hussein would reign over both banks of the Jordan for as long as possible, allowing Israel to avoid war and cross the nuclear threshold.

The Arab-Israeli crisis and war of May–June 1967, however, exposed all of the inherent weaknesses in the Israeli-Jordanian entente. In the face of public war fever, Hussein could no longer keep his distance from the other Arab states. Once Jordan joined Nasser's coalition, the Israelis felt they had no choice but war. They could not depend on American promises nor resort to nuclear deterrence. In the short, decisive war that followed, the Israelis conquered the West Bank, and their long-dormant expansionist urges were reawakened.

AFTERSHOCKS: JORDAN

The Israeli attack on Samu' marked the beginning of what Hussein described as the "worst week of his life."[1] At the time of the attack, the king had been at Amman's airport to meet Pakistani president Muhammad Ayub Khan. After learning of the raid, he hurried to the scene of the fighting, then to the bedside of his wife, Princess Muna, who had suffered a miscarriage the previous day. That night's state dinner for Ayub Khan was an unexpectedly solemn occasion. "I received the impression," noted US ambassador Findley Burns the following day, "that yesterday's events have thrown very cold water on the option that Jordan could live in at least de facto peace with Israel. Peace is just not in the cards no matter what Jordan and even the Israeli government desire."[2]

Some historians, echoing Burns, have drawn a straight line from Samu' to Hussein's decision to align with Nasser in May 1967. The raid, Samir Mutawi argues, convinced Jordan's leaders that "the Israelis made no distinction between one Arab nation and the other" and that "they needed to cooperate with the other Arab nations and seek to join them in a system of regional defense."[3] And indeed, there is a great deal of evidence from the immediate aftermath of the raid that supports Mutawi's argument. Previously, Hussein proclaimed, he had focused on the threat of Arab radicalism, while assuming that "our western border with Israel had by joint unwritten acknowledgment been neutralized." This "illusion," the king declared, "has been permanently shattered as far as I am concerned. It is now quite clear to all of us that, in the last analysis, Israel holds the critical key to our existence and is our major enemy."[4] The Israelis, Hussein argued, hoped that border violence would provide them with an excuse to seize the West Bank.[5] They hoped that the great powers would offer Israel a security guarantee in order to get the IDF to withdraw. The Israelis, according to Hussein, also hoped that if they took over the West Bank, his regime would collapse. A pro-Soviet, Palestinian-dominated regime would take control, forcing the Americans to draw closer to Israel.[6] In many post-Samu' conversations, Hussein emphasized that he felt personally betrayed by the Israelis. In one extraordinary meeting with Burns and CIA station chief Jack O'Connell, the king revealed that he had been meeting and corresponding with the

Israelis in hopes of eventually making peace. "As far as I am concerned," he said bitterly, "this attack was a complete betrayal by them of everything I had tried to do for the past three years in the interests of peace, stability, and moderation at high personal risk."[7]

Yet Hussein's bitter remarks and dark predictions did not mean that he was ready to fundamentally change his policy toward Israel. Certainly, he no longer showed much warmth toward the Israelis, even in private. Though Eshkol tried to restore direct contact with the king, Hussein would not meet with Israeli officials again until after the 1967 war.[8] But Hussein had no illusions that the regional balance of power had changed. He knew that no Arab "system of regional defense" could offer Jordan adequate protection from Israel. "The Arab countries," he told the Soviet ambassador to Jordan, "are not yet ready for a serious conflict with Israel."[9] Hussein feared that by inviting other Arab armies into Jordan, he might provoke an Israeli attack and endanger his regime. Allowing other Arab armies to enter Jordan, he told former US ambassador William Macomber, was "incompatible with Jordan's own interests."[10] To pacify the JAA's angry and embarrassed officers, the king instead sent Chief of Staff 'Amir Khammash to Washington to ask for $200 million in additional military aid.[11]

Once again, US officials complained that Hussein's requests were, as Walt Rostow put it, "stupendous." Yet the Americans still felt compelled to do something for the king.[12] If King Hussein fell, warned the CIA, his successors would turn the West Bank into a staging area for other Arab armies and terrorist organizations, sparking an Israeli invasion and a "major international crisis."[13] Johnson's NSC staffers recommended that the administration "try rebuilding what we can of the old tacit arrangement with Jordan."[14] The Americans thus proposed a much smaller aid package; in return, they expected Hussein to continue to repress the Palestinian guerrillas and keep non-Jordanian troops out of the West Bank.[15] As the negotiations progressed, Hussein engaged in some hard bargaining, even threatening to withdraw the JAA from the West Bank and turn the area over to an all-Arab "military directorate."[16] But the king was clearly bluffing. On December 21, when the two sides reached an agreement on a military aid package, Hussein swore to "do all that he could" to keep other Arab troops out of Jordan and to "prevent terrorist infiltration into Israel." Though Hussein remained suspicious of Israel, he made it clear that he did not want to alter Jordan's regional role in any way.[17]

During the winter and spring of 1967, neither the king nor anyone in his inner circle contemplated the kind of far-reaching concessions to Nasser and the PLO that they would later make that May. Some influential Jordanians, including Khammash and former prime ministers Bahjat al-Talhuni, Saʿid al-Mufti, and Sulayman al-Nabulsi, thought that Hussein should accommodate Palestinian grievances and settle his differences with Egypt, but even they did not want to appease Nasser at any price. In any event, it was Wasfi al-Tal who set the tone of Jordan's foreign policy.[18] On November 21, as demonstrations raged throughout the West Bank, al-Tal convened a press conference and castigated Egypt and Syria for not defending Jordan against Israel.[19] Though Hussein thought al-Tal's performance was "unfortunate," he refused to take Khammash's advice and dismiss him. Not wanting to look weak, the king kept al-Tal as prime minister and adopted a similarly belligerent tone.[20] On December 2, Hussein delivered a furious radio address, attacking Arab regimes that were "failing in their promises and treating Jordan as if she were the real enemy." He blasted Nasser for leaving Jordan to face Israel alone, while thousands of Egyptian soldiers went to Yemen to "fight [their] Arab brethren."[21]

Until the spring of 1967, Hussein assumed that there were "no prospects of rapprochement" with Nasser.[22] In February of that year, hoping to strengthen Jordan's ties with other conservative Arab states, the king toured the Persian Gulf states, where he received pledges of between 7.75 and 8.25 million dinars in aid, mainly from Saudi Arabia.[23] The king and al-Tal maintained ties to fifteen different Syrian groups plotting to bring down the neo-Baʿth regime, and groomed Salim Hatum and his followers as "a potential reprisal instrument" against Syrian-sponsored terrorism.[24] In public, Hussein seized every opportunity to contrast Nasser's brutality in Yemen with his timidity toward Israel. In January, the Jordanian government produced two Egyptian air force defectors, Muhammad Abu al-Muʿati ʿAbduh and Saʿid Muhammad ʿAli al-Fadhil, who claimed that the bombs dropped on Yemen could have "destroyed Israel in its entirety."[25] When Nasser responded by dubbing Hussein the "whore of Jordan," Hussein recalled Jordan's ambassador from Cairo and attacked Egypt even more viciously.[26] In a speech that March, Hussein proclaimed that Arab armies should be deployed against Israel, "not in Yemen to slaughter our brothers in Arabism and religion." Nasser's decision to allow UNEF into the Sinai, he added, had been the "greatest victory for [Israel] and our greatest defeat since the *nakba*"—the 1948 war.[27] On April 7, when Israeli planes shot down six Syrian MiGs in a dogfight, the Hashemite Broadcasting Service gleefully jeered at Nasser's inability to come to Syria's aid.[28] If the Jordanians were obsessed with Israel and desperately needed Egyptian protection, they did a remarkably good job pretending otherwise.

Hussein confronted his Palestinian opponents at home with similar harshness. He shared al-Tal's opinion that the West Bankers were a "naïve and gullible" mob led astray by a "craven upper crust."[29] Prominent Palestinians who criticized him for not defending the West Bank, Hussein sneered, were "the very men who contributed so much to the loss of Palestine in the first place."[30] The Jordanian press extolled the virtues of "unity of rank," implying that dissent would not be tolerated, and the government did its best to squelch all opposition.[31] In December, Hussein instituted mandatory conscription, which was essentially a way to keep young Palestinian men off the streets. Young West Bankers who refused to report for training were rounded up and trucked off to induction centers, which some Palestinians began calling "King Hussein's concentration camps."[32] In January, the Jordanian government closed the PLO's offices in Jerusalem.[33] The following month, the government passed harsh new press laws that shut down all existing newspapers and periodicals. Only publishers who parroted the official propaganda line were eventually allowed to return to work.[34]

Hussein did not want to act so aggressively forever. He certainly believed that he needed to show his Arab enemies and domestic opponents that he was firmly in control. But the king was more sensitive to public opinion than al-Tal. He hoped to eventually return to the path he had followed from 1964 to 1966: pursuing rapprochement with Egypt and his Palestinian subjects from a position of strength. Once the situation in Jordan calmed down, he told US officials, he planned to "promulgate a new constitution which would take into consideration some of the grievances of the West Bank."[35] By April 1967, Hussein started to cautiously rebuild some of the bridges that he and al-Tal had burned after Samuʻ. He formed a new government in which the former journalist and diplomat Saʻd Jumʻa replaced al-Tal as prime minister. Jumʻa was not as provocative or belligerent as al-Tal, but he was also not ardently pro-Egyptian like Bahjat al-Talhuni. He took office with a mandate to pursue rapprochement with Egypt and Syria "without sacrificing any of [Jordan's] interests."[36] Jumʻa called for returning to Arab summitry, but also for strengthening the Islamic Pact that Nasser so thoroughly despised. The Jordanian government briefly experimented with toning down its anti-Egyptian and anti-Syrian propaganda, but Radio Amman restarted its attacks as soon as Nasser attacked Hussein in a speech on May 2.[37]

Thus, at the beginning of May 1967, Hussein's national security policy remained unchanged despite Samuʻ. By appointing the Jumʻa government, the king had signaled that he was willing to pursue inter-Arab détente again, but not at great cost. Nor did the king's tentative overtures to Nasser reflect a desire for Egyptian protection from Israel. If anything, Hussein likely hoped that Nasser, for fear of being dragged into war by Syria, would have to court Jordan as a counterweight—just as the Egyptian president had done in late 1963. At the end of April, Hussein secretly invited UAC commander ʻAbd al-Munʻim Riyadh to Amman. The Syrian leadership, the king told the Egyptian general, had been penetrated by sinister forces, who were trying to draw Egypt into war.[38] Nasser's confidante Muhammad Hasanayn Haykal would later portray the Hussein-Riyadh meeting as evidence that the king was aware of a grand imperialist plot against Egypt. But there is a less conspiratorial explanation: Hussein still thought Nasser wanted to avoid war, and hoped to exploit his caution in order to drive a wedge between Egypt and Syria. In mid-May 1967, however, Hussein's cautious optimism about Nasser would be severely tested.

AFTERSHOCKS: ISRAEL

Contrary to what Hussein thought, Israel's leaders had not hoped to topple him, and they emerged from the Samuʻ affair a confused and regretful bunch. Both Eshkol and Rabin bemoaned the fact that the operation had escalated into a pitched battle with the Jordanian army.[39] The plan, Eshkol admitted, had been "not to hurt the prestige of the regime or the king."[40] Others were more critical of what had happened. The political opposition, led by Ben-Gurion's Rafi party, lambasted Eshkol for striking Syria rather than Jordan, and initially favorable press coverage soured once the raid's results became clearer.[41] Even within the cabinet, several ministers expressed anger over how the raid had been executed; the operation, snapped Minister of Health Yehuda Barzilai, had been "totally out of proportion."[42] The harshest response, however, came from abroad, particularly from Washington. President Johnson and his advisors were furious, and on November 25 they joined the rest of the Security Council in condemning Israel's raid. The attack on Samu', Robert Komer told Ambassador Harman, "put in jeopardy our whole policy of promoting Arab-Israel stability by subsidizing an independent Jordan."[43]

Eshkol responded to his critics by reminding them that there had been no clear evidence linking Syria to the mining that had preceded Samu', and that not reacting was not an option. "What is a deterrent?" he shouted at his fellow cabinet members. "What are we spending 1.5 billion lirot per year on. . . . Is it just so we can have a mezuzah? We tell the whole world that we have a deterrent, and then when our blood is spilled, we say *shema yisrael*—once, twice, three times—and don't react?!"[44] "Should we let ourselves be killed drop by drop, if we are not destroyed in the total war that Nasser promises further down the line?" he wrote to Hebrew University historian Yitzhak Baer. "Should we wait for articles by Ms. [Hannah] Arendt about our passivity?"[45] But while the prime minister felt obligated to justify what the IDF had done, there is no evidence that he or anyone else in the Israeli leadership were pleased to have undermined King Hussein. In high-level meetings, Eshkol, Rabin, and Yariv sought to justify the Samu' raid by arguing that the danger to the Hashemite regime was exaggerated and that the king would emerge from the episode stronger than before. The Jordanian army, Eshkol told the cabinet, had remained loyal throughout the crisis, and Hussein had demonstrated that he could crack down on the PLO and take a hard line against Nasser in the face of domestic upheaval. With time and effort, Israel could repair its relationship with Jordan.[46]

Though Hussein's weakness and unpopularity had been baldly exposed, the Israelis did not think the time had come to write him off. That winter, Abba Eban assembled a group of high-ranking Mossad, AMAN, and Foreign Ministry officials and asked them to answer two questions. First, was Israeli-Egyptian rapprochement possible? Second, was it in Israel's interest for King Hussein's regime to survive? Eban's working group discussed Jordan three times and gave the foreign minister their recommendations on January 13, 1967.[47] They argued resoundingly that the Israeli government should seek to keep Hussein in power for as long as possible.

Why did Israel's most experienced Arabists want to keep supporting Hussein? First, despite the most recent round of prophecies about Hussein's impending demise, the Israelis believed that the king's prospects were not so bad. Hussein, the working group noted, still had a loyal army and security services at his disposal. Jordan's impressive economic growth had given a larger number of his subjects a stake in his survival. The downward slide of Nasser's Egypt and staunch support from the United States also worked in the king's favor. Israel had to assume that Hussein might be assassinated, but he could just as easily survive for many more years.[48]

The working group agreed that any successor to Hussein would be far worse for Israel. Whatever Hussein's faults, the king did not want war. He would keep other Arab troops out of Jordan and make do with limited quantities of arms provided by the United States and its allies.[49] Moreover, as Mordechai Gazit, deputy director-general of the Foreign Ministry, pointed out, the longer Hussein stayed in power, the less likely Jordan was to break up or merge with another Arab state. Since "Arab nationalism" was "in the process of decline" and Nasser's regime was weakening, it was far better "that a clash between Israel and the Palestinians should occur in 1975 than in 1966." The working group assumed that even if Jordan remained independent after Hussein fell, it would likely become a "second Syria," politically unstable and a hotbed of guerrilla activity. The Israeli officials believed that no Palestinian figure, including al-Shuqayri, could establish a stable successor regime. Drawing an analogy to Vietnam, Gazit likened Hussein and his regime to "Marshal Ki and Saigon fighting the Viet Cong," and argued that Israel should not allow a Hashemite "Saigon" to be replaced by a Palestinian-controlled "Hanoi."

The working group also believed that Hussein's economic policies served Israel's interests. As late as 1961, Gazit recalled, Jordan had been widely regarded as economically unviable. Now, if economic development continued at its present pace and foreign aid was not cut off, the kingdom would achieve "self-sustenance" by the 1970s. Israel would no longer have to fear that the Jordan state would disintegrate if the monarchy were overthrown. Just as important, Gazit pointed out, the West Bank had become economically dependent on the East Bank. Most emigrants from Jordan were West Bankers, while approximately two hundred thousand West Bankers had migrated to the East Bank since King Abdullah annexed it. The Arab world's largest concentration of Palestinian refugees was being absorbed into their host society. Israel, the working group agreed, should try to ensure that these social and economic trends continued.[50]

The group did recognize that Jordanian control of the West Bank still posed major military problems for Israel. This point was argued most strongly by Shlomo Gazit, the head of AMAN's Research Division and a longtime confidante of Moshe Dayan. Whatever the king's merits, Gazit noted, the West Bank was a strategic "catastrophe" for Israel. The IDF leadership, he said, was "reconciled to the present situation, but would be happy for the opportunity to create a new and more comfortable status quo."[51] Gazit distributed an IDF paper to other members of the group that argued that "the continuity of the regime under any circumstances should not be seen as sacrosanct." If a "potentially intolerable danger for Israel" arose, there was "no doubt" that Israel would have to "intervene militarily to secure its interests in the West Bank."[52]

Nevertheless, Gazit made it clear that Israel's army chiefs still assumed that the superpowers would not allow Israel to hold conquered Arab territory. If the IDF preemptively seized the West Bank, its goal would be to "neutralize" the area, not to annex it to Israel. From Israel's standpoint, the best way to neutralize the West Bank would be to make it "an independent Palestinian state, connected to Israel with regard to foreign policy and decisively dependent on the IDF for defense and the preservation of order." The chances that Israel could create such a Palestinian dependency, however, "were not very high," because the great powers would not let Israel occupy the West Bank for long. Realistically, the best Israel could hope for was that a UN peacekeeping force might serve "as a barrier between Israel and a Jordanian state of one kind or another."[53] In the long run, Gazit added, the IDF leadership believed that the West Bank problem only mattered "so long as the region has not entered the nuclear era." He emphasized that "there are those who think that the moment that we enter the nuclear era, the thought of destroying Israel will no longer arise."[54]

And so, the working group concluded that Israel should continue to prop up King Hussein's regime. In their final report, they recommended that Israel deter Jordan's Arab enemies, encourage the Western powers to give Jordan economic aid, secretly cooperate with Jordan on economic initiatives, and maintain quiet contacts with Hussein to avoid unnecessary conflict. With Samu' in mind, the working group also advised Eshkol's cabinet to refrain from further reprisal raids against Jordan, while advocating "steps" against Hussein's enemies "that could have a positive effect on Jordan," including military action and "psychological warfare."[55]

On January 15, Eban informed the cabinet that the working group had completed their task, and suggested that the government discuss their conclusions.[56] A month later, the Israeli foreign minister told British foreign secretary George Brown that

> the Israeli government had exhaustively analyzed all the possible alterations in the status of the West Bank. Their conclusion was that every possible change would be harmful from Israel's point of view. The Israeli government certainly did not want to take over the West Bank. Even if they did so, they could not digest it; and in any case there were forces in the world that would not allow it. Israel therefore considered that the stabilization of the Hashemite regime was very much in their interests because by this means the *status quo* of the West Bank could be maintained while the centre of gravity of the state would remain the East.[57]

In short, Israel's Jordan policy had not changed. Its leaders still assumed that they could not enlarge their territory or carve a Palestinian puppet state out of the West Bank. For the time being, it was better for Hussein to remain in power. Whether or not the king ultimately survived, the dangers that could arise from his fall would only decrease with time. Jordan would become more economically viable. Egypt's power would continue to decline, and the dream of Arab unity would fade. And

Israel would acquire a nuclear capability, transforming the regional balance of power and making Arab-Israeli détente possible. The West Bank issue might no longer matter as much.

Yet Israeli policymakers already seem to have sensed that it would take considerable time and effort to translate their nuclear achievements into tangible strategic gains. By November 1966, the CIA estimated that Israel could assemble a nuclear weapon "in 6–8 weeks" if it wished. Israel was also projected to obtain ballistic missiles by late 1967 or early 1968.[58] And some members of the Israeli establishment still argued in favor of overt nuclear deterrence. After Samu', for example, Shimon Peres told Eshkol and Rabin that Israel did not need to strike Jordan or Syria to deter Arab provocations. Peres claimed that he did not advocate "war, or the conquest of the [Golan] Heights, or [the use of] planes." Rather, he was "convinced that we need to hit the Syrian officer corps with the things that they aspire toward. ... I am sure that the prime minister and the chief of staff know what I'm talking about."[59] Given Peres's close association with the nuclear project and the timing of his comments, it is almost certain that he was suggesting that Israel conduct an open nuclear test and frighten the Syrians into silence. Since no such test was conducted, however, it appears that Peres's views were marginal. Eshkol kept his promise not to "introduce" nuclear weapons into the Middle East.

But if Israel could not flaunt its nuclear achievements openly, could they still be used as a bargaining chip to end the regional arms race? Despite Eshkol's early hopes, the Middle East had not become the subject of serious US-Soviet dialogue. The Soviets did not want to push their Arab clients too far, particularly in light of growing Soviet-Chinese competition for Third World loyalties.[60] Neither Eshkol's overtures to the Soviets or comparable US efforts had any demonstrable effect on Soviet policy.[61] The Israeli intelligence community knew that the USSR had refused to help Egypt develop nuclear weapons and regarded the Soviets as essentially cautious, despite their support for Syria.[62] But no Israel officials believed that a breakthrough with the USSR would come anytime soon.

Nor had Israeli efforts to use Dimona as a bargaining chip with Nasser yielded serious results. "The issue that worries Egypt the most," concluded the Mossad, "is Israel's nuclear development." An end to the regional arms race might be the one "serious shared interest of the two sides."⁶³ Yet thus far, Meir Amit complained in November 1966, Israel's efforts to start a strategic dialogue with Egypt had not gone well. The basic contradictions between Nasser's hegemonic aims and Israel's fears of a unified Arab world were too strong.⁶⁴ Neither the Mossad nor AMAN thought that prospects for dialogue with Egypt were good. AMAN's Egypt analysts went so far as to argue that "as long as the current regime exists, basic hostility will persist." The real question was whether Arab-Israeli détente would be possible "after Nasser."⁶⁵ Yariv was not quite as pessimistic as his subordinates, but he also believed that serious Israeli-Egyptian dialogue was impossible in the short term. At best, he thought, Israel and Egypt could lay the groundwork for a future settlement by secretly acknowledging their shared interest in avoiding war.⁶⁶

An Arab-Israeli settlement was still just out of reach. Meanwhile, it was not totally clear what purpose Israel's nuclear capability would serve. Could nuclear weapons be used the way Peres suggested, as blunt instruments? Could Israel respond to, say, the entry of Iraqi troops into the West Bank by making nuclear threats? How severe a danger would Israel have to face before it could threaten to use, let alone actually use, a nuclear weapon?

Yet Israel's political and military leaders thought it unlikely that they would have to resolve their basic security dilemmas in the near future. The Arab world seemed completely unready to fight. "Aside from Syria," Eshkol told the Knesset Foreign Affairs and Defense Committee in late November 1966, "the Arab states do not currently seem interested in war with Israel. This is because of the balance of forces, the inter-Arab divide, and internal problems—Egypt in Yemen, the Iraqi army with the Kurds, and so on."⁶⁷ The IDF leadership was even quicker to dismiss the possibility of conflict. MACCABBI, the IDF's multiyear force structure and procurement plan, which was drawn up in the winter of 1967, assumed that the Arab states would not be ready to fight Israel until 1970.⁶⁸ As late as April 24, AMAN believed that "the Egyptians' basic point of departure is 'don't get entangled in a war with Israel.'"⁶⁹ "The problem," Rabin told Eshkol and the General Staff, "is not what the Arabs are capable of doing to us," but how Israel could strengthen itself "in the face of fragmentation in the Arab world."⁷⁰

Nevertheless, the General Staff did acknowledge that deteriorating inter-Arab relations might lead to "unexpected situations" that could lead to war. These unexpected situations might include a sharp spike in cross-border terrorism, increased fighting on the Israeli-Syrian border, Arab attacks on "objects vital to the development of Israeli research and strength" (e.g., the Dimona reactor), and the fall of the Jordanian monarchy.[71] If Israel wanted to avoid war and consolidate its power, it was essential to prevent small Arab provocations from growing into genuine threats. The main problem that Israel's leaders faced was how to respond to border violence in a way that served their larger goal of preserving the status quo. Should Israel rely on static defense to avoid unnecessary escalation? Or should it use its superior military strength to deter further provocations?

As before, Israel's political leadership leaned toward a more defensive approach. The Knesset voted to cancel a plan to shorten the length of military service, allowing the IDF to deploy more men on the border. The cabinet allocated more funding for the lighting and fencing of border settlements, and new fences went up in Jerusalem and Tiberias, and along the Tel-Aviv–Jerusalem railway.[72] But strengthening border defenses was expensive (a kilometer of fencing cost 750,000 lirot), and, more importantly, uncomfortable for the IDF. Rabin agreed that Israel needed to be better at guarding the Jordanian border, but cautioned Eshkol that it was impossible to hermetically seal it.[73] For the IDF chief of staff, the arguments against a purely static approach to border defense went beyond cost and logistics. Like the rest of the IDF leadership, Rabin thought that overreliance on static defense would weaken Israel's military credibility. He did not want Arab leaders to think that political considerations had made Israel less willing to fight. The General Staff thus lobbied against relying too heavily on static defense, and refused to accept US offers of anti-infiltration technology.[74] Through the spring of 1967, the IDF called for ever-tougher responses to Syrian-sponsored guerrilla operations and attacks on Israeli targets in the demilitarized zones along the Israeli-Syrian border.

In this final prewar round of border warfare, however, the Israeli leadership showed much greater respect for the fragility of Hussein's regime. As cross-border attacks escalated again, the IDF pressed for a "frontal clash" with Syria, but no longer insisted on holding each Arab state responsible for attacks launched from its soil. Between November 1966 and the end of March 1967, Palestinian operatives attempted roughly the same number of attacks from Jordan as they did from Syria.[75] Yet by February 1967, Israel adopted a policy of not blaming Jordan for incidents along its border in order to give Hussein time to recover from Samuʻ.[76] By March, the Israeli intelligence community thought the king was back on his feet. "We see that Hussein, who had everyone praying that he would not fall two months ago, has not only not fallen, but is attacking from all directions," Yariv told the General Staff. "The fact is that Hussein's position in the Arab world is stronger than it was before the Samuʻ affair."[77] Indeed, Israel's leaders believed that by confronting Syria aggressively, they could bolster Hussein's position in the Arab arena. After the Israeli air force shot down six Syrian planes in a dogfight in April, Yariv referred to the MiGs that fell in Jordanian territory as a "gift from God" for Hussein, ripe for "maximum propaganda exploitation."[78] Abba Eban also thought that the April 7 incident would benefit Hussein.[79] Neither seemed worried that Israel's clashes with Syria might eventually embroil Jordan as well.

THE CRISIS BEGINS

May 13, 1967, marked the beginning of what Michael Hadow, Britain's ambassador to Israel, described as the period of "overtaken intelligence appreciations" in the Middle East.[80] For reasons that remain hotly debated, Soviet officials informed the Syrian and Egyptian governments that Israel had massed large numbers of troops on the Syrian border. The warning was false, as Egyptian chief of staff Mahmud Fawzi learned when he visited Damascus a few days later. Yet by this point, Nasser had committed himself to an exercise in brinksmanship from which he could not (or did not want to) retreat without losing face. Large numbers of Egyptian troops had already begun to deploy in the Sinai. On May 16, the Egyptian government requested that UNEF withdraw from its bases. Three days later, UN secretary-general U Thant agreed to pull the peacekeepers out, setting the stage for Nasser's announcement on May 23 that he would close the Straits of Tiran to Israeli shipping.[81]

Initially, the Israeli leadership viewed Nasser's moves as no more than a bluff, designed to show that Egypt would not sit idly by while the IDF pounded its Syrian ally. Egypt, Eshkol told the cabinet on May 16, would attack Israel only "in the event of a wide-scale attack [on Syria], including the conquest and seizure of territory."[82] But by May 19, the Israelis changed their minds. AMAN estimates indicated that Egypt now had enough troops in the Sinai to launch an attack, and more soldiers were arriving from Yemen. Egyptian MiG-21s had swooped into the Negev and photographed the Dimona reactor in broad daylight. With UNEF about to withdraw, Nasser seemed certain to take even greater risks.[83] The Egyptian president, Rabin warned the cabinet on May 21, "had not yet embarked on any adventure with a clear head. He got entangled in Syria and also in Yemen."[84] It seemed that Nasser was about to get entangled with Israel as well.

When Nasser announced that he would close the Straits of Tiran, the Israelis faced an agonizing choice. By remilitarizing the Sinai and closing the Gulf of Aqaba, the Egyptian president had crossed two of Israel's strategic "red lines." If Israel did not respond, it would signal that it could live with what its leaders had previously deemed an act of war. And if war was inevitable, it was better for Israel to act as soon as possible. An Egyptian first strike might destroy Eilat, Dimona, or Israel's handful of airfields. Even if Nasser did not land the first blow, each passing day sapped any element of surprise that Israel might enjoy, diminishing its chances of victory and raising the number of casualties it would suffer. These arguments were made most forcefully by the General Staff, who urged Eshkol to act.[85] The prime minister and a majority of his cabinet, however, wanted to delay a decision for war. First and foremost, Israel's ministers were preoccupied with how the United States would react to an Israeli first strike. No matter how grave the threat of war, Israel could not afford to alienate its most powerful patron. When Egypt closed the straits, Johnson declared that he regarded Nasser's act as "illegal and potentially disastrous to the cause of peace," but no one knew whether the president would tolerate an Israeli strike against Egypt or whether he would come to Israel's aid if Nasser attacked.[86]

Over the grumblings of the IDF leadership, Eshkol dispatched Eban for talks in Paris, London, and, most importantly, Washington.[87] Israel, Eban told Johnson on May 26, "is confronted with two alternatives:

to surrender or to stand, and we are confident that if we stand we will win." But Israel still wanted to explore a possible "international solution." What would the United States do, he asked, "to carry out its commitments to keep the Straits and the Gulf open?" Johnson urged Eban to wait while the United States organized a coalition of maritime states that would send a naval force into the Straits of Tiran to challenge Egypt's blockade. The president admitted that he could not guarantee international support for this plan, or that Congress would allow the US Navy to take part in it. But Israel, he said, "must not make itself responsible for initiating hostilities." Israel, Johnson emphasized, "will not be alone unless it decides to go it alone."[88] Shortly after he met with Eban, Johnson wrote to Eshkol to inform him that the Soviets had threatened to "give aid" to the Arab states if Israel struck first. "As your friend," Johnson added, "I repeat even more strongly what I said yesterday to Mr. Eban. Israel just must not take any preemptive military action and thereby make itself responsible for the initiation of hostilities."[89]

When Eshkol convened his cabinet on May 28, the Soviets' threats and Johnson's warnings tipped the balance in favor of Israel's doves. Israel, remarked Minister of Justice Zerah Warhaftig, might be a "nation that dwells alone," but it could not afford to be a "nation that fights alone." When Rabin warned the cabinet that further delay would make it harder for the IDF to win, he met fierce opposition, particularly from Eban. Johnson, Eban said, had wagered American prestige on his ability to open the straits, and would have to make good on his promise. The foreign minister recognized that Israel would take a risk by waiting, but he argued that a preemptive attack could be more dangerous. If America's assurances turned out to be "a bluff or an illusion," he added, "then we can sober up." The cabinet decided to wait two to three weeks for the United States to try and break the blockade, while keeping the IDF's reserves mobilized and on high alert.[90] According to Avner Cohen, the leading historian of Israel's nuclear program, Armaments Development Authority employees hastily assembled two primitive atomic explosive devices that same day. Faced with the threat of a devastating surprise attack, Israel had finally crossed the nuclear threshold.[91]

During these tense two weeks, the Jordanian front occupied a low place on Israel's list of strategic worries. Preoccupied with the Egyptian troops pouring into Sinai, the Israelis did not spend much time worrying about the West Bank, where there was no comparable military buildup. It seemed "that war would pass over Central Command," recalled Col. Yisrael Lior, Eshkol's military aide.[92] Yet as Israel's government postponed an attack, the General Staff grew increasingly worried that Jordan would join the Arab coalition. In the eyes of Israel's generals, Nasser had undermined not only Israel's credibility, but also the internal stability of Egypt's Arab rivals. Rabin believed that Hussein would weaken as the crisis dragged on.[93] "If our situation gets worse," Operations Branch chief Ezer Weizman warned on May 25, "the Jordanians will act. Jerusalem, in particular, will be endangered."[94] "The Jordanians have said they won't 'play,' but this can't be taken for granted. They need to be watched," argued Yariv on May 27.[95]

The cabinet's May 28 decision to wait made the General Staff even more anxious that Hussein would join the Arab war effort. When Eshkol met with the IDF's commanders that night, Yariv warned that a feeling that "soon Palestine shall be returned" was sweeping through Jordan's refugee camps. The JAA, he thought, might disobey orders and spontaneously attack Israel.[96] By May 29, Yariv, like many of his IDF compatriots, was despondent. As long as Israel waited, he declared, "national chauvinism will ignite the Arab countries, and Hussein's regime will be especially endangered." Jordan was "more likely to act militarily against Israel than before."[97] Even if the Jordanians did not attack, it would be far more difficult for Israel to strike Egypt if Hussein joined the Arab coalition. If Hussein mobilized all his forces, Weizman warned, the resulting threat from the West Bank might make a preemptive strike against Egypt impossible.[98] Had the IDF's commanders known how prescient their fears were, they might have been even more worried.

"JORDAN WILL STAND STILL"

Like Israel's leaders, Hussein and his inner circle initially viewed Nasser's moves as little more than posturing. By May 17, the Jordanian government had put the JAA on alert, and issued a statement that an attack on any Arab state was an attack on them all.[99] Such rhetoric, Hussein privately acknowledged, "was designed for internal consumption," to demonstrate that the Jordanian government was not "asleep at the switch."[100] Jordan, Jum'a told Burns on May 21, "desperately wanted to stay out of any possible Arab-Israeli conflict."[101] Hussein nevertheless realized that he could benefit if Israel moved rapidly against Egypt or Syria. From the king's standpoint, the best possible end to the crisis was either a swift Israeli attack or a swift Egyptian retreat from the brink. During the first week of the crisis, Hussein tried unsuccessfully to encourage both.

Hussein first attempted to encourage an Israeli attack. Israel, he told Ambassador Burns on May 18, would probably attack Syria. If Egypt did not react, he said, "Jordan will stand still." If Nasser moved, Jordan would have to take "sufficient action to keep from being a conspicuous scapegoat," but "this would not entail a direct armed clash with Israel so long as an Israeli attack on Syria were of limited duration." Hussein nevertheless worried that Israel might attack Jordan if another terrorist attack occurred. What would the United States do to assure Jordan's security? he asked. Essentially, the king was offering the Americans a deal. If the United States promised to keep Israel out of the West Bank, he would not act if Israel attacked Egypt and Syria. But Burns made no promises. The United States, he said, would uphold the territorial integrity of Middle Eastern states. However, since there was no evidence that Israel wanted to invade Jordan, the United States could not justifiably issue the kind of warning Hussein had in mind.[102]

Having failed to get the Americans to unleash Israel, Hussein tried to convince Nasser to avoid war. On May 19, the king sent 'Amir Khammash to Cairo to meet 'Ali 'Ali 'Amir and 'Abd al-Mun'im Riyadh, the UAC's top two commanders. The Jordanian chief of staff had been ordered to confront the Egyptians and convince them to back down. Khammash asked the Egyptians to convene an emergency meeting of the UAC. To see whether the Egyptians seriously wanted war, he also told 'Amir and Riyadh that Jordan would accept troops from Saudi Arabia and Iraq, something Israel had always regarded as a casus belli.[103] Yet while the Egyptians spurned Khammash's offer of help, they showed no sign of backing away from confrontation with Israel during the days that followed. Nasser's behavior, Hussein remarked, "mystified" him and his advisors. He worried that the USSR was playing a "major backstage role in a game of brinksmanship."[104] Then came the closure of the Straits of Tiran.

For Hussein, Nasser's decision to close the straits was "incomprehensible and extremely dangerous."[105] The king and his advisors now believed that the Egyptians had no fear of an Israeli attack, and might even be ready to attack Israel themselves.[106] Yet Nasser still showed no interest in rapprochement with Hussein, or even in bringing Jordan into his coalition. Perhaps the Egyptian leader wanted to keep Jordan isolated in the hope of bringing down the monarchy. Yet there was still a way for Hussein to avoid defeat. If Israel attacked quickly enough, Hussein might survive the crisis unscathed. Political tensions in Jordan would not yet have reached a boiling point, and Hussein could still credibly protest that Nasser had spurned his help.

So Hussein tried one last time to persuade the Americans to allow Israel to attack. On May 26, he sent President Johnson a message. The United States, Hussein stated, was "risking [the] hostility of the entire Arab world" by supporting Israel's navigational rights in the Straits of Tiran. If Johnson tried to solve Israel's problems, Nasser could force his Arab rivals to punish the United States, through measures ranging "from oil nationalization to severance of diplomatic relations." Nasser, he warned, did not want to fight Israel, but to wage a "political war" against the United States and its Arab allies, with Soviet encouragement. What Johnson should do, Hussein said, was to act neutral and allow the crisis to remain a "purely UAR-Israeli confrontation." If the United Nations failed to solve the problem, then Israel could send a ship through the straits. "Nasser could then meet this challenge by forcibly stopping them," Hussein predicted. "Regardless of the outcome, [the United States] would be in the position of peacemaker, not that of partisan."[107]

When Walt Rostow forwarded Hussein's message to Johnson, he added a brief note of his own. "Our Arab friends," he wrote, "really find it difficult to remember what President Eisenhower had to do to get the Israeli troops out of Sinai."[108] Johnson's national security advisor had clearly not grasped what Hussein meant. The king obviously did not care what happened in Sinai so long as the IDF stayed away from the West Bank. Hussein was suggesting that the United States allow Israel to go it alone. The IDF could humiliate Nasser on the battlefield, and conservative Arab regimes would not be forced to break their ties to the United

States. The superpowers could then intervene and impose a settlement on the parties. But over the next two days, neither the Americans nor the Israelis did what Hussein wanted. Johnson played for time, and the Israelis grudgingly followed his lead. In Jordan, popular enthusiasm for war grew. "The Jordanians," observed Foreign Minister Ahmad Tuqan on May 27, "are a volatile people, and the emotionalism of the man in the street is on the upswing."[109] Equally important were the grumblings of the JAA, whose officers warned Hussein that if war came, "lack of coordination with other fronts would seriously penalize Jordan, affect its performance and multiply its losses in manpower and territory."[110]

Hussein's overture to Nasser at the end of May 1967 was the product of his weaknesses: military weakness in the face of Israel and political weakness in the face of domestic discontent and war fever. The latter was made worse by Israel's apparent weakness, which bolstered Nasser's prestige and made war attractive to ordinary Jordanians. But in the end, it was the Jordanian elite's changed reading of Nasser's intentions that drove the king to join the Arab coalition. By May 30, Hussein concluded that he could take Nasser's side at a tolerable cost, and that doing so could actually reduce Jordan's losses in the event of war.

HUSSEIN'S FATEFUL GAMBLE

Hussein's trip to Cairo on May 30 should not be seen as a last-minute grasp for Egyptian protection. In fact, he could now safely conclude that Israel would attack Egypt, not Jordan, first, regardless of Israel's purported designs on the West Bank. JAA intelligence indicated that the IDF was rapidly building up its forces in the Eilat area, and was preparing for a major amphibious operation to break Egypt's blockade. In contrast, Israeli activity on the Jordanian front seemed entirely defensive.[111] Hussein, in other words, could assume that Jordan could take Egypt's side without great military risk. Egypt seemed likely to absorb the brunt of the IDF's assault. By the time Israel could move against Jordan, the superpowers might have already intervened to stop the fighting.

Rather, the king's visit was motivated primarily by political considerations, namely, the hope that Nasser would allow Jordan to join his coalition without demanding an intolerable price in return. In a speech on May 26, Nasser had claimed that he wanted to cooperate with every Arab state bordering Israel, but there were "obstacles" to doing so, specifically, "Wasfi al-Tal, the spy of the Americans and the British."[112] Prominent Jordanian opponents of al-Tal, including 'Abd al-Mun'im al-Rifa'i, Hazim Nusayba, and Ahmad Tuqan, thought that Nasser was signaling his willingness to reconcile with Hussein if al-Tal were sidelined.[113] Al-Tal begged Hussein not to align with Nasser and risk losing the West Bank. According to one Jordanian source, al-Tal even asked Hussein to appoint him prime minister until the crisis ended. If war came and Jordan was maligned for staying out, he said, the king could blame him.[114] But Hussein, who had sided with al-Tal over his rivals up to this point, finally changed his mind. On the night of May 28, the king approached Egypt's ambassador in Amman to request a meeting with Nasser.[115]

Nasser agreed, but insisted that Hussein's visit remain a secret until they reached an agreement. By complying with this request, Hussein closed himself off to voices of caution. The king warned only a few of his closest advisors of his impending trip, and no one alerted US or Saudi officials in Jordan.[116] When the king's plane touched down in Cairo on May 30, he discovered that he had been tricked. The Egyptians greeted him with "full publicity." Long before Hussein's meeting with Nasser ended, the Egyptian government had already sent out press releases and scheduled a televised signing ceremony for an Egyptian-Jordanian agreement.[117] Essentially, Nasser had the power to make Hussein agree to whatever he wanted. "Since your visit is a secret, what would happen if we arrested you?" he jokingly asked the king.[118]

But Hussein was too valuable a prize to jail, and there was business to be done. The Egyptians were deeply suspicious of Hussein's motives. "I've felt that you believe that I will enter the battle with the Jews and the Jews will hit us," Nasser remarked. The IDF, 'Abd al-Hakim 'Amir added, was deployed to hit Egypt and Syria. The Israelis were not massing on the Jordanian border. So what had really made Hussein change his mind and come to Egypt? Hussein dodged the Egyptians' accusations, insisting that he wanted to serve the Arab cause. He blamed Ahmad al-Shuqayri for poisoning his relationship with Egypt. After a while, Nasser relented and invited the PLO chairman to come and reconcile with Hussein so that they could get on with the task of negotiating a military alliance.[119]

Yet the agreement that Hussein finally signed was more a surrender

King Hussein and Gamal Abdul Nasser signing their mutual defense pact, May 30, 1967. AP Photo/Stf/Calvert.

than a pact. The king agreed to allow Iraqi troops to deploy in Jordan, and offered 'Abd al-Mun'im Riyadh command of the JAA.[120] Not satisfied with taking military control of the Jordanian front, Nasser forced the king to make major political concessions as well. The king agreed to exile Salim Hatum and his fellows from Jordan, signifying that his proxy war against Syria was over.[121] When al-Shuqayri arrived at the meeting, Nasser told him that he would accompany Hussein back to Amman. Perhaps wanting to balance these demands with a gift (or a poisoned chalice), Nasser also offered Hussein control of the Gaza Strip.[122]

For Nasser, his meeting with Hussein marked the high point of his prewar maneuvering. He and Field Marshal 'Amir had previously considered a preemptive strike against Israel—Operation FAJIR—but canceled their plans just before H-hour on May 27, fearing that the United States might intervene on Israel's side.[123] To gain time, Nasser had told Soviet officials that he would consider a Soviet plan to invite Eshkol to Moscow and negotiate an end to the crisis.[124] Following his meeting with

Hussein, however, Nasser refused to accept the Soviet initiative. He had previously hoped that a visit by Eshkol to Moscow would postpone an Israeli attack, he said. But now, he was not so worried. Two hundred Iraqi tanks and an infantry division were headed for Jordan. Egypt, Nasser said, "practically occupied" the Hashemite kingdom.[125] The Egyptian-Jordanian defense pact had clearly bolstered Nasser's confidence that Egypt could absorb an Israeli first strike and go on to win.[126]

Yet the king and his compatriots still believed they could eventually wriggle out of Nasser's clutches. They had coped with Nasser's waves of popularity before and apparently thought they could do so again. Even as popular enthusiasm for war soared, the Jordanian leadership quietly began to prepare for the day after the crisis ended. The king was aware that "the post pact celebrations in Jordan were pro-Nasir, not pro-Husayn," and was determined to correct the impression "that Jordan's basic policies had altered."[127] On June 2, Hussein gave a speech warning his subjects against "individualistic action."[128] Privately, he and his advisors told US officials that they still distrusted Nasser and that al-Shuqayri would not be permitted to raise money or bring PLA troops into Jordan.[129] Hussein also claimed he had "agreed to put Jordanian forces under Egyptian control in the event of hostilities so that, in the event of a military reverse, Nasser and not he would take the blame."[130]

Indeed, the Jordanian elite seems to have believed that it might still be possible for Jordan to avoid war altogether. The Jordanian government, Khammash told US officials, still hoped to avoid war, and was "counting on the sense of let-down in the Arab man in the street to turn to dissatisfaction with Nasser, who was responsible for whipping up the war fever in the first place." The prospect of an Israeli attack did not seem to bother the Jordanian chief of staff; no "alarming Israeli troop dispositions" had yet been spotted along the armistice line.[131] The Jordanian leadership remained preoccupied with the image, not the substance, of hostility toward Israel. Hussein and his inner circle do not seem to have pondered how far they could go before the entire charade spun out of control.

THE CLOSING OF THE RING

"More and more, I feel that the political-military ring is closing around us, and I don't think that anyone will open it," Rabin told the General Staff and the cabinet defense subcommittee on June 2.¹³² For the chief of staff and most other Israelis, the three days following Hussein's visit to Cairo had been some of the tensest in their country's short history. Hussein's pact with Nasser meant that an all-Arab attack was now an imminent possibility. The problem, Eshkol told the cabinet on June 1, was no longer just the Straits of Tiran. The pronouncements and actions of Nasser and other Arab leaders indicated that "their goal is to turn the wheels of history back to before 1948."¹³³ With time, Rabin warned the next day, "Arab military cooperation will grow stronger and stronger." If Israel did not act, it would face an ever-growing military threat on all of its borders, especially the West Bank front.¹³⁴ By June 3, the IDF leadership believed that Nasser was planning a surprise attack to seize Eilat or the entire southern Negev in which the JAA, bolstered by Iraqi troops, would play a key role.¹³⁵

Hussein's pact with Nasser effectively annulled the Israeli cabinet's May 28 decision to give American diplomacy a chance. Between nuclear deterrence and preemptive war, the two remaining options, there was never really much of a contest. Despite the fact that Eshkol had apparently ordered the arming of two nuclear devices before Hussein's trip to Cairo, Israel's bomb was not brought out of the basement. On June 1, at Eshkol's invitation, Rafi, Ben-Gurion's pro-nuclear party, joined a national unity government along with Menachem Begin's Gahal party. Yet newly appointed defense minister Moshe Dayan did not press Eshkol to play the nuclear card.¹³⁶ The only Rafi member to favor a display of atomic prowess was Shimon Peres, who claims to have begged Dayan to consider "a certain proposal which . . . would have deterred the Arabs and prevented the war"—presumably a nuclear test. According to Peres, his proposal was "considered . . . and rejected," and probably with good reason.¹³⁷ There are hints in the archival record that Israel might have detonated a nuclear device had Egypt struck Israel's population centers from the air or used poison gas.¹³⁸ According to former chief of staff and Dayan confidante Tsvi Tsur, Sayeret Matkal, the IDF's elite commando unit, prepared to "fly to a high place in the Sinai desert, unload a certain object from the helicopter, activate it and get out fast."¹³⁹ But the Israeli government appears to have had no desire to introduce nuclear weapons into the Middle East, and for good reason. An Israeli nuclear test could have alienated the United States, provoked Soviet intervention, or put intolerable pressure on Nasser to acquire nuclear weapons later.[140]

Instead, Eshkol again tried to convince the Americans that Israel had to act. "A point is being reached at which counsels to Israel will lack any moral or logical basis," he wrote to Johnson on May 30.[141] The following day, the prime minister dispatched Mossad chief Meir Amit to learn how the Johnson administration would react to an Israeli first strike in light of the Egyptian-Jordanian pact.[142] When Amit arrived in Washington, he found that the Americans were no longer so rigidly opposed to Israeli preemption.[143] While Johnson formally urged Eshkol to give diplomacy a chance, many prominent US officials had accepted the idea of Israel going it alone.[144] Other maritime states did not want to confront Nasser, Congress was wary of military action, and pro-Western states like Jordan were moving into Nasser's camp. "If we follow our present course," NSC staffer Harold Saunders warned Walt Rostow, "it is hard to see how we can make good our commitment without paying a tremendous price in the Arab world. . . . We ought to consider admitting that we have failed and allow fighting to ensue."[145] The CIA concurred. "The US cannot expect to receive any sympathy if it employs force in the Strait, but it will also not get any gratitude if it fails to do so," argued the agency's analysts.[146] Indeed, Walt Rostow wrote to Johnson on June 4—perhaps an Israeli attack on Egypt would have long-term benefits for America's position in the Middle East: "The moderate Arabs—and in fact, virtually all Arabs who fear the rise of Nasser as a result of this crisis—would prefer to have him cut down by the Israelis rather than by external forces. . . . Just beneath the surface is the potentiality for a new phase in the Middle East of moderation; a focusing on economic development; regional collaboration; and an acceptance of Israel as part of the Middle East if a solution to the refugee problem can be found. But all this depends on Nasser's being cut down to size."[147]

The Americans' ambivalence was not lost on Amit. When he warned Secretary of Defense Robert McNamara that Israel had no choice but to attack, the American merely thanked him "for his candid discussion and indicated that he, the Secretary, would be seeing the President shortly and would convey Amit's views to him."[148] (According to Amit's account,

McNamara said, "I read you loud and clear."[149]) CIA officials who met with Amit, including Director of Central Intelligence Richard Helms, also did not seem strongly opposed to Israeli preemption.[150] Unsurprisingly, Amit interpreted the Americans' tight-lipped responses in a way that justified what Israel's generals wanted to do anyway. "My conclusion after the first round in Washington is that we need to wait a little bit longer for the naval breakthrough plan and then strike," he cabled to Jerusalem. "Public opinion is in favor. The CIA is in favor. The only ones opposed at this point are the State Department people."[151] Two days later, the Israeli cabinet finally voted to strike Egypt.

While the Egyptian-Jordanian pact accelerated Israel's march toward war, the Israelis still did not fundamentally rethink their strategy or war aims. Until the war started, Rabin refused to put Central Command on an offensive footing. "The central problem is the degree of the blow that Nasser receives," he told Operations Branch officers on May 31. "A plan for the conquest of the West Bank should not distract us from the principal thing."[152] Rabin did authorize planning for Operation PARGOL, a battle plan that called for seizing the West Bank's central ridge if Jordanian armor assumed offensive positions on the West Bank, if an Iraqi division entered Jordan, or if the JAA attacked Israel.[153] On the eve of the war, IDF Central and Northern Commands had orders that called for them to seize parts of the northern West Bank, the Latrun salient, and the approaches to Jerusalem if Jordanian armor deployed on the West Bank.[154] But Israel's basic aim, Rabin reiterated on June 4, was "to concentrate the effort against Nasser. It is forbidden to deviate from that. After that blow, the face of the Middle East will change."[155] He ordered Central Command to maintain its defensive posture, and rebuffed many of Gen. Uzi Narkiss's demands for additional troops. "Central Command's defense," Narkiss recalled after the war, "was definitely based on [expectations of] miracles, such as that the enemy would not attack."[156] This was more or less accurate. Rabin believed that the Jordanians would not attack immediately but would "participate according to the results of the battle [in the Sinai]."[157]

Neither the Israeli military nor the political leadership thought that war with Jordan was inevitable, even after Hussein's pact with Nasser. Offensive action against Jordan was still treated as a last resort. Talk of taking the West Bank, so ubiquitous in the run-up to Suez, was seldom heard in these prewar discussions, and was certainly not incorporated into the IDF's operational orders. The objective of PARGOL, as well as of the scaled-down version of the plan authorized on June 4, was to keep the JAA from reaching Israel's population centers, not to seize territory. Indeed, the IDF leadership viewed a quick attack on Egypt not only as a way to prevent greater *military* threats from arising on the Jordanian front, but also as a way to save the *political* status quo in Jordan from collapse. AMAN predicted that if the crisis persisted, the Hashemite regime would surely fall, but that Hussein might survive if Israel attacked quickly and deflated Nasser's bloated prestige.[158] "I think, at this stage," Rabin told the cabinet defense subcommittee on June 1, "that Jordan's not the problem. I believe—and we've got signs—that they're worried and saying *nu, nu* [i.e., hurry up]! I think they know that their fate depends on our behavior."[159] Bizarrely, some IDF generals even talked about helping Hussein politically when they planned how to respond to a Jordanian attack. "We must remember that Hussein has a personal interest in Egypt's downfall," argued Gen. David "Dado" Elazar, head of Northern Command. "He will give the order to fire according to the circumstances, but is likely to pull back quickly if we help him out with limited attacks like the conquest of the Hebron hills or pressure on the Jenin sector." Elazar thought Hussein could benefit from Nasser's humiliation while posing as a courageous Arab leader—"a hero fighting off a Jewish attack."[160] Here, in a nutshell, was what the IDF wanted: a phony war with Hussein and a decisive showdown with Nasser.

It seemed that Hussein was going to get the "purely UAR-Israeli confrontation" that he wanted. The Israelis had finally realized that their passivity in the face of Nasser's threats forced even his bitterest Arab rivals to line up behind him. A critical mass of US officials had decided that American interests were best served by allowing Israel to go it alone. The IDF's efforts were to be directed southward, away from the West Bank. And it would all happen before the domestic situation in Jordan got out of control, and just as Iraqi troops began entering the kingdom.

THREE DAYS OF WAR

On the morning of June 5, 1967, both Hussein and the Israeli government still wanted to avoid war with each other. The problem was that Hussein had been stripped of operational control over his armed forces. With ʿAbd al-Munʿim Riyadh in command, the JAA would act on misinformation supplied by the Egyptian military leadership. By the time Hussein was in a position to make his own demands for a ceasefire, he had already provoked the Israelis to conquer the West Bank.

At nine o'clock on the morning of June 5, Hussein received a message from ʿAbd al-Hakim ʿAmir, who claimed that the IDF had attacked Egypt earlier that morning. He said that 75 percent of the enemy's air force had been destroyed, and Egypt had launched a counteroffensive. Accordingly, he had ordered Riyadh to attack Israeli targets from the Jordanian front. ʿAmir's report was completely false. Beginning at a quarter to eight that morning, Israeli planes had destroyed most of Egypt's air force on the ground. But Hussein did not know this, and the JAA had already begun to move. At a quarter to ten, Jordanian troops began firing across the border into Israel, followed by artillery barrages two hours later. Riyadh had also planned for combined Iraqi-Syrian-Jordanian air strikes, though it was not until eleven o'clock that Iraqi planes linked up with the Jordanian air force and headed for Israel.[161] Misled by reports that the Egyptian Army was advancing into the Negev, Riyadh also moved the JAA's Sixtieth and Fortieth Armored Brigades southward, making a concentrated attack on Israel's heartland impossible. If the JAA had not been under Egyptian command, Hussein's advisor Zayd al-Rifaʿi later told Yaʿakov Herzog, it could have "reached the coast in four to five hours," or turned East Jerusalem into an "Arab Stalingrad."[162]

Shortly after Riyadh ordered Jordan's air force into action, Hussein received a message from Eshkol through Odd Bull, the head of UNTSO, the UN observer force that monitored the armistice lines. Eshkol informed the king that Egyptian-Israeli hostilities had begun, and that if Jordan did not intervene, Israel would leave it alone. Hussein brushed off the message. "They started the battle," he told Bull. "Well, they are receiving our reply by air."[163] At 11:50 AM, Jordanian Hawker Hunters began bombing Netanya, Kfar Sirkin, and Kfar Saba. At 12:30 PM, JAA troops crossed the armistice line into south Jerusalem, seizing UNTSO's headquarters on Government House Ridge.

At this point, the Israelis finally lost patience. From Government House Ridge, Jordanian infantry could easily conquer the Jewish neighborhoods below. Uzi Narkiss had also begun to worry that the Jordanians would attack Israel's isolated enclave on Mount Scopus.[164] At an early afternoon meeting with the General Staff, Dayan authorized air strikes against Jordan's airfields, and ordered the IDF to seize the Jenin area to stop the JAA's shelling. The defense minister also authorized limited operations in Jerusalem aimed at stopping Jordanian artillery barrages, protecting Mount Scopus, and pushing the JAA back from Government House Ridge. Yet Dayan warned the General Staff not to let soldiers enter Jenin itself, if possible, and rejected suggestions that Israel occupy the Latrun salient. The Israelis were still operating within the parameters of the "mini-PARGOL" plan that Rabin had authorized a day earlier. "We are already screwing their air force," boasted Rabin. "What do we need to take territory for at this point?" For the moment, Dayan seemed to agree. "See if it's possible to talk to the Jordanians about holding their fire," he told Rabin.[165] But another Israeli request for a ceasefire sent that evening through State Department channels also went unheeded by Hussein.[166]

Had Hussein understood how fast Israeli attitudes were changing, he might have reined in his troops. By nightfall on June 5, Menachem Begin and Yigal Allon, the cabinet's most ardent expansionists, began calling for Israel to take the entire West Bank. Earlier that day, Allon had told the General Staff that moving troops into the Jenin sector would require them to conquer the entire northern West Bank, "which would permit us to take the whole area."[167] That evening, he and Begin called on Eshkol to go beyond the IDF's original plans and take the Old City of Jerusalem. Eshkol, wary of the potential diplomatic consequences, decided not to decide, and Dayan backed him.[168]

Yet Hussein gave the Israelis even more time to change their minds. By the morning of June 6, Jordan's military situation was desperate. Most of the Jordanian air force had been destroyed. JAA command and control had completely broken down, leaving units to fight isolated battles all over the West Bank. At six o'clock that morning, the Jordanian army was losing a tank every ten minutes.[169] Desperate to cut his losses, Hussein summoned the US, British, and French ambassadors and begged them to stop the Israelis. Still, he could not agree to an official ceasefire. "We must stop the fighting," he told Burns, "but for God's sake, the Israelis must not announce anything publicly concerning this matter.

Otherwise it would result in internal anarchy here."[170] Though the king begged Nasser for permission to answer the UN's call for a ceasefire, the Egyptian president did not agree to do so until a quarter past eleven that night. By this point, it seemed unlikely that Jordanian troops could stay on the West Bank any longer anyway. The JAA, Hussein told US officials, "scarcely exists as an organization.... If we do not withdraw tonight, we will be chewed up."[171]

In any case, the Israelis were now bent on completing their takeover of the West Bank. On the afternoon of June 6, the cabinet defense subcommittee voted to complete the conquest of the West Bank's central mountain ridge.[172] As Allon later pointed out, once this decision was made, there was virtually no resistance to the idea of pushing onward to the Jordan River. The IDF was already being pulled into a position of de facto control over the West Bank's major population centers. There seemed to be no reason for the IDF not to take the sparsely populated Jordan Valley and establish a more defensible ceasefire line.[173] That night, the cabinet also voted to allow the IDF to surround the Old City of Jerusalem.[174] New Jordanian requests for a ceasefire, conveyed by Ambassador Barbour, now inspired little Israeli interest.[175] On June 7, the IDF entered the Old City and took the remainder of the West Bank, as the JAA's shattered forces withdrew across the Jordan.

"Even if we conquer the West Bank and the Old City," Eshkol had warned his colleagues on the night of June 5, "we will be forced to leave them."[176] Would the prime minister be proven right? And if Israel managed to hang on to the West Bank, what would the future hold for it?

NOTES

1. Amman to State, November 19, 1966, NA/RG59/DOSCF 1964–1966/DEF 19–8 US-JORDAN.
2. Amman to State, November 14, 1966, NA/RG59/DOSCF 1964–1966/POL 7 PAK.
3. Mutawi, *Jordan in the 1967 War*, 77.
4. Amman to State, November 15, 1966, NA/RG59/DOSCF 1964–1966/POL 32–1 ISR-JORDAN.
5. Amman to State, November 14, 1966, NA/RG59/DOSCF 1964–1966/POL 32–1 ISR-JORDAN.
6. Amman to State, November 23, 1966, NA/RG59/DOSCF 1964–1966/POL 32–1

ISR-JORDAN.

7. Amman to State, December 11, 1966, LBJL/NSF/Country Files/Jordan, box 146.

8. On the Israelis' attempts to restore contact with Hussein, see Levavi to London, February 24, 1967, and London to Jerusalem, March 12, 1967, YHP.

9. Hussein-Sliusarenko memcon, January 4, 1967, in Naumkin, *Blizhni vostochni konflikt*, doc. 242.

10. Amman to State, December 22, 1966, *FRUS*, 1964–1968, 18: doc. 373.

11. Amman to State, November 24, 1966, LBJL/NSF/Country Files/Jordan, box 146.

12. Rostow to Johnson, December 2, 1966, *FRUS*, 1964–1968, 18: doc. 355.

13. "The Jordanian Regime: Its Prospects and the Consequences of Its Demise," CIA memo, December 13, 1966, LBJL/NSF/Country Files/Jordan, box 146.

14. Wriggins and Saunders to Rostow, November 16, 1966, *FRUS*, 1964–1968, 18: doc. 337.

15. Rostow to Johnson, December 12, 1966, *FRUS*, 1964–1968, 18: doc. 363.

16. Amman to State, December 11, 1966, *FRUS*, 1964–1968, 18: doc. 362.

17. Amman to State, December 22, 1966, *FRUS*, 1964–1968, 18: doc. 373.

18. Amman to State, December 11, 1966, NA/RG59/DOSCF 1964–1966/POL 23–9 JORDAN.

19. "Mulabasat ma'rakat al-samu'," reprinted in Tal, *Kitabat fi al-qadaya al-'arabiyya*, 241–244.

20. Amman to State, November 26, 1966, NA/RG59/DOSCF 1964–1966/POL 15–1 JORDAN; Amman to State, December 20, 1966, LBJL/NSF/Country Files/Jordan, box 146.

21. Quoted in Amman to State, December 3, 1966, NA/RG59/DOSCF 1964–1966/POL 15–1 JORDAN.

22. Amman to State, February 27, 1967, NA/RG59/DOSCF 1967–1969/POL JORDAN-UAR.

23. Figures cited in Central Command monthly intelligence summary no. 2, IDFA/1338/79/40.

24. Amman to State, December 29, 1966, NA/RG59/DOSCF 1964–1966/POL 32–1 JOR-SYR.

25. *al-Difa'*, January 10, 1967.

26. *al-Difa'*, February 28, 1967.

27. *Filastin*, March 21, 1967.

28. Fortescue to Beemish, April 12, 1967, BNA/FCO 17/473.

29. Amman to State, December 11, 1966, NA/RG59/DOSCF 1964–1966/POL 23–9 JORDAN.

30. Amman to State, December 6, 1966, NA/RG59/DOSCF, 1964–1966/POL 23–9 JORDAN.

31. For an example of the regime's calls for internal unity, see *al-Difa'*, January 24, 1967.

32. Jerusalem to State, December 8, 1966, NA/RG59/DOSCF 1964–1966/POL 23–9 JORDAN.

33. Amman to FCO, January 9, 1967, BNA/FCO/17/231.

34. Dann, *King Hussein*, 158. The laws took effect at the end of March.

35. Rostow to Johnson, December 17, 1966, LBJL/NSF/Country Files/Jordan, box

146.
36. Amman to FCO, April 29, 1967, BNA/FCO 17/211. See also Jum'a, *al-Mu'amara wa-ma'rakat al-masir*, 185–186.
37. Amman to FCO, May 10, 1967, BNA/FCO 17/211.
38. Haykal, *al-Infijar*, 435–440.
39. Yitzhak Rabin, remarks at a meeting of the General Staff, November 14, 1966, in Rosenthal, *Yitzhak Rabin*, 420. See also Rabin's remarks in cabinet minutes, November 13, 1966, ISA.
40. Cabinet minutes, November 27, 1966, ISA.
41. For the reaction of the opposition and the Israeli press, see KFADC minutes, November 22, 1966, ISA/A/8161/3; KFADC minutes, December 13, 1966, ISA/A/8161/4; Hadow to Brown, December 21, 1966, BNA/FO 371/16840.
42. Editorial note, in Lammfromm and Tsoref, *Levi Eshkol*, 520; cabinet minutes, November 27, 1966, ISA.
43. For US reactions to the Samu' operation, see, for example, Washington to Jerusalem, November 16, 1966, ISA/FM/4030/7; Rostow to Johnson, November 15, 1966, *FRUS*, 1964–1968, 18: doc. 333; memorandum for the record, November 15, 1966, *FRUS*, 1964–1968, 18: doc. 334; State to Tel Aviv, November 22, 1966, *FRUS*, 1964–1968, 18: doc. 343. For the text of UN Security Council Resolution 228, November 25, 1966, see UNISPAL, https://unispal.un.org/DPA/DPR/unispal.nsf/9a798adbf322aff38525617b006d88d7/1a03c7bfb8d6c049852560c3004a4aaf?OpenDocument. Komer's remarks to Harman are summarized in memorandum for the record, November 16, 1966, *FRUS*, 1964–1968, 18: doc. 336.
44. Quoted in editorial note, in Lammfromm and Tsoref, *Levi Eshkol*, 520. The *shema*, a prayer proclaiming the oneness of God, is closely associated with Jewish concepts of martyrdom. Historically, Jewish victims of religious persecution recited it before their deaths.
45. Eshkol to Baer, January 11, 1967, in Lammfromm and Tsoref, *Levi Eshkol*, 526.
46. Cabinet minutes, November 27, 1966, ISA. The Hashemite regime, Rabin told Eshkol and a small group of other high-ranking Israelis on December 28, was "stable, in Middle Eastern terms." See "Consultation in the Prime Minister's Office," December 28, 1966, ISA/A/7935/7. On January 2, Yariv told the General Staff that while the internal situation in Jordan was tense and the Syrians were actively trying to foment instability there, "Hussein's chances of prevailing are good." Yariv also believed that Nasser did not want to topple Hussein, for fear of war with Israel. More likely, he sought to mobilize just enough domestic opposition against the king to get him to appoint a more neutral government and adopt policies that were more amenable to Syria and Egypt. See General Staff minutes, January 2, IDFA/117/70/205.
47. Gazit to Eban, January 13, 1967, ISA/FM/4092/9.
48. Untitled Foreign Ministry memorandum (working group concluding report), January 8, 1967, ISA/FM/4092/9.
49. Ibid.
50. Working group minutes, December 12, 1966, ISA/FM/4092/9.
51. Ibid.
52. "Israel's Policy toward Jordan," undated, ISA/FM/4094/10. A draft of this document was discussed at the working group's meeting on December 19, then slightly revised and submitted to Mordechai Gazit on December 23. See also working group

minutes, December 19, 1966, ISA/4094/10.

53. "Israel's Policy toward Jordan," undated, ISA/FM/4094/10.

54. Working group minutes, December 19, 1966, ISA/4094/10.

55. Untitled Foreign Ministry memorandum (working group concluding report), January 8, 1967, ISA/4092/19.

56. Cabinet minutes, January 15, 1967, ISA.

57. Brown-Eban memcon, February 21, 1967, BNA/PREM/13/1617.

58. Cohen, *Israel and the Bomb*, 232. See also Cohen, "Crossing the Threshold."

59. KFADC minutes, November 22, 1966, ISA/A/8161/3.

60. See especially Laron, "Playing with Fire." On the larger implications of détente and the Sino-Soviet split for the USSR's relations with Third World regimes, see Westad, *Global Cold War*, 158–170.

61. Dean Rusk, for example, told Eban in October 1966 that Soviet foreign minister Andrei Gromyko "had shown no interest in dampening down [the] arms race in [the] area, excepting nuclear weapons." Eban-Rusk memcon, October 8, 1966, FRUS, 1964–1968, 18: doc. 328. For similar US conclusions, see meeting of the interdepartmental regional group for the Near East and South Asia, March 28, 1967, FRUS, 1964–1968, 18: doc. 400; Katzenbach to Johnson, May 1, 1967, FRUS, 1964–1968, 18: doc. 415.

62. On Israel's knowledge of the Soviet response to Egypt's request for nuclear assistance, see Yariv's remarks in General Staff minutes, March 6, 1967, IDFA/70/205. For the Israeli intelligence community's view that Soviet hostility to Israel had clear limits, see the AMAN estimates cited in Heller, *Yisrael veha-milhamah ha-karah*, 503.

63. Appendix C, "Topics for Dialogue with Egypt," undated (late 1966), ISA/FM/4091/19. The Mossad estimated that the Israeli nuclear program was five to ten years ahead of Egypt's, and that it was beyond Egypt's means to allocate significant amounts of money to nuclear weapons development.

64. "Meeting at the Home of General Meir Amit," November 27, 1966, ISA/FM/4091/19.

65. "Appendix B: Egypt-Israel," undated (late 1966), ISA/FM/4091/19.

66. "Meeting at the Home of General Meir Amit," November 27, 1966, ISA/FM/4091/19.

67. KFADC minutes, November 22, 1966, ISA/A/8161/3.

68. Cited in Golan, *Milhamah be-shalosh hazitot*, 21.

69. See David Carmon's remarks in General Staff minutes, April 24, 1967, IDFA/117/70/206.

70. Remarks at a conference of senior IDF commanders, February 27, 1967, in Rosenthal, *Yitzhak Rabin*, 433.

71. "Draft of Working Order for the Year 1967/68," in Rosenthal, *Yitzhak Rabin*, 429. See also Golan, *Milhamah be-shalosh hazitot*, 21.

72. KFADC minutes, November 22, 1966, ISA/A/8161/3.

73. Remarks at a meeting of the General Staff, December 12, 1966, in Rosenthal, *Yitzhak Rabin*, 422.

74. See, for example, Davies to Rusk, February 8, 1967, FRUS, 1964–1968, 18: doc. 388.

75. See "Sabotage and Mines," unsigned, undated (spring 1967), ISA/A/7936/5. The document initially states that nine attacks were launched from Jordan and nine from Syria during the months in question, but handwritten corrections elsewhere in the

document indicate that the number launched from Jordan was slightly higher.
76. Tel Aviv to State, February 10, 1967, NA/RG59/DOSCF 1967–69/POL 27–14 ISR-SYR.
77. General Staff minutes, March 6, 1967, IDFA/117/70/205.
78. General Staff minutes, April 8, 1967, IDFA/117/70/206.
79. Cabinet minutes, April 9, 1967, ISA.
80. Michael Hadow, "The Second Arab-Israeli War: The Preliminaries," June 29, 1967, BNA/FCO 17/526.
81. Oren, *Six Days of War*, 54–85.
82. Cabinet minutes, May 16, 1967, ISA.
83. "Discussion of ROGEL," May 19, 1967, IDFA/192/74/1176.
84. Cabinet minutes, May 21, 1967, ISA.
85. See especially Gluska, *Eshkol*, 267–304.
86. Lyndon B. Johnson, "Statement by the President on Rising Tensions in the Near East," May 23, 1967, the American Presidency Project, http://www.presidency.ucsb.edu/ws/index.php?pid=28265.
87. Eban's mission, Rabin told the General Staff on May 23, "seems like it will not have a good effect." "Chief of Staff Discussion," May 23, 1967, IDFA/192/74/1176.
88. Johnson-Eban memcon, May 26, 1967, FRUS, 1964–1968, 19: doc. 77. See also minutes of the same talk in ISA/FM/5937/30.
89. State to Tel Aviv, May 27, 1967, FRUS, 1964–1968, 19: doc. 86.
90. Cabinet minutes, May 28, 1967, ISA.
91. Cohen, *Israel and the Bomb*, 273–274.
92. Haber, *Ha-Yom tifrots milhamah*, 175.
93. "ROGEL—Chief of Staff Discussion," May 22, 1967, IDFA/192/74/1176.
94. "Operations Branch Head Discussion," May 25, 1967, IDFA/192/74/1176.
95. "Chief of Staff Discussion," May 27, 1967, IDFA/192/74/1176.
96. "Chief of Staff Discussion," May 28, 1967, IDFA/192/74/1176.
97. "Chief of Staff Discussion," May 29, 1967, IDFA/192/74/1176.
98. "General Staff Discussion," May 29, 1967, IDFA/192/74/1176.
99. "Tasrih al-sayyid Sa'd Jum'a," May 17, 1967, in *al-Watha'iq al-urduniyya, 1967*, 9.
100. Amman to State, May 17, 1967, NA/RG59/DOSCF 1967–1969/POL 32–1 ISR-JORDAN.
101. Amman to State, May 21, 1967, NA/RG59/Lot Files/68D135, box 4.
102. Amman to State, May 18, 1967, FRUS, 1964–1968, 19: doc. 12.
103. Amman to State, May 23, 1967, LBJL/NSF/NSC Histories/Middle East Crisis, box 22. See also "UAR/Jordanian Discussion regarding Jordan's Role in Current Crisis and UAR Assessment of Present Situation," CIA cable, May 25, 1967, LBJL/NSF/Country Files/Middle East Crisis, box 105.
104. Amman to State, May 23, 1967, LBJL/NSF/NSC Histories/Middle East Crisis, box 22.
105. Amman to FCO, May 23, 1967, BNA/PREM 13/1617.
106. Amman to State, May 22, 1967, LBJL/NSF/Country Files/Middle East Crisis, box 115.
107. State to White House, May 26, 1967, LBJL/NSF/NSC Histories/Middle East Crisis, box 17.
108. FRUS, 1964–1968, 19: doc. 107n1.
109. Amman to State, May 27, 1967, LBJL/NSF/NSC Histories/Middle East Crisis,

box 22.

110. "Background on Jordan/UAR Defense Pact and Re-examination of Jordan Position as Result of It," CIA cable, June 4, 1967, LBJL/NSF/Country Files/Middle East Crisis, box 106.

111. State to White House, May 28, 1967, LBJL/NSF/Country Files/Middle East Crisis, box 105.

112. Quoted in Shuqayri, *al-Hazima al-kubra*, 1:122. Al-Shuqayri confirms that Nasser meant this speech to serve as an overture to Hussein.

113. Amman to State, May 26, 1967, NA/RG59/DOSCF 1967–1969/POL 15–1 UAR; Amman to State, May 27, 1967, LBJL/NSF/NSC Histories/Middle East Crisis, box 22.

114. Rashid, *Hisab al-saraya wa-hisab al-qaraya*, 149.

115. Jum'a, *al-Mu'amara wa-ma'rakat al-masir*, 187.

116. Amman to State, May 30, 1967, NA/RG59/DOSCF 1967–1969/POL 7 JORDAN.

117. CIA memo, May 30, 1967, DDRS/CK3100562546.

118. Lauer and Vance, *Hussein of Jordan*, 44.

119. Haykal, *al-Infijar*, 656–660.

120. Ibid., 660–661.

121. Amman to State, May 31, 1967, LBJL/NSF/NSC Histories/Middle East Crisis, box 22.

122. Jum'a, *al-Mu'amara wa-ma'rakat al-masir*, 188; Shuqayri, *al-Hazima al-kubra*, 1:125–126.

123. Oren, *Six Days of War*, 119–121.

124. The idea, in fact, was Eshkol's, and had been transmitted to the Soviets by Moshe Sneh, head of MAKI, Israel's Communist party. See Raoul Teitelbaum, "What Now, Comrade Sneh?," *Ha'aretz*, May 27, 2009; as well as Laron, "Playing with Fire," 16.

125. Nasser-Pozhdidaev memcon, June 1, 1967, in Naumkin, *Blizhni vostochni konflikt*, doc. 260.

126. Captured Egyptian documents, in fact, indicate that Nasser and 'Amir fully expected an Israeli attack, and thought it would serve their aims. Egypt could counterattack, seize Israeli territory, and put the United States in an even more awkward position, allowing Nasser to settle the "Palestine problem" in postwar negotiations, if not on the battlefield. See Shemesh, *Arab Politics*, 213–216.

127. "Background on Jordan/UAR Defense Pact and Re-examination of Jordan's Position as a Result of It," CIA cable, June 4, 1967, LBJL/NSF/Country Files/Middle East Crisis, box 106.

128. "Arab States," unsigned, undated FM memo, ISA/A/7920/4.

129. Amman to State, June 3, 1967, LBJL/NSF/NSC Histories/Middle East Crisis, box 23.

130. "King Hussein's Attitude toward Israel Prior to the Hostilities of June 5 and His Actions Thereafter vis-à-vis Israel," unsigned briefing paper, June 28, 1967, LBJL/NSF/Country Files/Jordan, box 148.

131. Amman to State, June 3, 1967, LBJL/NSF/NSC Histories/Middle East Crisis, box 23.

132. "Presentation of Facts to the Cabinet," June 2, 1967, IDFA/192/74/1176.

133. Cabinet minutes, June 1, 1967, ISA.
134. "Presentation of Facts to the Cabinet," June 2, 1967, IDFA/192/74/1176.
135. "Planning Session with Deputy Chief of Staff," June 3, 1967, IDFA/192/74/1176.
136. On the formation of the national unity government, see Oren, *Six Days of War*, 132–139.
137. Peres, *Battling for Peace*, 167.
138. See the examples cited in Ginor and Remez, *Foxbats over Dimona*, 33, 224–225n26; Helms to Johnson, June 2, 1967, George Washington University, National Security Archive, http://www.gwu.edu/~nsarchiv/NSAEBB/NSAEBB265/19670602 .pdf; Rabin-Warnke memcon, November 12, 1968, FRUS, 1964–1968, 20: doc. 317.
139. Amir Oren, "Former IDF Chief Reveals New Details of Israel's Nuclear Program," *Ha'aretz*, September 16, 2011.
140. Cohen, *Israel and the Bomb*, 275–276.
141. Harman to Rusk, May 30, 1967, FRUS, 1964–1968, 19: doc. 102.
142. Oren, *Six Days of War*, 145–149.
143. For similar assessments, see Quandt, "Lyndon Johnson"; and Gat, "Let Someone Else."
144. See, for example, Johnson to Eshkol, June 3, 1967, FRUS, 1964–1968, 19: doc. 139.
145. Saunders to Rostow, May 31, 1967, FRUS, 1964–1968, 19: doc. 114.
146. Board of National Estimates to Helms, June 1, 1967, FRUS, 1964–1968, 19: doc. 126.
147. Rostow to Johnson, June 4, 1967, FRUS, 1964–1968, 19: doc. 144.
148. McNamara-Amit memcon, June 1, 1967, FRUS, 1964–1968, 19: doc. 124.
149. Segev, *1967: Veha-arets shintah et penehah*, 350–352.
150. See Oren, *Six Days of War*, 146–147.
151. Head of the Mossad to the Mossad, June 2, 1967, ISA/FM/5937/30.
152. "Chief of Staff Discussion," May 31, 1967, IDFA/192/74/1176.
153. "PARGOL: Planning Order," June 1, 1967, IDFA/192/74/1176.
154. "Operation Mozart," June 5, 1967, IDFA/192/74/1176.
155. "Branch Heads Meeting with the Deputy Chief of Staff," June 4, 1967, IDFA/192/74/1176.
156. IDF Central Command, "The Six Day War: Concluding Report, Part 1, Section 1," IDFA/901/67/7.
157. "Branch Heads Meeting with the Deputy Chief of Staff," June 4, 1967, IDFA/192/74/1176.
158. Appendix C, "Situation Evaluation: Jordan," IDFA/192/74/1176.
159. Quoted in editorial note, in Rosenthal, *Yitzhak Rabin*, 480.
160. "Chief of Staff Discussion," May 31, 1967, IDFA/192/74/1176.
161. Mutawi, *Jordan in the 1967 War*, 127.
162. Ya'akov Herzog, "Details on 1967," September 17, 1968, YHP. See also Shlaim, *Lion of Jordan*, 247.
163. Lauer and Vance, *Hussein*, 65.
164. IDF Central Command, "The Six Day War, Concluding Report, Part 1, Section 1," IDFA/901/67/7.
165. Quoted in Haber, *Ha-Yom tifrots milhamah*, 227–228.

166. State to Amman, June 5, 1967, *FRUS*, 1964–1968, 19: doc. 160.
167. Yigal Allon oral history, ISA/A/5001/19.
168. Haber, *Ha-Yom tifrots milhamah*, 229–230.
169. Amman to State, June 6, 1967, LBJL/NSF/Country Files/Middle East Crisis, box 107, 1 of 2.
170. Amman to State, June 6, 1967, NA/RG59/Lot Files/68D135, box 4.
171. State to White House, June 6, 1967, LBJL/NSF/Country Files/Middle East Crisis, box 107, 1 of 2.
172. Golan, *Milhamah be-shalosh hazitot*, 245.
173. Yigal Allon oral history, ISA/A/5001/19.
174. Haber, *Ha-Yom tifrots milhamah*, 232–233.
175. "US Policy and Diplomacy in the Middle East Crisis," DOS Historical Study, January 1969, 125–134, LBJL/NSF/NSC Histories/Middle East Crisis, box 20.
176. Quoted in Haber, *Ha-Yom tifrots milhamah*, 231.

SIX

THE HARVEST OF WAR, JUNE-NOVEMBER 1967

NEITHER KING HUSSEIN NOR ISRAEL'S LEADERS WENT TO WAR expecting to spend years bargaining over the West Bank. Yet by the time the guns fell silent, it was clear just how fragile their prewar marriage of convenience had been. The question now was what would replace it.

At first, neither Hussein nor the Israelis really wanted to negotiate with each other. Eshkol and many of his colleagues would have preferred to impose a settlement upon the local Palestinians. Hussein hoped that the great powers would simply force the Israelis to withdraw. In the end, neither side could influence the United States or manipulate the West Bank Palestinians effectively enough to get what they wanted. By the time the UN Security Council adopted Resolution 242 in November 1967, it seemed as though the king and his Jewish neighbors might finally have to come to terms with one another.

THE DIMENSIONS OF THE AFTERMATH

Following six days of combat, the amount of territory under Israeli control quadrupled from 20,250 to 88,000 square kilometers. At the same time, the length of Israel's borders shrank from 985 to 650 kilometers. The ceasefire lines, Defense Minister Dayan proclaimed on June 29, were strategically ideal for Israel. They were shorter than the armistice lines, were based on natural boundaries, and were far from Israel's population centers and military bases. Israelis would no longer have to live in fear of being overwhelmed in a devastating surprise attack.[1] The sight of Israeli soldiers praying at Jerusalem's Western Wall and patrolling the biblical landscape of the West Bank also sparked deep emotion among both religious and secular Israeli Jews. On June 14, an estimated two hundred thousand Israelis flocked to the Western Wall to celebrate the holiday of Shavu'ot.[2] Not far removed from the Holocaust, Israelis from all walks of life had spent the weeks before the war terrified that they would be slaughtered en masse by Arab soldiers. Many believed that they owed their lightning victory to divine intervention, and that their return to Jerusalem's Old City and the West Bank heralded the coming of the messiah. Though an estimated six out of ten Jewish Israelis thought that some occupied territory could be traded for peace, few could say exactly what land they would be willing to give up: 90 percent opposed the return of the Old City to Jordan, 85 percent opposed giving the Golan Heights back to Syria, and nearly three-quarters opposed withdrawal from the Gaza Strip and the West Bank.[3]

Living within Israel's newly conquered territories, however, were approximately one million Arab civilians. Only about 70,000 Arabs lived in the vast Sinai desert, and most of the Golan Heights' inhabitants had fled during the war. But in the West Bank and the Gaza Strip, huge numbers of Arabs remained. Though many Palestinians fled to the East Bank both during and after the war, nearly 600,000 stayed put, as did an additional 70,000 in East Jerusalem. In the Gaza Strip, Israel now ruled over 356,000 Palestinians, of whom 172,000 were refugees.[4]

Any Israeli government would have found it difficult to decide how to administer the occupied territories, but Levi Eshkol's cabinet was particularly unsuited to the task. The national unity government that Eshkol had formed on the eve of the war was the largest in Israel's history. Every faction except for Israel's ultra-Orthodox and Communist parties was represented. Not only would Eshkol find it difficult to control this unwieldy mob, but he deeply resented the fact that he had been seen as too weak to lead Israel by himself in a time of crisis. He was especially angry that Moshe Dayan had taken his place as defense minister and claimed the glory of victory for himself.[5] These two bitter enemies and their deeply divided government would soon have to make some of the most fateful decisions in Israel's history.

The 1967 war transformed King Hussein's state as well. On the surface, the Hashemite kingdom's prospects seemed bleak. The West Bank

Israel and the Occupied Territories, 1967.

had been conquered, and the East Bank was flooded with Palestinians who had fled across the Jordan River. By August 1967, the Jordanian government estimated that some 250,000 West Bankers had crossed the river, swelling the East Bank's population by 25 percent.[6] Approximately 190,000 of these refugees found temporary lodging with relatives or friends, but most still needed aid, which was mainly supplied by foreign governments and international relief agencies.[7] At the beginning of July, Israel announced that it would allow West Bank refugees to apply to return home, but only 17,000 managed to do so before "Operation Refugee" ended that September.[8] Jordan was also nearly defenseless against external threats. The Jordanian armed forces had been eviscerated by the IDF. Only four of the JAA's eleven brigades remained operational, and 80 percent of its armor and nearly its entire air force were gone.[9]

Still, the war had not been a total disaster for the Hashemite monarchy. Hussein's position in the Arab arena had dramatically improved. The king's principal Arab enemy, Nasser, now bore responsibility for a catastrophic Arab defeat. Hussein, on the other hand, had demonstrated that he was not afraid to fight Israel, and had proven that he was no mere lackey of Britain and the United States. As the king himself put it, he had "fought the hardest and lost the most," and was therefore "in a unique position to speak for a moderate course."[10] The king's stronger inter-Arab position was acknowledged by the Americans and the Israelis as well. "Even without the West Bank, Hussein is in a stronger position vis-à-vis Nasser than before," AMAN Chief Yariv told the IDF General Staff.[11]

The war also provided Hussein with an opportunity to resolve longstanding intra-Jordanian tensions from a position of strength. Neither the king nor any of his top advisors thought that Jordan would be better off without the West Bank at this stage. The West Bank Palestinians, Hussein said, had caused him "a great deal of trouble in his lifetime," but they would cause "even more trouble if they were not returned to Jordan." The king believed that the Arab world would never forgive him if he allowed Israel to turn the West Bank into a Palestinian puppet state.[12] Rather than part ways with his restive West Bank subjects, Hussein hoped to bring them back into the Jordanian fold and grant them greater autonomy. Bahjat al-Talhuni, who replaced Sa'd Jum'a as prime minister that fall, told US officials that he and Hussein wanted "a new relationship between the West Bank and Amman if and when Israeli withdrawal could be effected," involving "substantial decentralization of the central government's authority."[13] The war had dealt Jordan a devastating blow, but it had also given Hussein a chance to rebuild his state on more stable foundations.

In the meantime, it seemed as though the East Bank could survive on its own, at least for a while. Some elite Jordanians, such as former foreign minister Hazim Nusayba, thought that "Jordan's economy had no future without the West Bank."[14] But such arguments belied the fact that the West Bank, except for the Jerusalem area, had actually been an economic burden prior to the war.[15] The economy of the East Bank did suffer in the immediate postwar period, but mainly because of the stresses that the new refugee crisis imposed upon the East Bank. Notably, Hussein generally refrained from using economic arguments to justify his efforts to retrieve the West Bank. When one interviewer asked him if Jordan could survive without the West Bank, he tactfully replied, "The West Bank is an important part of Jordan, just as Jordan is part of the Arab nation. The question is not a matter of survival, but of right."[16]

Hussein wanted to regain the West Bank, but it was not indispensable to him. So long as his army remained loyal, foreign aid continued to flow, and the "new refugees" did not become an unbearable burden, his kingdom could survive. For the moment, the king would have the luxury of being able to refuse Israeli offers that entailed too high a political price.

SUEZ REDUX?

As the 1967 war drew to a close, the center of the Arab-Israeli struggle moved from the battlefield to the halls of the United Nations. All of the parties expected that the Soviets, who had broken off diplomatic relations with Israel, would back Arab demands for a return to the status quo ante. The Americans, who had ties to both the Arab states and Israel, could conceivably align with either side. And so, both Hussein and the Israeli government concentrated on winning over the Johnson administration.

The Israelis and the Jordanians wanted very different things from the United States. From the moment the prewar crisis began, Eban later recalled, the Israeli government sought to ensure that there would be no repeat of 1957, when the superpowers forced Israel to withdraw from Sinai and Gaza without a peace settlement.[17] The Israelis wanted to end what Eban called the "intermediate status between war and peace" that had existed since 1949.[18] Going forward, Eshkol told the Knesset, Israel would insist on negotiating directly with the Arabs, and would reject any solutions imposed from outside.[19] But to hold out for a negotiated peace, Israel needed US support. Only the United States could deter the Soviets from intervening militarily in the Middle East, a possibility that worried some prominent Israelis, including Dayan and Eban.[20] And only the United States could keep the United Nations from demanding Israel's immediate withdrawal.

For Hussein, on the other hand, Suez offered an encouraging precedent. The king hoped that Johnson, like Eisenhower, would force Israel to withdraw for fear of losing the Arab world to the Soviets. "Everyone is suspicious of your position and the Arab countries are in ferment because they think your guarantees of territorial integrity apply only to Israel," he warned US ambassador Findley Burns. The Soviets, Hussein added, were making inroads all over the Arab world, and "your silence on Israeli withdrawal will cost you heavily."[21] Hoping to force the Americans to distance themselves from Israel, Hussein joined Nasser in accusing Britain and the United States of providing air support for the IDF, an allegation that came to be known as "the Big Lie." When Burns confronted him about these claims, Hussein responded, "Can the US promise to get me back on the West Bank?"[22] The king soon realized that the so-called "Big Lie" deeply angered the Americans, and at the end of June, he publicly renounced it.[23] Still, the king's calls for Israel's unconditional withdrawal were basically indistinguishable from the line taken by other Arab states. The international community's duty, Hussein told the UN General Assembly on June 26, was the "swift condemnation of the aggressor and the enforcing of the return of Israeli troops to the line held before the attack of 5 June."[24]

Unfortunately for the king, his hopes for a second Suez were not shared in Washington. Broadly speaking, the Americans supported Israel's position that occupied lands should be traded for peace. America's postwar goal, Walt Rostow told Johnson on June 7, should be "to move from the present situation to as stable and definitive a peace as possible."[25] Whatever reservations US officials might have had about Israel going it alone, they did not want to follow in Eisenhower's footsteps. Johnson's advisors presumed that the Israelis would never withdraw in exchange for another set of external guarantees. "Israel," Secretary of Defense McNamara argued, "won't ever depend on guarantees. Eban [was] given a lesson in US constitutional processes and he won't ever forget it."[26] Even Secretary of State Rusk, who was generally much less sympathetic to Israel, thought the United States could not "make Israel accept [a] puny settlement."[27]

Still, Rusk, along with most of his colleagues, also worried that "Israel's keeping territory would create a revanchism for the rest of the twentieth century."[28] Though US policymakers shed few tears for Nasser, they were concerned that the Arabs' desire for revenge would give the Soviets an opportunity to expand their influence in the Middle East.[29] While the Americans did not think the Israelis should give up their conquests for nothing, they also did not want Israel to humiliate the Arabs by redrawing the prewar map. "We're in a heck of a jam on territorial integrity," grumbled McNamara.[30]

The way out of that "jam" was for President Johnson to spell out some general principles for a settlement while not "setting [the Israelis'] feet in concrete," as he put it.[31] On June 19, as the UN General Assembly convened for a special session on the Middle East, Johnson laid out his "five principles" for Arab-Israeli peace, which included both "the recognized right of national life" and "political independence and territorial integrity for all." "The main responsibility for the peace of the region depends upon its own peoples and its own leaders," Johnson said.[32] It was a way of proclaiming America's desire for a peace settlement without demanding that either side do anything specific.

Yet privately, Johnson's cabinet officers hoped to rebuild the prewar Israeli-Jordanian entente. Despite Hussein's role in propagating "the Big Lie," the king had a history of close relations with the United States and secret dealings with Israel. He was also the only Arab belligerent who had not broken diplomatic relations with the United States. "If there were any sign of a magnanimous peace between [Hussein] and the Israelis, we should encourage it," argued McGeorge Bundy, whom Johnson had pulled away from his new job at the Ford Foundation to head the NSC's Special Committee on the Middle East.[33] The problem with a Jordan-first approach, however, was that it enjoyed little backing in Israel.

A "STATE OF ISHMAEL"?

Before the 1967 war, Israel's leaders assumed that if they ever conquered the West Bank, they would be quickly forced out. At best, some sort of peacekeeping force would deploy on the West Bank, which would buy Israel some time to develop nuclear weapons. The events of May and June 1967 effectively killed this strategy. Having witnessed how quickly UNEF withdrew from the Sinai, Eshkol and his colleagues did not want to trust their security to another international peacekeeping force. Those who knew their country's nuclear secrets must have also lost faith in the idea that atomic weapons would compensate for Israel's small size. Most importantly, the Israelis had reason to hope that they might not need to withdraw so quickly after all. Perhaps the Americans would decide that they had made a mistake in 1956, and allow Israel to redraw its borders.

Had the West Bank been more sparsely populated, many of Israel's leaders might have considered annexing part or all of the area. Indeed, during and immediately after the war, Dayan, Central Command chief Uzi Narkiss, and many lower-ranking IDF commanders took steps designed to reduce the size of the West Bank's population and consolidate Israel's hold over strategically crucial territory. During the war, Dayan had deliberately slowed down the IDF's advances so that Palestinian civilians would have time to flee. The aim, he told Rabin, was to "empty the West Bank of its inhabitants."[34] The military government went out of its way to help Palestinians who wished to depart, and made it difficult for those who left to return. Dayan and Narkiss also permitted and even encouraged the destruction of several West Bank border villages to ensure that the armistice line could never be precisely reconstructed. None of these actions were authorized by the cabinet, and in a few cases, Eshkol intervened to stop the army.[35] But in general, Israel's government quietly accepted the facts that the IDF created on the ground, and decided to create some itself. By June 11, Eshkol and his fellow ministers had already agreed to merge the Jewish and Arab halves of Jerusalem.[36]

Yet most of the West Bank's residents did not leave, and that meant that Israel could not simply absorb the region. Influential voices within Israel's national security establishment called for the creation of a Palestinian state instead. As early as June 6, Ambassador Avraham Harman urged Eshkol to mobilize Palestinian notables in the occupied territories in support of "a Palestinian state in the West Bank and Gaza Strip tied to Israel by military and economic pacts."[37] The Foreign Ministry's foremost Arabist, Moshe Sasson, likewise envisioned a West Bank state linked strategically and economically to Israel.[38] Many IDF officers made similar suggestions. Rehavam Ze'evi, deputy chief of the IDF's Operations Branch, called for a "state of Ishmael" to be established in the West Bank, with Nablus as its capital.[39] A committee of senior IDF officers hastily convened by Dayan drew up proposals for two different "Palestinian options." AMAN's Shlomo Gazit envisioned an independent, demilitarized Palestinian state in the West Bank and the Gaza Strip, while Yuval Ne'eman, a prominent physicist and longtime strategic planner, called for setting up a Palestinian autonomous regime in the West Bank and the Gaza Strip, federated with Israel.[40] Regardless of their differences, Israel's proponents of the Palestinian option all believed that it had been a grave mistake to allow Egypt and Jordan to keep the West Bank and Gaza Strip in 1949. The Arab states could never again be allowed to project their power so close to Israel's heartland.

Ultimately, though, the future of the occupied territories would not be decided by soldiers or bureaucrats, but by Israel's politicians. Between June 15 and June 19, Eshkol discussed Israel's terms for peace with his cabinet—first the smaller cabinet defense subcommittee, then the entire national unity government. "The moment we meet with serious people in the United States, they'll ask us to tell them what we want," the prime minister warned his colleagues. "Perhaps they'll agree, perhaps not, but they'll want to know what they're supposed to support." If Israel could not say what kind of settlement it wanted, Eshkol predicted, the Americans might lose their patience and impose one instead.[41]

After several long, agonizing debates, the cabinet authorized Abba Eban to tell the Johnson administration that Israel would conclude peace treaties with Egypt and Syria on the basis of Mandatory Palestine's international borders, so long as the Golan Heights and the Sinai Peninsula were demilitarized. Israel's freedom of navigation in the Straits of Tiran and the Suez Canal would also need to be guaranteed, along with access to the headwaters of the Jordan. The cabinet ministers concurred that Israel should annex the Gaza Strip and resettle its refugees elsewhere. And they likewise agreed that Israel should extend its jurisdiction to East Jerusalem (though they thought that Eban should not mention this to the Americans).[42]

But Eshkol's government could not decide what to do with the West Bank. At first the ministerial defense committee wanted to declare that the Jordan River was Israel's eastern border.[43] When the full cabinet discussed this option a few days later, obvious questions arose. If the Jordan became Israel's border, did that mean Israel had annexed the West Bank? Would the West Bank's Arab residents become Israeli citizens? And if not, who was responsible for them?

None of the cabinet's ministers wanted to immediately annex the West Bank. Even Menachem Begin feared doing anything that would leave Israel internationally isolated. He thought that Israel should simply wait for the world to lose interest in the West Bank. In the meantime, he predicted, many Jewish immigrants would arrive in Israel, shifting the demographic balance in favor of annexation. Begin did not want to grant the Palestinians autonomy, which he believed would lead to statehood. And he was equally unwilling to return the West Bank to Jordan. "Did we send our sons into battle to establish another Arab state, or to give an Arab state part of the land of Israel, so that we can have an enclave within the land of Israel from which it's possible to shoot at Tel Aviv?" he asked.[44]

On the opposite end of the spectrum were Zalman Aranne, minister of education and culture; Pinhas Sapir, minister of finance; Ya'akov Shimshon Shapira, minister of justice; and Eliyahu Sasson, minister of police. All of them wanted to return the West Bank to Jordan in exchange for peace. The Damascus-born Sasson had spent years negotiating secretly with Arabs, including King Abdullah, and knew that his judgment regarding Arab politics carried special weight. He urged his colleagues to negotiate with Hussein, whom he regarded as the most realistic of all the Arab leaders.[45] Aranne and Sapir, both veteran Mapainiks of Eshkol's generation, warned that prolonged entanglement with the West Bank would harm Israel's democratic character, economy, and international image. "Ha-kadosh barukh-hu [the Holy One blessed be He] has done us a great kindness and given us something called Hussein," Aranne joked.[46] Shapira, though he hailed from the National Religious Party, did not see Israel's conquest of the West Bank as a harbinger of messianic times. At a time when imperial powers were in retreat throughout the world, Shapira argued, Israel had no business acquiring colonies of its own.

The rest of the Israeli cabinet did not want to return the West Bank to Jordan or annex it. A small plurality of ministers, including Eshkol, Dayan, and Allon, wanted to place the West Bank under some form of Palestinian self-rule, allowing Israel to keep a strategic foothold there without assuming full responsibility for its population. They hoped to prevent the West Bank from ever being linked to the wider Arab world again. An Israeli-Jordanian peace treaty, argued Gahal's Yosef Sapir, "would not be worth the paper that it's written on" as long as "the nature of the Jordanian state" could change. Israel could never rule out the possibility that Hussein could fall and Jordan would merge with another Arab state, argued Minister of Welfare Yosef Burg. Israel would have to accept the "political and social difficulties of keeping the population without citizenship within the state of Israel" while exploring "different types of independent administration."[47]

It was Minister of Labor Yigal Allon who argued most passionately against giving the West Bank back to Jordan. For the former war hero and longtime opponent of Ben-Gurion's strategy, the 1967 war affirmed that he had been right not to give up his dream of conquering the West Bank. Had Israel conquered the West Bank in 1948, Allon proclaimed, "it's doubtful that war would have been necessary in 1956 or today." If Israel wanted to assure its future security, he said, "the last thing [it should do] is return one inch of the West Bank." Allon scorned the idea of giving up the West Bank for peace with Hussein, "a flesh-and-blood phenomenon, who will live for a maximum of sixty years, if he doesn't take a bullet in the meantime."[48]

Like his colleagues, Allon warned that Jordan might fall into the clutches of more radical rulers, allow other Arab armies to enter, or merge with another Arab state. "Today it's Hussein, tomorrow it'll be [former prime minister Sulayman al-] Nabulsi, two days from now some Syrian will rule over them," he predicted. But Allon added a worry of his own: Hussein's successor would likely sign "a defense pact with the USSR or China." "The combination of the West Bank with stronger Arab forces and international support—that's very dangerous," he warned.[49] Though Allon did not refer directly to Israel's nuclear program, his remarks hinted at how the Arabs could effectively neutralize Israel's atomic deterrent through pacts with nuclear-armed superpowers. It was an argument that undoubtedly resonated with the several ministers in the cabinet who feared that the Soviets might intervene militarily in the Middle East.

The solution, Allon argued, was for Israel to annex strategically important, sparsely populated parts of the West Bank. He thought Israel should annex Jerusalem, most of the Hebron hills, and a strip of territory between seven and eight kilometers wide along the length of the Jordan Valley. By annexing these areas, he asserted, Israel could cut the West Bank off from its Arab hinterland. Any Arab army advancing through the East Bank would have to break through a fortified defensive line running along the Jordan River. To consolidate Israel's hold over the Jordan Valley, Allon added, the government should encourage Jewish settlement there. According to Allon, Israel could do all of this without taking responsibility for the West Bank's Arabs. He thought that the bulk of the Palestinians, who lived on the West Bank's central mountain ridge, could be offered an "independent Arab state . . . swallowed and surrounded by Israeli territory . . . even independent in its foreign policy."[50]

Though Allon acknowledged that such an entity was far from what the West Bank Palestinians would want, he brushed off the possibility that they would later threaten Israel. The important thing, he argued, was to get the Americans and the Palestinians to accept his plan before it was too late. If Israel did not move immediately, he said, "the shock of conquest will wear off, the despair and frustration with Arab leaders will pass, and an Arab nationalist movement will get started. What we can get done with Arab leaders today, we will not be able to do in two years."[51] But the cabinet did not vote on Allon's or anyone else's plan. After days of debate, Eshkol's deeply divided government voted simply to leave the fate of the West Bank open for further discussion.

Thus, Eban returned to the United States unable to tell the Americans what Israel could offer Jordan in return for peace. When the Israeli foreign minister met Rusk on June 21, he revealed that Israel would be willing to return Sinai and the Golan to Egypt and Syria, and planned to annex Gaza and resettle most of its refugees. But when Rusk asked what Israel planned to do with the West Bank, Eban could only allude to contacts with local Palestinians. This was not what Rusk wanted to hear. The Israelis might be angry with Hussein, he warned, but they "should not sell him short."[52] When Eban met with McGeorge Bundy soon afterward, the president's advisor likewise argued that Israel should negotiate with Hussein. Bundy pointedly warned Eban that the United States would oppose the creation of a Palestinian state, and would not provide such an entity with aid.[53] Eban now believed that Israel should negotiate with Hussein, if only to keep the Americans on its side. "I have the impression that we can improve our position in Washington and London as well as Tehran if we agree to establish contact with Hussein, even without reaching an immediate agreement," he wrote to Eshkol.[54]

Eshkol did not know how to take the Americans' pro-Hashemite advice. The prime minister had not received any official guidance about how to handle the West Bank issue, and felt personally conflicted about both the "Jordanian option" and the future of the occupied territories as a whole. Though he claimed to have a "soft spot" for the Hashemite family, he shared Allon's view that Israel should grant the Palestinians autonomy while keeping strategically important, sparsely populated territory for itself.[55] Even before the war ended, he had worried aloud about the dangers that could arise from prolonged occupation. He doubted that Israel would ever receive enough Jewish immigrants to absorb the occupied territories and preserve a Jewish majority, and he thought that prolonged occupation could harm the Israeli economy. And yet Eshkol was clearly not immune to the euphoria felt by so many of his countrymen. By June 8, he was speaking of the "liberation of the West Bank" to his fellow Mapai members.[56] "For the first time since the establishment of the State, Jews pray at the Western Wall, the relic of our holy Temple and our historic past, and at Rachel's Tomb. For the first time in our generation, Jews can pray at the Cave of Machpela in Hebron, the city of the Patriarchs. The prophecy has been fulfilled: 'There is recompense for the work, the sons have returned to their borders,'" he proclaimed to the Knesset.[57]

Thus, Eshkol responded to the Johnson administration's call for Israeli-Jordanian negotiations by doing what he did best. The prime minister chose to keep his options open, delegate hard thinking to others, and block outside pressure. At Eshkol's request, Ya'akov Herzog put together a small group of Mossad, Defense Ministry, and Foreign Ministry officials to consult with Palestinian notables and then recommend what to do about the West Bank and the Gaza Strip.[58] Shortly thereafter, Herzog flew to London to meet with Hussein, who had just finished meeting with President Johnson and his advisors in Washington.[59]

Hussein and Herzog convened at Emmanuel Herbert's house on July 2. Unlike their prewar meetings, when both men had arrived eager to cooperate against Nasser, this time they shared no common purpose. Not only did Herzog have no official position that he could present to the king, but he did not personally believe that Israel should give the West Bank back to Jordan. The deeply religious Herzog viewed Israel's victory as an act of God, and would subsequently become a fervent advocate of Jewish settlement in the West Bank.[60] As for Hussein, he still had not decided whether to give up on the United Nations and negotiate directly with Israel.

The meeting thus served mainly as an opportunity for the two men to test each other's moods. Herzog stated that his government had not planned to attack Jordan, and had been shocked when Hussein joined the Arab coalition. Hussein responded by describing how he felt after Samu', and denied that the Arabs had really wanted war. "With the Arabs, words do not have their ordinary meaning. The threats meant nothing. There had been no cooperation, no joint planning for attack," he said.[61]

Both Herzog and Hussein spoke of a deeper psychological gap between Arabs and Israelis. Arab leaders, Herzog said, saw the Zionist movement as "an artificial movement without basic roots." They did not understand that centuries of persecution had led Jews to feel responsible for one another; nor did they understand "the undying attachment of the Jews to the land of Israel."[62]

"What you have said earlier about the historic link with the land I have understood for some time now; others have not," Hussein answered. "This is the most difficult point for Arabs to accept. Our basic problem now is how to maintain Arab identity in the area. Not only you have rights. We also have rights. Do not push us into a corner."[63]

Both men, however, were vague about what their governments would do next. Herzog spoke hazily of his preference for "economic union . . . leading to a confederation," but emphasized that he had no power to negotiate. Hussein indicated that he would be willing to reach a separate peace with Israel, claiming that if the Arab governments failed to formulate a common policy, "each country individually would be free to act as it wished." But as for what an Israeli-Jordanian settlement would entail, Hussein said little, except that it would have to be a peace of "dignity and honor."[64]

When Herzog returned to Israel, he met with Eshkol and Mossad chief Meir Amit, and recommended that Israel mobilize its contacts in Morocco, Tunisia, Libya, and Iran to back Hussein if he chose to negotiate. The purpose of doing so would not be to achieve Israeli-Jordanian peace, but to avoid pressure at the United Nations. "If a split develops within the Arab world on this issue, it will strengthen our position," Herzog summed up, "as well as the chances that international pressure for withdrawal without real peace will weaken." Eshkol approved Herzog's proposal.[65] The prime minister clearly felt no need to pursue serious negotiations with Jordan so long as his cabinet remained divided, the "Palestinian option" remained open, and the debate in New York continued.

"A MAJOR ACT OF COURAGE"

By the time Hussein met with Herzog in London, he must have felt quite hopeless. On June 27, the Israeli Knesset voted to extend Israeli "law, jurisdiction, and administration" to East Jerusalem.[66] By doing so, the Israelis effectively annexed the demographic and economic center of the West Bank, and there was no telling what they would do with the rest of the area. What was certain was that the United Nations was unlikely to force the IDF out of the West Bank before Israel absorbed more of it. During his talks with Johnson and his advisors in Washington and New York, Hussein begged for the United States to vote for a nonaligned resolution that called for Israel to withdraw immediately and unconditionally from the occupied territories. With Johnson looking on, Bundy and Undersecretary of State Nicholas Katzenbach bluntly informed the king that the administration would not force Israel to pull back without peace.[67] Clearly, Suez would not repeat itself. If Hussein wanted to get the West Bank back, he needed to show the Americans that he was willing to talk to the Israelis.

To negotiate, the king needed permission from his fellow Arab leaders, and on July 10, he went to Cairo to get it. Unlike the last time he and Nasser had met, Hussein was tough, direct, and demanding. The king told Nasser that the war had been uniquely disastrous for Jordan, which had "lost half of its being after building it from nothing." If the Arab governments did not show some flexibility, Hussein added, there was no way that the United Nations would force Israel to withdraw.[68]

To the king's pleasant surprise, Nasser agreed to allow Jordan to resort to diplomacy in order to recover the West Bank. The Egyptian president vowed to regain his own land by force, but recognized that Hussein could not follow the same path. Since the West Bank Palestinians were incapable of waging a "useful struggle" and Jordan was dependent on US aid, Hussein would have to negotiate. Nasser had only two conditions: that Hussein not negotiate directly with Israel, and that he not sign a treaty with the Jewish state.[69]

When Hussein returned to Amman, he confidently told the US and British ambassadors that he was ready for "a unilateral settlement with Israel." Hussein claimed that he wanted "to be able to live in peace and to develop Jordan along economic, educational and other lines of peace and reason." If he failed, he would feel that he had "done his best to avert [war] and would abdicate." The king indicated that he would agree to minor border modifications, but insisted that East Jerusalem be given back to Jordan. Hussein also wanted the Israelis to consider giving him the Gaza Strip so that Jordan would have an outlet to the Mediterranean Sea.[70]

Hussein had timed his peace overture to coincide with new and promising developments in New York. American and Soviet diplomats had begun drafting a joint resolution in hopes of breaking the impasse at the United Nations. Hussein hoped the superpowers would force Arab governments to put "an end to their state of belligerency with Israel," giving him diplomatic cover for a bilateral deal.[71] There were also signs that the United Nations might force Israel to reverse course on Jerusalem.

On July 14, the General Assembly voted by a large majority to condemn Israel's de facto annexation of the eastern half of the city. Hussein now pressed US and British diplomats hard on the Jerusalem question. "Israeli sovereignty over all Jerusalem," he told Burns, "would bring out the worst in the way of religious rivalry and fanaticism and would plant the seed of future conflict in the area."[72] The king obviously hoped that by showing that he wanted peace, he would encourage the Americans to compromise with the Soviets and undo Israel's Jerusalem decision before it became an established fact.

For a moment it seemed like Hussein's efforts might succeed. Rusk informed Eban of the king's initiative—calling it "a major act of courage"—and suggested that Eshkol announce that "administrative arrangements recently placed in effect" in Jerusalem were only temporary.[73] Typically, Eshkol played up his domestic political problems in order to deflect US pressure, telling Barbour that he had "stretched his cabinet like a rubber band" over the Holy City.[74] Eban played the direct negotiations card, telling Rusk that if Hussein wanted peace, he should appoint representatives to meet with Israeli officials.[75] But if Israel's foreign minister hoped that the king would reject his offer, he was mistaken. On July 19, the CIA informed the Israeli government that Hussein was willing to meet Israeli representatives for talks in Europe.

Eshkol was perturbed by the news. If he tried to delay a meeting with Hussein, the Johnson administration might conclude that Israel could not make a decision about the West Bank. The Americans would then try to force Israel to decide, and his cabinet would tear itself apart. Eban wanted to meet with Hussein, but Herzog and 'Adi Yafeh, Eshkol's private secretary, advised Eshkol against letting him do so. If Hussein wanted to know the Israeli cabinet's position on the West Bank, they noted, Eban could not just plead ignorance. Yet when Herzog suggested that Eshkol could meet with Hussein himself, Eshkol shot down the idea. How could he meet with Hussein, he asked, without consulting Dayan?[76] The possibility of a clash with his formidable defense minister was apparently too much for Eshkol to handle, even for the sake of a meeting with an Arab head of state.

For a brief moment, it seemed as though the Americans and the Soviets might force Eshkol's hand anyway. On July 21, the US and Soviet UN delegations agreed on a draft resolution and presented the final text to Israeli and Arab diplomats. The Israelis recoiled from the draft. Eban described it as a collection of "vague formulas which put the emphasis on withdrawal, without obligating the Arabs to do deeds."[77] But in the end, the Israelis were saved by the Arab bloc, whose delegates unanimously rejected the resolution. The USSR withdrew its cosponsorship of the draft, and it was never put to a vote.[78] The General Assembly voted to adjourn the special session that same day.[79]

The Arab rejection of the US-USSR draft robbed Hussein of an opportunity to drive a wedge between the United States and Israel and win back the West Bank. At the end of July, the king told Burns that "his own position was too weak to try to undertake bilateral negotiations with the Israelis at the moment." Better, the king thought, not to negotiate for three or four months. "Who knows?" Hussein asked. "Nasser may crack before then and be forced to reach a settlement with the Israelis, in which case the danger of my doing so would be immeasurably reduced."[80] Disappointed, US officials had no choice but to accept Hussein's decision. If the king would not negotiate, there was not much the Johnson administration could do for him. "As long as the Arabs are adamant, I doubt if we can or should make the Israeli view of Jerusalem or the West Bank into a federal case," McGeorge Bundy told Johnson. "We can't tell the Israelis to give things away to people who won't even bargain with them. We may well be headed toward a de facto settlement on the present ceasefire lines."[81]

For the time being, a "de facto settlement on the present ceasefire lines" satisfied the Israelis. When Eban returned from New York at the end of July, he informed his Mapai colleagues that a "positive impasse, unlike in 1956" prevailed at the United Nations. The cabinet did not need to make any decisions about the future of the West Bank. Israel, said Eban, should simply wait for Hussein to take the initiative. Golda Meir agreed. "Why do we need to talk?" she asked. "Nothing's pressing on us. Let Hussein do the talking."[82]

Only Yigal Allon seemed disappointed with the way the special session had ended. Israel, he complained, had missed an opportunity to get the Americans to agree to its ideas, and might later have to return the entire West Bank to Hussein.[83] Of course, Allon's disappointment was personal, since the ideas he wanted the Americans to hear were his own. By this time, he had condensed his vision for the West Bank into a nine-point plan, which he distributed to his fellow ministers.[84] The cabinet did not vote on the so-called "Allon Plan." As Eshkol later told Allon, there was no point in breaking up the national unity government for the sake of a resolution that would not pass.[85] Additionally, by the end of July, the "Palestinian option," one of the Allon Plan's basic pillars, no longer seemed realistic.

THE PALESTINIAN OPTION IN ECLIPSE

By July 1967, Israeli officials had grown skeptical about reaching a settlement with the West Bank Palestinians. The Johnson administration strongly opposed the idea. It was also clear that the West Bank's economy would likely collapse if it were isolated from Jordan. "In the West Bank there is almost no industry; the residents almost never sustained themselves. They were always practically a province of the East Bank," Uzi Narkiss told the Knesset Foreign Affairs and Defense Committee.[86] Though the Israelis did not want West Bankers to feel dependent on Jordan, they realized that they could not cut the ties between the two banks, either. Ongoing trade between the East and West Banks, Narkiss told the General Staff, "lowers the tension ... and our job is to lower the tension."[87]

Mainly, the Israelis lost interest in the Palestinian option because prominent West Bankers no longer wanted to negotiate with them. Immediately after the war, noted Moshe Sasson and Shaul Bar-Hayim, who handled the occupied territories policy committee's contacts with West Bank notables, Palestinian leaders had been willing to negotiate with Israel. Now, those willing to discuss a separate peace were primarily "collaborators and traditional quislings." According to Sasson and Bar-Hayim, "memories of our withdrawal from Gaza in 1956, the lack of quiet on the borders, Russian naval activity, and the ongoing discussions in the UN" had overtaken the shock of defeat. Palestinian notables now had to consider what would happen to them if they flirted with Israel and ended up back under Jordanian rule. Sasson and Bar-Hayim noted that West Bank notables did not want to jeopardize their family, property, business interests, and bank accounts on the East Bank, or their access to remittances from abroad. The two Israelis concluded that the "decisive majority" of West Bank notables would not want to negotiate with Israel so long as there remained a chance of an Israeli-Jordanian accord.[88]

When the members of Eshkol's occupied territories policy committee drew up their recommendations for how Israel should deal with the West Bank, most of them thought that Israel should opt for the Jordanian, not the Palestinian, option. Yet they did not think that Jordan should be allowed full sovereignty over the West Bank. Instead they called for an Israeli-Jordanian confederation, or joint rule over the West Bank. Within this framework, Israel would have the upper hand on just about every issue. The IDF would stay on the West Bank to make sure that no Arab forces entered it. Israel and Jordan would sign a mutual defense pact that would "permit the IDF to march to the East Bank in the event of a hostile change that undermines the peace agreement." Israel would also be the senior partner in Jerusalem. Hussein would have some sort of guardianship over the city's Islamic holy sites, but no political role there. At the same time, the committee expected Jordan to help resolve the Palestinian refugee problem and prop up the West Bank's economy.[89]

In short, while the occupied territories policy committee called for talks with Hussein, they too hoped to extend an Israeli security umbrella over the West Bank without taking responsibility for the people who lived there. The chiefs of Israel's intelligence services, who approved the committee's proposals, acknowledged that there was virtually no chance that Hussein would accept such demands. The way to change his mind, they thought, was to convince him that Israel's occupation was "impossible to undermine."[90] Over the next few months, the Israelis would become even more convinced that they needed to stand fast as the Palestinians tried and failed to dislodge them from the West Bank.

THE BATTLE FOR PALESTINIAN SUPPORT

For King Hussein, who watched the West Bank leadership closely, waning Palestinian interest in a separate peace was a heartening trend at an otherwise frustrating time. Since June, the Jordanian government had worked hard to thwart an Israeli-Palestinian settlement. "Every one of you is still a Jordanian citizen and will remain so," Prime Minister Jum'a warned the West Bankers in a speech on June 21. Palestinians who acted "in service of the aims of aggression" would "be punished to the utmost degree."⁹¹ Lest the United States consider the Palestinian option, Jum'a assured US diplomats that "only a handful of Palestinian notables were willing to lend their support to promoting an autonomous West Bank."⁹²

By the end of July, Hussein could take comfort in the fact that the West Bank elite were moving back into his camp. On July 22, former members of Jordanian Jerusalem's municipal council, led by ex-mayor Ruhi al-Khatib, announced that they would not join an Israeli-run municipal government.⁹³ Two days later, a group of Jerusalem notables and Islamic jurists petitioned the military government, decrying the merger of East and West Jerusalem and accusing Israel of violating their religious rights.⁹⁴ Prominent West Bank women, professional associations of lawyers, doctors, and engineers, and Muslim clerics issued similar statements during the weeks that followed. Other groups of notables from Hebron and Bethlehem likewise proclaimed their loyalty to Hussein and their commitment to the unity of the two banks.⁹⁵

There is no clear evidence that the Jordanian regime instigated these Palestinian protests. Indeed, well-informed US officials believed that the West Bank notables had acted independently in order "to win support for what they conceive[d] to be King Hussein's objectives."⁹⁶ Nevertheless, Hussein tried to capitalize on Palestinian discontent. In conversations with US diplomats, the king and Jum'a played up rising West Bank tensions, warning that they could undermine East Bank support for a settlement and encourage radical Arab governments to sponsor guerrilla warfare. The only solution to the "deteriorating situation," Jum'a proclaimed, was a "Security Council resolution coupling Israeli withdrawal with an end to belligerency."⁹⁷ Radio Amman broadcast the West Bankers' statements over Jordan's airwaves. To keep Palestinians from being co-opted by Israel, the Jordanian government began paying the salaries of its former civil servants, judges, and lawyers.⁹⁸

At the same time, Hussein feared that West Bank unrest could spin out of control and destabilize his regime. Privately, he worried that violent West Bank resistance would provoke a harsh Israeli crackdown that could force him to retaliate and risk another military catastrophe.⁹⁹ While Hussein encouraged civil resistance to Israeli occupation, he also quietly sought to keep Syrian-trained militants from infiltrating the occupied territories.[100] And though the king urged the West Bankers not to cooperate with the Israelis, he grudgingly worked with Eshkol's government in order to stem the flow of refugees to the East Bank. After some initial resistance, Hussein allowed Jordanian Red Crescent officials to meet secretly with Israeli diplomats to negotiate how refugees could return.[101] To keep the West Bank economy afloat, the Jordanian government agreed to help residents of the occupied territories receive money from abroad, and allowed the Palestinians to keep bringing produce and other goods to the East Bank.[102] In the fall, the king quietly agreed to allow Israel to rebuild the bridges over the Jordan River, permitting people and goods to flow freely between the two banks once again.[103]

Hussein's functional cooperation with Israel, culminating in his acceptance of its "open bridges" policy, certainly helped Jordan maintain its ties to the West Bank and prevent further Palestinian flight. Yet the king's compromises also validated the opinions of Israelis who thought he needed to be convinced that Israel would not budge.

At the end of July, Israeli policymakers had feared a "civil rebellion" in the West Bank.[104] Realizing that the Jordanians would exploit harsh Israeli action for propaganda purposes, Dayan resolved not to confront the Palestinians "face to face," but to "not let anarchy reign" either.[105] Dayan had Anwar al-Khatib and a few other prominent signatories of anti-Israeli petitions sent into "internal exile" within Israel, but did not crack down hard on those engaged in nonviolent resistance. Confident that time was on Israel's side, Dayan responded to those who refused to cooperate with the military government by ignoring them. He notified striking West Bank judges that they were free not to work, but that other judges, perhaps Israeli ones, would be employed in their place.[106] By the end of August, nearly all the Jordanian civil servants who had been offered the opportunity to work for Israel had taken it.[107] The Israelis believed that Hussein and the West Bankers were learning that they needed Israel's day-to-day cooperation more than Israel needed theirs. By August 14, Aharon Yariv thought that Jordanian efforts to incite Palestinian resistance were slackening. "The reason is clear," he said. "They have an interest in having the refugees return."[108]

The final chapter in Jordan's efforts to mobilize the West Bankers against Israel's military government unfolded that September. At the beginning of the academic year, Palestinian students and teachers went on strike. Shortly thereafter, the Jordanian government encouraged the West Bankers to expand the school protests into a general strike, timed to coincide with the opening of the UN General Assembly. Dayan was not greatly concerned by the school strike, but the prospect of mass Palestinian resistance was another matter. The Israeli defense minister did not want to have to break up large civilian demonstrations and draw unwelcome attention from abroad.[109]

In the end, Dayan's fears of an all-out West Bank rebellion proved unfounded. Only Nablus, historically a stronghold of opposition to foreign rule, fully observed the general strike. Rather than confront the Nabulsis head on and hand Hussein a propaganda victory, the military government selectively targeted individual notables and neighborhoods, and sought to isolate Nablus from the rest of the West Bank. The Israelis closed the nearby Damiya Bridge to traffic, directed Israeli wholesalers to other West Bank cities, and froze government lending to local residents. By early October, Nablus mayor Hamdi Kan'an gave up, promising Dayan that he would end the school strike if the military government lifted sanctions against his city. Not until the outbreak of the intifada in 1987 would the West Bank's Palestinians again attempt collective resistance on such a major scale.[110]

For the Israelis, the Palestinian "civil rebellion" in the West Bank demonstrated that they needed to behave as though they felt no pressure to withdraw anytime soon. To soothe Palestinian discontent, the military government would allow West Bankers to maintain economic ties with Jordan and would try not to involve itself in their day-to-day lives. But Israel would not tolerate displays of civil disobedience and would not permit the West Bank elite to unite against the occupation. And Israel also needed to show Hussein and the Palestinians that it was determined to keep vital portions of the West Bank no matter what.

Thus, on August 21, with the West Bank simmering with discontent, Moshe Dayan presented his plan for the West Bank to the cabinet. The defense minister thought Israel should build five military bases on the West Bank's central mountain ridge, adjoining civilian settlements. "We must decide now. Otherwise we will eventually regret that we did not do so," he warned. "Once these conditions are ensured, it will be possible to think about solutions for the Arab population." Israel, in other words, needed to unilaterally consolidate its hold over the high ground in the West Bank before it was too late. Hussein and the Palestinians would have no choice but to come to terms with new realities.

As with the Allon Plan, the cabinet was too divided to vote on Dayan's proposal for allowing Israeli civilians to settle in the West Bank. But this time, the cabinet did something new: it took a separate vote on Dayan's proposal to build bases, which passed with eleven votes. Only five ministers voted against what Pinhas Sapir disparagingly called "not deciding on the one hand and creating facts on the other." Eshkol, despite his rivalry with Dayan, supported his call for bases, which he thought was a good way to put pressure on Hussein.[111]

As it turned out, "creating facts" of a military kind quickly led to the creation of other "facts" on political and ideological grounds. Since June, Eshkol and his colleagues had been sought out by the former residents of Gush 'Etsiyon, a bloc of kibbutzim that the Jordanians had captured in 1948, massacring many Jewish fighters in the process. Many of the survivors and their children now wanted to rebuild Jewish settlements on the same site.[112] While Eshkol may have hesitated to allow Dayan to take credit for establishing civilian settlements in the West Bank, he proved unable to resist the opportunity to do so himself. Shortly after the cabinet discussed Dayan's plan for the West Bank, Eshkol asked the Foreign Ministry's legal counsel, Theodore Meron, for his opinion regarding the legality of settlement in the occupied territories. "My conclusion," Meron replied, "is that civilian settlement in the administered territories contravenes the explicit provisions of the Fourth Geneva Convention."[113] Eshkol was not dissuaded. On September 24, he told the cabinet that he had approved the establishment of a "NAHAL outpost" at Gush 'Etsiyon, denying that this conflicted with the government's previous decision. NAHAL, after all, was an IDF brigade in which soldiers combined military service with agricultural work; its numerous settlements within Israel proper usually doubled as military bases. But the outpost established at Gush 'Etsiyon was in fact a civilian settlement populated by young religious Zionists, many of them from families that had survived the massacre of 1948. Eshkol insisted on calling it a "NAHAL outpost" in order to dodge the issue of the illegality of civilian settlement in the West Bank.[114]

By establishing the settlement at Gush 'Etsiyon, Eshkol acted against the judgment of his legal advisors and with scant consideration for how the international community would react. Still, he could not resist the urge to reverse one of 1948's most traumatic defeats and one-up Dayan in the process. Not for the last time, the Israeli government made a decision of tremendous strategic importance based on the political calculations and personal rivalries of powerful politicians. When Eban complained that settling Gush 'Etsiyon undermined his efforts at the United Nations, Eshkol brushed him off. "There is also a public in Israel," he informed Eban, "and it has a pulse, mood, needs."[115]

FROM KHARTOUM TO RESOLUTION 242

Eshkol might have wanted his fellow Israelis' approval more than he feared the wrath of the international community, but the possibility that the United Nations might compel Israel to relinquish the occupied territories never left his mind. By the fall of 1967, the Israelis faced yet another Jordanian effort to put international pressure on them. Since July, Hussein had hoped that the Arabs would finally show some interest in a political settlement, allowing the superpowers to act on their behalf. At the end of August, the king got his wish when the Arab League convened for a summit in Khartoum.

At Khartoum, Ahmad al-Shuqayri ruefully recalled, "oil triumphed over the Arabs."[116] The summit marked the end of the long Saudi-Egyptian struggle for Arab leadership, in favor of the Saudis. Nasser finally agreed to withdraw unconditionally from Yemen. No longer afraid of the Egyptian president, the Saudis offered to bankroll him, pledging to contribute £95 million in oil revenues to Egypt and another £40 million to Jordan. Nasser accordingly proposed a strategy that reflected his new benefactors' caution rather than the militancy of his former Syrian and Palestinian allies. For now, Nasser said, "we have to resort to the political solution until we become capable of resorting to the military solution." If the UN route failed, he added, the Arab League should allow King Hussein to reach a settlement with Israel through the United States. Otherwise, Nasser warned, Israel would absorb both the West Bank and Jerusalem.[117]

Nasser's call for Arab diplomacy proved far too much for al-Shuqayri. The PLO chairman proclaimed that the Arabs would never get back the West Bank via the United Nations, "not in months and not in years and not in centuries!" On the final day of the Khartoum conference, al-Shuqayri stormed out.[118] The rest of the Arab leaders, however, lined up in favor of political action. Unlike at the pre-1967 summits, the Arab League did not call for war with Israel; the closest thing was a resolution stressing the "need to strengthen military preparation to face all eventualities." But the Arabs refused to come to terms with Israel's existence. The Arab leaders made it clear that they would not accept Israel's legitimacy by adopting three "no" resolutions—"no peace with Israel, no recognition of Israel, and no negotiations with her."[119] In theory, the "three nos" left room for half measures—nonbelligerency agreements, indirect negotiations, and so on. Still, the Khartoum consensus came nowhere close to the Israeli position, with its emphasis on direct negotiations and contractual peace.

Yet Hussein regarded the summit as a triumph. Khartoum, he told US officials, was a "complete victory for the moderates, exceeding all expectations." "If the West nurtures this," he exclaimed, "real peace is within [our] grasp."[120] With Egypt on his side, Hussein hoped to get the superpowers to revive their draft resolution and compel the Israelis to withdraw. At the end of September, Hussein visited Moscow to coordinate Soviet and Arab policy before the next round of UN discussions.[121] After returning to Jordan, the king informed President Johnson that he and Nasser would accept a revised version of the US-Soviet resolution, and had received Soviet approval for the idea. "Sir," he implored Johnson, "I really hope that I might be right in feeling that the United States government has not made her choice to back Israel and to forsake her other friends and interests in the area."[122]

Hussein, however, was not the only one heartened by Khartoum. Much of the existing historiography maintains that the "three nos" hardened the Eshkol government's position, and this was certainly how the Israeli government chose to present matters at the time.[123] "The stances of the Arab heads of state," Eshkol publicly stated on September 3, "strengthen Israel's determination to abide by its decision not to return to conditions that allow its ill-wishers to undermine its security, and to plot against her sovereignty and the essence of her existence."[124] But privately, Israeli policymakers felt relieved that the Arabs had not chosen to act more flexibly. "No one among us is frustrated that the Arabs rejected the idea of peace negotiations," Ya'akov Herzog wrote in his diary. "It's becoming increasingly clear that the present situation, so long as it persists, is in our favor. There is no serious chance of renewed war.... There is no sign that the Russians are interested in escalating tensions. In the meantime, we hold on to the territories, and we have the leisure to think and plan and maybe even act."[125] The Israelis did not so much harden their position after Khartoum as use the Arabs' rhetoric to justify decisions they already wanted to make. Eshkol's decision to resettle Gush 'Etsiyon was the obvious case in point.

What worried the Israelis was not the persistence of Arab rejectionism, but the reopening of the General Assembly later that month. Israel had emerged triumphant from the previous round of UN discussions, and its leaders wanted to prevent another bout from ending with an imposed settlement. "The objective now," Eban told the cabinet, "is to get through the regular Assembly safely."[126] Israel, he thought, could use the "three nos" of Khartoum to convince the world that Israel was not responsible for diplomatic deadlock.[127] Since July, Eban and his diplomats had been urging US officials not to revive the US-Soviet resolution.[128] Now they redoubled their efforts, arguing that Khartoum proved that the Arabs were unready for peace.

Privately, US officials did not accept the Israeli government's gloss on the Khartoum resolutions and worried about mounting Israeli intransigence. Johnson told British officials that he "believed in the genuineness of the new mood of moderation displayed by the Arabs at Khartoum," and that if the Israelis' attitudes kept "hardening," they might "get themselves into a corner."[129] But the president and his advisors continued to accept the Israeli argument that a return to the armistice regime was unacceptable. "The United States Government played a central role in bringing about Israeli withdrawal in 1957, but at that time no such mutually accepted basis for coexistence was established," Johnson wrote to Saudi Arabia's King Faysal. "Those arrangements accordingly did not endure. I do not think it possible to travel the same road again."[130] While the Americans might have discerned a slight change in the Arab stance after Khartoum, it was a matter of too little, too late. As Rusk told Johnson, there had been "considerable movement on the Arab side but not enough."[131] The new interpretation of the US-Soviet draft resolution that emerged from Soviet-Arab diplomacy particularly displeased US officials. "[The Soviets] want a loose resolution calling for Israeli withdrawal which states Arab obligations loosely enough that they can be disregarded," Walt Rostow complained.[132] It was time to draw up a new resolution, Rostow argued, with the goal of giving the Arabs and the Israelis a text "which each party could, for the time being, interpret in his own way until they became gripped of a negotiating process via an intermediary."[133]

But by the time Hussein arrived in the United States for another visit that November, the Americans were worried that they were running out of time to push a suitable resolution on the Middle East through the Security Council.[134] Johnson's advisors were concerned that if they did not move quickly, the Soviets and the Egyptians might rally support for a resolution that Israel would reject. Arthur Goldberg, the US ambassador to the United Nations, did not want to "get into a tactical position of looking negative and defensive."[135] He and other US officials hoped to put forward their own draft in the Security Council, but needed some Arab support in order to muster a majority vote and prevent the USSR from using its veto. They saw Hussein as the solution: the king could convince the Egyptians and the Soviets to allow an American draft to pass. "If the king does not enter the fray," Rusk warned, "the snows will have fallen heavily before any resolution passes."[136]

Initially, the Jordanians demanded a resolution that called for Israeli withdrawal before the parties reached an agreement. Goldberg stood firm, telling Hussein that the "notion of instant peace is nonsense."[137] To mollify the king, Goldberg promised him that the United States would "support a return of the West Bank to Jordan with minor boundary rectifications" and seek "a role" for Jordan in Jerusalem.[138] Having gotten nowhere with the Americans since June, Hussein finally decided to support a more ambiguous resolution in the Security Council with the hope that the Americans would be tougher on the Israelis in private. After all, he told Lord Caradon, Britain's UN ambassador, he was "concerned more with what happens on the ground at home than in words in New York."[139]

With the king now onboard, Goldberg handed his draft off to the British. The US diplomat's resolution, which was submitted by Lord Caradon and adopted by the Security Council as Resolution 242 on November 22, was a case study in what diplomats call "constructive ambiguity." While it called for Israel to withdraw from "territories occupied in the recent conflict," it did not spell out how far Israel would withdraw or how a settlement would be attained.[140]

While Hussein and the Israelis would interpret Resolution 242 differently, they both regarded it as the end of postwar stocktaking. Hussein now believed that a US-brokered settlement was just around the corner. "This was not the end of the road," he told Goldberg, "but the beginning."[141] Meeting with Herzog in London on November 19, Hussein stated that "if the people of the Western Bank approached him, he would be free to enter into negotiations on his own and without seeking the agreement of other Arab states." The king wanted to know Israel's position on the West Bank: what were "the limits of the land?" he asked.[142] Herzog had no answer to this question, but his boss understood that Israel might need to find one soon. "I have pressed the government a number of times to reach a decision on our plans for the future of the territories and our conditions for peace, so that we can at least speak clearly with the Americans," Levi Eshkol complained to his cabinet that same day. "We have not reached that point, only alternating partial decisions. Soon enough, we'll be told that the Americans are waiting for our suggestions. We will need to give them something whole."[143]

NOTES

1. Editorial note, in Rosenthal, Yitzhak Rabin, 525.
2. Rosenak, "Religious Reactions," 215.
3. Segev, 1967: Israel, 551.
4. See Appendix A in Gazit, Carrot and the Stick, 297–299.
5. See, for example, Ya'akov Herzog diary, June 25 and July 14, 1967, ISA/A/4511/3; Haber, Ha-Yom tifrots milhamah, 272–274.
6. Amman to State, July 29, 1967, NA/RG59/DOSCF 1967–1969/POL 27-14 ARAB-ISR/SANDSTORM.
7. J. P. Tripp, "The Refugee Problem in Jordan," August 3, 1967, BNA/FCO 17/214.
8. Gazit, Carrot and the Stick, 48.

9. Mutawi, Jordan in the 1967 War, 164.

10. Hussein-Johnson memcon, June 28, 1967, FRUS, 1964–1968, 19: doc. 331.

11. General Staff minutes, June 19, 1967, IDFA/117/70/206. For US intelligence assessments that made similar arguments, see "Special Assessments on the Middle East Situation: King Husayn's Current Position," CIA memo, June 27, 1967, LBJL/NSF /Country Files/Middle East Crisis, box 110; and "Special Assessments on the Middle East Situation: Postwar Leadership of the Arab Bloc," CIA memo, August 1, 1967, LBJL/NSF/Country Files/Middle East Crisis, box 111.

12. Amman to State, July 28, 1967, FRUS, 1964–1968, 19: doc. 393.

13. Amman to State, October 17, 1967, NA/RG59/DOSCF 1967–1969/POL 27 ARAB-ISR.

14. Amman to State, June 10, 1967, NA/RG59/Lot Files/68D135, box 1.

15. See chapter 4 of this volume.

16. "Mu'atamar sahafi li-jalalat al-malik Husayn," June 19, 1967, in al-Watha'iq al-urduniyya, 1967, 88.

17. Mapai party secretariat minutes, September 14, 1967, LPA/2-24-1967-91.

18. Tel Aviv to State, June 13, 1967, FRUS, 1964–1968, 19: doc. 277. See also Jerusalem to Washington, June 13, 1967, ISA/FM/4078/5.

19. "Statement to the Knesset by Prime Minister Eshkol, 12 June 1967," Israel Ministry of Foreign Affairs,

http://www.mfa.gov.il/MFA/ForeignPolicy/MFADocuments/Yearbook1 /Pages/23%20Statement%20to%20the%20Knesset%20by%20Prime%20Minister%20Eshk.aspx.

20. See Eban to Eshkol, June 29, 1967, ISA/A/7938/10; as well as Dayan's remarks to the General Staff on July 3, 1967, quoted in editorial note, in Rosenthal, Yitzhak Rabin, 530. The General Staff and AMAN tended to be somewhat more skeptical about the prospect of Soviet intervention. Yariv, for example, thought that the USSR would threaten Israel "as in 1956" if war resumed and "Cairo were conquered," but would not otherwise be willing to risk confrontation with the United States. See General Staff minutes, July 31, 1967, IDFA/117/70/206.

21. Amman to State, June 10, 1967, LBJL/NSF/Country Files/Middle East Crisis, box 108.

22. State to White House, June 12, 1967, LBJL/NSF/Country Files/Middle East Crisis, box 108.

23. Ashton, King Hussein of Jordan, 121.

24. The text of Hussein's June 26 address to the General Assembly is available through the Official Document System of the United Nations, at http://www.un.org /ga/search/view_doc.asp?symbol=A/PV.1536.

25. Rostow to Johnson, June 7, 1967, FRUS, 1964–1968, 19: doc. 189.

26. NSC Special Committee meeting notes, June 13, 1967, FRUS, 1964–1968, 19: doc. 280.

27. NSC meeting notes, June 7, 1967, FRUS, 1964–1968, 19: doc. 197.

28. NSC Special Committee meeting notes, June 14, 1967, FRUS, 1964–1968, 19: doc. 287.

29. See, for example, Eugene Rostow's comments in Washington to FCO, June 27, 1967, BNA/PREM 13/1622.

30. NSC Special Committee meeting notes, June 12, 1967, FRUS, 1964–1968, 19: doc. 263.

31. Ibid.
32. "Address by President Johnson, 19 June 1967," Israel Ministry of Foreign Affairs, http://www.mfa.gov.il/MFA/ForeignPolicy/MFADocuments/Yearbook1/Pages/26%20Address%20by%20President%20Johnson-%2019%20June%201967.aspx.
33. Bundy to Johnson, June 21, 1967, FRUS, 1964–1968, 19: doc. 311.
34. Quoted in Golan, Milhamah be-shalosh hazitot, 258.
35. Raz, Bride and the Dowry, 103–125.
36. Cabinet minutes, June 11, 1967, ISA.
37. Harman to Eshkol, June 6, 1967, ISA/A/7920/3.
38. Sasson to director-general, undated, ISA/A/7920/3.
39. Gluska, Eshkol, 402.
40. Pedatzur, Nitsahon ha-mevukhah, 39–40.
41. Cabinet minutes, June 19, 1967, ISA.
42. Ibid.
43. Ya'akov Herzog diary, June 15, 1967, ISA/A/4511/3.
44. Cabinet minutes, June 19, 1967, ISA.
45. Cabinet minutes, June 18, 1967 (second session), ISA.
46. Ibid.
47. Cabinet minutes, June 19, 1967, ISA.
48. Ibid.
49. Ibid.
50. Ibid.
51. Ibid.
52. New York to State, June 22, 1967, FRUS, 1964–1968, 19: doc. 314; Jerusalem to European embassies, June 22, 1967, ISA/FM/4078/5.
53. Washington to Jerusalem, June 21, 1967, ISA/FM/4296/7.
54. New York to Jerusalem, June 22, 1967, ISA/FM/4078/5.
55. Eshkol's remarks to the Mapai secretariat, June 8, 1967, in Lammfromm and Tsoref, Levi Eshkol, 565; cabinet minutes, June 19, 1967, ISA.
56. Eshkol's remarks to the Mapai secretariat, June 8, 1967, in Lammfromm and Tsoref, Levi Eshkol, 565–569.
57. "Statement to the Knesset by Prime Minister Eshkol, 12 June 1967," Israel Ministry of Foreign Affairs,
http://www.mfa.gov.il/MFA/ForeignPolicy/MFADocuments/Yearbook1/Pages/23%20Statement%20to%20the%20Knesset%20by%20Prime%20Minister%20Eshk.aspx.
58. Herzog to director-general, June 26, 1967; Eshkol to Herzog et al., July 4, 1967, ISA/A/7921/2. The interagency committee included Moshe Sasson and Shaul Bar-Hayim of the Foreign Ministry, David Kimche of the Mossad, and Gen. Chaim Herzog, Ya'akov's brother and a senior Defense Ministry official. In the immediate aftermath of the war, Chaim Herzog had served as military governor of the West Bank.
59. Ya'akov Herzog diary, June 26, 1967, ISA/A/4511/3.
60. See especially Bar-Zohar, Yaacov Herzog, 298–299, 310.
61. Ya'akov Herzog, "Meeting with Charles on Sunday, July 2nd, from 8:10 P.M. to 9:45 P.M.," July 2, 1967, YHP.
62. Ibid.
63. Ibid.
64. Ibid.

65. Ya'akov Herzog diary, July 7, 1967, ISA/A/4511/3.
66. On the decision to merge East and West Jerusalem, see cabinet minutes, June 26, 1967, ISA; Wasserstein, Divided Jerusalem, 211–215.
67. Johnson-Hussein memcon, June 28, 1967, FRUS, 1964–1968, 19: doc. 331.
68. "Meeting in Cairo on 11 July 1967 of Presidents Nasir and Boumedienne and King Husayn," CIA cable, July 24, 1967, LBJL/NSF/Country Files/Middle East Crisis, box 110.
69. "Extracts from Cable from Ambassador Burns in Jordan," July 19, 1967, LBJL/NSF/Country Files/Middle East Crisis, box 113; "Meeting in Cairo on 11 July 1967 of Presidents Nasir and Boumedienne and King Husayn," CIA cable, July 24, 1967, LBJL/NSF/Country Files/Middle East Crisis, box 110. See also Fawzi, Harb al-thalath sanawat, 191–192.
70. Copy of Burns cable for Battle, July 13, 1967, LBJL/NSF/Country Files/Jordan, box 148. See also Amman to FCO, July 16, 1967, BNA/PREM 13/1622; and Khammash's comments on Gaza in Amman to State, July 18, 1967, NA/RG59/DOSCF 1967–1969/POL 27–14 ARAB-ISR SANDSTORM.
71. Amman to State, July 22, 1967, LBJL/NSF/Country Files/Middle East Crisis, box 113.
72. Ibid. See also Amman to FCO, July 17, 1967, BNA/PREM 13/1622.
73. State to New York, July 13, 1967, FRUS, 1964–1968, 19: doc. 360.
74. Tel Aviv to State, July 14, 1967, LBJL/NSF/Country Files/Middle East Crisis, box 113.
75. Rusk-Eban memcon, July 15, 1967, FRUS, 1964–1968, 19: doc. 367.
76. Ya'akov Herzog diary, July 19, 1967, ISA/A/4511/3.
77. Jerusalem to New York, July 21, 1967, ISA/FM/4078/7.
78. Ro'i, "Soviet Policy," 31–35.
79. Dishon, Middle East Record, 1967, 84.
80. Amman to State, July 28, 1967, FRUS, 1964–1968, 19: doc. 393.
81. Bundy to Johnson, July 31, 1967, FRUS, 1964–1968, 19: doc. 399.
82. Mapai political committee minutes, July 29, 1967, ISA/A/7921/2.
83. Ya'akov Herzog diary, July 30, 1967, ISA/A/4511/3.
84. For the text of Allon's plan, see "The Future of the Liberated Territories of the Western Land of Israel and Ways of Dealing with the Arab Refugee Problem," July 26, 1967, ISA/A/7921/2.
85. Yigal Allon oral history, ISA/A/5001/19.
86. KFADC minutes, June 28, 1967, ISA/A/8161/7.
87. General Staff minutes, July 17, 1967, IDFA/117/20/207.
88. Sasson and Bar-Hayim, "Summary of Impressions from Conversations with West Bank Notables, July 6–18, 1967," ISA/A/7921/2.
89. Special Interdepartmental Committee for Political Contacts in the Occupied Territories to the Prime Minister, July 20, 1967, ISA/A/7921/2.
90. Committee of Service Heads to the Prime Minister, July 27, 1967, ISA/A/7921/2.
91. "Bayan al-sayyid Sa'd Jum'a," June 21, 1967, in al-Watha'iq al-urduniyya, 1967, 97.
92. Amman to State, July 4, 1967, NA/RG 59/DOSCF 1967–69/POL 27 ARAB-ISR.

93. "Mudhakirrat majlis amanat al-quds," July 22, 1967, in al-Watha'iq al-urduniyya, 1967, 137–138.
94. "Mudhakirrat zu'ama al-dafa al-gharbiyya al-muslimin," July 24, 1967, in al-Watha'iq al-urduniyya, 1967, 139–142.
95. For the texts of these various statements, see al-Watha'iq al-urduniyya, 1967, 146–159, 175–176, 181–183.
96. Jerusalem to State, August 23, 1967, NA/RG59/DOSCF 1967–1969/POL 28 JORDAN.
97. Amman to State, July 28, 1967, FRUS, 1964–1968, 19: doc. 393; Amman to State, July 29, NA/RG59/DOSCF 1967–1969/POL 27–14 ARAB-ISR/SANDSTORM.
98. Jerusalem to State, August 23, 1967, NA/RG59/DOSCF 1967–1969/POL 28 JORDAN.
99. Amman to FCO, August 8, 1967, BNA/FCO 17/279.
100. These efforts were confirmed by Israeli intelligence sources. See, for example, David Carmon's remarks in Tel Aviv to State, September 6, 1967, NA/RG59/DOSCF 1967–1969/POL 27 ARAB-ISR; and Jerusalem to embassies, September 5, 1967, ISA/FM/4296/7.
101. Amman to State, July 31, 1967, LBJL/NSF/Country Files/Middle East Crisis, box 110; Yosef Tekoa, "Returning the Arabs to the West Bank: A Conversation with Jordan's Representative," undated, ISA/FM/3835/5; Jerusalem to posts, August 6, 1967, ISA/FM/3835/5.
102. Dishon, Middle East Record, 1967, 285; FM Research Division to Hillel, July 24, 1967, ISA/FM/4296/7.
103. On the development of the "open bridges" policy, see especially Gazit, Carrot and the Stick, 176–194.
104. See Sasson to Eban, undated (late July 1967), ISA/FM/4088/10; Ya'akov Herzog diary, July 25, 1967, ISA/A/4511/3.
105. Braun, Hotem ishi, 192.
106. Ben-Hurin to Foreign Minister, July 29, 1967, ISA/FM/4088/8.
107. Jerusalem to State, August 23, 1967, NA/RG59/DOSCF 1967–1969/POL 28 JORDAN.
108. General Staff minutes, August 14, 1967, IDFA/117/20/206.
109. Rafi party secretariat minutes, September 3, 1967, LPA/5-3-1967-24.
110. Gazit, Carrot and the Stick, 278–286.
111. Ya'akov Herzog diary, August 21, 1967, ISA/A/4511/3; "Notes on Moshe Dayan's Positions in Cabinet Meetings, June 1967–January 1969," unsigned, YLE.
112. Gorenberg, Accidental Empire, 103–109.
113. FM Legal Counsel to Foreign Minister, September 14, 1967; FM Legal Counsel to Yafeh, September 18, 1967, ISA/A/7921/3.
114. See Gorenberg, Accidental Empire, 112–118.
115. Jerusalem to Washington, September 26, 1967, ISA/A/7938/10.
116. Shuqayri, al-Hazima al-kubra, 2:140. See also Mahgoub, Democracy on Trial, 139–142.
117. Farid, Nasser, 55–58; Shuqayri, al-Hazima al-kubra, 2:143–145.
118. Shuqayri, al-Hazima al-kubra, 2:146, 152.
119. For the Arabic text of the resolutions, see al-Watha'iq al-urduniyya, 1967, 213–216.

120. Unsigned, undated memo, LBJL/NSF/Country Files/Jordan, box 147.
121. On Hussein's visit to Moscow, see Amman to State, October 8, 1967, DDRS/CK 3100545575.
122. Hussein to Johnson, October 9, 1967, DDRS/CK3100501442.
123. See, for example, Oren, Six Days of War, 321–322; Gorenberg, Accidental Empire, 110.
124. Eshkol's summary statement, September 3, 1967, ISA/A/7921/6.
125. Ya'akov Herzog diary, September 3, ISA/A/4511/3.
126. Ya'akov Herzog diary, September 10, 1967, ISA/A/4511/3.
127. Mapai secretariat minutes, September 14, 1967, LPA/2-24-1967-91.
128. For pre-Khartoum Israeli efforts to prevent the revival of the US-Soviet draft, see Tel Aviv to State, August 7, 1967, FRUS, 1964–1968, 19: doc. 409; Tel Aviv to State, August 16, 1967, FRUS, 1964–1968, 19: doc. 420; Tel Aviv to State, August 28, 1967, FRUS, 1964–1968, 19: doc. 430; Rostow-Evron memcon, August 29, 1967, FRUS, 1964–1968, 19: doc. 431.
129. Washington to FCO, September 27, 1967, BNA/PREM 13/1623.
130. Johnson to Faisal, September 25, 1967, FRUS, 1964–1968, 19: doc. 447.
131. Memcon of Johnson with Rusk et al., October 3, 1967, FRUS, 1964–1968, 19: doc. 453.
132. Rostow to Johnson, October 12, 1967, FRUS, 1964–1968, 19: doc. 467.
133. Rostow to Johnson, October 13, 1967, FRUS, 1964–1968, 19: doc. 471.
134. Rostow to Johnson, October 31, 1967, LBJL/NSF/Country Files/Jordan, box 147.
135. Rostow to Johnson, November 6, 1967, FRUS, 1964–1968, 19: doc. 510.
136. Memo for the record, November 6, 1967, FRUS, 1964–1968, 19: doc. 509.
137. New York to State, November 4, 1967, FRUS, 1964–1968, 19: doc. 501.
138. State to Tel Aviv, November 30, 1968, FRUS, 1964–1968, 19: doc. 506; Rusk to Johnson, undated, FRUS, 1964–1968, 19: doc. 513.
139. New York to FCO, November 6, 1967, BNA/PREM 13/1624.
140. UNSC Resolution 242, November 22, 1967, FRUS, 1964–1968, 19: doc. 542.
141. New York to State, November 11, 1967, DDRS/CK3100120742.
142. Ya'akov Herzog, "Two Meetings with Charles," undated (November 1967), YHP.
143. "Remarks of the Prime Minister to the Cabinet," November 19, 1967, ISA/A/7921/6.

SEVEN

A CHANCE FOR PEACE?

1968

UNLIKE 1967, 1968 IS NOT USUALLY REGARDED AS A WATERshed year in the Arab-Israeli dispute. Yet while no wars were fought and no peace accords were signed in 1968, it was nevertheless a time of great consequence for Israel, Jordan, and the West Bank Palestinians. For the first time, Israel and Jordan tried and failed to compromise on the future of the West Bank, while the fida'iyyun organizations came to dominate the Palestinian national movement. No one yet predicted that King Hussein would renounce his claims to the West Bank, but he had already begun to cede ground to an increasingly expansionist Israel and increasingly militant Palestinians.

Throughout 1968, it was Hussein, rather than the Israelis, who truly wanted to resolve the West Bank issue. Levi Eshkol and his colleagues believed that as long as the military balance remained in Israel's favor, they could get a better deal by waiting. They thought that Palestinians in the West Bank and the Gaza Strip would grow reconciled to occupation, and that Arab leaders would eventually come forward to negotiate on Israel's terms. At the same time, Israel's leaders knew they could not hold on to their conquests without US support, especially if the Soviets intervened on the side of the Arabs.

By negotiating with Hussein, the Israelis mainly hoped to prevent the Johnson administration from presenting plans of its own. Most highly placed Israelis, particularly senior IDF officers, were skeptical that a separate peace with Jordan was worth sacrificing the strategic advantages offered by the West Bank. And Prime Minister Levi Eshkol's fears were not limited to the diplomatic arena; they included the domestic front as well. Like his colleagues, Eshkol worried about an imposed settlement. Unlike them, he worried that he would be held personally responsible for unpopular concessions.

Yet even bolder and more forthcoming Israeli leaders would have found it hard to make peace with Jordan in 1968. Recent studies that portray Hussein as a bold and imaginative leader, whose efforts for peace were scuttled by intransigent Israelis, overstate the case.[1] Certainly, Hussein wanted peace, and his Israeli interlocutors knew it. "[Hussein's] desire to have substantive discussions with us is clear and in good faith," Abba Eban admitted. "Whoever thinks that we want peace with Jordan and that Jordan is running away from it—it is difficult to imagine a less truthful depiction."[2] Still, the human drama of Hussein's meetings with Israeli representatives should not obscure the fact that he was a weak ruler who could not afford to push his domestic or Arab opponents too far. As a monarch, Hussein could take certain types of personal risks that a democratically elected politician like Eshkol could not. But historians should not confuse the king's willingness to test the diplomatic waters with the capacity to navigate more dangerous seas for the sake of peace. If the Israelis behaved intransigently toward Hussein, they did so in part because trends within Jordan and in the wider Arab world validated their fears and allowed them to avoid difficult decisions.

But Israel's indecision had fateful consequences. The diplomatic stalemate of 1968 brought Jordan to the edge of chaos and helped the Palestinian guerrilla organizations become the official standard-bearers of their people's struggle. By 1969, it was clear that Hussein would eventually need to confront the fida'iyyun, even if doing so cost him the West Bank.

AN UNBRIDGEABLE GAP

By October 1967, the IDF's strategic planners assumed that peace was unlikely within a year. Israel, they declared, needed to build up its military strength and hold fast until the Arabs agreed to negotiate.[3] Since France still would not supply Israel with more weapons, the Israelis desperately wanted the United States to help them match Egypt's rapid military buildup. The Israelis wanted the Johnson administration to sell them twenty-seven Skyhawk jets in addition to forty-eight that they already had under contract. They also desperately hoped to purchase fifty Phantom jet fighters, whose speed and weapons systems surpassed anything that the Israeli air force possessed.[4]

But the Americans gave Israel no sign that they would supply the coveted warplanes. On November 27, after Eshkol made his case for why the United States should sell Israel the aircraft, Ambassador Barbour gave him an unexpectedly frosty answer. The Johnson administration, he said, did not believe that the Arabs could threaten Israel anytime soon. "As the events of May and June receded in people's memory," Barbour warned, "Israel will have to give increasing attention to her image in the world. Her position as the victim of an attempt by her neighbors to annihilate her becomes less credible the longer she sits in her present posture as an occupying power in large areas."[5] The ambassador's message was clear: the Johnson administration did not think that Israel needed more planes, and did not want to reward Israeli intransigence.

On December 5, Eshkol met with the IDF General Staff and offered a grim prognosis. "We can assume it is possible for the situation to remain as it is for two or three years, but afterward it will have to change," he predicted. The Arab states would rearm with the help of the USSR. "From where will our salvation come?" Eshkol asked. The prime minister noted that he was not looking forward to an upcoming visit to the United States, since President Johnson had a reputation for asking "nasty questions." "As of right now," Eshkol speculated, "the United States favors Hussein, and we need to be able to explain our stance to them." Eshkol wanted to know whether his generals could provide him with a formula for a West Bank deal "that will give us security" but "not oblige us to bring all these Arabs into our state."[6]

Few of Eshkol's generals had high hopes for an Israeli-Hashemite peace. The issue, remarked Aharon Yariv, was not just what kind of border Israel could accept. The key fact was that "the Arabs are not ready for a fundamental change in their relations with us." Without this sort of "fundamental change," Yariv argued, Israel should try to keep the occupied territories "until someone holds us at gunpoint. Then, we can consider whether to 'die with the Philistines' or find another solution. We can then weigh whether this or that border is good for us." No treaty with Hussein, Yariv said, would be worth much if the rest of the Arab world remained hostile to Israel. "If we close a deal with Hussein, who will guarantee that he'll be there a month or two years later?" the IDF intelligence chief asked. An agreement with Hussein, he added, would not solve the Palestinian problem, either. There would "still be hundreds of thousands of refugees, and what will happen with Fatah and the other organizations?" Yitzhak Rabin also doubted that a separate peace with Hussein would be worthwhile. "It's a hypothetical question, not reality, to think about the conditions for returning [the West Bank] when you have Egypt, Iraq, Syria, and the whole Arab world as it is." Overwhelmingly, the IDF brass agreed that Israel should only sign a separate peace agreement with Egypt. The generals thought that if the Americans asked Eshkol about Jordan, he should tell them that a separate peace would weaken Hussein's regime. Perhaps he could suggest that the West Bank should be made into a Palestinian state.[7]

Eshkol did not especially like the answers that his generals gave him. He had come to dislike the idea of a separate Palestinian entity. A West Bank state, he said, would become a source of Arab irredentism. The West Bankers would insist on Palestinian rule for Gaza, and lay claim to Arab-populated areas in Israel. "What if Nazareth wakes up one day and says it wants to join a Palestinian entity?" Eshkol asked. The prime minister was also skeptical that Israel could ensure that a Palestinian entity on the West Bank would remain demilitarized. "Will they have an army? Will they have police?" he asked Rabin. "You can say that you don't want it, but the question is whether it's your right to intervene." Eshkol's greatest doubts, however, concerned how Johnson would react if he told the president that Hussein could not survive a separate peace. "Johnson can say to me, 'Trust me. We'll supply arms and watch over Jordan with or without Hussein, in case they kill him. And Moscow won't enter. But don't sit on the Jordan,'" he predicted.[8]

Only Deputy Chief of Staff Hayim Bar-Lev, who would succeed Rabin as chief of staff in January 1968, offered Eshkol an idea of what to do if Johnson insisted that he talk to Hussein. Perhaps, Bar-Lev suggested, Jordanian civil administration could be restored over the West Bank, but the IDF could keep troops in the Jordan Valley and on the West Bank's central ridge until an overall Arab-Israeli settlement was reached. "At a moment of change in Jordan—if there is a change in the regime there—we are in place. The moment the Jordanians try to insert any sort of military forces—we are in place," he told Eshkol.[9] Eshkol evidently took Bar-Lev's ideas to heart. Immediately afterward, he had his advisors Aviad Yafeh and Ya'akov Herzog draw up plans for an Israeli-Jordanian peace deal that were nearly identical to Bar-Lev's suggestions.[10]

But before Eshkol could discuss anyone's ideas with Johnson, he needed permission from his cabinet. At the end of December, the cabinet defense subcommittee met yet again to discuss the future of the occupied territories, and again failed to agree on a plan. With the exception of Yigal Allon, most of the subcommittee now opposed the idea of a Palestinian state. But while Mapai and Mapam moderates like Eban, Eliyahu Sasson, and Yisrael Barzilai wanted to return the West Bank to Jordan in exchange for peace, hard-liners like Menachem Begin and Ahdut ha-'Avodah's Yisrael Galili thought Israel should control the area permanently.[11] Nor could Israel's politicians agree on what sort of new borders they could accept. According to Rabin, who later disclosed the details of these meetings to US officials, there was an "80 to 85 percent" consensus in favor of the Allon Plan, but the subcommittee did not put that plan to a vote.[12] Most likely, Eshkol did not want to challenge Moshe Dayan, who had the power to bring down the national unity government or wreck a long-planned merger of Rafi, Mapai, and Ahdut ha-'Avodah into a unified Labor Party.[13] During the cabinet subcommittee's discussions, Dayan made it clear that he had no interest in returning the West Bank to Jordan. The defense minister claimed that if Israel could maintain bases on the West Bank's central ridge, establish settlements throughout the area, and keep East Jerusalem, he could see turning the 1949 armistice line into Israel's "political border." Yet since Hussein would never consent to such arrangements, Dayan added, "the reality which exists today in the territories—that's my plan."[14]

The result was continued indecision. Not only did the cabinet members not authorize Eshkol to tell Johnson what Israel would be willing to give up, but they made it almost impossible for him to negotiate on his own. Henceforth, the government ruled, no Israeli minister could offer territorial concessions without the cabinet's permission.[15] Eshkol left for the United States with nothing new to tell Johnson. All he could say was that Israel would hold the occupied territories until peace was made, and that Israel's borders should be determined in direct negotiations.[16]

Moshe Dayan and Levi Eshkol, 1968. Israel Government Press Office/Ilan Bruner.

But the Americans were impatient. When Eshkol met with Johnson at his Texas ranch on January 7, the president seemed unmoved by Eshkol's talk of direct negotiations and his requests for Phantoms. "Phantoms won't determine security," Johnson told Eshkol. "Planes won't change things that basically. The big problem is how two and a half million Jews can live in a sea of Arabs." Secretary of State Dean Rusk asked Eshkol "what kind of Israel [he] want[ed] the Arabs to live with and the American people to support." At the moment, he added, it was "difficult for us to describe the Israelis the Arabs are expected to live with." Eshkol responded that Israel wanted real peace; his countrymen could not "live forever with the feeling that they are untouchable." As for "what kind of Israel" he wanted, though, all Eshkol could say was that "Israel is not ready to return to the Israel of June 4."[17]

Eshkol's visit did not end on a high note. Johnson agreed to sell Israel twenty-seven additional Skyhawk aircraft, speed up the delivery of planes that Israel had already bought, and take steps to ensure that

Israel could be supplied with Phantom jets on short notice. But Johnson still made no promise to supply Israel with the desired planes. Before the United States provided Israel with Phantoms, "the Soviets and Arabs must prove the Israelis are right," the president told Eshkol.[18] "The sense that time is working against Israel followed us the whole time," Herzog told the KFADC afterward. Most ominously, Herzog said, Rusk had told him that should Israel remain inflexible, "if the Soviets threaten you, we will not go to Congress to counter the Soviet threat." There seemed to be a "deep gap, impossible to bridge" with the Americans, Eshkol's advisor warned. "I fear that in the coming months the dispute with them will sharpen."[19]

THE MATCHMAKER

The confrontation with the Americans over the occupied territories did not arrive quite as quickly as Eshkol and his colleagues feared. The day of reckoning was postponed by UN envoy Gunnar Jarring, who spent the winter of 1968 shuttling between Israel, Egypt, and Jordan. Neither the Israelis nor the Egyptians particularly wanted to work with Jarring, a mild-mannered Swede who knew little about the Middle East. The Israelis thought Jarring should do nothing more than lay the groundwork for direct negotiations. As Eshkol quipped, there was nothing wrong with "a matchmaker who will bring the bride and groom to the *hupa* [wedding canopy], but afterward he should get lost."[20] They cooperated with Jarring mainly to keep the UN Security Council from taking up the Arab-Israeli issue again. As Eban acknowledged, Israel had no interest in seeing Resolution 242 replaced by a resolution in which "territories and withdrawal would be among the first issues."[21] Nasser likewise had little use for Jarring, but thought Egypt should show the world that it "was not obstructing the efforts that are being made to establish peace in the region." If nothing else, the Egyptian president thought, the UN mediator's mission could give Egypt more time to prepare for war. "Israel will not withdraw from our land as the result of the US applying pressure on it, nor will it withdraw as a result of the efforts of the United Nations. But it will withdraw when we become capable of carrying out military action to drive it out of the occupied land," he told his advisors.[22]

In fact, Nasser had more room to drive a wedge between the Israelis and the Americans than he realized. The Johnson administration was growing nervous about the Arab-Israeli impasse. Presidential advisor Eugene Black, who toured the Middle East that winter, warned Johnson of "bitter frustration" in the Arab world.[23] At an NSC meeting on February 21, Undersecretary of State Nicholas Katzenbach warned that if Jarring did not succeed, America's regional position would become "absolutely intolerable."[24] Moreover, US officials were increasingly inclined to blame Jarring's lack of progress on Israel. They resented the Israelis' insistence on direct negotiations and their refusal to unequivocally accept Resolution 242. The United States had "bled in the halls of the UN" for the resolution, Walt Rostow complained. "The Arabs," he worried, "are beginning to believe that we aren't even trying to press Israel."[25] Even the staunchly pro-Israel Johnson was coming to share his advisors' frustration. When Rostow sent him a memo on Israel's requests for Phantoms, the president scribbled on it, "Tell Israel they better work out peace plan."[26]

Yet Nasser's inflexibility allowed the Israelis to regain the diplomatic initiative. Early in February, Eban suggested that Jarring hold Arab-Israeli talks modeled on the armistice negotiations of 1949, when UN mediator Ralph Bunche had scurried back and forth between Arab and Israeli delegations housed on different floors of a hotel on the isle of Rhodes.[27] The Americans supported Eban's idea, and on March 10, Jarring proposed that he would invite all of the parties to meet with him on Cyprus. The Egyptians, however, responded rigidly. Egyptian foreign minister Mahmud Riyadh again argued that Israel needed to not only "accept" Resolution 242 but "implement it," meaning withdraw from the occupied territories before talks even began.[28] Regardless of what the Egyptians said about "accepting" Resolution 242, UN ambassador Arthur Goldberg complained to Rusk, the "plain fact is that when Jarring put his specific proposal to them, they rejected it."[29] From Jerusalem, Eban watched with satisfaction. The more obstinately Nasser behaved, the less Israel had to fear outside pressure. "We are talking about a tactical-diplomatic campaign, not about peace," Eban told the KFADC on March 19. "It's clear that no Arab state is ready to move forward for peace. The thing to do is to minimize pressure and put the blame for the deadlock on the other side. That's what they're dealing in, that's what we're dealing in."[30]

Unlike Israel's and Egypt's leaders, Hussein did not welcome deadlock. By the winter of 1968, the king and his advisors were getting anxious.[31] The refugees from the 1967 war continued to test the strength of the Jordanian state. Approximately 53,000 Palestinians who had fled the West Bank remained crowded in newly constructed camps in the Jordan Valley, where winter rains had turned the dust to mud and "led to a population explosion among the local vermin." Another 188,000 Palestinians who had fled the occupied territories had settled in Amman and other cities, where international relief agencies and the government struggled to provide for them.[32] To prevent economic collapse and political upheaval, Hussein desperately needed diplomatic progress.

Initially the king had hoped the Arab League might give him a mandate to negotiate. In December 1967, Hussein asked Nablus mayor Hamdi Kan'an to organize a West Bank delegation to take part in an upcoming Arab summit in Rabat. The king hoped the West Bank Palestinians could persuade the Arab leaders that their situation was intolerable and that Hussein could relieve their plight by making peace with Israel.[33] By January 1968, when it became clear that the Rabat summit would be delayed, Hussein began toying with the idea of an interim solution for the West Bank. "Piecemeal progress," he told US officials, was necessary to "get out of the present box." Israel, he suggested, could withdraw from the West Bank, and Jordan would administer the area. However, Jordan would move no forces into the West Bank until the Israeli and Jordanian governments negotiated agreements on Jerusalem, refugees, and borders.[34] The king did not formally transmit his proposal to Israel, claiming there was no point in doing so before it received Arab endorsement or Israel accepted Resolution 242.[35] Instead, he sent his West Bank supporters to tell the Israelis that he was ready to negotiate if they would first give him their terms. Moshe Sasson, who had begun another round of talks with West Bank notables, suddenly found himself swamped with Jordanian peace feelers. "We can help you and ourselves in finding a solution and convincing the Arab world," Anwar Nusayba told him.[36]

The Israelis did not appreciate Hussein's overtures. By serving as the king's go-betweens, the West Bank notables signaled that they still believed that Jordan could rescue them from occupation. "Jarring's running around and Hussein and Nasser's diplomatic activity leave room for hopes and delusions," Sasson told Eshkol late in January 1968. Local notables thought of themselves as "part of the *Arab world*, the *kingdom of Jordan*, and the *Palestinian people*," not as West Bankers.[37] The Israelis, of course, wanted the West Bankers to tell Hussein that they were losing faith in the Arab governments and were on the verge of making a separate deal with Israel. Indeed, Dayan had asked Sasson to begin his latest round of contacts in order to "increase our ability to maneuver vis-à-vis Hussein, and perhaps even as an alternative."[38] The Israelis were in no hurry to negotiate with Hussein, and believed that the more desperate he became, the better.

Eshkol thus responded haltingly to Hussein's feelers. He and Eban met with Nusayba, and they assured Barbour and Jarring that Israel was happy to deal with Hussein's emissaries.[39] Still, Eban's February 20 meeting with Nusayba did not produce a meeting of the minds. Again, Nusayba stated that Hussein could not move forward if Israel did not define its terms for peace. In order to "allow the Arabs to get out of their psychological morass," he suggested that Israel should accept the 1947 partition plan as a starting point for talks. Eban responded that his government wanted peace and a "compact," solidly Jewish Israel, but it could discuss its "peace map" only with Hussein himself.[40] When Nusayba reported his conversation to the king, Hussein asked him to tell the Israelis that he wanted peace, but needed to know what kind of agreement his Jewish neighbors wanted before he could negotiate.[41] An increasingly familiar pattern had played out once again: Hussein, eager for the Israelis to withdraw, asked them for a peace plan. The Israelis, determined to hang on to whatever they could, demanded that Hussein agree to negotiate first.

Given the choice, Eshkol probably would have kept up this diplomatic shadowboxing indefinitely. Unfortunately for the prime minister, he and Hussein were negotiating not in a vacuum, but against a backdrop of escalating violence along the Jordan River.

THE ROAD TO KARAMEH

Between June 1967 and mid-March 1968, Palestinian militants killed or wounded 168 Israelis.[42] Yasir Arafat and his Fatah compatriots had been stunned by the Arab defeat, but they viewed Israel's occupation of the West Bank and Gaza as an opportunity. At first, they set up their headquarters on the West Bank and unsuccessfully tried to mobilize the local population for "popular war" against the Israeli occupiers.[43] The Palestinian guerrillas quickly discovered, however, that the portion of the Jordan Valley east of the river offered an excellent alternative base. New refugee camps that had been hastily erected there following the war offered the Palestinian militants a haven where they could plan and train beyond Israel's reach while staying within striking distance of Israeli border patrols and farms.[44] From the east side of the river, the fida'iyyun shot at Israeli soldiers and farmers, lobbed mortar shells at kibbutzim and moshavim (cooperative agricultural communities), and crossed the river to plant explosives and ambush Israelis.[45] In response, the IDF razed abandoned villages along the Jordan and expelled members of the Nusayrat tribe, suspected of helping the militants, to the East Bank.[46] IDF ambushes, together with helicopter and jeep patrols along the ceasefire line, were stepped up.[47] Yet Israel's preventive measures could not stop the fida'iyyun. By mid-February 1968, the air was ripe for a large-scale Israeli reprisal.

Hussein and his advisors were unsure of what to do about the fida'iyyun. The king genuinely feared that "those bastards," as he called them, would provoke a major Israeli attack.[48] He and his advisors also worried that the Palestinian organizations threatened internal law and order. Reports of armed fida'iyyun prowling the streets of Amman, demanding "contributions" from businessmen, were already becoming common.[49] Still, the king and his inner circle were mindful of the guerrillas' popularity within Jordan and of the support they enjoyed from other Arab governments. While only Syria had backed the Palestinian guerrillas before June 1967, other states, including Egypt, now supported them as well.[50] While Nasser had once worried that the guerrillas would drag Egypt into war, he and his advisors now hoped they would help prevent Israel from consolidating its occupation.[51]

Before the Jordanians could decide how to deal with the guerrillas, the ceasefire line exploded. On the night of February 14–15, Palestinian militants shelled the Kfar Ruppin kibbutz in the Beit She'an Valley. Israeli troops fired back, drawing a JAA artillery barrage against nearby Kibbutz Ma'oz Hayim. The following afternoon, Israeli artillery and tanks shelled JAA batteries and the East Ghor Canal. By the time a ceasefire took hold, three Israelis had been killed and seventeen wounded. Ten Jordanian soldiers and between 23 and 46 civilians were killed, while over 150 were wounded.[52] The clashes sent shock waves through Jordan. In Amman, sixty thousand angry mourners attended the funerals of fallen soldiers. An estimated seventy thousand residents of the Jordan Valley fled their homes. Top Jordanian intelligence officials like Muhammad Rasul al-Kaylani and Ma'an Abu-Nuwar reported a dramatic upswing in anti-Israeli sentiment and support for the fida'iyyun.[53]

But perhaps the most significant result of the February 15 violence was that it opened a public rift between Hussein and Bahjat al-Talhuni over how to handle the guerrillas. On February 16, Hussein delivered a speech praising his army and criticizing the Palestinian militants. "Jordan has never accepted, and will never accept upon its territory, [activity] which conflicts with the higher Arab interest," he warned.[54] The following day, Minister of the Interior Hasan al-Kayid vowed that the Jordanian government would "strike with an iron hand at the hands of those who play around with security."[55] Yet the king immediately found himself undercut by his prime minister. Al-Talhuni, who had advocated rapprochement with Nasser prior to 1967, now championed accommodating the fida'iyyun. He gave a speech repudiating al-Kayid's statement, claiming that it represented al-Kayid's personal opinion, not Jordanian policy.[56] Despite the fact that his address amounted to an attack on the king, al-Talhuni suffered no consequences, at least not in public. Indeed, many elite Jordanians appeared to be firmly on his side. On February 21, a number of prominent Jordanians, led by former prime minister Sulayman al-Nabulsi, gathered in Amman and issued a statement calling on Hussein to provide money and weapons to the fida'iyyun.[57]

Before February 15, the Israeli intelligence community believed that Hussein might be capable of clamping down on the Palestinian guerrillas but wanted to use border violence to put pressure on Israel.[58] Afterward they concluded, as Yariv later recalled, that "Hussein would have been unable to deal with the terrorists even if he wanted (and his willingness was questionable), for a number of reasons."[59] Not only were the Israelis impressed by al-Talhuni's and al-Nabulsi's public displays of defiance, but they had intelligence indicating that both men had challenged the king even more brazenly in private. According to a well-placed Jordanian source, after al-Talhuni criticized Hasan al-Kayid, Hussein had asked him to resign in order to let a Palestinian-dominated government take over and negotiate with Israel. Al-Talhuni declared that he would refuse, and warned Hussein that the fida'iyyun, Iraqi troops still stationed in Jordan, and half the Jordanian army would back him. Al-Talhuni then urged al-Nabulsi to assemble his supporters and declare their backing for the guerrillas. According to the Israelis' source, Hussein had then gone to al-Nabulsi's house and told him and his guests that he, Hussein, could "go to Switzerland and not have to deal with all these problems," or invite "American paratroopers" into Jordan and make peace with Israel. However, the king stated, he did not want to do either. He then revealed that Nasser had given him permission to negotiate separately with Israel. When al-Nabulsi asked if Nasser had done so in writing, the king admitted that he had not. Al-Nabulsi and his supporters then ignored the monarch and issued their proclamation anyway.[60]

Thus, by March the Israelis were leaning toward neutralizing the fida'iyyun themselves. On March 6, David Carmon, deputy chief of AMAN, told the cabinet defense subcommittee that Fatah was preparing for a major spring offensive. Hussein, Carmon added, could do nothing to stop the guerrillas; the IDF would have to do the job. Bar-Lev then outlined a plan for ousting Fatah from its major base in the East Bank town of Karameh. IDF troops, he said, would have to penetrate the East Bank, seize control of Karameh, comb the area, and kill or capture any fida'iyyun they found. Dayan asked the subcommittee to approve Bar-Lev's plan in principle so it could be carried out immediately after the next attack. It was only luck, Dayan said, that Fatah's attacks had not killed more Israelis. One day, "a bus full of children could hit a mine."[61] Eban, however, argued that authorizing an operation in advance would make it difficult to adjust it to political circumstances. Bar-Lev's plan, he added, would cause civilian casualties and harm Israel's international position. The other ministers sided with Eban, and no plan of attack was approved. On March 18, however, a bus full of children headed for Eilat struck a mine, killing two and wounding twenty-seven.[62] Dayan's dark prophecy had come true. That night, the cabinet defense subcommittee approved Bar-Lev's plan. This time Eban voiced no opposition.

The following day, however, an apologetic message from Hussein arrived via the US embassy. Eban and Foreign Ministry director-general Gideon Rafael implored Eshkol to wait. Yet when the cabinet defense subcommittee convened again that evening, Yariv and Dayan overwhelmingly carried the day. Yariv argued that Hussein had effectively lost control of his country to al-Talhuni, and could not solve Israel's fida'iyyun problem. Dayan scoffed at the possibility of diplomatic fallout. If the Arab states came to Fatah's aid, he added, he would welcome the opportunity to fight them. The subcommittee overwhelmingly reaffirmed Bar-Lev's plan. No one, including Eshkol, seemed willing to challenge Dayan.

Still, on March 20, Eban got one final chance to convince the government to hold back the IDF. Jarring, who had recently passed through Amman, informed the Israelis that he wanted to visit. Eban suspected he was carrying a message from Hussein. The Israeli foreign minister had also received a frantic phone call from Barbour, who told him that Hussein was ready to fire al-Talhuni, have Iraq withdraw its troops from Jordan, send senior JAA officers to meet with Israelis, and crush the fida'iyyun. It would be a "disaster" if Israel now attacked Jordan, Barbour warned.[63] That same day, an accident at an archaeological dig left Dayan hospitalized. Eban, now convinced that he could get a fairer hearing, implored the cabinet defense subcommittee to cancel the raid that afternoon.[64] "As a doctor of US-Israeli relations, I don't know how it will be possible to heal the relationship," he warned. When the subcommittee regrouped that evening, another message from Barbour arrived. The US ambassador warned that the Johnson administration would view an Israeli raid as "a fatal blow to US interests and to the Jarring mission." Eban argued that Israel had already "brought Hussein to his knees" and forced him to act. Attacking now would yield no benefit, but would seriously damage US-Israeli relations and "destroy the chances" that Israel would get Phantom jets.

Yet in the end, the subcommittee decided to authorize the raid by a margin of one vote. For Eshkol, who voted in favor, the decision was based as much on politics as on principle. When Eban urged the prime minister to delay a reprisal earlier that day, Eshkol had complained that he did not want it to look like the government could not act without Dayan. Happy for an opportunity to look decisive, he too voted for the raid. The IDF would cross the Jordan hours later.

"THE BEGINNING OF A PROCESS"

The battle of Karameh on March 21, 1968, actually involved two coordinated IDF operations—one at Karameh and the other at Safi, south of the Dead Sea. The operation against Karameh was by far the larger, involving some 1,300 IDF troops, one hundred armored personnel carriers, and seventy-five Centurion and Sherman M-51 tanks. Because of bad weather, Israeli paratroopers arrived at Karameh late, only to find that there were far more fida'iyyun and weapons caches in the camp than they had expected. The Israelis thus spent far more time than planned combing the camp and got caught in fierce firefights with Palestinian militants. Nine IDF soldiers were killed, as were an estimated 170 fida'iyyun. Even tougher fighting took place outside the camp, where JAA and IDF tanks traded numerous volleys of shells. By the end of the day, twenty-seven IDF troops had been killed, along with at least forty Jordanian soldiers.[65]

Immediately after Karameh, the IDF's commanders depicted the battle as a victory. The IDF had sacrificed more men than in any prewar retaliatory raid, Yariv and Bar-Lev told the cabinet, but its losses were not high given the scale of the operation. The army had accomplished its immediate objective—to clear Karameh of fida'iyyun and thwart Fatah's plans for a spring offensive. Many Fatah members had been killed, and it would take months before the fida'iyyun could rebuild their base.[66]

Yet it rapidly became clear that Karameh had in fact empowered the fida'iyyun. Fatah, Eshkol told the cabinet on March 31, had retaken Karameh. Waves of new guerrillas were pouring into the East Bank— raw recruits as well as men trained in Syria and Egypt.[67] Although the fida'iyyun had played little role in determining the battle's outcome, the fact that they had stood and fought made them the heroes of an Arab world still reeling from defeat. *Al-Ahram* likened them to the Algerian *mujahidin*, the Viet Cong, and anti-Nazi resistance movements in wartime Europe.[68] In addition to fresh recruits and good press, the guerrillas' performance yielded major political gains. The leaders of the fida'iyyun organizations now felt confident enough to push Yahya Hammuda, who had succeeded al-Shuqayri as chairman of the PLO, to grant them a majority of seats on the Palestine National Council.[69] King Hussein, who had been on the verge of cracking down on the guerrillas before the battle, was now forced to express solidarity with them. "It is difficult for me to distinguish between fida'iyyun and others," he told reporters on March 23. "We may reach a stage soon when we all become fida'iyyun."[70]

Given the king's plight, the "Palestinian option" now regained some cachet among the Israeli leadership. They were not ready to go so far as to talk to the PLO or Fatah. When West Bank notable Walid Shakʻa informed Sasson that the leaders of both organizations wanted to talk to Israel about establishing a Palestinian state, Dayan responded dismissively. "The way to deal with [the fida'iyyun]," he said, "is to kill them."[71] But there was nevertheless a great deal of talk in Jerusalem about negotiating with local Palestinian notables and establishing some kind of Palestinian dependency on the West Bank. "Tell [the West Bank notables] we'll sit along the length of the Jordan and the mountain ridge," Eshkol suggested to Sasson. "From what's left, they can establish something independent of their own, with a parliament of their own. They can establish a state."[72]

This time, however, Israel's leaders also spoke of making a deal with a Palestinian-dominated government in Amman. The logic was simple: the West Bank was not viable on its own, but Hussein would never agree to give up any part of it to Israel. If the Palestinians took control of the East Bank, however, Israel would have interlocutors in Amman who might be more willing to trade some of the West Bank for peace. The principal advocate of this position was Dayan. "[The Palestinians] should take over there [i.e., on the East Bank]," the defense minister told Sasson. "If they were in power in Jordan, we could reach an agreement with them."[73] The Palestinians, Dayan argued, were "the only actors in the Arab world who are ready to sit with us to discuss peace with the knowledge that it will entail major territorial revisions."[74]

Yet the idea of cutting off contact with Hussein or trying to overthrow him did not gain much ground in Jerusalem. Most of Israel's leaders do not appear to have believed that the advantages of having a Palestinian-dominated regime in Amman were worth alienating the Johnson administration or opening Jordan to Soviet influence. When Eban addressed the KFADC on April 9, he spoke at length about the damage that Hussein's downfall could do to the US-Israeli relationship.

Israel, Eban emphasized, also had "a great deal to fear from [an area of] continuous Soviet control stretching from Syria to Jordan to Egypt."[75] Even Dayan, the most forceful proponent of agreement with an Amman-based Palestinian government, was careful to state that such a settlement should be reached "under the auspices of the king."[76] He claimed to be "against toppling Hussein, against the idea of occupying Amman," unless the Americans were fully onboard.[77] Like Eban, Dayan and the General Staff worried that Hussein's fall might result in a US-Israeli rift so wide that the Soviets would no longer feel deterred from intervening militarily in the Middle East. Israel's military men were also keenly aware of the growing Soviet presence in Syria and Egypt and did not want the USSR to establish a similar foothold along the Jordan River. Hussein's fall was not "axiomatic," Bar-Lev remarked, and a pro-Soviet regime in Jordan could be far worse.[78]

Moreover, the Israelis needed Hussein to keep Jarring's mission alive and hold off an imposed settlement. The diplomatic fallout from the Karameh raid had been severe. Just a few hours after the battle began, a letter from Johnson arrived, belatedly warning the Israelis not to attack.[79] When the cabinet convened that evening, Eban warned his colleagues that the president's cable was "only the beginning of a process." He worried that the Security Council would discuss not just the Karameh raid, but also the larger question of why Jarring had made such little progress.[80] Though Security Council Resolution 248, adopted on March 24, did not condemn Israel too harshly, it nevertheless marked the first time since the 1967 war that the superpowers both lined up against the Jewish state.[81]

During the weeks that followed, the Israelis saw more and more signs that pointed toward an imposed settlement. On March 31, Johnson announced that he would not run for a second term. No longer concerned with Jewish votes, the president might prove more sympathetic to the State Department's calls for pressure on Israel, warned Rabin, now ambassador to the United States.[82] The following week, Hussein met with Nasser in Cairo. Their talks, which the king described as "the most difficult and arduous he had ever had with any leader," began on a low note. Nasser stated "flatly that [the] Jarring Mission could not succeed, that only [a] military solution was feasible and that [the] UAR military was therefore preparing for that solution."[83] But in the end, the Egyptian leader agreed that Jarring could meet with the parties' UN ambassadors in New York, so long as the Israelis first agreed to "implement" Resolution 242. Most likely, Nasser hoped to keep Jarring in the field and gain time to prepare for war. But the king was desperate enough to portray Nasser's small gesture as a major breakthrough. If the United States could get the Israelis to say the magic words, he told Ambassador Burns, "then Jordanian and Egyptian representatives would be in New York in a matter of [a] few days ready to talk under Jarring's auspices."[84] Though the Americans still did not accept the Arab interpretation of Resolution 242, they were impressed by Hussein's desire for peace, and believed that an Israeli-Jordanian settlement might be the only way to keep the Jarring mission alive and prevent another bout of violence.[85] Walt Rostow and other US officials now pressed the Israelis to clarify their terms in order to allow Hussein to negotiate.[86]

"We need to get used to the idea," Eban told the KFADC on April 9, "that soon we are going to have to either refuse to meet with Hussein or tell him what the conditions [for peace] are."[87] With demands for diplomatic progress mounting, Eban and his diplomats believed that Israel could no longer avoid defining its position on the West Bank. The Israelis had to show that they were actively talking peace with Hussein in order to prevent the Johnson administration from proposing a plan of its own. "The stubbornness of our neighbors can help us out of sensitive situations, but I still think it would be better if we could begin negotiations as soon as possible," Eban wrote to Rabin later that month. "I don't feel that time is working in our favor unless the passage of time is accompanied by activity in search of peace."[88]

By the end of April, Eshkol decided to listen to his diplomats and open high-level talks with the king. The prime minister took pains to ensure that these negotiations did not ignite a cabinet crisis over Israel's future borders. Though Eban and Golda Meir urged Eshkol to meet with Hussein himself, he refused.[89] Instead he sent Eban, Herzog, and Bar-Lev to London to meet with the king, specifically instructing them not to "open negotiations or obligate the government at this stage." Since Israel had no official negotiating position on the West Bank, Eban and Herzog were told to speak of "schools" in the cabinet, one favoring annexation, one a deal with the Palestinians, and one an Israeli-Jordanian settlement involving "substantial changes" to the prewar boundaries.⁹⁰

Yet while Eshkol refused to decide what to offer Hussein, he raced to tell the Americans that he had decided to talk to the king. On April 30, he sent Johnson a letter warning that no "formulation" could "bridge the gap" between Nasser's calls for the "implementation" of Resolution 242 and a negotiated peace. Thus, Israel had chosen to privately explore "whether Jordan is willing, on its own account, to discuss a settlement with us." While Israel clarified Hussein's views, Eshkol added, the United States should keep Jarring "available" and provide Israel with the Phantom jets that he had requested back in January.⁹¹ While Eshkol was disinclined to take personal risks or offer major concessions for peace, he clearly hoped to use the negotiations with Hussein to gain as much time and weaponry as possible.

On May 3, Hussein and his private secretary, Zayd al-Rifa'i, met with Eban and Herzog in Emmanuel Herbert's London home. Typically, the verbose Eban did most of the talking, describing at length Israel's "three schools" of thought on the West Bank. The king and al-Rifa'i listened politely, but offered little response. Mainly the Jordanians seemed determined, even desperate, to bring the Egyptians to New York for talks with Israel under UN cover. Token Egyptian participation in New York talks, Hussein said, would allow Jordan to "negotiate fully with Israel and at [the] ministerial level. But it must be possible to say that 'the UAR is in the conference.'"⁹²

Later that month, Herzog would tell Eshkol, Allon, Dayan, and Eban that Jerusalem was the one issue on which Hussein seemed closed to compromise.⁹³ But in any event, the Israelis' next moves had little to do with anything the king had told them. Eshkol and his advisors would continue to talk to Hussein because they feared an imposed settlement, while the prime minister's concern for his personal standing prevented him from deciding what to offer the king.

"AN EGG THAT HASN'T HATCHED"

Through May 1968, Israel's leaders were gripped by a sense of impending crisis. Intelligence reports indicated that West Bank notables were growing skeptical about the prospects for a negotiated settlement. To break the deadlock, the Palestinian leadership might launch another "civil rebellion."[94] Israel was losing its ability to use the West Bankers as a lever on Hussein, Moshe Sasson warned. The West Bank notables now believed that Jarring's mission would soon end and that the Jordanians would come back.[95]

Bad news also trickled in from abroad. On May 10, the Egyptian government proposed to break the deadlock in the Jarring mission. The Egyptians suggested that Jarring or the superpowers could call upon Israel and the Arabs to "implement" a settlement according to a predetermined timetable. Arab and Israeli diplomats would work out the details in "separate rooms," and no peace treaty would be signed.[96] US policymakers had reservations about Egypt's proposal, but hoped it might provide Hussein with cover to negotiate. The United States, Walt Rostow told Rabin, would not insist on "something akin to the Congress in Vienna in 1815."[97] In light of Egypt's newfound "tactical flexibility," Eban worried that the Americans would hold Israel responsible if the diplomatic stalemate continued. "We are turning into the Egyptians," he said, "and they—the Israelis."[98] Eshkol shared Eban's fears.[99] President Johnson was "friendly to Israel," he told the cabinet, "but American interests have prevailed."[100]

With the diplomatic horizon darkening, further contacts with Hussein offered Israel a way to delay the collapse of the Jarring mission and avoid an imposed settlement. Eban, the main champion of this strategy, argued for it over and over again. "As long as the superpowers believe that we have independent contacts," Eban told Eshkol, Dayan, and Allon, "it holds off Jarring and America."[101] "I am in favor of contacts with the Arabs even if they lead nowhere, to a lack of contact, which subjects us to external forces," he remarked shortly afterward."[102] Eshkol accepted his foreign minister's recommendation to keep the channel to Hussein open, but clearly never intended for the negotiations to lead anywhere. He believed that Hussein sincerely wanted an agreement, and might even defy Nasser if offered the right terms. "If we offered [Hussein] an honorable settlement, he would reach a settlement with us," Eshkol admitted.[103] Yet when Eban again suggested that Eshkol meet with Hussein, the prime minister made it clear that he did not really want negotiations to advance that far. What if Hussein refused to accept Israel's conditions for peace? he asked. Could Israel still maintain foreign support afterward, when the Arabs opted for war again?[104]

Notably, Eshkol never bothered to consider whether Israel should scale back its demands. Doubtless he believed that he could not remain in office if he did so. With Israeli elections approaching in 1969, the government's hawks were shoring up their positions by taking hard-line public stances. Discussions about the future of contacts with Hussein took place in the shadow of a cabinet crisis staged by Dayan and Begin, who attacked Eban and the Foreign Ministry for making statements that seemed too accepting of Resolution 242.[105] Allon was also engaging in demagoguery. In April, when Rabbi Moshe Levinger and his followers held a Passover seder at Hebron's Park Hotel and refused to leave, Allon joined Begin and the National Religious Party's Zerah Warhaftig in visiting them and proclaiming his support.[106] After the government moved Levinger and company to the local IDF headquarters, Eshkol angrily told Allon that his behavior recalled the *porshim*, the right-wing movements that had refused to accept the authority of the Zionist mainstream during the Mandate period.[107]

With the Americans bearing down on him and his cabinet veering out of control, Eshkol decided to stall on all fronts. To pacify the Johnson administration and Jarring, he had Herzog remain in contact with the Jordanians. To placate Dayan, he agreed to explore one of the defense minister's pet ideas—the possibility of a modus vivendi with West Bank notables, involving greater administrative autonomy for the Palestinians and expanded economic ties between Israel and the occupied territories. For Dayan, the modus vivendi plan was a step toward his ultimate goal of "functional partition" between Israel, Jordan, and the West Bank.[108] Eshkol apparently went along with the idea for less grandiose reasons. He was in fact skeptical that functional partition could serve as the basis of a settlement, arguing that it smacked of colonialism. "There have been imperial powers bigger than us, and they made sure to teach them their language. They created Anglophones and Francophones.... The people learned what they learned and then they knew how to say, 'Enough, we don't want you here anymore,'" he warned.[109] But of course, Eshkol had a personal interest in mollifying Dayan. Most likely, he also accepted

Herzog's argument that Israel could use the modus vivendi concept to deflect outside pressure.[110]

Yet while Eshkol indulged Dayan by experimenting with functional compromise, he also gave a larger share of the limelight to Allon. On June 3, he invited Allon to present his plan for the West Bank to the Labor Party political committee.[111] When the plan leaked to the press soon afterward, Eshkol grudgingly appointed Allon deputy prime minister.[112] As with Dayan, however, Eshkol's choice to appease Allon reflected his desire to keep his rivals in check rather than any kind of genuine policy decision. Though the prime minister's advisors believed that Allon's plan enjoyed wide support within the Labor Party, Eshkol knew that no one outside of Israel was seriously interested in it.[113] He also knew that if he gave the plan his wholehearted backing, Dayan would try to break up the government. On June 3, the defense minister had told his colleagues that he was willing to have the Allon Plan presented to Hussein on an unofficial basis, since it was too early to "break up the national unity government over an egg that hasn't hatched."[114] But he left no doubt that he would fight the plan in the unlikely event that Hussein actually accepted it. To Herzog, Dayan proclaimed that "when it came to Zionism, he was a religious Jew." He vowed that if "Eban and others" put forward proposals for withdrawal, he would oppose them, "and there's no doubt whose side the public will stand on."[115] Eshkol thus trod lightly. When McGeorge Bundy and American UN ambassador George Ball visited Israel in mid-July, Eshkol allowed Allon to present his plan to them, but had Eban make clear that it was "not endorsed by [the] government."[116]

Eshkol could put his domestic political considerations first because the Johnson administration gave him little reason to do otherwise. Overall, America's failure to advance a major Middle East initiative in the summer of 1968 probably had little to do with anything happening in the region. Johnson and his advisors were preoccupied with Vietnam, rising antiwar sentiment, and race riots across the United States. They did not have much time or energy left for the Middle East.[117] Yet Israel's contacts with Jordan also helped restrain the Americans from responding to Egypt's timetable proposals with an initiative of their own. Johnson and his advisors were already skeptical that they could reach an agreement with the Soviets on the Middle East, and did not want to set off an internal Israeli crisis that would bring a more hard-line government into power.[118] Israeli-Jordanian contacts, which Rostow and CIA director Richard Helms followed through secret channels, provided a convenient reason to avoid difficult and potentially counterproductive choices. "Whether we take a Middle East initiative depends, in fact, on whether Israel-Jordan talks work out," Rostow told Johnson. And while the talks did not look promising, they had "not yet broken off."[119]

Knowledge of Israeli-Jordanian contacts had a similarly calming effect on Jarring. Later in June, Jarring told Eban that he would not end his mission yet, since the Jordanians had told him they were still exploring Israel's position.[120] In mid-July, after Bundy and Ball left Israel, Eban confidently told the cabinet that there was no danger that the Security Council would discuss the Middle East before September, when the General Assembly reconvened. Eban's remarks, Herzog noted in his diary, carried *"a degree of calm which I cannot remember since before his departure for the discussions at the Security Council last November."*[121]

For their part, Hussein and his advisors seem to have felt they had no choice but to play the Israelis' game. When Herzog met al-Rifa'i in London on June 19, he asked that Jordan not press for talks in New York while secret clarifications remained ongoing. Al-Rifa'i obliged. "The goal of setting another meeting with Hussein," Herzog cabled home, "while recruiting [the Jordanians] to relax Jarring and prevent another approach to the Security Council was achieved."[122]

Why were the Jordanians so passive? It is doubtful that Hussein refrained from turning to the Security Council because he believed that his talks with Israel would actually lead to negotiations in New York. The Israelis had still not conceded anything to him. And by late July, Egypt's position had hardened to such a degree that Nasser's promise to let the Jordanians talk with Jarring and the Israelis in New York meant nothing. The Egyptians now insisted that Resolution 242 could not be implemented "by any Arab state if the Israelis were left in occupation of Arab territories"—including the Golan Heights. In other words, the Egyptians were now tying their willingness to accept an Israeli-Jordanian peace to an *Israeli-Syrian* settlement, despite the fact that the neo-Ba'th rejected Resolution 242 and refused to deal with Jarring at all.[123]

The Jordanians, however, had other reasons to keep the talks with the Israelis going, most importantly to reduce the threat of a major Israeli attack. Late in May, fida'iyyun attacks on the Beit She'an Valley had escalated again. On June 4, after more than one hundred shells hit Israeli agricultural settlements in a single day, the IDF shelled Irbid, killing between twenty-five and thirty people.[124] On August 4 the Israeli air force bombed targets in Salt, killing an estimated twenty-five fida'iyyun, six JAA and Iraqi soldiers, and twenty civilians.[125] In response to this spike in violence, Hussein requested new equipment for Jordan's internal security forces, established direct links with the JAA's Bedouin divisional commanders, and created the all-Bedouin Desert Forces units, commanded by his uncle Sharif Nasir.[126] Yet so long as there was no political settlement in sight, Hussein hesitated to confront the Palestinian militants.[127] He knew that border violence would continue, along with the threat of Israeli reprisals. The king needed some way to restrain the Israelis, and presumably, as long as he remained in contact with them, they would not try to bring down his regime. By keeping the Jarring process alive, Hussein also ensured that the United States maintained a stake in his regime and would try to restrain Israel from attacking Jordan. The irony was that the king's policy also helped Israel avoid an imposed settlement.

Still, the Israelis could not assume that Hussein would continue to wait on them forever. No matter how badly the Jordanians feared them, there was still the danger that they would get impatient and cut off contact. By September 1968, Eshkol and his colleagues began to feel this sense of risk more acutely, as the local, regional, and international horizons darkened once again.

"A SENSE OF RISING PRESSURE"

By mid-August, Israel's efforts to reach a modus vivendi with the West Bank Palestinian leadership fell apart. At the end of June, Muhammad 'Ali al-Ja'bari, the mayor of Hebron, had told the Israelis that he would be willing to head a West Bank civil administration. Anticipating strong resistance from the cities of the northern West Bank, Dayan and Eshkol decided to try a "Hebron district–first" approach, and al-Ja'bari agreed.[128] By mid-July, the Jordanians got wind of the idea, and al-Talhuni appeared on Jordanian television and radio, warning the West Bankers against cooperating with Israel. Local notables in Bethlehem, Hebron, and Beit

Sahur worried that the Jordanian government would harm their family members and business interests on the East Bank if they took part in a regional administrative body.[129] On August 26, twenty West Bank mayors submitted a petition to Dayan, declaring their "utter rejection ... of the dark shadow of occupation," and demanding "nothing less than an end to occupation and hence the reunion with the East Bank of the Hashemite kingdom of Jordan."[130] The Israelis' attempt to reach a modus vivendi with the Palestinians thus came to an ignominious end.

The Israelis' failure to court the West Bankers coincided with escalating violence. In August, a string of grenade attacks rocked Jerusalem, and the Tel Aviv central bus station was bombed.[131] On September 8, Egyptian artillery batteries opened fire on Israeli positions along the northern sector of the Suez Canal, killing ten and wounding eight.[132] Increasingly, the stalemate over the occupied territories appeared to be on the verge of devolving into yet another major Arab-Israeli confrontation.

And if Arabs and Israelis did meet on the battlefield again, they would do so in an international context wherein the United States seemed determined to compromise with the Soviet Union, a possibility that the Israelis had feared ever since the 1967 war ended. In August, when the Soviets invaded Czechoslovakia to snuff out Alexander Dubcek's government, Eshkol briefly hoped the United States might take a harder line against the Soviets in the Middle East. After all, he reminded his cabinet, the Czechoslovak coup of 1948 had led to the formation of NATO.[133] By the beginning of September, however, Eshkol's hopes had largely been dashed. The Americans, Rabin reported from Washington, seemed determined to engage the Soviets on the Middle East despite Czechoslovakia.[134] For the Israelis, ongoing US-Soviet dialogue was particularly ominous in light of the USSR's most recent proposal for a settlement, submitted to Rusk on September 4. Like Egypt's timetable proposal, the Soviet initiative called for Israel and the Arabs to "implement" Resolution 242 in phases. Israel would first withdraw its troops thirty to forty kilometers away from the canal and from part of the Golan, then back to the armistice lines. The Arab states would then give the UN statements proclaiming an end to belligerency. UN troops would deploy in Gaza, in Sinai, and at Sharm al-Shaykh. The United States, the Soviet Union, Britain, and France would guarantee the prewar borders.[135]

In essence, the Soviet proposal was everything the Israelis had been fighting against since June 1967. It called for full withdrawal to the prewar lines, did not mention direct negotiations, and substituted multilateral guarantees and nonbelligerency pledges for peace treaties. Yet, Rabin warned, "there is no question that there's a school in the State Department which is prepared to see the Soviet initiative as a possible chance to reach a Middle East solution."[136] On September 19, Eban addressed the cabinet, stressing the need to strengthen US opposition to the Soviet plan. The general feeling, Herzog wrote afterward, was that "we are standing before a new and serious phase in the diplomatic struggle." And according to Eban, "Our only hope is the contact with [Hussein]."[137]

Yet while diplomatic developments reinforced the tactical arguments for a high-level meeting with the king, the Israelis still could not agree on who should meet with Hussein or what he should be told. As before, Eshkol let Israeli domestic politics guide him. He remained determined not to spark a cabinet crisis by making it look as if he were prepared to give Hussein too much. Eshkol still refused to meet with Hussein himself. Eban, who was charged with meeting with the monarch instead, was again instructed to make it clear that the government had no defined position on the future of the West Bank, and to instead speak of three schools of thought regarding the occupied area. To be absolutely sure that Eban did not make any offers of his own, Eshkol proposed that Allon or Dayan accompany the foreign minister to London.[138] Since Dayan refused to meet with Hussein, Eshkol decided to send Allon and allow him to present his plan to Hussein, though not as the official position of the Israeli government. "The intention is not to enter into negotiations at this stage or to obligate the government to a specific plan," Eshkol told the cabinet on September 24. "I don't hold the view that the time has come for the cabinet to decide on the various proposals regarding the West Bank."[139] With the exception of Menachem Begin, the cabinet agreed. "There was a sense of rising pressure, but formally, in any case, the government stuck to its positions," Herzog later noted. The only new decisions the cabinet had made, he added, involved enlarging Israel's outposts in Gush 'Etsiyon and Hebron.[140]

The Allon Plan.

THE LONDON TALKS AND BEYOND

"Is this final?" King Hussein asked Abba Eban. It was the afternoon of September 27, and Hussein had just heard Eban explain the Allon Plan. Hussein commented that he saw "some difficulties" with Eban's proposal, prompting Yigal Allon to step in. "The main point," argued Israel's deputy prime minister, "was security." Unlike the Arabs, Allon said, Israel could not lose even one war and survive. An IDF presence in the Jordan Valley, Allon argued, "would contribute to the security of Jordan and indeed, of the entire area. Once linked in peace with such a military disposition, no outside force would be able to interfere."[141]

"What is security?" Hussein asked Allon, and then answered his own question. "What is important," he said, "is how people feel, and not so much maps and defensive positions.... Security does not depend on a few kilometers here and there, but on a true and fair solution." Allon disagreed, and launched into a lecture about the importance of terrain in modern warfare and the topography of the Jordan Valley. "Topography was more important than the goodwill of the people," he told Hussein. "War had its consequences." The discussion went on for a while longer, and in the end, Eban, Allon, Herzog, Hussein, and al-Rifa'i parted cordially. But the following day, al-Rifa'i informed Herzog that Hussein could not accept the Allon Plan. An Israeli military presence in the Jordan Valley, al-Rifa'i stated, was "wholly unacceptable," and the "principle of inadmissibility or acquisition of territory by force" should also apply to Jerusalem.[142]

The two sides had not moved much since May, yet neither party left London planning to cut off contact. Before they left, al-Rifa'i and Herzog agreed to set a date for another high-level meeting after Eban returned to Israel at the end of October.[143] The question now was what purpose another high-level meeting would serve. Would it simply help Israel stave off pressure from the United States until the General Assembly ended? Or would it coincide with talks under Jarring's guidance in New York? With the Jarring mission at a breaking point, the Soviet timetable proposal in the air, and the foreign ministers of Jordan, Egypt, and Israel gathering in New York, Hussein hoped for one last chance to secure UN cover for negotiations. Perhaps the Israelis would finally declare that they would "implement" Resolution 242. If the Israelis issued such a statement, Hussein told British prime minister Harold Wilson, he would let his foreign minister negotiate with Israel under Jarring's auspices.[144] According to Zayd al-Rifaʿi, Hussein thought that talks in New York were Jordan's "last chance to reach a peaceful settlement" before Nasser opted for war again.[145]

Had it been up to Eban, the king might have gotten his wish. Writing to Eshkol shortly after meeting with Hussein, Israel's foreign minister again emphasized "the tactical goal of guaranteeing the continuation of the contacts." Yet Eban thought the Americans might force Israel to come out more strongly in support of Resolution 242 and negotiate under the umbrella of the Jarring mission. Israel, he told Eshkol, could not afford to put forth a "negative position" if faced with such pressure.[146] Eban believed that his country's remaining diplomatic capital might be best spent preempting the Jordanians and securing US backing for a settlement that Israel could accept. After arriving in the United States, Eban told Rusk what he and Allon had proposed to the Jordanians. He asked Eshkol to let him tell Jarring as well, and to have Herzog arrange for Jordan's foreign minister to meet him in New York.

Eshkol rejected the idea. He scolded Eban for telling Rusk what he had proposed to Hussein, warning that "if you give [the Americans] a finger, they will want the whole hand, if not the whole head." Under no circumstances, he added, was Eban to disclose the details of his meeting with Hussein to Jarring. Eban glumly wrote back that this sort of attitude "worked against any peace proposal, in any case and at any time," but nevertheless accepted the prime minister's orders.[147] With Jarring, Eban limited his talk of Israeli-Jordanian contacts to generalities, while Herzog flew to London to secure al-Rifaʿi's promise that Jordan would not push for New York meetings so long as secret talks continued.[148] The centerpiece of Eban's trip to the United States was his speech to the General Assembly, in which he argued that Resolution 242 should be "implemented through negotiation." It was an ingenious way for him to appropriate Arab calls for "implementation" while sticking to Israel's previous position, showing some flexibility without causing a crisis at home. Predictably, it was ignored by Egyptian foreign minister Riyadh, who demanded that the Security Council "undertake the supervision and guarantee the implementation of its Resolution 242 of 22 November 1967," which meant the "withdrawal of the Israeli forces from every inch of the occupied Arab territories."[149] Between Eban's and Riyadh's unbending positions, there was just not much room left for Hussein to maneuver.

The Johnson administration might have induced the Israelis to change their minds, but again, Egyptian rigidity dampened their inclination to do so. The president and his inner circle knew what Hussein and the Israelis had discussed in London, and still regarded Israeli-Jordanian talks as the "best hope" for an Arab-Israeli settlement.[150] Rusk and Rostow urged Johnson to "strengthen [Eban's] hand and that of other moderates in the Israeli cabinet" in order to bring the Israelis, Jordanians, and Jarring together.[151] When Johnson met Eban on October 22, the president urged the Israeli foreign minister to make peace with Jordan, and vowed that the United States and Britain would intervene "like in 1958" to defend Hussein's regime.[152] The following day, Johnson sent a terse letter to Eshkol, urging him to "resist those who find it easier to risk Israel's future on today's expanded boundaries than to reach out for real peace."[153] But the Americans' parallel efforts to soften Egypt's stance failed. Even after Rusk told Riyadh that the United States would support Israel's withdrawal from all of Sinai in exchange for opening the Suez Canal, maintaining an international presence at Sharm al-Shaykh, and putting "something in writing to which Israel was also a signatory," the Egyptians barely budged.[154] The Israelis no longer worried about a crisis at the United Nations. Even Rusk, Eban told his party colleagues, was "fed up" with Egypt. The Egyptian government, he added, "took a stand that is so clearly against peace that it could not use its numerical advantage in the General Assembly, and it passed without them trying to start a discussion there or in the Security Council."[155]

Given Egyptian attitudes, the Johnson administration had little incentive to spend its final months pressing for an Israeli-Jordanian settlement. At the end of 1968, the administration sent former Pennsylvania governor William Scranton to Israel and Jordan in order to try and "move Israel off the Allon plan" and start another round of Israeli-Jordanian negotiations.[156] But the Americans did not feel the time was yet ripe to back their calls for greater Israeli moderation with real pressure. Notably, when US officials began to negotiate the terms of a Phantom aircraft sale to Israel that fall, they chose not to link the supply of the planes with progress toward a peace settlement. There was no way to guarantee that "if we asked for something and received it, the Arabs would respond in such a way as to translate the Israeli concession into real progress," argued one State Department memorandum.[157]

Though Allon, Eban, and Herzog met with Hussein and al-Rifaʻi again at the end of November, by this time the chances of an Israeli-Jordanian agreement were dim. The meeting, which was held on November 19 on a ship in the Gulf of Aqaba, amounted to nothing more than a long rehash of both sides' positions on a territorial settlement and Resolution 242.[158] The king and the Israelis did not cut off contact, but their secret talks seemed increasingly pointless. The negotiations appeared unlikely to produce a settlement that both sides could accept, and no longer even held much tactical value for Israel.

Meanwhile, Hussein's domestic political fortunes deteriorated. On November 2, fida'iyyun affiliated with the small Kata'ib al-Nasir (Battalions of Victory) organization stormed a police roadblock outside the US embassy in Amman. The following day, Jordanian police and security forces arrested the group's leader, Tahir Dablan, and began rounding up his supporters in Amman. The ensuing resistance shocked Hussein's inner circle. It took nearly a full division of JAA troops to root out Dablan's group.[159] Since neither the king nor the leaders of the larger fida'iyyun organizations wanted the Dablan affair to escalate into an all-out confrontation, they negotiated a draw of sorts. The Jordanian government agreed not to suppress the fida'iyyun so long as the latter pledged to abide by certain rules—not firing into Israel from the East Bank, coordinating infiltration into the occupied territories with the JAA, not wearing uniforms or carrying weapons in Jordanian cities, and respecting government roadblocks and security regulations.[160] By December, however, the Palestinian militants were violating all of these conditions at will.[161] In February 1969, the Jordanian government suffered another blow when Yasir Arafat was appointed chairman of the PLO. The fida'iyyun now dominated the official representative body of the Palestinian national movement. More than ever, confronting the Palestinian guerrillas could leave Hussein isolated in the Arab world.

Hussein, according to the US embassy in Amman, was "temporarily still ahead of his opposition, but his margin of control over the situation is likely to narrow slowly in the absence of genuine, timely movement toward a settlement."[162] By 1969, it seemed doubtful that there would be such movement. And it was also unlikely that Hussein could make peace with Israel without confronting the fida'iyyun first, regardless of how such a confrontation might affect his claim to the West Bank.

NOTES

1. See especially Shlaim, *Lion of Jordan*; Raz, *Bride and the Dowry*.
2. KFADC minutes, May 21, 1968, ISA/A/8161/12.
3. Chief of staff order, October 18, 1967, in Rosenthal, *Yitzhak Rabin*, 546–547.
4. Rostow to Johnson, September 12, 1967, FRUS, 1964–1968, 19: doc. 436.
5. Tel Aviv to State, November 27, 1967, FRUS, 1964–1968, 19: doc. 3. See also Jerusalem to Washington, November 27, 1967, ISA/A/7938/11.
6. "Protocol of Meeting with the Prime Minister," December 5, 1967, ISA/A/7921/3.
7. Ibid.
8. Ibid.
9. Ibid.
10. Yafeh to Eshkol, December 6, 1967, ISA/A/7936/4; Yafeh to Eban, February 6, 1968, and enclosure, ISA/A/7921/4.
11. Editorial note, in Rosenthal, *Yitzhak Rabin*, 561–562. All of the ministers except Begin and Galili believed that Israel would have to cooperate if the Americans tried to get them to negotiate with Hussein.
12. Saunders-Rabin memcon, June 25, 1969, NA/RG59/DOSCF 1967–1969/POL ISR-US.
13. This, incidentally, was what Yigal Allon believed. See Yigal Allon oral history, ISA/A/5001/19.
14. Quoted in Segev, *1967: Veha-arets shintah et panehah*, 616.
15. This resolution was referred to repeatedly during subsequent cabinet discussions on the negotiations between Israeli officials and Hussein. See, for example, Ya'akov Herzog diary, September 24, 1968, ISA/A/4511/4.
16. Editorial note, in Rosenthal, *Yitzhak Rabin*, 561–562.
17. Eshkol-Johnson memcon, January 7, 1968, FRUS, 1964–1968, 20: doc. 39.
18. Eshkol-Johnson memcon, January 8, 1968, FRUS, 1964–1968, 20: doc. 41.
19. KFADC minutes, February 9, 1968, ISA/A/8161/10.
20. KFADC minutes, November 7, 1967, ISA/A/8161/9.
21. KFADC minutes, February 27, 1968, ISA/A/8161/11.
22. Farid, *Nasser*, 93, 115–116.
23. Black to Johnson, February 14, 1968, FRUS, 1964–1968, 20: doc. 80.

24. Memo for the record, February 21, 1968, FRUS, 1964–1968, 20: doc. 91.
25. Rostow to Johnson, February 5, 1968, FRUS, 1964–1968, 20: doc. 68.
26. Rostow memo for Johnson, February 29, 1968, FRUS, 1964–1968, 20: doc. 94.
27. Tel Aviv to State, February 4, 1968, LBJL/NSF/Country Files/Israel, box 141.
28. State to Tel Aviv, March 10, 1968, FRUS, 1964–1968, 20: doc. 106; Cairo to State, March 14, 1968, FRUS, 1964–1968, 20: doc. 113.
29. New York to State, March 15, 1968, DDRS/CK3100139282.
30. KFADC minutes, March 19, 1968, ISA/A/8161/11.
31. J. P. Tripp, "Jordan in the Doldrums," January 24, 1968, BNA/FCO 17/219.
32. D. G. Crawford, "The Refugee Situation on the East Bank," December 11, 1967, BNA/FCO 17/217.
33. Sasson to Eshkol, December 24, 1967; minutes of the ministerial committee for West Bank affairs, December 24, 1967, ISA/A/7921/3.
34. Amman to State, January 15, 1968, LBJL/NSF/Country Files/Jordan, box 147.
35. Amman to State, January 25, 1968, NA/RG59/DOSCF 1967–1969/POL 27 ARAB-ISR.
36. Sasson, "An Arab-Israeli Peace Agreement—Is It Possible, and How? Summary of Views of Arab Personalities in Jerusalem, Judea, and Samaria," January 30, 1968, ISA/A/7921/4.
37. Sasson, "A First Attempt at a Diplomatic Initiative and Its Lessons," January 22, 1968, ISA/A/7921/4 (emphases in the original).
38. "Diplomatic Contacts with Palestinian Leaders: A Conversation with the Prime Minister," November 21, 1967, ISA/A/7921/3.
39. Tel Aviv to State, February 20, 1968, LBJL/NSF/Country Files/Israel, box 141.
40. Eban-Nusayba memcon, February 20, 1968, AECID/Abba Eban Papers/C-0001 F-0007.
41. Sasson report on Hussein-Nusayba meeting, February 24, 1968, ISA/A/7921/4.
42. Israeli Defense Ministry figures cited in "Terrorism and Internal Security in Israel and Jordan," Special National Intelligence Estimate 30–1–68, April 18, 1968, DDRS/CK3100562605.
43. Sayigh, *Armed Struggle*, 163.
44. Ibid., 177.
45. For a portrait of the border violence in the upper Jordan Valley, see Goren, *ha-Gevul she-lo hutash*.
46. Jerusalem to FCO, December 14, 1967, BNA/FCO 17/630.
47. KFADC minutes, December 19, 1967, ISA/A/8161/9.
48. Amman to State, January 15, 1968, NA/RG59/DOSCF 1967–1969/POL 27 ARAB-ISR.
49. Amman to State, February 15, 1968, and enclosure, LBJL/NSF/Country Files /Jordan, box 147.
50. Abu Iyad, *My Home, My Land*, 57.
51. On Egyptian support for the Palestinian guerrillas, see Sayigh, *Armed Struggle*, 175–176; as well as *al-Ahram*, January 28, 1968.
52. KFADC minutes, February 20, 1968, ISA/A/8161/10.
53. Amman to State, February 20, 1968, LBJL/NSF/Country Files/Jordan, box 147.

54. "Risalat al-malik Husayn ila al-usra al-urduniyya," February 16, 1968, in *al-Watha'iq al-urduniyya, 1968*, 46.
55. "Tasrih al-sayyid Husayn al-Kayid," February 17, 1968, in *al-Watha'iq al-urduniyya, 1968*, 48.
56. Dishon, *Middle East Record, 1968*, 587.
57. *al-Ahram*, February 21, 1968.
58. See David Carmon's remarks in KFADC minutes, February 9, 1968, ISA/A/8161/10. This impression was shared by Moshe Sasson, whose talks with Nusayba led him to conclude that "the king has no interest in allowing the river to become a calm, stable borderline" so long as there was no chance of a settlement on the horizon. See Sasson to Eshkol, February 15, 1968, ISA/A/7921/4.
59. KFADC minutes, March 26, 1968, ISA/A/8161/11.
60. Ya'akov Herzog, "A Special Chapter on Jordan," undated (early April 1968), YHP.
61. Ibid. Unless otherwise noted, my account of the Israeli government's pre-Karameh decision-making is based on this document.
62. Casualty figures cited in *FRUS, 1964–1968*, 20: doc. 116n4.
63. See also KFADC minutes, April 9, 1968, ISA/A/8161/11.
64. On the galvanizing effect that Dayan's injury had on the Foreign Ministry, see also Rafael, *Destination Peace*, 202.
65. My account of the fighting at Karameh is based largely on Bar-Lev's testimony to the KFADC, March 26, 1968, ISA/A/8161/11.
66. Ya'akov Herzog, "A Special Chapter on Jordan," undated (April 1968), YHP.
67. Eshkol's remarks to the cabinet, March 31, 1968, ISA/A/7921/6.
68. *al-Ahram*, March 24, 1968.
69. Sayigh, *Armed Struggle*, 218–220.
70. Quoted in Dishon, *Middle East Record, 1968*, 588.
71. "Discussion with the Minister of Defense," unsigned [Moshe Sasson], April 6, 1968, ISA/A/7921/4.
72. Moshe Sasson, "A Report and Directives from the Prime Minister," April 9, 1968, ISA/A/7921/4.
73. "Discussion with the Minister of Defense," unsigned [Moshe Sasson], April 6, 1968, ISA/A/7921/4.
74. Moshe Dayan, "Assessment of the Diplomatic Situation," April 18, 1968, ISA/A/7921/4.
75. KFADC minutes, April 9, 1968, ISA/A/8161/11.
76. "Discussion with the Minister of Defense," unsigned [Moshe Sasson], April 6, 1968, ISA/A/7921/4.
77. Moshe Dayan, "Assessment of the Diplomatic Situation," April 18, 1968, ISA/A/7921/4.
78. Bar-Lev's remarks, undated (April 18), ISA/A/7921/4.
79. State to Tel Aviv, March 21, 1968, *FRUS, 1964–1968*, 20: doc. 119.
80. Ya'akov Herzog, "A Special Chapter on Jordan," undated (early April 1968), YHP.
81. For the text of the resolution, see *New York Times*, March 24, 1968.
82. Rabin's cables are quoted by Eban in KFADC minutes, April 9, 1968, ISA/A/8161/11.

83. Amman to State, April 8, 1968, *FRUS, 1964–1968*, 20: doc. 136. See also Farid, *Nasser*, 117–122.
84. Amman to State, April 10, 1968, *FRUS, 1964–1968*, 20: doc. 142.
85. See Rostow's comments in Washington to FCO, April 30, 1968, BNA /FCO/17/550.
86. See, for example, Rostow-Evron memcon, April 26, 1968, *FRUS, 1964–1968*, 20: doc. 152.
87. KFADC minutes, April 9, 1968, ISA/A/8161/11.
88. Eban to Rabin, April 18, 1968, AECID/Abba Eban Papers/C-0001 F-0007.
89. See Eban-Meir memcon, April 16, 1968, ISA/A/7936/4.
90. Unsigned, untitled memo, April 25, 1968, ISA/A/7936/4.
91. Rabin to Rusk, April 30, 1968, *FRUS, 1964–1968*, 20: doc. 157.
92. Ya'akov Herzog, "Record of Meeting Held on May 3, 1968," YHP.
93. Eshkol-Dayan-Allon-Eban memcon, May 29, 1968, ISA/A/7921/4.
94. David Farhi, "Moods of the Political Leadership in East Jerusalem and Nablus," May 5, 1968, ISA/A/7921/4.
95. "Consultation on the Subject of the Arabs in the Administered Territories," May 21, 1968, ISA/A/7921/4.
96. Cairo to State, May 14, 1968, *FRUS, 1964–1968*, 20: doc. 173.
97. Rabin-Rostow memcon, May 17, 1968, *FRUS, 1964–1968*, 20: doc. 177.
98. "Meeting with General Y. Rabin," May 24, 1968, ISA/A/7938/11.
99. Labor Party political committee minutes, June 3, 1968, ISA/A/7921/13.
100. Eshkol's remarks to the cabinet, undated (May 1968), ISA/A/7921/6.
101. Eshkol-Eban-Allon-Dayan memcon, May 29, 1968, ISA/A/7921/4.
102. Labor Party political committee minutes, June 3, 1968, ISA/A/7921/13.
103. Ibid.
104. Eshkol-Eban-Allon-Dayan memcon, May 29, 1968, ISA/A/7921/4. For similar remarks, see Labor Party political committee minutes, June 3, 1968, ISA/A/7921/13.
105. On this episode, see Ya'akov Herzog, "From June 12 to July 20, 1968," ISA/A/4511/4.
106. See especially Gorenberg, *Accidental Empire*, 143–151.
107. Eshkol's remarks to the cabinet, undated (May 1968), ISA/A/7921/6.
108. "Consultation on the Subject of the Arabs in the Administered Territories," May 21, 1968, ISA/A/7921/4.
109. Eshkol-Eban-Allon-Dayan memcon, May 29, 1968, ISA/A/7921/4.
110. Herzog had argued that "in a situation of heavy international pressure, we can say that we're partaking in an experiment with [the West Bank Palestinians] and that we ask that they give us time for things to play out." See "Consultation on the Subject of the Arabs in the Administered Territories," May 21, 1968, ISA/A/7921/4.
111. Labor Party political committee minutes, June 3, 1968, ISA/A/7921/13.
112. Ya'akov Herzog, "From June 12 to July 20, 1968," ISA/A/4511/4.
113. By early July, the Israeli cabinet had received reports that the Allon Plan had made a "bad impression" in the United States. Ya'akov Herzog, "From June 12 to July 20, 1968," ISA/A/4511/4.
114. Labor Party political committee minutes, June 3, 1968, ISA/A/7921/13.
115. Ya'akov Herzog, "From June 12 to July 20, 1968," ISA/A/4511/4.
116. Amman to State, July 17, 1968, *FRUS, 1964–1968*, 20: doc. 217.

117. For a vivid portrait of the American political scene in 1968, see Lafeber, *Deadly Bet*.
118. Meeting notes, June 25, 1968, FRUS, 1964–1968, 20: doc. 199. See also Rusk to Johnson, May 23, 1968, FRUS, 1964–1968, 20: doc. 180.
119. Editorial note, FRUS, 1964–1968, 20: doc. 186.
120. KFADC minutes, July 5, 1968, ISA/A/8162/1.
121. Ya'akov Herzog, "From June 12 to July 20, 1968," ISA/A/4511/4 (emphasis in the original).
122. Herzog to Eban, June 19, 1968, YHP.
123. Amman to State, July 24, 1968, LBJL/NSF/Country Files/Jordan, box 148.
124. Tel Aviv to FCO, June 10, 1968, BNA/FCO 17/636; DOD memo, June 4, 1968, DDRS/CK3100186123.
125. Amman to FCO, August 7, 1968, BNA/FCO 17/637.
126. Amman to State, May 31, 1968, NA/RG59/DOSCF, 1967–1969/POL 23 JORDAN; J. P. Tripp, "Jordan's Prospects following the Israeli Attack on 4 August," August 27, 1968, BNA/FCO 17/637; Dishon, *Middle East Record, 1968*, 591–592.
127. See, for example, his comments to Bundy in Amman to State, July 20, 1968, FRUS, 1964–1968, 20: doc. 221.
128. Sasson-Dayan memcon, June 30, 1968; "Summary of Discussion of the Committee on Arab Contacts, Headed by the Prime Minister, July 3, 1968," ISA/A/7921/5.
129. "Consultation on Our Conduct in the Administered Territories, July 23, 1968," ISA/A/7921/5.
130. Petition by West Bank notables, August 26, 1968, ISA/A/7921/5.
131. On these attacks, see Gazit, *Carrot and the Stick*, 270–271.
132. Korn, *Stalemate*, 93.
133. Eshkol's remarks to the cabinet, August 21, 1968, copy in ISA/A/4511/4.
134. Rabin cable, September 11, 1968, reproduced in Ya'akov Herzog diary, ISA/A/4511/4.
135. Rusk-Dobrynin memcon and attachment, September 4, 1968, FRUS, 1964–1968, 20: doc. 245.
136. Rabin cable, September 14, 1968, reproduced in Ya'akov Herzog diary, ISA/A/4511/4.
137. Ya'akov Herzog diary, September 16, 1968, ISA/A/4511/4.
138. Ya'akov Herzog diary, September 15, 1968, ISA/A/4511/4.
139. Ya'akov Herzog diary, September 24, 1968, ISA/A/4511/4.
140. Ya'akov Herzog diary, undated summary (probably October 1968), ISA/A/4511/4.
141. Ya'akov Herzog, "Meeting with Charles on September 27th, 1968, in London (15:30–17:30 P.M.)," YHP.
142. Ibid.
143. Ibid.
144. FCO to Amman, September 28, 1968, BNA/FCO 17/54.
145. State to Amman, October 7, 1968, LBJL/NSF/Country Files/Jordan, box 147.
146. Eban to Eshkol, September 29, 1968, YHP.
147. Ya'akov Herzog, "Additional Notes on the Conversation with Charles, September 27, 1968," YHP.
148. Herzog's report to the cabinet, October 27, 1968, YHP.

149. Eban's October 8 and Riyadh's October 10 speeches to the General Assembly are quoted in *Yearbook of the United Nations, 1968: The Situation in the Middle East*, UNISPAL, https://unispal.un.org/DPA/DPR/unispal.nsf/9a798adbf322aff38525617b006d88 d7/9d181d3b2925e6b785256cc6007496aa?OpenDocument.

150. Rostow to Johnson, September 30, 1968, *FRUS*, 1964–1968, 20: doc. 267.

151. Rusk memo to Johnson, October 21, 1968, NA/RG59/DOSCF 1967–1969/POL ISR-US; Rostow to Johnson, October 23, 1968, NA/RG59/DOSCF 1967–1969/POL ISR-US.

152. KFADC minutes, October 30, 1968, ISA/A/8162/2. For the much less revealing American account of this conversation, see Eban-Johnson memcon, October 22, 1968, *FRUS*, 1964–1968, 20: doc. 284.

153. Johnson to Eshkol, October 23, 1968, *FRUS*, 1964–1968, 20: doc. 285.

154. UN to State, November 3, 1968, *FRUS*, 1964–1968, 20: doc. 301.

155. Labor Party political committee minutes, December 27, 1968, ISA/A/7921/13.

156. Harold Saunders, "Mid-East Scenario for the Next Month," November 25, 1968, LBJL/NSF/Country Files/Jordan, box 147.

157. Hart to Rusk, October 15, 1968, NA/RG59/DOSCF 1967–1969/DEF 12–5 ISR.

158. Ya'akov Herzog, "Meeting Held on November 19, 1968," YHP.

159. See Zayd al-Rifa'i's and Hussein's accounts in, respectively, Amman to State, November 6, 1968, NA/RG59/DOSCF 1967–1969/POL 23–8 JORDAN; Amman to State, November 11, 1968, NA/RG59/DOSCF 1967–1969/POL 23 JORDAN.

160. FM Research Division to Director-General, November 24, 1968, ISA /FM/4296/9.

161. KFADC minutes, December 24, 1968, ISA/A/8162/3.

162. Amman to State, November 27, 1968, NA/RG59/DOSCF 1967–1969/POL 1 JORDAN-US.

EIGHT

THE JORDANIAN CIVIL WAR AND THE SEEDS OF DISENGAGEMENT, 1969–1970

BETWEEN JANUARY 1969 AND SEPTEMBER 1970, THE HASHEM-
ite monarchy nearly collapsed. During this period, Israel's leaders stopped asking themselves whether they could reach a settlement with King Hussein. Instead, they began to wonder whether Israel still had a stake in the Hashemite monarchy's existence.

There were, in fact, influential Israelis who argued that it would be better if the Palestinians took control of the East Bank. A Palestinian regime in Amman, they claimed, would enjoy greater legitimacy than Hussein and might eventually agree to resolve the West Bank issue in a way that Israel could accept. But when Hussein and the fida'iyyun finally confronted each other in September 1970, Golda Meir's government felt compelled to act on the king's behalf. The US government was determined to ensure Hussein's survival, and the Israelis did not want to part ways with their American patrons.

As a result, Hussein's regime survived, but he could no longer mobilize Arab or Palestinian backing for his claims to the West Bank. The struggle for the West Bank began to evolve into an Israeli-Palestinian contest in which Jordan played an increasingly marginal role.

A STATE WITHIN A STATE

By 1969, the Palestinian guerrilla organizations had established what one US estimate called "almost a state within a state" in Jordan.[1] The Jordanian government barely controlled large parts of its territory, particularly north of Amman. Even 'Abd al-Mun'im al-Rifa'i, who alternated with Bahjat al-Talhuni as prime minister through the summer of 1970, admitted that the Jordanian government was "not in complete control of the situation in some parts of Jordan."[2] The fida'iyyun moved about fully armed nearly everywhere outside the capital. An atmosphere of lawlessness prevailed. Bands of armed fida'iyyun were frequently spotted roaming around Petra and Jerash, the kingdom's major tourist sites. The number of burglaries in Amman rose sharply, as did cases of fida'iyyun extorting local businessmen for "contributions." During 'Id al-Adha, armed eleven- and twelve-year-olds stopped traffic on Amman's downtown streets, demanding money for the PFLP.[3] Even Hussein and his family did not escape harassment. In July 1969, a Fatah guerrilla strolled into one of the king's palaces fully armed. He was arrested but was released after claiming that he merely wanted to "pay his respects" to Hussein. Shortly thereafter, Princess Muna's car was held up by fida'iyyun, who interrogated her at gunpoint.[4]

Hussein and his government nevertheless made little effort to clamp down on the Palestinian organizations. After a year of fruitless contacts with Israel, they believed that border violence might help them achieve what diplomacy had not. Like the Egyptians, who began shelling Israeli positions along the Suez Canal in March 1969, Hussein and his inner circle believed that more border clashes might finally convince the Americans to impose a settlement on Israel.[5] In April, the king told President Richard Nixon that "the Arabs were prepared to sign any document with Israel except a formal peace treaty," and that if the Israelis were "less vague" about the Gaza Strip, he could offer "substantial" concessions on the West Bank.[6] Yet only after Israel withdrew from the West Bank, Zayd al-Rifa'i told Assistant Secretary of State Joseph Sisco, would Jordan "turn its security forces loose."[7] Meeting with Allon, Eban, and Herzog, Hussein warned that "in the absence of progress on the political front, it would be impossible [to completely] stop [the] incidents."[8] The king even briefly allowed the JAA to shoot at IDF vehicles near the ceasefire line and to fire back when the IDF shelled the Palestinian guerrillas' positions.[9]

When the IDF responded by bombing the East Ghor Canal, the Jordanian government reined in its troops, but Hussein made no effort to hold back the fida'iyyun at any point in 1969.[10] The closest he came was in June, when he appointed his uncle Sharif Nasir and Muhammad Rasul al-Kaylani, two known opponents of the Palestinian guerrillas, as JAA commander in chief and minister of the interior, respectively.[11] But in the end, Hussein did not order the JAA to act. By late August, Zayd al-Rifa'i claimed that the king was "resigned" to the closure of the East Ghor Canal and pessimistic about ever bringing the fida'iyyun under control.[12]

No matter how punishing the IDF's reprisals were, Hussein did not yet want to take a stand against the Palestinian guerrillas. Not only did the king not want to make life easier for the Israelis, but he and his advisors genuinely feared they might lose if they challenged the fida'iyyun. 'Amir Khammash, whose tenure as chief of staff ended in 1969, thought the monarchy would "probably lose out" in a confrontation with the guerrillas.[13] On paper, the Palestinian militants were no match for the JAA. Even in September 1970, the major Palestinian groups fielded no more than about fourteen thousand relatively lightly armed fighters. The JAA, in contrast, numbered about fifty-eight thousand troops, including two full infantry divisions and an armored division.[14] Nevertheless, a JAA-fida'iyyun clash could provoke a Syrian or Iraqi invasion and alienate the Arab oil producers who were sustaining Jordan's economy. In the event of a showdown, the fida'iyyun would also likely have the support of Jordan's Palestinian majority and many urban East Bankers, particularly in Irbid, which had always been susceptible to anti-Hashemite sentiment and bore the brunt of many Israeli reprisals.[15]

The fida'iyyun even cultivated some support within the East Bank's major tribal confederations, traditionally the bedrock of the monarchy's power. A number of the Bani Sakhr, one of the largest and most powerful East Bank tribes, joined Fatah. Deputy Prime Minister 'Akif al-Fayiz, one of the Bani Sakhr's leading figures and a longtime fixture in Jordanian cabinets, went so far as to have his house placed under Fatah guard.[16] Al-Fayiz's affinity for Fatah was unusual for a member of the East

Bank establishment, but indicative of the sympathy that some members of the Jordanian political elite felt for the guerrillas. A number of prominent East Bankers, including ʻAbd al-Munʻim al-Rifaʻi, al-Talhuni, and Khammash, hoped to bring the Palestinian national movement into the mainstream of Jordanian politics. They called for curbing smaller leftist groups like the PFLP while seeking a modus vivendi with Fatah, ostensibly the least "ideological" of the Palestinian organizations.[17]

Hussein thus pursued short-term rapprochement with the fida'iyyun while quietly preparing for confrontation. The king moved East Bank officers into operational roles, shifted Palestinian officers into staff positions, and enlarged Sharif Nasir's all-Bedouin Desert Forces.[18] The first test of strength between Hussein and the fida'iyyun in February 1970, however, indicated that the king was still unwilling or unable to confront the guerrillas. In January, at the urging of his army officers, Hussein informed US officials that he planned to move against the fida'iyyun, and asked them to restrain the Israelis while he moved troops off the ceasefire line and into the East Bank's cities.[19] On February 10, the Jordanian government issued a new set of internal security guidelines aimed at regulating fida'iyyun behavior in urban areas.[20] When the internal security forces attempted to enforce these new measures, the Palestinian militants resisted. Fida'iyyun seized several of Amman's seven hills, including Jabal Ashrafiyya, Jabal Taj, and Jabal Hussein. In Irbid, Palestinian guerrillas captured much of the city center.[21] It appeared that the time for a clash had finally come.

But the JAA never received its marching orders. For another week Hussein thought about forcing a confrontation. He readied Jordanian warplanes to bomb Iraqi or Syrian troops that might join up with the fida'iyyun, and again asked the Americans to restrain the Israelis and provide arms for his supporters.[22] Yet by February 12, the king capitulated. The government announced a "freeze" on the new security regulations, which was followed by an "agreement of viewpoints" between Hussein and the fida'iyyun on February 22. The details of the agreement were kept secret, but Hussein privately indicated that he had granted the Palestinian guerrillas a role in enforcing internal law and order.[23] Interior Minister al-Kaylani, whom the Palestinians hated, resigned—probably because the guerrillas had demanded that he step down.

Following the February clashes, Hussein and Zayd al-Rifaʻi tried to put a brave face on what had happened. In conversations with American, British, and Israeli officials, they claimed that aggressive JAA officers wanted "to sort the [fidaʼiyyun] out once and for all," but the government had wisely chosen to avoid bloodshed and enlisted Fatah to bring more militant organizations under control. Moreover, Hussein and al-Rifaʻi claimed, so long as Israel remained politically inflexible, there was no point in risking a JAA-fidaʼiyyun confrontation.[24] But in fact, the February showdown appeared to mark what US ambassador Harold Symmes called "the lowest trough of Hashemite authority" since 1967. The king, Symmes reported, now ruled largely on the "sufferance" of his "disunited adversaries." In the meantime, the regime's traditional pillars of support—the major East Bank tribes and Jordan's ethnic and religious minorities—were coming to see Hussein as incapable of defending their interests.[25]

As it turned out, the US ambassador spoke too soon. "The lowest trough of Hashemite authority" really arrived in June 1970. On June 6, after fidaʼiyyun severely beat a Jordanian soldier outside Amman's Hussein mosque, gunfights between soldiers and guerrillas broke out all over the city. The next day, members of the Syrian-backed al-Saʻiqa group fired on JAA troops in Zarqa. In the ensuing battle, one soldier and seven fidaʼiyyun and civilians were killed. An even worse round of fighting then began in Amman.[26] Fidaʼiyyun attacked Amman's radio, television, and power stations, shelled Hussein's palaces, and fired at Hussein's motorcade.[27] Mayor Ahmad Fawzi estimated that $1.5 million worth of municipal stores were destroyed.[28] Fidaʼiyyun also kidnapped US diplomat Morris Draper, raped the wives of two other US officials, and murdered US military attaché Robert Perry.[29] The PFLP briefly seized the Philadelphia and Intercontinental Hotels, taking some sixty foreigners hostage.[30] The JAA responded by indiscriminately shelling the areas where the guerrillas had holed up. Amman's Wahdat refugee camp suffered seventeen direct hits from JAA artillery batteries on June 10. Mass graves were dug for the dead; the nearby hospital could not accommodate all of the wounded.[31] Official estimates claimed that seventy-eight civilians, fourteen soldiers, and four security personnel were killed before a ceasefire was reached on June 10, but the real total was probably higher.³² "It is hard to avoid the feeling that we are witnessing the general disintegration of the state," commented one British diplomat.³³

Hussein still tried to placate the guerrillas. Bowing to the PFLP's demands, the king forced Sharif Nasir and Zayd Bin Shakir, commander of the JAA's Third Armored Division, to resign their posts.³⁴ The king appointed Mashur Haditha al-Jazi, known for his sympathy for the guerrillas, as JAA chief of staff.³⁵ He formed a new cabinet, and out of its seventeen ministers, seven had signed statements in support of the fida'iyyun during the June crisis.³⁶ The king also agreed to allow an Arab League committee composed of Egyptian, Sudanese, Libyan, and Algerian officials to mediate between him and the Palestinian guerrillas. There was virtually no sign that the king would use force to regain control over his kingdom.

"We visualize a day coming when Jordan might become little more than a convenient battleground, into which various fedayeen and Arab forces ... would move from time to time," predicted the US embassy in Amman.³⁷ It was not the first time that foreign diplomats had warned of Jordan's impending descent into anarchy. In the past, the JAA had crushed the king's internal opponents, while powerful external forces deterred other Arab states from intervening. The difference this time was that Hussein no longer controlled one of the most strategically sensitive pieces of territory in the Middle East. Would Israel and the United States still try to keep the Hashemite monarchy in power?

ISRAEL, THE UNITED STATES, AND THE FUTURE OF JORDAN, 1969–1970

Richard Nixon, who became president in 1969, had little interest in a "Jordan-first" approach to resolving the Arab-Israeli conflict. Though Nixon, a solitary, profane, and deeply insecure man, had clawed his way to prominence with a series of nasty red-baiting campaigns, he was determined to enlist the Soviets in ending the war in Vietnam. He and his national security advisor, the German-Jewish political scientist Henry Kissinger, believed that the way to get the Soviets to cooperate was to seek "linkages" between Vietnam and other areas of superpower conflict, including the Middle East.³⁸ In the Arab-Israeli context, this meant that the United States would direct its energies toward resolving the conflict between Israel and Egypt, the superpowers' two main clients. "We don't think Hussein could survive a separate settlement," Secretary of State William Rogers told the NSC in February 1969.[39] "A UAR plan," he commented a few months later, "is the place to start."[40] When the Nixon administration launched the so-called Two Power talks with the Soviets on the Arab-Israeli dispute, they conspicuously chose not to discuss Israeli-Jordanian matters, leaving those for the far less important Four Power talks with the Soviets, the French, and the British.[41] By September 1969, Zayd al-Rifa'i was complaining that Jordan had been "set aside and neglected" by the superpowers.[42]

In theory, the Israelis might have had a great deal to fear from the Nixon administration's new approach to Arab-Israeli diplomacy. After all, since June 1967 they had worried that the superpowers would join together and force them to withdraw from the occupied territories. And indeed, Israeli officials initially responded to the Two Power and Four Power talks just as they had responded to the Jarring mission—by playing up their bilateral contacts with Hussein.[43] By the spring of 1969, however, the Israelis abandoned this tactic. The Nixon administration, Rabin told his government, knew what had occurred between Israel and Jordan on Johnson's watch, and would no longer play Israel's game.[44] The tactical value of Israel's contacts with Hussein had run out.

Yet the Israelis were not terribly dismayed when the Nixon administration abandoned Johnson's Jordan-first approach to peacemaking. Partly this reflected a change in leadership: Levi Eshkol died in office in February 1969, and was replaced by Golda Meir. The new prime minister disdained both Eban and Herzog for their intellectualism, and still resented both for outshining her during her years as foreign minister. She would soon relegate Hussein's interlocutors to the margins, relying instead on Rabin, who remained ambassador in Washington, and Dayan, whom she valued for his military expertise and blunt hawkishness.[45]

But there were also more substantive reasons for the Israelis to cheer the shift in US policy away from Jordan. The Israelis had never wanted the United States to put forward its own ideas for a West Bank deal. Declining outside interest in an Israeli-Jordanian settlement and quiet on the West Bank, Herzog concluded, meant that "on this front, time is definitely working to our advantage."[46] The fact that America's new Middle

East policy depended heavily on Soviet and Egyptian flexibility could also serve Israel's interests. The initial phase, in which the Americans probed Soviet intentions, was bound to be tense. As Rabin noted in his memoirs, "March–July 1969 were difficult and uncomfortable months for us."⁴⁷ But the Israelis knew that Kissinger saw Soviet policy as the taproot of regional tension, and that he disliked the State Department's efforts to work out the terms of a settlement with the USSR.⁴⁸ They understood that if US-Soviet talks dragged on long enough, Kissinger could win Nixon over, and the threat of an imposed settlement would disappear.

Still, Meir and her colleagues worried that stalemate in the US-Soviet talks might lead the Americans *back* to a Jordan-first approach, and tried to block off that route as well.⁴⁹ "Any separate settlement between Israel and Jordan seems remote," Herzog told Kissinger, Rogers, and other US officials in the fall of 1969.⁵⁰ In December, when Assistant Secretary Sisco suggested to Eban that they meet secretly with Zayd al-Rifa'i and "get Israeli-Jordanian negotiations started," Eban brushed the idea aside. "There was no communications problem between Israel and Jordan at this point," he said.⁵¹ Yet at the same time, the Israelis downgraded their bilateral contacts with Hussein. Eban and Allon stopped meeting with the king. After May 1969, talks with Jordanians were handled primarily by Herzog and, on a few occasions, Chief of Staff Bar-Lev. The Israelis used these conversations mainly to probe for information about Arab politics and to urge Hussein to repress the fida'iyyun. The parties largely stopped discussing the future of the West Bank.⁵²

By the end of 1969, Israel's diplomatic strategy appeared to have succeeded. Deadlock in the Two Power talks convinced Nixon that Kissinger was right. The Americans could not easily "deliver" the Israelis, and by trying too hard to do so, they stood to help the Soviets. The turning point came in December, when the USSR, Egypt, and Israel all rejected peace proposals put forward by Rogers. "From now on," said Nixon, "we're going to go it alone in the peace process. The Soviets have had their opportunity."⁵³ The fact that Jordan accepted the so-called Rogers Plan was irrelevant to the president. It was indicative of how marginal a role Hussein had come to play in Arab-Israeli diplomacy.

The breakdown of internal order in Jordan and Hussein's declining stature were bound to raise certain questions in the US and Israel. What exactly was the king's regime worth to them? Would Hussein's fall lead to greater instability and violence, or could it produce a Palestinian successor regime that might eventually reach a settlement with Israel?

The Israelis had clearer reasons to see the possible upsides to Hussein's fall. Many of them no longer believed that the fida'iyyun would pose a worse threat without him. "Since 1965, the Palestinian organizations have wanted to turn Jordan into North Vietnam. . . . In effect, they have achieved that," Aharon Yariv told the Knesset Foreign Affairs and Defense Committee in February 1969.[54] Intelligence estimates prepared for Meir's September 1969 visit to the United States argued that the Palestinian organizations enjoyed "almost complete freedom of action" in Jordan.[55] If anything, the Israelis believed that Hussein made their fida'iyyun troubles worse than they might have been otherwise, since his ties to the United States prevented Israel from responding more forcefully to guerrilla attacks. The Israeli government constantly had to weigh the benefits of retaliatory operations against the Foreign Ministry's fear of alienating the Americans.[56] "We are limited in our ability to fight them in Jordan," Yariv admitted.[57]

But there were broader strategic reasons for the Israelis to conclude that Hussein's downfall might not be such a bad thing. After all, the king refused to consider the sort of West Bank agreement that Israel's leaders wanted. And so long as Hussein remained in power, Israel could not pursue a separate "Palestinian option" on the West Bank. But what if the Palestinians took power on the East Bank? Then, perhaps the endless triangulation among Israel, the Hashemite monarchy, and the West Bankers would end. A Palestinian-dominated government on the East Bank would also have a broader political base and might therefore find it easier to make territorial concessions and keep the peace along the border. And a Palestinian entity that encompassed both banks of the Jordan would be more viable than a truncated West Bank cut off from the Arab world.

Certainly, Israel's leaders did not think it would be impossible to make peace with a Palestinian-dominated regime. If the king fell, Dayan told a small group of cabinet ministers and generals in October 1969, Israel could pursue a "Palestinian peace."[58] Israel, Eban told British foreign secretary Michael Stewart, would have no problem if Jordan "decided to call itself Palestine." "Our problem," Eban argued, "is what Israel will look like in the event of peace. Once we establish secure borders, what goes on beyond them is the Arabs' business."⁵⁹ Even Meir, supposedly an arch-foe of Palestinian nationalism, had no problem with the idea of dealing with a Palestinian-led Jordan. "I don't want to conduct negotiations with Arafat while he heads an organization whose goal is to murder us," she told the General Staff in the spring of 1970. "But if he is Jordan's chosen representative and wants to conduct peace negotiations, I can imagine sitting with him."⁶⁰

Still, it was not only the Palestinians that Israel's leaders had to consider. If Hussein's regime collapsed, Syrian or Iraqi forces would probably try to carve up Jordan. "The conquest of Jordan," Dayan told Meir and the General Staff in 1969, "has always been on the Iraqis' minds."⁶¹ And if the IDF tried to counter a Syrian or Iraqi takeover of Jordan, they could find themselves facing Soviet troops. In December 1968, when British ambassador Michael Hadow asked Yariv whether Israel would benefit from Hussein's fall, the AMAN chief responded, "I'd rather have you on my back than the Russians." The Israelis, Hadow thought, had clearly been influenced by the situation along the Suez Canal, where they faced "an Egypt both unwilling and unable to make peace with Israel and backed by Russian arms and technicians down to the battalion level."⁶² By the spring of 1970 a ten-thousand-man Soviet air defense division had deployed in Egypt. Soviet fighter pilots were flying missions on Egypt's behalf, and Soviet-manned SAM-3 batteries were approaching the canal line.⁶³ The USSR was clearly willing and able to provide its Arab clients with a security umbrella under which they could wage war against Israel. The implications for the Jordanian front were ominous.⁶⁴

In such circumstances, the Israelis could not just let events in Jordan take their course. To intervene in Jordan, Israel would need backing from the United States, the only power that could keep the Soviets out. If Hussein fell, Dayan told Meir and the General Staff in October 1969, the IDF might seize small parts of the East Bank "for the sake of Israel's defense," but further Israeli moves would depend on US approval. Only with US backing, Dayan argued, could Israel "prevent pro-Soviet extremists from taking over" or "prevent the entry of Syrian and Iraqi forces into Jordan."⁶⁵ In light of the USSR's expanding role in the Middle East, Israel needed the shield of US power to shape whatever new order developed on the East Bank.

What this meant was that the Israelis needed to cultivate the Americans very carefully. Meir's government did not want the Nixon administration to blame Israel for Hussein's collapse. When Hussein asked Israel for "breathing space" in February and June 1970, Meir responded favorably through US channels.[66] Regardless of whether the king managed to defeat his Palestinian rivals, such restraint could still earn Israel some diplomatic points in Washington. At the same time, top Israeli officials tried to convince the Americans that Hussein's regime might have outlived its usefulness. The fall of his regime, Rabin told Sisco in August 1969, might not be such a bad thing. "In hindsight," he said, "perhaps Israel erred by not conquering all of Jordan [in 1967], even more so than [not conquering] Cairo and Damascus." Had Israel conquered both banks of the Jordan, Rabin argued, there would be no danger of a pro-Soviet regime taking power in Amman. With US aid, Israel could have resettled massive numbers of refugees and implemented far-reaching development programs. "After World War II," Rabin remarked, "the Americans implemented plans in Japan and Germany to repair and alter the character of the [societies under occupation], which could serve as a model for the Middle East." Most importantly, Israel could have dealt with all the Palestinians on both banks at once. "There is no room in the original Palestine (1920) for more than two states: Israel and a Jordan which is the state of the Palestinians," Rabin asserted.[67]

Sisco's response, however, indicated that such Israeli overtures were premature. Though Rabin got the impression that "the United States would rather have us there [i.e., on the East Bank] than a Soviet linked-regime," Sisco avoided discussing the subject any further.[68] A few weeks later, Sisco told Israeli diplomat Shlomo Argov that the United States "had not yet written [Hussein] off" and so there was no need to plan for what would follow his demise.[69] When Meir visited Washington soon afterward, she was advised to downplay Hussein's importance, but not to go any further.[70]

The Israelis waited until April 1970 to sound out the Americans about Jordan's future again. When Sisco met with Dayan in Israel, the Israeli defense minister commented that he did not want to find himself later in the position of "having seen the overthrow of the Hashemite regime coming but having done nothing about it." According to Dayan,

Israel would not act to "save a Jordanian regime . . . which was falling and had little or no chance of survival." Rather, the defense minister wanted the Americans to tell him what Israel should do in "a situation in which a struggle might be going on" between Hussein's regime and "other elements" in which Israeli intervention could "tip the balance." Whatever Israel did, Dayan emphasized, would be done only with the explicit blessing of the United States. If Hussein asked Israel to intervene, Israel could "do it physically and legally but not unless you concur and support."[71] Dayan seems to have wanted to secure US support for Israeli intervention in Jordan regardless of the ultimate outcome. Ostensibly, the goal of an Israeli attack on Syrian or Iraqi forces would be to "tip the balance" in Hussein's favor, but Dayan surely knew that Israel could not guarantee that Hussein would survive. Nevertheless, if Israel's leaders knew the Americans would support their intervening, they could rest assured that they could secure their interests in Jordan without fear of a clash with the USSR.

Yet while Nixon and his advisors had little faith that Hussein could play a major role in regional diplomacy, they worried much more than the Israelis about his possible overthrow. "We can see nothing but trouble from a regime like Iraq's or Syria's in Jordan," Kissinger told Nixon in April 1969.[72] The "greatest USSR victory," Rogers remarked that same month, "would be [a] radical takeover in Jordan."[73] Nixon also wanted to preserve the Hashemite regime, and disliked the Israelis' "fatalistic attitude" toward it. "That kind of thinking," he snapped, "is a death wish. They must not be given any encouragement."[74]

By the spring of 1970, American thinking on Jordan began to shift somewhat. Before Symmes left Amman at the beginning of May, he drafted a long cable in which he urged the Nixon administration to reconsider its backing for Hussein. The outgoing ambassador argued that the king's long-term prospects were poor, and that he could not help to resolve the fate of the West Bank even if he managed to stay in power. The time had come for the United States to reconsider its policy of exclusive support for the Hashemite monarchy. "The fundamental problem with exclusive support," Symmes argued, "is that it supposes that Hussein can still remain an authentic spokesman on behalf of Palestinian rights, when clearly the initiative in this respect is passing to others." Symmes called for the United States to adopt a policy of "slow disengagement" from the Hashemite monarchy, and to "deal directly but discreetly with the forces of Palestinian nationalism, including the [fida'iyyun]." Peace, Symmes wrote, "may lie in [the] premise that 'Palestine is Jordan, and Jordan is Palestine.'"[75]

In principle, Symmes's ideas appealed to some other US officials. Sisco, for instance, had concluded that neither Jordan nor Lebanon could play a productive role in the peace process; at most, the United States could maintain "holding operations" there. "Only Israel, the Palestinians, and the UAR retain any room for maneuver," he told Kissinger.[76] Harold Saunders, who remained on the NSC staff, also thought the United States should consider reaching out to Palestinian nationalists. While a "Palestinian entity created on the West Bank by Israel" could not work, Saunders argued, "a 'partition of Palestine' negotiated by the Israelis and Arab Palestinians would have at least a chance of looking like a real solution."[77]

Nevertheless, even if some US officials recognized the long-term desirability of coming to terms with Palestinian nationalism, they feared the short-term consequences of the Hashemite regime's collapse more. When the Washington Special Actions Group (WSAG), the NSC's special subcommittee for crisis management, discussed Jordan in June, no one argued that the United States should stand aside if Hussein called for outside help. Though military support for Hussein "would seem one of the last moves we should contemplate," Kissinger told Nixon, the United States could lose the trust of other "moderate" Middle Eastern governments by ignoring Hashemite pleas. Moreover, "an Iraqi-Syrian-fedayeen takeover" in Jordan could provoke Israeli intervention, giving the Soviets "cause for entrenching themselves on the Eastern front."[78] To maintain American credibility, prevent regional war, and deter Soviet intervention, Nixon's advisors felt they must support Hussein.

Still, there were limits on what the United States could do for the king. Perhaps the only important US policymaker who actually wanted to use force on Hussein's behalf was Nixon himself. The president thought that a crisis in Jordan would give him an opportunity to demonstrate his toughness to the USSR and the American public. "There comes a time when the US is going to be tested as to its credibility in the area," he told the NSC. "The real question will be, will we act? .... We must be ready."[79] But Nixon's advisors were not so bellicose. The possibility of military intervention in Jordan had been considered and ruled out by the State Department and the NSC staff as early as the spring of 1969. Washington's Middle East experts assumed that US military intervention on Hussein's behalf would not keep him in power and could provoke major Soviet countermoves.[80] Even as officials like Kissinger and Sisco began to plan for possible military intervention in Jordan in the summer of 1970, they hoped to avoid actually sending US troops there. Sisco feared that US intervention on Hussein's behalf could "polarize the Middle East" and badly damage America's position in the Arab world. "I personally would want to use American troops and aircraft only as a last resort," he said. Kissinger felt the same. "I assume that we would intervene only if US lives were in danger," he told the WSAG.[81]

It was as if the American and Israeli positions were mirror images of each other. The Israelis, who could easily intervene in Jordan, were not terribly eager to save Hussein. The Americans, who did not want to get militarily involved in the Middle East, wanted to keep Hussein in power. The gap between the US and Israeli positions was substantial enough for both sides to avoid discussing the Hashemite kingdom with each other through the summer of 1970. Despite Dayan's overture in April, the Americans did not involve Meir's government in their contingency planning for Jordan, and the Israelis did not raise the kingdom's future with the Americans again. By mid-June 1970, Rabin concluded that the United States would not intervene in Jordan even if "Palestinian extremists seize power as the result of the present regime's collapse." Still, the Americans would be "happy and satisfied if the present situation lasted for a while," and did not want Israel to do anything that "embarrassed" Hussein. The question of whether the United States would allow Israel to intervene in Jordan if Hussein fell, Rabin thought, should not be raised yet. Israel needed to wait for the right moment.[82]

THE PATH TO CIVIL WAR

Though the roots of Jordan's civil war lay in the political stalemate and border violence that followed the 1967 conflict, it was the prospect of diplomatic progress that finally ignited it. By the spring of 1970, US policymakers feared that the War of Attrition could escalate into a regional war, with the Soviets deeply involved. In July, after months of negotiations, Sisco and Rogers convinced Egypt and Israel to agree to a ninety-day ceasefire and renewed talks under UN auspices.[83] For Hussein, the Israeli-Egyptian ceasefire finally tipped the scales in favor of confronting the fida'iyyun.[84] The ceasefire offered renewed hope for an Arab-Israeli settlement and left the PLO estranged from Egypt, its main partner in border warfare against Israel. On July 26, the Jordanian government declared its support for the American proposals, aligning itself with Egypt against the PLO, Iraq, Algeria, and Syria.

From this point, it was only a matter of time before the Jordanian government and the Palestinian guerrillas clashed. The PFLP and PDFLP now called upon the other guerrilla organizations to capitalize on popular opposition to the ceasefire and seize power. At an extraordinary session of the Palestinian National Council held on August 27–28, the PDFLP called for the "establishment of a revolutionary nationalist authority [in Jordan]." Since most of the other guerrilla organizations, particularly Fatah, were not ready to call openly for regime change, the PDFLP's proposal was rejected. Even Fatah's relative restraint, however, reflected the overconfidence of its leaders more than a desire to avoid confrontation. Arafat and his comrades believed that the fida'iyyun were growing stronger with time, and that Hussein was unlikely to move against them.[85] Indeed, Arafat's rhetoric increasingly echoed the speeches of his more radical counterparts. On August 15, for example, he proclaimed that Amman would become the "Hanoi of the Revolution" and a "cemetery for conspirators."[86]

The fida'iyyun leaders' verbal attacks on the ceasefire and Hussein coincided with numerous strikes, demonstrations, and violent clashes between the JAA and the guerrilla groups. At the end of August, a series of violent incidents erupted in Amman, peaking on September 1, when Palestinian gunmen tried once again to assassinate the king. Five days later, PFLP guerrillas landed two hijacked commercial airliners at Dawson's Field, a former British airstrip outside Zarqa. A third hijacked plane landed there on September 9. By September 12, the guerrillas had blown up the planes and fled, taking fifty-four passengers with them as hostages.[87] In the meantime, the remainder of the Palestinian organizations finally committed themselves to ousting Hussein. On September 8, Fatah's revolutionary council adopted a resolution calling for Hussein's overthrow; the PLO central committee did the same a day later.[88]

Hussein had never had such obvious cause for an all-out assault upon the fida'iyyun. The hijackings and the positions adopted by Fatah and the PLO amounted to open declarations of war upon his regime. There was not a moment to lose. The longer the Jordanian government waited, the more time the fida'iyyun would have to consolidate their positions in Amman and rally popular support. By September 14, the General Intelligence Directorate already had solid intelligence that the PLO planned to declare a general strike in Amman on September 17, with the goal of igniting an uprising. The king's inner circle also worried that by hesitating, they would also lead the US and British governments to believe that the Hashemite monarchy was a lost cause.[89]

Additionally, the Jordanian leadership had reason to believe that Nasser would tolerate a crackdown on the fida'iyyun, who had also criticized Egypt for its acceptance of the ceasefire. At the end of August, Nasser had advised Hussein to be patient and deal with the guerrillas "through political action." "Do not forget that the Prophet Job lived by the River Jordan," he told Hussein.[90] But Nasser's calls for restraint were not especially strong, certainly when compared with the tough stance he had taken after Karameh. And there were other indications that Nasser would not take a hard line against the Jordanian government. The Egyptian government publicly condemned the hijackings, and the Jordanians also possessed reliable intelligence indicating that Nasser had warned fida'iyyun leaders not to overthrow Hussein.[91] The king could safely assume that Nasser would not blame a confrontation solely on him.

Hussein had considered an all-out offensive against the guerrillas even before the hijacked planes landed at Dawson's Field. On August 31, he informed a US official that the JAA was spoiling for a fight, and that "continued disorder in Amman ... might at some point force his hand."[92] By September 14, he made up his mind. After meeting with Rashid, who painted a bleak picture of Jordan's internal situation, Hussein summoned Wasfi al-Tal and Habis al-Majali, whom he had appointed JAA chief of staff following Mashur Haditha's resignation on September 9. All three agreed that the time had come to move.[93] On September 15, the king informed the US and British ambassadors, L. Dean Brown and J. F. S.

Phillips, that he would form a military government the next day. "The army," he said, "would then surround Amman and settle accounts with the [fida'iyyun]."[94]

THE EARTHQUAKE

In the early morning hours of September 17, JAA troops entered Amman, moving in a "picture book pincer movement" toward the city center.[95] By five o'clock in the afternoon, the army controlled most of the city, with the exception of Jabal Hussein and the Wahdat refugee camp, both fida'iyyun strongholds.[96] Fighting in the capital, however, continued to rage over the next two days, as the JAA fought block by block to kill or capture guerrillas interspersed throughout Amman's neighborhoods. JAA tanks had trouble moving into densely populated areas, and the infantry units that accompanied them often pulled back as soon as engagements with the fida'iyyun began. As a result, much of the fighting involved JAA tanks and artillery batteries firing haphazardly at lightly armed Palestinians who moved between buildings along narrow residential streets.[97] Inevitably, large numbers of Palestinian civilians were caught in the crossfire. Hospitals were crammed with the wounded; many more injured people were left lying in the streets. By the afternoon of September 19, Hussein believed that he had "5,000 casualties to deal with, excluding the dead"—whose numbers he did not estimate. The situation in Amman, he said, resembled "the aftereffects of an earthquake."[98]

By this point, Amman was no longer Hussein's main preoccupation. He believed that if the JAA could keep fighting in the capital, victory—albeit ugly and costly—was virtually assured there.[99] The monarch's major problems now lay elsewhere. Other Arab governments, led by Egypt, were calling for Hussein to allow the Arab League to mediate between Jordan and the PLO. An Arab League delegation led by Egyptian chief of staff Muhammad Sadiq traveled to Amman and demanded a ceasefire, while Tunisian president Habib Bourguiba called for an emergency Arab summit in Cairo.[100] If Hussein did not win a speedy victory, he might have to bow to Arab pressure and accept a ceasefire before he decisively defeated the fida'iyyun.

An early ceasefire would also leave much of northern Jordan under PLO control. At the outset of the fighting, the PLO central committee had declared the districts of Balqa, Irbid, 'Ajlun, and Jerash a "liberated area."[101] On the morning of September 20, the JAA had still not retaken Irbid, the second-largest city on the East Bank and the key to the control of northern Jordan.[102] Hussein needed to secure Irbid before he agreed to outside mediation, but it was not clear that he would have time. Increasingly, it looked as if the Syrian army might arrive there first.

Prior to the hijackings, Hussein and his advisors had viewed Iraq, not Syria, as their most threatening Arab neighbor. Following the assassination attempt on Hussein on September 1, the Iraqi government had threatened to help the fida'iyyun, and some of the Iraqi troops stationed in Jordan since 1967 helped the PFLP land their hijacked planes in the kingdom.[103] Nevertheless, the Jordanian leadership believed that the Iraqis were shocked by the international community's anger at the hijackings and feared foreign intervention. By the time the Jordanian army went on the offensive, Hussein was more worried that Syria would intervene on the side of the guerrillas.[104] On the night of September 19–20, the Syrian armed forces finally threw their weight behind the fida'iyyun.[105] By the morning of September 21, approximately three hundred Syrian tanks had deployed around Irbid.[106]

Well before the crisis began, Hussein expected that he might have to ask for American or Israeli help. In the event of Syrian or Iraqi intervention in a Jordanian civil conflict, the king had told US officials in August, he did not rule out the possibility that "he might be driven to request American military action."[107] On September 15, when Hussein informed the US embassy of his intention to act, he commented that he might "need to call for [American] and Israeli assistance."[108] Now the time had come. "We would welcome Israeli or other air intervention or threat thereof," Hussein told British officials on the morning of September 20.[109] At three o'clock in the morning Jordanian time on September 21, the king sent the US embassy a similar message for Nixon. "The situation," Hussein asserted, was "critical." He called for "immediate physical intervention both air and land as per the authorization of government," and stated that "immediate air strikes on invading forces from any quarter plus air cover are imperative."[110]

"A LITTLE EXCITEMENT"

Though Hussein asked both the British and the US governments for help, Britain had no desire to get involved in Jordan's civil war. Prime Minister Edward Heath's government did not think the survival of Hussein's regime warranted damaging Britain's economic interests elsewhere in the Arab world. When Heath's cabinet met on September 20, they agreed that Britain would not intervene militarily in Jordan.[111] The British preferred that Israel attack Syria's forces "without it appearing that such action was encouraged or instigated by Western governments."[112]

It thus fell to the Americans and the Israelis to decide whether to support Hussein's regime. Though US policymakers had begun debating that summer whether to intervene in Jordan, they were still groping their way toward a policy when the civil war began. US officials agreed on one key issue: a Palestinian victory would not serve US interests. When Kissinger's WSAG discussed the possible outcomes of a Jordanian civil war on September 15, the participants all thought it would be better if Hussein won. Even if the guerrillas only managed to force Hussein to appoint a weak, pro-PLO government, the consequences for US interests could be dire. "[Arab-Israeli] negotiations would be out of the question," Kissinger wrote to Nixon. Border violence would escalate, prompting Israel to seize parts of the East Bank. The Persian Gulf monarchies would be destabilized. A Palestinian victory, Kissinger summed up, "could not produce the stability that is necessary for peace."[113] "Are we all agreed that victory for Hussein is essential from our point of view?" he asked the WSAG two days later. According to the meeting's minutes, "all agreed emphatically."[114]

But did this mean that the United States would use force to preserve the Hashemite monarchy? From the beginning of the crisis, Nixon's senior advisors wanted to avoid military action. When the WSAG discussed the hijackings on September 9, the participants concluded that "Israeli troops would be preferable to US troops for an operation in support of King Hussein against the [fida'iyyun] and possibly the Iraqis." Some, like Admiral Thomas Moorer of the Joint Chiefs of Staff, wanted the Israelis to do the job because America's armed forces were already overextended in Vietnam. Other US policymakers, particularly Sisco, opposed US intervention on political grounds. US forces, Sisco argued, could provide only a "temporary prop" for Hussein's regime. There was no point in risking American lives and prestige if Hussein were doomed to fall as soon as US soldiers left. Moreover, if Iraq and Syria intervened in Jordan, the Israelis would certainly do so as well. US intervention in Jordan would thus become "a US-Israel operation.... The whole Arab world would have to come out in support of Iraq and Syria."[115] When the WSAG met again on September 15, its participants still thought that if Hussein could not defeat the fida'iyyun alone, "the US should stand aside." If Hussein proved "unable to handle the Iraqis," it "would be preferable for Israel to begin any air attacks necessary."[116]

Nixon, on the other hand, thought the United States alone should help Hussein. Initially, he even considered using US ground forces. "I am not concerned about the long occupation.... I still think it is better for us to go and support the king," he said.[117] The president wanted to show the Soviets and domestic audiences that he would use force to protect American interests. Nixon thought there was "nothing better than a little confrontation now and then, a little excitement."[118] US military support for Hussein, he told Kissinger, "shows guts." If the Iraqis or the Syrians attacked Jordan, the United States should "use American air and knock the bejesus out of them."[119] Nixon also hoped to prevent Israel from intervening. "If the Israelis did it, the ceasefire would go out the window," he told Kissinger.[120] When Kissinger informed Nixon that his advisors favored Israeli intervention, Nixon was furious. "*No* without my approval at the time," he scrawled on Kissinger's memo. "We shall not support Israel in *any way* if they attack Jordan on their own."[121] Since Meir was in the United States when the crisis began, Nixon also worried that the United States would be accused of colluding with Israel if the IDF moved. "It wouldn't be very good if... Meir walked out of the meeting [with me] and said they were going to move into Jordan," he told Kissinger.[122]

Thus, the US government made no effort to involve the Israeli government in its military planning during the first phase of the Jordanian civil war. When Meir and Nixon met on September 18, they mainly discussed the situation along the Suez Canal. Regarding Jordan, Nixon simply noted that it would be better for Israel if Hussein stayed in power, and hinted that Meir's government should not undermine him.[123] In the meantime, the US armed forces prepared to intervene. By September 18, the United States had two aircraft carriers, a cruiser, and fourteen destroyers deployed off Cyprus, along with a Marine task force near Crete. Additional ships, including a third aircraft carrier, the *John F. Kennedy*, were on their way. The Joint Chiefs of Staff prepared to launch air operations from Europe.[124]

Once Syria invaded Jordan, however, the question of whether the Nixon administration should ask Israel to act became increasingly pressing. By the evening of September 20, the WSAG began to fret that the United States would not be able to intervene before it was too late. They decided to inform Rabin that Hussein had asked the British for help without explicitly requesting that Israel act. Apparently, the Americans did not want to ask Israel to intervene until they were certain that there was no alternative.[125]

Kissinger and Sisco phoned Rabin, informed him of Hussein's request for "an Israeli air strike on Syrian forces," and asked whether Israel could provide intelligence on Syria's troop positions. Yes, Rabin answered, but did "the US government look favorably to this request? What is your position?" Before they could talk any further, an aide walked into Kissinger's office with a cable. It was Hussein's desperate request for "air strikes... from any quarter." Kissinger told Rabin, "You had better call us back in ten minutes," then hung up.[126]

The national security advisor next called Nixon to persuade him that the United States needed Israel's help. "By tomorrow morning," he told the president, "we may reach the decision point as between US and Israeli action." While US forces could launch two hundred sorties per day from its aircraft carriers, they had no access to nearby land bases and could not follow up "unless we want to get ground forces fighting the Syrians." On the other hand, if the Israelis bombed Hussein's opponents, "they can follow it up and they can escalate more easily than we." Moreover, Kissinger added, "as hated as they are, [the Israelis] are at least recognized to have a local interest in the thing while we... would be the imperialists coming in."[127]

Nixon was not totally convinced. If Israel intervened, he thought, the Arab states would be "more likely to reunite against the Israelis." Nevertheless, the president now seemed more resigned to the idea of Israeli intervention. "It's too bad we don't have more land bases," he sighed.[128]

Kissinger then called Rabin, and told him that the United States "would look favorably" upon Israeli air strikes, compensate Israel for materiel losses, and "hold the situation under control vis-à-vis the Soviets."[129]

But would the Israelis play their part? After all, Kissinger acknowledged earlier that day, the Israelis might not "mind it if Hussein should topple. They would have no more West Bank problem."[130] Indeed, it does not appear that on the eve of the civil war the Israeli government was greatly concerned with the fate of Hussein's regime. AMAN briefing papers prepared for Meir's trip to Washington described the Hashemite monarchy as "probably doomed" but did not advise her to lobby on its behalf.[131] In fact, another briefing paper prepared for Eban recommended the exact opposite. The foreign minister was instructed to tell the Americans that "a radical change in the Jordanian regime might help in solving the Arab-Israel conflict rather than exacerbating it."[132] And Eban and Meir had no problem making such arguments to the Americans even after the crisis in Jordan shifted in Hussein's favor. "The world would not come to an end if [Hussein] departed from the scene," Eban told Charles Yost, the US ambassador to the UN, on September 23. According to Yost, Eban "seemed to imply that, sooner or later, Israel had to find an accommodation with the Palestinians and that it might in the long run be easier if they dominated the state of Jordan."[133] Meir made similar remarks to US chargé d'affaires Owen Zurhellen on September 27. "If there is peace and Israel determines defensible borders for itself," she said, "what remains of the West Bank, together with Jordan, can be Palestine." What mattered to her was not who ruled Jordan, but that "neither Jordan's army nor Arafat's army nor any hostile army will be able to cross the Jordan River."[134]

Far from being eager to intervene on Hussein's behalf, the Israeli government was reluctant to involve itself in the Jordanian crisis. On September 17, the cabinet voted to authorize air strikes against Iraqi or Syrian forces in Jordan if Hussein specifically requested them "with US endorsement or knowledge." On September 20, before Kissinger approached Rabin, Meir further modified these conditions. Israel would only bomb targets in Jordan in *coordination* with the United States, she told the cabinet.[135]

For the Israelis, the main reasons to support Hussein had to do with US-Israeli relations. If they deliberately ignored Hussein's requests for help, the Americans might think they had deliberately allowed him to fall. On the other hand, once assured of US support, Israel could gain a great deal by intervening. If the king survived, he might prove more willing to make peace on Israeli terms. If he did not, Israel would still find it easier to prevent Syria and Iraq from swallowing Jordan.

At first, even the Syrian invasion of Jordan did not prompt the Israelis to act. Early on September 21, when Allon, Dayan, and Bar-Lev considered how to respond to Syria's incursion, they did not discuss the possibility of intervening militarily to save Hussein. Dayan did not even want to deploy additional armored units on the Golan. The defense minister maintained that Jordan was not in danger of being partitioned by Syria and Iraq, and that moving tanks toward the battlefront would only anger the Americans.[136]

By the time the meeting ended, however, news of Hussein's request for help reached Israel. When the cabinet met later that morning, Bar-Lev maintained that Israel could not oust the Syrians and the Iraqis with air strikes alone. The Syrians had nearly 300 tanks in Jordan; the Iraqis had approximately 250. To drive these forces out of Jordan, the IDF would have to intervene massively on the ground, which could lead to fighting on the Golan and along the Suez Canal.

Essentially, the Israeli government had to decide whether saving Hussein's regime and pleasing the United States was worth the risk of regional war. Dayan and Peres led the anti-interventionist camp. An Israeli incursion into Jordan, Dayan argued, could lead to all-out war, Soviet intervention, and massive Israeli casualties. It would also make the IDF look like "mercenaries trying to save a failed regime." Dayan thought the IDF should only intervene if Hussein directly requested Israel's help and promised to sign a secret peace treaty. Otherwise, Israel should not act unless it was absolutely clear that Iraq and Syria were going to take over the East Bank. In that case, Israel should "move the lines eastward along the length of the mountain ridge [i.e., take over the Irbid heights]."[137] Peres also believed that Israel should not act as America's lackey on behalf of a doomed Arab regime. "It might not be possible to save [Hussein]," he told Herzog, "but it may be possible to stain our reputation."[138]

But most of the Israeli cabinet, led by Allon, felt otherwise. To intimidate the Syrians and the Iraqis, the government decided to have the

IDF move armored units to the Golan, and send planes on low reconnaissance flights over Syria's and Iraq's forces in Jordan.[139] The cabinet agreed, however, that the IDF would not actually attack the Syrians until Meir returned home and until the United States promised to support Israel. At 10:25 AM in Washington, Rabin called Kissinger and told him that Israel would "respond positively" to Hussein's request, but only if the Americans formally asked Israel to intervene, explained what they would do to deter the Soviets, and pledged to back Israel at the UN.[140]

The Americans responded haltingly to Rabin's demands. Early in the morning on September 21, Nixon decided to "tell [Rabin] go." He believed that Israeli air strikes on Syria's forces in Jordan "could have a psychological effect and could turn this thing right around." Still, he worried that the Israelis would try to hold on to parts of the East Bank. The Israelis had "mixed motives," Nixon told Kissinger. "They'd like to go in there, you know, and fuck a little of the ground."[141] Nixon wanted the Israelis to "announce ... that they will withdraw when the Syrians withdraw from Jordan. . . . If things come apart, then they break their word and we understand."[142] When the NSC met a few hours later, the president and his advisors decided to tell the Israelis that the United States approved of IDF action "in principle," but that US approval was "contingent on the king's acquiescence," and that Israel should stick to air strikes if possible.[143]

When the Americans informed the Jordanians that Israel was willing to act, however, al-Rifaʻi indicated that they would prefer that Israel attack Syria itself.[144] Nixon liked the idea. An Israeli attack on Syria, he thought, would "give King Hussein the best break... without jeopardizing the king's position in the Arab world."[145] That afternoon, Sisco told Rabin that the Jordanians would prefer that Israel strike Syria.[146] It was not until ten thirty that night in Washington that the Americans finally told the Israelis what they would do for them in return. While the Nixon administration agreed to back the Israelis at the UN and deter the USSR, they remained unwilling to provide them with written pledges of support.[147] When the Israeli cabinet met on the morning of September 22, they accepted the Americans' response but refused to consider attacking Syria.[148] "We have got caught up in the excitement of Dr. Strangelove Kissinger and Rabin," grumbled Gideon Rafael.[149]

THE CAIRO AGREEMENT AND THE END OF THE CIVIL WAR

The Americans and the Israelis never resolved their differences over where the IDF should intervene, but in the end, it did not matter. The IDF's show of strength on the Golan, along with fierce resistance by Jordanian ground troops, was enough to stop the Syrians. CIA sources reported that "the Syrians were very concerned about Israeli intervention."[150] Syrian defense minister Hafiz al-Asad, who seized power in a coup shortly thereafter, later recalled that he did not use his air force against the Jordanians "because I wanted to prevent escalation"—presumably implying a clash with Israel.[151] Safe from air attack, the JAA managed to regroup and push the Syrians back over the border. By the afternoon of September 23, Syria withdrew its three armored brigades from Jordanian territory.[152] When Hussein met Ambassador Brown the following day, he thanked "[Nixon] and Mrs. Meir for the effective spooking operation," which he regarded as a "major contribution to the Syrian withdrawal."[153]

For Hussein, victory in the north came just in time. Desperate to end the fighting, on September 22 the Arab League sent another delegation, headed by Sudanese president Ja'far al-Numayri, to urge Hussein and Arafat to attend an emergency summit in Cairo. Hussein could now agree without fear of forfeiting victory. On September 27, Hussein and Arafat, both carrying guns, strode into the Cairo Hilton for five hours of tense discussions with their fellow Arab leaders. By evening, Nasser (who died of a heart attack the following day) rallied most of the Arab League behind a compromise solution. The Cairo Agreement, as it came to be known, called for both sides to cease fire, release prisoners, and withdraw their forces from Jordan's cities. A follow-up committee, headed by Tunisian prime minister Bahi Ladgham, would oversee implementation of the agreement.[154]

In theory, the Cairo Agreement might have favored the guerrillas. In some ways it was not so different from previous agreements that Hussein had reached with the fida'iyyun. This time, however, the balance of power on the ground favored the monarchy. Though the PLO remained relatively unscathed in northern Jordan, it had been crippled in Amman,

King Hussein (left) and Yasir Arafat (center) at the emergency Arab summit in Cairo, September 1970. AP Photo.

the civil war's most important theater. In a week and a half of fighting, the fida'iyyun had suffered severe losses in manpower and materiel. Between 910 and 960 guerrillas had been killed.[155] The PLO leadership was in disarray; many commanders of different guerrilla organizations were dead or had been taken prisoner. Palestinian civilians in Amman, whom the guerrillas had drawn on for sanctuary and support, seemed reluctant to face another round of fighting.[156] Though the PLO's civilian casualty estimates (which ranged from 15,000 to 30,000) were almost certainly exaggerated, a large number of Palestinian civilians had indeed been killed or wounded. As of October 7, the Jordanian government estimated that 700 civilians had been killed and 1,600 wounded in Amman.[157] Even if these figures underestimated total civilian casualties, they still represented significant loss of life and limb. Food supplies were also running low, and many Palestinian neighborhoods in Amman and elsewhere had been nearly destroyed. Only a large-scale US-led disaster relief effort prevented humanitarian catastrophe in Jordan.[158]

In contrast, the JAA had suffered relatively light casualties—three hundred dead and two thousand wounded—about a third of which were inflicted by the Syrians.[159] Though the Jordanian army was running low on ammunition and had lost tanks fighting Syria's forces, it was swiftly rearmed by the United States.[160] Most importantly, unlike the fida'iyyun, Hussein's troops were in high spirits. Many soldiers had deserted during the fighting: according to Rashid, an estimated three thousand JAA troops fled to Syria at the start of the civil war.[161] But the mass mutiny that Palestinian leaders yearned for never came. The JAA remained largely intact, and its Bedouin-dominated combat units were keen to finish what they had started.[162] They got their chance when Hussein appointed Wasfi al-Tal prime minister for a third and final time late in October.

Publicly, al-Tal paid lip service to the notion that the "sovereignty of the Jordanian state" and "true *fida'i* freedom of action" could coexist."[163] In reality, he wanted to drive the PLO out of Jordan, and Hussein did not restrain him. Sporadic clashes between the JAA and the guerrillas resumed in November 1970, and were followed by major engagements in December and in January 1971. Once Bahi Ladgham ended his mission in mid-April, the JAA was free to drive the fida'iyyun from their surviving strongholds in northern Jordan. This time the monarchy's victory came easily. The guerrillas were disorganized and badly weakened, and could no longer draw on outside help. Iraq had withdrawn all of its troops from Jordan by March 1971.[164] Syria, now dominated by al-Asad, showed no interest in intervening in Jordan again. When Arafat asked al-Asad to let Palestinian forces operate from his territory, the Syrian leader refused.[165] After a series of fierce battles in the 'Ajlun area in mid-July, Hussein and his advisors concluded that the fida'iyyun were "virtually finished" as an "organized, independent movement in Jordan."[166]

BACK TO THE PALESTINE QUESTION

Having repulsed external threats and crushed internal ones, King Hussein again sought to make peace with Israel. In March 1972, the king unveiled his "United Arab Kingdom" plan. According to this scheme, Jordan would be reorganized into a "Jordan region" and a "Palestine region," the latter comprising the West Bank and "any other liberated Palestinian lands" (presumably the Gaza Strip). The monarchy and a national parliament would rule the kingdom as a whole, but each region would have its own legislature and ministerial council.[167]

Hussein quickly discovered, however, that his plan had no takers in Jerusalem. The Israelis still had no interest in giving up the West Bank. Indeed, in the fall of 1970, Meir's government had passed up a chance to reach a deal with Hussein that would have offered Israel much more than the United Arab Kingdom plan. Less than a week after the king signed the Cairo Agreement, he had met with Yigal Allon, who proposed that Jordan and Israel establish "a Palestinian framework in the West Bank that would serve as an alternative to the terrorist leadership and would later link up with Palestinian elements in the East Bank."[168] The objective, Allon later recalled, was to reach an interim agreement on the West Bank that would allow the IDF to remain in key strategic locations while Hussein regained a political foothold there.[169] Hussein told Allon that he accepted the idea in principle.[170] When Allon raised his plan with the Israeli cabinet, however, they rejected it. Meir and Dayan, Allon later remembered, did not want to "speed up the pace of the debate on the future of the territories."[171] Not surprisingly, Meir also rejected the United Arab Kingdom plan. Later in 1972, she indicated that she might offer Jordan something along the lines of the Allon Plan as the basis for an interim settlement. But when Hussein refused, Meir did not consider modifying her terms.[172]

Certainly, Meir felt no great pressure to treat Hussein more generously. By the beginning of 1973, the Egyptian front had been peaceful for nearly two years. Superpower efforts at Middle East peacemaking had slowed to a crawl. There were few signs of unrest in the occupied territories, which were experiencing an economic boom. Per capita income on the West Bank had doubled since 1967. Unemployment had dropped from 7 percent to 2 percent. An estimated thirty-five thousand West Bankers and twenty-five thousand Gazans, about a third of the labor force of each territory, worked in Israel. For many Israelis, Dayan's dream of an Israeli-Palestinian modus vivendi appeared to be coming true, and at a very low cost. Annual Israeli expenses for civil administration between 1968 and 1971 ran slightly higher than $10 million for the West Bank and $15 million for the Gaza Strip.[173] There seemed to be no reason for Meir's government to rush toward a politically controversial and strategically risky settlement with Jordan.

Only the trauma of the 1973 Yom Kippur War forced the Israeli government and public to abandon their standstill mentality. Even so, the postwar cabinets led by Meir and Rabin were far less interested in peace with Jordan than in peace with Egypt. In a handful of fruitless postwar meetings with Hussein, the Israelis refused to consider Hussein's idea of an interim agreement that restored part of the Jordan Valley to his kingdom. They offered to give him Jericho, but nothing more.[174]

Meir and Rabin did not offer Hussein terms that he could accept, for the same reasons that Eshkol had not. They felt little pressure from the United States and greatly feared the domestic political consequences of withdrawing from the West Bank. Kissinger, now secretary of state, did not strongly urge the Israelis to reach a disengagement agreement with Jordan. Partly this was because Jordan did not take part in the 1973 war and the situation on the West Bank was far less explosive than in Sinai or on the Golan. But Kissinger's lack of interest in Israeli-Jordanian negotiations derived mainly from his overarching desire to remove Egypt from the Arab coalition without granting the Soviets a larger regional role or weakening Israel. He had long recognized that the West Bank was "the key issue and constituted the strategic crux of the matter for Israel," and did not want it to get in the way of an Israeli-Egyptian settlement.[175] And while the Americans did not seem especially determined to press the West Bank issue, the forces within Israel who opposed withdrawal were too powerful to ignore. The number of settlers in the occupied territories remained small; as of 1977, about eleven thousand lived there.[176] Still, the 1973 war had dealt a powerful blow to the Labor Party and boosted right-wing factions who wanted Israel to keep and settle the occupied territories, including the increasingly militant National Religious Party and Menachem Begin's newly formed Likud.

Yet even if the Americans had been tougher or the Israeli right had been weaker, Meir and Rabin still would have had to consider all of the strategic problems that remained linked with the West Bank's future. The idea that Israel might substitute nonconventional might for strategic depth never regained its former popularity among the country's leaders. The Israelis no longer feared that a US president would try to make them give up their nuclear program altogether. The Nixon administration abandoned even the pretense of trying to get Israel to sign the Non-Proliferation Treaty (NPT), in part because Kissinger thought doing so undermined the chances for a settlement. "One of the consequences of pursuing an Arab-Israeli settlement that would require Israel to give up the security provided by expanded borders is that we would probably have to relax on the nuclear issue," Nixon's advisor argued.[177] But the Americans were still not ready to condone an Israeli policy of overt nuclear deterrence. Just as importantly, the threat of Soviet military intervention in the Middle East had proven quite real during the War of Attrition, and hardly disappeared afterward.

As a result, even in the darkest moments of the 1973 war, when Dayan proposed that Israel prepare to use nuclear weapons, Meir reportedly refused.[178] Another, more traumatic war passed without Israel bringing its nuclear option into the open, almost certainly because its leaders feared how the superpowers would respond. And these anxieties continued to shape Israel's nuclear strategy, or lack of one. "I do not think Syria gives a damn whether Israel possesses nuclear weapons because it is sure that as long as it operates on the conventional level there are Soviet missiles to neutralize any nuclear threat against Syria," Rabin remarked in 1983.[179]

When the Cold War began to wind down, the Israelis still had to bear in mind that Egypt, Syria, and Iraq were building up stockpiles of chemical weapons, and that one of its regional enemies might acquire nuclear weapons of its own.

Israel's leaders thus continued to view the West Bank through the lens of the conventional balance of forces, which they believed made a return to the armistice lines impossible. "The problem for Israel, as far as an overall settlement is concerned, is not to be in a position that in a few years, whenever they move, we have to go to a preemptive war. The real fact that they can move near to our borders means that we would have to mobilize and they then can destroy our economy by requiring total mobilization," Rabin told President Gerald Ford and Kissinger in 1975. "A return to the 1967 borders and the establishment of a Palestinian state means that Israel cannot survive."[180] Even in the 1990s, after Israel signed a peace treaty with Jordan and the Iraqi army had been trounced by the United States, the Israelis remained haunted by visions of Arab armies marching toward the Mediterranean from the West Bank. In October 1995, two years after he signed the Oslo Accords with the PLO, Rabin proclaimed that "the security border of the State of Israel will be located in the Jordan Valley, in the broadest meaning of that term."[181]

Of course, it might be argued that the Israelis' fears were overblown and that they did not take into account the role that external guarantees and demilitarized zones might play. It could also be argued that Israel missed an opportunity to make peace with Hussein before the Arab League designated the PLO the "sole legitimate representative of the Palestinian people" in 1974.[182] Certainly, not only revisionist historians have made such arguments. Yigal Allon termed Meir and Dayan's unwillingness to consider an interim settlement with Hussein in 1970 a "cardinal error."[183] Henry Kissinger felt the same. "If Israel had moved with Hussein... the most moderate Arab of all, there would have been no Rabat decision," he complained in 1974.[184]

Regardless of whether a window of opportunity for an Israeli-Jordanian settlement existed between 1971 and 1974, however, it is clear that any such settlement, even one based on total Israeli withdrawal from the West Bank, would have rested on a shaky foundation. The Jordanian civil war badly tarnished Hussein's claims to represent Palestinians living under Israeli occupation. West Bank Palestinians, according to US reports, were "horrified at the carnage and bloodshed visited upon their relatives and friends."[185] On September 19, 1970, the mayors of all major West Bank towns published a statement holding Hussein "responsible before God and history" for the bloodshed on the East Bank.[186] By October, five West Bank members of the Jordanian parliament resigned their posts; their compatriots only narrowly ruled out resigning en masse. Even men like Ma'zuz al-Masri and Hilmi Hanun, the mayors of Nablus and Tulkarm, respectively, and self-described "loyal unionists," believed that Hussein would have to do significant "fence-mending" if he ever wanted to rule the West Bank again.[187]

Initially Hussein disregarded the West Bankers' anger. Emboldened by his victory over the PLO, the king was sure that most West Bankers would eventually calm down and recognize that he was the only person capable of bringing the Israeli occupation to an end. Hussein understood that many West Bankers had reservations about reunifying with Jordan, but he thought he could assuage their suspicions. The United Arab Kingdom Plan, he told US officials in 1972, would almost certainly be accepted by a "silent majority" of Palestinians.[188] But other than a few visits by West Bank notables to Amman that summer, allegedly in exchange for bribes (Shaykh Ja'bari reportedly received a "new Dodge sedan"), there were few signs that Hussein's ideas enjoyed much support in the occupied territories.[189] Most West Bankers, reported the US consul in Jerusalem, would ideally prefer that the United Nations force Israel to withdraw from the occupied territories, whereupon the area would be sealed off "from all outside influences" and its residents would freely determine their future.[190] Hussein's plan was not greeted with any enthusiasm in the occupied territories and received no support elsewhere in the region. The king was denounced as a traitor in the Arab press, and Egypt broke off diplomatic relations with Jordan—which Syria, Algeria, and Libya had already done in 1970.

Over the next two years, Arab and Palestinian backing for Hussein's claims to the West Bank continued to fade. Following the 1973 war, Hussein told other Arab leaders and Palestinian notables that if he regained the West Bank, he would hold a "plebiscite" that would let its residents determine the terms of their relationship with the Jordanian state. According to Ahmad Tuqan, Hussein thought he could use such a referendum to "defeat PLO efforts to become [the] sole Palestinian spokesman."[191] But by December 1973, Tahir al-Masri, who held the West Bank portfolio in Hussein's cabinet, admitted that a "popular vote would easily go to the PLO," and that "under these circumstances, traditional vote rigging methods are unworkable."[192] Pro-PLO trends on the ground dovetailed with Arab efforts to make the organization the official representative of the Palestinians. At the Algiers summit of November 1973, all the Arab states except Jordan voted to recognize the PLO as the "sole representative of the Palestinian people." The following year at Rabat, the Arab League adopted a resolution declaring the PLO the "sole legitimate representative of the Palestinian people." This time, Hussein had no choice but to join in the chorus.[193]

Hussein also found that the domestic political rewards for reclaiming the West Bank were rapidly shrinking. Even on the East Bank, there was not much popular support for the king's efforts—and not only because of Palestinian anti-Hashemite sentiment. The tumult of the 1968–1970 period left an enduring mark upon the kingdom's Transjordanian minority. Many native East Bankers had no desire to see the West Bank restored to Jordan, since this would leave them a much smaller minority within the kingdom.[194] By the early 1970s, many powerful Transjordanians, particularly in military circles, had already begun to press Hussein to cut his ties to the West Bank.[195] There were also few economic benefits to be gained by retrieving the West Bank. Even before 1967, the area had been a liability, and the East Bank was proving that it could function without it. Despite the devastation wrought by the 1970 fighting, the Jordanian economy made a "remarkable recovery," thanks to US and Saudi help.[196] Though Jordan still relied heavily on foreign aid, the return of the West Bank would have done nothing to solve the country's economic problems. In fact, it probably would have made them worse. As a CIA report pointed out in 1973, if the West Bank rejoined Jordan, it would have to compete with the East Bank for funds.[197]

As early as November 1973, Hussein thought that "if the other Arab states select [the] PLO as the sole spokesman [for the Palestinians], then Jordan has no greater interest in Jerusalem and the West Bank than any other non-confrontation Arab state."[198] Indeed, it was primarily the

PLO's refusal to accept Resolution 242 (and a corresponding lack of US pressure on Israel to negotiate with the organization) that kept Hussein from renouncing his claims to the West Bank until 1988. So long as the PLO did not take part in the peace process, Jordanian disengagement would have looked too much like a decision to abandon the West Bankers, with obvious negative implications for Hussein's relations with other Arab leaders and the East Bank's Palestinian majority. Moreover, there were benefits to keeping Jordan's claims alive. In light of what the PLO had done in 1970, Hussein was in no hurry for it to set up a state on his western border. Until the late 1980s, Jordan's claims to the West Bank also helped the king secure US aid.

Nevertheless, by the early 1970s, the pre-1967 Israeli-Jordanian entente had little chance of being rebuilt. The stage was set for a protracted Israeli-Palestinian struggle over the West Bank's future—a struggle that has yet to be resolved.

NOTES

1. "The Fedayeen Movement: Growing Strength and Influence," INR memorandum, January 23, 1969, NA/RG59/DOSCF 1967–1969/POL 27 ARAB-ISR.
2. State to Jidda, May 3, 1969, NA/RG59/DOSCF 1967–1969/POL 27 ARAB-ISR.
3. Amman to State, April 4, 1969; "Jordan: Lawlessness Approaches the Limits of the Government's Tolerance," INR memorandum, September 26, 1969, NA/RMNPM/NSF/Country Files/Jordan, box 613.
4. Appleyard to Tripp, July 29, 1969, BNA/FCO 17/806.
5. Amman to State, July 29, 1969, NA/RG59/DOSCF 1967–1969/POL 27 ARAB-ISR.
6. Nixon-Hussein memcon, April 8, 1969, NA/RMNPM/NSF/Country Files /Jordan, box 613.
7. State to Amman, April 11, 1969, NA/RMNPM/NSF/Country Files/Jordan, box 613.
8. Ya'akov Herzog, "Main Points in Meeting of May 25," YHP.
9. Amman to State, June 2, 1969, NA/RG59/DOSCF 1967–1969/POL 27 ARAB-ISR.
10. Amman to State, August 29, 1969, NA/RG59/DOSCF 1967–1969/POL 27 ARAB-ISR.
11. See, for example, US ambassador Harold Symmes's prediction that al-Kaylani's and Nasir's appointments would place Hussein on a "collision course" with the Palestinian guerrillas. Amman to State, June 30, 1969, NA/RG59/DOSCF 1967–1969 /POL 27 ARAB-ISR. See also "Jordan and the Fedayeen: Both Sides Geared for Pos-

sible Showdown," INR memorandum, July 16, 1969, NA/RG59/DOSCF 1967–1969 /POL 23 JORDAN. For Israeli views of the situation in Jordan, see Ya'akov Herzog, "Charles: From December 1968 through the End of August 1969," YHP. For Sharif Nasir's message, see Amman to State, July 12, 1969, NA/RG59/DOSCF 1967–1969 /POL 27 ARAB-ISR.

12. Amman to State, August 29, 1969, NA/RG59/DOSCF 1967–1969/POL 27 ARAB-ISR.

13. J. P. Tripp, "Major General Khammash's Views on the Jordanian Scene," July 28, 1969, BNA/FCO/17/827.

14. CIA briefing paper for the NSC meeting on September 23, 1970, NA /CIA-RDP79T00827A002200040002-8.

15. Amman to FCO, June 26, 1970, BNA/FCO 17/1402.

16. Amman to State, July 24, 1969, NA/RMNPM/NSF/Country Files/Jordan, box 613; Amman to FCO, September 27, 1969, BNA/FCO 17/806.

17. Amman to State, July 24, 1969, NA/RMNPM/NSF/Country Files/Jordan, box 613. On al-Rifa'i's sympathies for the fida'iyyun, see also Tarawna, *Rihlati ma'a al-urdun*, 105.

18. Amman to State, July 23, 1969, NA/RG59/DOSCF 1967–1969/POL 23–3 JORDAN.

19. Tel Aviv to State, January 26, 1970, NA/RMNPM/Country Files/Jordan, box 614.

20. Amman to FCO, February 11, 1970, BNA/FCO/17/1038.

21. Amman to State, February 12, 1970, NA/RG59/DOSCF 1970–1973/POL 23 JORDAN.

22. Amman to MOD, February 20, 1970, BNA/FCO/17/1038; Herzog–al-Rifa'i memcon, March 6, 1970, ISA/A/7434/7; Amman to State, February 16, 1970, NA /RMNPM/NSF/Country Files/Israel, box 605; Amman to State, February 16, 1970, NA/RMNMP/NSF/Country Files/Jordan, box 614.

23. Amman to FCO, February 24, 1970, BNA/FCO 17/1038.

24. For these arguments, see Amman to FCO, February 24, 1970, BNA/FCO 17/1038; Amman to State, February 27, 1970, NA/RG59/DOSCF 1970–1973/POL 23 JORDAN; Herzog–al-Rifa'i memcon, March 6, 1970, ISA/A/7434/7; Amman to FCO, May 11, 1970, BNA/FCO/17/1040.

25. Amman to State, April 30, 1970, NA/RG59/DOSCF 1970–1973/POL 23 JORDAN. Though Symmes did not mention it, by this time he numbered among those who felt betrayed by Hussein. Earlier that April, fida'iyyun had attacked the US embassy and burned down the US cultural center, leading Assistant Secretary Sisco to cancel a planned visit to Jordan. Hussein blamed Symmes for Sisco's decision and demanded that the State Department transfer him elsewhere. See Amman to State, April 16, 1970; Kissinger to Nixon, April 22, 1970, NA/RMNPM/NSF/Country Files /Jordan, box 614.

26. Amman to MOD, June 9, 1970, BNA/FCO/17/1040.

27. Dishon, *Middle East Record, 1969–1970*, 804.

28. Amman to State, June 17, 1970, NA/RG59/DOSCF 1970–1973/POL 23 JORDAN.

29. De Atkine, "Amman 1970," 77.

30. Dishon, *Middle East Record, 1969–1970*, 805.

31. Amman to FCO, June 11, 1970, BNA/FCO 17/1041, no. 258; Amman to FCO, June 13, 1970, BNA/FCO 17/1041, no. 275.
32. Dishon, *Middle East Record, 1969–1970*, 810.
33. Amman to FCO, June 11, 1970, BNA/FCO 17/1041.
34. Ibid.
35. On Haditha's views of the Palestinian guerrillas, see Tarawna, *Rihlati ma'a al-urdun*, 105.
36. Amman to FCO, June 29, 1970, BNA/FCO 17/1042.
37. Amman to State, July 4, 1970, NA/RMNPM/NSF/Country Files/Jordan, box 615.
38. On Nixon's foreign policy in general, see Bundy, *Tangled Web*; Dallek, *Nixon and Kissinger*. On the administration's application of "linkage" to the Middle East, see Daigle, *Limits of Détente*, 17–25.
39. NSC minutes, February 1, 1969, *FRUS, 1969–1976*, 24: doc. 3.
40. NSC minutes, April 25, 1969, DNSA/KT00019.
41. NSC minutes, February 1, 1969, *FRUS, 1969–1976*, 24: doc. 3. On the Americans' reluctance to discuss Jordan in the Two Power talks, see also Rogers to Nixon, October 14, 1969, NA/RMNPM/Country Files/Middle East—General, box 644.
42. Amman to State, September 11, 1969, NA/RMNPM/NSF/Country Files/Jordan, box 613.
43. See, for example, Eban's remarks to Rogers in State to Tel Aviv, March 15, 1969; Nixon-Eban memcon, March 17, 1969, NA/RMNPM/NSF/Country Files/Israel, box 604.
44. Ya'akov Herzog, "Charles: From December 1968 through the End of August 1969," YHP.
45. Siniver, *Abba Eban*, 283–290.
46. Ya'akov Herzog, "Charles: From December 1968 through the End of August 1969," YHP.
47. Rabin, *Pinkas sherut*, 247.
48. On the internal US debate, see especially Daigle, *Limits of Détente*, 31–82.
49. Ya'akov Herzog, "Charles: From December 1968 through the End of August 1969," YHP.
50. DOS memcon, September 26, 1969, NA/RG59/DOSCF 1967–1969/POL 7 ISR.
51. State to Tel Aviv, December 18, 1969, NA/RG59/DOSCF 1967–1969/POL 27-14 ARAB-ISR/SANDSTORM.
52. Ya'akov Herzog, "Report on Jordan following the Conversation with Hayim's Counterpart and the Advisor on September 28, 1969," YHP.
53. Quoted in Daigle, *Limits of Détente*, 82.
54. KFADC minutes, February 25, 1969, ISA/A/8162/4.
55. "The Internal Position and Stability of the Regimes in the Principal Arab Countries," unsigned briefing paper for Meir, undated (September 1969), ISA/FM/7328/5.
56. For examples of such concerns, see Rafael to Eban, December 20, 1968; Rafael to Eban, February 26, 1970, AECID/Abba Eban Papers/C-0001 F-0007. See also Arthur Lurie's comments in Tel Aviv to FCO, June 12, 1970, BNA/FCO 17/1066.
57. KFADC minutes, February 25, 1969, ISA/A/8162/4.
58. Ya'akov Herzog, "Report on Jordan following the Conversation with Hayim's Counterpart and the Advisor on September 28, 1969," YHP.

59. Foreign Ministry to London, December 27, 1969, AECID/Abba Eban Papers/C-0001 F-0007.
60. Quoted in Gai, *Bar-Lev*, 204.
61. Ya'akov Herzog, "Report on Jordan following the Conversation with Hayim's Counterpart and the Advisor on September 28, 1969," YHP.
62. Tel Aviv to FCO, December 3, 1968, BNA/FCO/17/810.
63. Adamsky, "How American and Israeli Intelligence," 113; State to Tel Aviv, May 23, 1970, NA/RMNPM/NSF/Country Files/Israel, box 607.
64. For evidence that Israeli fears of a Soviet presence in Jordan increased in tandem with developments on the Egyptian front, see Sharon, *Warrior*, 246.
65. Ya'akov Herzog, "Report on Jordan following the Conversation with Hayim's Counterpart and the Advisor on September 28, 1969," YHP.
66. See Tel Aviv to State, February 17, 1970, NA/RMNPM/NSF/Country Files/Israel, box 605; Tel Aviv to State, June 4, 1970, NA/RMNPM/NSF/Country Files/Israel, box 607.
67. Washington to FM, August 12, 1969, ISA/A/7433/5.
68. Ibid.
69. Ya'akov Herzog, "Charles: From December 1968 through the End of August 1969," YHP.
70. Meir was advised to urge the Americans to back the Persian Gulf monarchies, Lebanon, Tunisia, and Morocco. Jordan was deliberately excluded from this list. Instead Meir was instructed to argue that US backing for Hussein should be conditional on his willingness to distance himself from Nasser and "extremist forces in his kingdom." "The Arab World and Israel," unsigned briefing paper for Meir, undated (September 1969), ISA/FM/7328/5.
71. Tel Aviv to State, April 15, 1970, NA/RMNPM/NSF/Country Files/Jordan, box 614.
72. Kissinger memo to Nixon, April 5, 1969, NA/RMNPM/NSF/Country Files/Jordan, box 613.
73. NSC minutes, April 25, 1969, DNSA/KT00019.
74. NSC minutes, February 1, 1969, *FRUS*, 1969–1976, 24: doc. 3
75. Amman to State, May 2, 1970, NA/RG59/DOSCF 1970–1973/POL 23 JORDAN.
76. Joseph Sisco, "Current Appraisal of Arab-Israeli Situation," April 28, 1970, NA/RMNPM/NSF/Country Files/Middle East—General, box 645.
77. Saunders to Kissinger, May 5, 1970, NA/RMNPM/NSF/Country Files/Jordan, box 614.
78. Kissinger to Nixon, June 11, 1970, NA/RMNPM/NSF/Country Files/Jordan, box 614.
79. NSC minutes, June 17, 1970, *FRUS*, 1969–1976, 24: doc. 26.
80. NSCIG/NEA Contingency Study on Jordan, May 27, 1969, DNSA/PR00425.
81. WSAG minutes, June 11, 1970, DNSA/KT00148.
82. Washington to FM, June 11, 1970, ISA/A/7428/22.
83. Korn, *Stalemate*, 235–258.
84. See his remarks in Amman to FCO, August 6, 1970, BNA/FCO 17/1042.
85. Sayigh, *Armed Struggle*, 255–259.
86. J. F. S. Phillips, "Jordan: Annual Review for 1970," January 6, 1971, BNA/FCO 17/1411.

87. Ibid.
88. Sayigh, *Armed Struggle*, 260.
89. Rashid, *Hisab al-saraya wa-hisab al-qaraya*, 173–176.
90. Farid, *Nasser*, 203.
91. Dishon, *Middle East Record, 1969–1970*, 840; Rashid, *Hisab al-saraya wa-hisab al-qaraya*, 174.
92. Amman to State, September 1, 1970, NA/RG59/DOSCF 1970–1973/POL 15-1 JORDAN.
93. Rashid, *Hisab al-saraya wa-hisab al-qaraya*, 176.
94. Amman to FCO, September 15, 1970, BNA/FCO 17/1043; Kissinger to Nixon, September 15, 1970, *FRUS, 1969–1976*, 24: doc. 246.
95. Haig to Kissinger, September 17, 1970, *FRUS, 1969–1976*, 24: doc. 253.
96. Amman to FCO, September 17, 1970, BNA/FCO 17/1043.
97. De Atkine, "Amman 1970," 78–79.
98. Amman telex, September 19, 1970, BNA/PREM 15/124.
99. Amman to State, September 19, 1970, NA/RG59/DOSCF 1970–1973/POL 23–9 JORDAN.
100. Rashid, *Hisab al-saraya wa-hisab al-qaraya*, 179; R. Beaumont, "President Nasser's Last Summit," October 7, 1970, BNA/FCO 17/1053.
101. Amman to State, September 17, 1970, NA/RG59/DOSCF 1970–1973/POL 23–9 JORDAN.
102. Tel Aviv to MOD, September 20, 1970, BNA/FCO 17/1043.
103. On the Iraqi threats following the September 1 assassination attempt, see Amman to FCO, September 3, 1970, BNA/FCO 17/1042. On Iraqi aid to the PFLP hijackers, see intelligence information cable, September 12, 1970, *FRUS, 1969–1976*, 24: doc. 229; as well as Hussein's remarks in Ya'akov Herzog, "Meeting at Charles' Initiative of Charles and the Advisor with Herzog and Allon," October 3, 1970, YHP.
104. Hoskinson to Kissinger, September 16, 1970, *FRUS, 1969–1976*, 24: doc. 250. See also Amman to State, September 16, 1970, NA/RMNPM/NSF/Country Files /Jordan, box 615.
105. Kissinger to Nixon, September 20, 1970, NA/RMNPM/NSF/Country Files /Jordan, box 615.
106. Tel Aviv to Amman, September 21, 1970, NA/RG59/DOSCF 1970–1973/POL 23–9 JORDAN; Tel Aviv to MOD, September 21, 1970, BNA/FCO 17/1043.
107. Amman to State, September 1, 1970, NA/RG59/DOSCF 1970–1973/POL 15-1 JORDAN.
108. State to embassies, September 15, 1970, NA/RG59/DOSCF 1970–1973/POL 23–9 JORDAN.
109. Amman to FCO, September 20, 1970, BNA/FCO 17/1043.
110. Amman to State, September 21, 1970, *FRUS, 1969–1976*, 24: doc. 284.
111. Cabinet minutes, September 20, 1970, 10:30 PM, BNA/CAB 130/479.
112. State to White House, September 21, 1970, NA/RMNPM/NSF/Country Files/Jordan Crisis, box 619.
113. Kissinger to Nixon, September 16, 1970, *FRUS, 1969–1976*, 24: doc. 247.
114. WSAG minutes, September 17, 1970, *FRUS, 1969–1976*, 24: doc. 254.
115. Combined WSAG and Review Group minutes, September 9, 1970, *FRUS, 1969–1976*, 24: doc. 214.
116. Kissinger to Nixon, "Contingency Planning for Jordan," September 16, 1970,

NA/RMNPM/NSF/Country Files/Jordan, box 615.

117. Nixon-Kissinger telcon, September 12, 1970, FRUS, 1969–1976, 24: doc. 233.

118. Nixon-Kissinger telcon, September 17, 1970, 2:40 PM, NA/RMNPM/Kissinger Telcons, box 30.

119. Nixon-Kissinger telcon, September 17, 1970, FRUS, 1969–1976, 24: doc. 256.

120. Nixon-Kissinger telcon, September 17, 1970, FRUS, 1969–1976, 24: doc. 262.

121. See Nixon's handwritten notes on Kissinger to Nixon, "Contingency Planning for Jordan," September 16, 1970, NA/RMNPM/NSF/Country Files/Jordan, box 615 (emphases in the original).

122. Nixon-Kissinger telcon, September 17, 1970, FRUS, 1969–1976, 24: doc. 262.

123. Nixon-Meir memcon, September 18, 1970, FRUS, 1969–1976, 23: doc. 162.

124. WSAG minutes, September 18, 1970, FRUS, 1969–1976, 24: doc. 264.

125. WSAG minutes, September 20, 1970, FRUS, 1969–1976, 24: doc. 281.

126. Rabin-Kissinger telcon, September 20, 1970, FRUS, 1969–1976, 24: doc. 283.

127. Nixon-Kissinger telcon, undated (September 20, 1970), FRUS, 1969–1976, 24: doc. 286.

128. Ibid.

129. Kissinger-Rabin telcon, September 20, 1970, FRUS, 1969–1976, 24: doc. 287.

130. WSAG minutes, September 20, 1970, FRUS, 1969–1976, 24: doc. 281.

131. "Assessment of the Situation in the Middle East," AMAN memo, September 9, 1970, ISA/A/7529/7.

132. Rubinovitz, "Blue and White 'Black September.'"

133. CIA memo, September 24, 1970, FRUS, 1969–1976, 24: doc. 325.

134. Gazit to Washington, September 27, 1970, ISA/FM/9341/10.

135. Herzog to Meir, "Memo on US-Israel Contacts on the Syrian-Jordan Situation," September 25, 1970, YHP.

136. Yigal Allon oral history, ISA/A/19/5001. See also Rafael, *Destination Peace*, 247.

137. Unsigned cable to Rabin, September 21, 1970, ISA/FM/9341/10.

138. Peres note to Herzog, September 21, 1970, YHP.

139. Yigal Allon oral history, ISA/A/19/5001.

140. Rabin-Kissinger telcon, September 21, 1970, FRUS, 1969–1976, 24: doc. 301.

141. Nixon-Kissinger telcon, September 21, 1970, FRUS, 1969–1976, 24: doc. 292.

142. Nixon-Kissinger-Rogers-Haig telcon, September 21, 1970, FRUS, 1969–1976, 24: doc. 294.

143. NSC minutes, September 21, 1970, FRUS, 1969–1976, 24: doc. 299; Kissinger-Sisco telcon, September 21, 1970, FRUS, 1969–1976, 24: doc. 302; WSAG minutes, September 21, 1970, FRUS, 1969–1976, 24: doc. 303. For the message given to Rabin, see State to White House, September 21, 1970, NA/RMNPM/NSF/Country Files/Jordan Crisis, box 619.

144. FRUS, 1969–1976, 24: doc. 304n7.

145. NSC minutes, September 21, 1970, FRUS, 1969–1976, 24: doc. 307.

146. Herzog to Meir, "Memo on US-Israel Contacts on the Syrian-Jordan Situation," September 25, 1970, YHP.

147. State to Amman and Tel Aviv, September 22, 1970, FRUS, 1969–1976, 24: doc. 311.

148. Herzog to Meir, "Memo on US-Israel Contacts on the Syrian-Jordan Situation," September 25, 1970, YHP.

149. Rafael note to Herzog, September 22, 1970, YHP.
150. See Helms's remarks in NSC minutes, September 22, 1970, *FRUS, 1969–1976*, 24: doc. 313.
151. Quoted in Seale, *Asad*, 159.
152. NSC minutes, September 23, 1970, *FRUS, 1969–1976*, 24: doc. 318.
153. Kissinger to Nixon, September 25, 1970, NA/RMNPM/NSF/Country Files /Jordan, box 615.
154. Farid, *Nasser*, 208; Rashid, *Hisab al-saraya wa-hisab al-qaraya*, 186; Kissinger to Nixon, September 28, 1970, *FRUS, 1969–1976*, 24: doc. 330.
155. Sayigh, *Armed Struggle*, 267.
156. Amman to State, October 5, 1970, NA/RG59/DOSCF 1970–1973/POL 23-9 JORDAN.
157. Amman to State, October 7, 1970, NA/RG59/DOSCF 1970–1973/POL 23-9 JORDAN.
158. On relief efforts, see Irwin to Nixon, September 26, 1970, NA/RMNPM /NSF/Country Files/Jordan, box 615.
159. Amman to State, September 30, 1970, NA/RG59/DOSCF 1970–1973/POL 23-9 JORDAN; Amman to State, October 7, 1970, NA/RG59/DOSCF 1970–1973 /POL 23-9 JORDAN.
160. State to Rogers, *FRUS, 1969–1976*, 24: doc. 334.
161. Rashid, *Hisab al-saraya wa-hisab al-qaraya*, 178.
162. See al-Rifa'i's remarks in Amman to State, September 27, 1970, NA/RG59 /DOSCF 1970–1973/POL 23-9 JORDAN.
163. "Ahdath elul," in Tal, *Kitabat fi al-qadaya al-'arabiyya*, 498.
164. Shai, "Ha-me'oravut ha-iraqit," 71.
165. Amman to State, July 17, 1971, NA/RG59/DOSCF 1970–1973/POL 23-9 JORDAN.
166. Amman to State, July 24, 1971, NA/RG59/DOSCF 1970–1973/POL 23-9 JORDAN.
167. "Khitab jalalat al-malik al-Husayn hawla al-mashru' al-ittihad bayn difatai al-mamlaka," in *al-Watha'iq al-urduniyya*, 1972, 16–17.
168. Ya'akov Herzog, "Meeting at Charles' Initiative of Charles and the Advisor with Herzog and Allon," October 3, 1970, YHP.
169. Yigal Allon oral history, ISA/A/5001/19.
170. Ya'akov Herzog, "Meeting at Charles' Initiative of Charles and the Advisor with Herzog and Allon," October 3, 1970, YHP.
171. Yigal Allon oral history, ISA/A/5001/19.
172. Shlaim, *Lion of Jordan*, 351–356.
173. "Economic Interdependence of the West Bank and Gaza Strip with Israel and Jordan," CIA memo, August 1973, NA/CIA-RDP85T0087R001500190009-3.
174. Shlaim, *Lion of Jordan*, 378–388.
175. Kissinger-Allon memcon, April 26, 1971, DNSA/KT00264. On Kissinger's post-1973 strategy, see Yaqub, "Weight of Conquest," 236–244.
176. Gorenberg, *Accidental Empire*, 358. These figures do not include Israeli residents of East Jerusalem.
177. Kissinger to Nixon, September 10, 1969, NA/RMNPM/NSF/Country Files /Middle East, box 651. He made similar remarks a few months later: "If we use our leverage on the NPT, can we use it again on the terms of peace?" he asked. See "Meet-

ing of Special NSC Review Group on Israeli Assistance Requests," January 26, 1970, George Washington University, National Security Archive, http://www.gwu.edu/~nsarchiv/NSAEBB/NSAEBB189/IN-27.pdf. On Nixon, Israel, and the NPT, see Cohen and Burr, "Israel Crosses the Threshold."

178. See the transcript of Avner Cohen's January 2008 interview with Arnan "Sini" Azaryahu, Wilson Center Digital Archive, http://digitalarchive.wilsoncenter.org/document/117848.

179. Quoted in Inbar, *Rabin and Israel's National Security*, 116.

180. Rabin-Kissinger-Ford memcon, June 11, 1975, DNSA/KT01664.

181. Quoted in Luft, "All Quiet on the Eastern Front?," 7.

182. For this argument, see Shlaim, *Lion of Jordan*.

183. Yigal Allon oral history, ISA/A/5001/19.

184. Kissinger meeting with bipartisan leadership, December 17, 1974, GRFL/National Security Adviser memcons, box 8.

185. Amman to State, September 22, 1970, NA/RG59/DOSCF 1970–1973/POL 23–9 JORDAN.

186. Jerusalem to State, September 24, 1970, NA/RG59/DOSCF 1970–1973/POL 23–9 JORDAN.

187. Jerusalem to State, September 30, 1970, NA/RG59/DOSCF 1970–1973/POL 23–9 JORDAN.

188. Amman to State, April 3, 1972, NA/RG59/DOSCF 1970–1973/POL 7 JORDAN.

189. Amman to State, August 26, 1972, NA/RG59/DOSCF 1970–1973/POL 28 JORDAN.

190. Jerusalem to State, April 2, 1972, NA/RG59/DOSCF 1970–1973/POL 28 JORDAN.

191. Amman to State, November 23, 1973, NA/RMNPM/NSF/Country Files /Jordan, box 618.

192. Amman to State, December 6, 1973, NA/RMNPM/NSF/Country Files/Jordan, box 618. For a similarly pessimistic US assessment, see "Present West Bank Political Attitudes," CIA memo, January 29, 1974, NA /CIA-RDP85T00353R000100010007-8.

193. Shemesh, *Palestinian Entity*, 272–310.

194. On this issue, see Abu-Odeh, *Jordanians, Palestinians, and the Hashemite Kingdom*.

195. See, for example, Zayd al-Rifa'i's comments in Amman to State, June 20, 1973, NA/RMNPM/NSF/Country Files/Jordan, box 618.

196. Amman to State, April 6, 1973, NA/RG59/DOSCF 1970–1973/POL 2–5 JORDAN.

197. "Economic Interdependence of the West Bank and Gaza Strip with Israel and Jordan," CIA memo, August 1973, NA/CIA-RDP85T0087R001500190009-3.

198. Amman to State, November 27, 1973, NA/RMNPM/NSF/Country Files /Jordan, box 618.

CONCLUSION

DURING THE 1950S AND 1960S, ISRAEL'S LEADERS HAD LIMITED strategic choices, most of them bad ones. They had the unenviable task of figuring out how to secure the survival of a small state in a profoundly hostile environment, and they operated without the luxury of time and direct insight into the thinking of their adversaries enjoyed by historians. While some of Israel's choices had unfortunate, indeed tragic, results, it behooves us to consider why they were made in the first place, and what alternatives, if any, were available. And while this book is primarily a study of Israeli policy, it also behooves us to remember that almost all of the Israelis' choices regarding the West Bank were influenced by the behavior of the Arab states, the Palestinians, and the great powers.

1949–1967

From 1949 until 1967, Israel's leaders grappled with whether they should try to acquire more territory or find a way to live within the armistice lines. The archival evidence clearly indicates that they would have preferred to conquer the West Bank and transform it into some sort of Palestinian vassal state. They believed that over time, the regional military balance would shift in favor of the Arab states, and that the surest way to prevent the Arab states from projecting their power into the West Bank was to conquer it. As late as 1966, the IDF held that the ideal way to solve the West Bank problem would be to create "an independent Palestinian state, connected to Israel with regard to foreign policy and decisively dependent on the IDF for defense and the preservation of order."[1] In other words, an Israeli colony.

Nevertheless, from the winter of 1957 until the next Arab-Israeli war broke out ten years later, Israel's leaders generally assumed that they had no chance of realizing their dream of wider borders. After being forced to withdraw from Sinai and the Gaza Strip, they came to terms with the fact that the United States and the Soviet Union were not going to permit them to expand. They could not in fact choose conquest. And so the Israelis changed course, adopting a strategy specifically designed to serve as an alternative to territorial expansion. They pursued a nuclear deterrent and strategic alignment with the United States, and tacitly supported Middle Eastern opponents of Pan-Arabism, including King Hussein.

This was the strategy that Israel was still wedded to on the morning of June 5, 1967, and this was the strategy that Israel's leaders would have been happy to pursue to fruition. Yet in the end, it contained the seeds of its own destruction. While the decline of Pan-Arabism strengthened Hussein's regime and the Jordanian state, it also contributed to the resurgence of Palestinian nationalism that forced the king to fight in 1967. And while the superpowers may not have wanted Israel to widen its borders, they were even more strongly opposed to Israel becoming a declared nuclear power. Since neither the United States nor the Soviet Union was willing to pay a price to uphold the status quo in the Middle East, the Israelis, when confronted, chose war. Levi Eshkol's government did not want to go to war in June 1967, but not to do so, as Avi Shlaim has written, would have been an act of faith, not statesmanship.[2]

It is possible that Israel might have been able to further delay the onset of war by adopting more static, defensive responses to border violence. But Nasser, the Palestinians, and the Syrians all saw that the regional balance of power was shifting in Israel's favor, and would have probably tried at some other point to force a crisis before an Arab victory became impossible.

1967 AND BEYOND

Following the 1967 war, Israel's leaders were suddenly confronted with another major choice: whether to try to keep conquered territory or trade it to the Arabs for peace. The Israelis insisted that they were, as Moshe Dayan famously put it, waiting for an Arab phone call, and that when

Arab leaders offered them real peace, they would happily give them back their land. At the same time, they insisted that they could never return to the 1967 armistice lines, and took numerous unilateral steps designed to keep parts of the occupied territories deemed important for either strategic or ideological reasons. When King Hussein did offer to negotiate, the Israelis presented him with terms that they knew he would refuse.

Were these wise or foolish choices? We will never know whether an agreement between King Hussein and the Israeli government that restored the West Bank to Jordan would have stood the test of time. But it is both understandable and unsurprising that the Israelis shunned the king's initial overtures. During the previous two decades, they had witnessed Hussein nearly succumb to his local and Arab opponents numerous times, and they had suffered the consequences of his decision to appease Nasser in May 1967. They had good cause to wait to negotiate with Hussein until Egypt, whose generals had recently commanded the Jordanian army, changed course. And they had good cause not to be satisfied with Hussein's word that the West Bank would never again become a base for aggression.

Yet while the Israelis might have had sound reasons not to rush toward a settlement with Hussein, the way they dealt with the West Bank in the meantime was unnecessary and unsound. The Israelis were arguably justified in holding out until they could be sure that peace with Hussein would be worth something. But they did not have to adopt policies that made it unlikely that he would ever agree to compromise with them over the West Bank. They did not have to effectively annex a vastly enlarged East Jerusalem or establish civilian settlements in the occupied territories.

Israel's leaders made these decisions knowing that Hussein would insist that they be reversed, and knowing that this would be politically impossible. They did not care. Eshkol, Allon, and Dayan placed nationalist and religious ideology and concerns for their personal power and popularity over the possibility of future peace. They believed that the social and political costs of occupation and even the risk of renewed war were preferable to internal political strife or an imperfect settlement.

The Israelis could act as they did because neither the Johnson nor the Nixon administration gave them any reason not to do so. The Johnson administration adopted a "Jordan-first" approach in theory while making little effort to foster Israeli-Jordanian peace. By the time Nixon took office, it was already too late for such an approach to have any real chance of success. Hussein's victory in 1970 merely ensured that for another eighteen years, the Israelis could avoid coming to terms with Palestinian nationalism.

By 1988, Hussein finally renounced his claims to the West Bank, and the PLO emerged as Israel's primary interlocutor over the fate of the occupied territories. In a way, this turn of events reflected what some Israelis had always wanted. As early as 1949, Ben-Gurion had argued that it would be better for Israel if the West Bank were a separate state rather than part of a larger Arab entity. Yet whatever strategic advantages the "Palestinian option" held for Israel, it also posed a whole series of much more vexing questions about the very nature of Zionism and Palestinian nationalism. It remains unclear whether Israelis and Palestinians can answer those questions.

NOTES

1. "Israel's Policy toward Jordan," undated, ISA/FM/4094/10. See also chapter 5 of this volume.
2. Shlaim, "Israel: Poor Little Samson," 55.

SOURCES

ARCHIVES AND PRIVATE PAPERS

Israel

Abba Eban Centre for Israeli Diplomacy, Hebrew University, Jerusalem (AECID)
    Abba Eban Papers
Ben-Gurion Archives, Sedeh Boker (BGA)
    Ben-Gurion Diary
Israel Defense Forces Archives, Tel ha-Shomer (IDFA)
    Central Command Records
    General Staff Records
    Operations Branch Records
Israel Intelligence Library, Glilot (IIL)
    Captured Jordanian Documents File
Israel State Archives, Jerusalem (ISA)
    Cabinet Minutes
    Foreign Ministry Files (FM)
    Golda Meir Papers
    Knesset Foreign Affairs and Defense Committee Minutes
    Levi Eshkol Papers
    Prime Minister's Office Files
    Record Group 130.15, Records of the Foreign Ministry's Middle East Division, 1949–1967
    Ya'akov Herzog Papers
    Yigal Allon Oral History
Labor Party Archives, Beit Berl (LPA)
    Mapai Party Secretariat Minutes
    Rafi Party Secretariat Minutes
Moshe Dayan Center Arabic Press Archive, Tel Aviv University, Ramat Aviv
Ya'akov Herzog Papers, Jerusalem (YHP). With the kind permission of Shira Herzog.
Yad Levi Eshkol, Jerusalem (YLE). With the kind permission of Miriam Eshkol.

United Kingdom

British National Archives, Kew (BNA)
Cabinet Office Files
Foreign and Commonwealth Office Files (FCO)
Foreign Office Files (FO)
Prime Minister's Office Files (PREM)

United States

Gerald R. Ford Presidential Library, Ann Arbor, MI (GRFL)
National Security Adviser memcons
John F. Kennedy Presidential Library, Boston (JFKL)
George Ball Papers
National Security Files (NSF)
Country Files
Robert Komer Papers
President's Office Files (POF)
Lyndon B. Johnson Presidential Library, Austin, TX (LBJL)
National Security Files (NSF)
Country Files
NSC Histories
United States National Archives and Records Administration, College Park, MD (NA)
Record Group 59: General Records of the Department of State (RG59)
Central Files (DOSCF)
Decimal Files (1960–1962)
Subject-Numeric Files (1963–1973)
Lot Files
Records of the Central Intelligence Agency, via the CIA Records Search Tool (CREST)
Richard M. Nixon Presidential Materials (now housed at the Nixon Presidential Library, Yorba Linda, CA) (RMNPM)
Henry A. Kissinger Office Files
National Security Files (NSF)
Country Files

PUBLISHED OFFICIAL DOCUMENTS

Israel

Israel State Archives. *Documents on the Foreign Policy of Israel*. Vol. 3, *Armistice Negotiations*. Jerusalem: Israel State Archives, 1983.
———. *Documents on the Foreign Policy of Israel*. Vol. 5, *1950*. Jerusalem: Israel State Archives, 1988.
———. *Documents on the Foreign Policy of Israel*. Vol. 6, *1951*. Jerusalem: Israel State Archives, 1991.

———. *Documents on the Foreign Policy of Israel.* Vol. 7, 1952. Jerusalem: Israel State Archives, 1992.
———. *Documents on the Foreign Policy of Israel.* Vol. 8, 1953. Jerusalem: Israel State Archives, 1995.
———. *Documents on the Foreign Policy of Israel.* Vol. 11, 1956. Jerusalem: Israel State Archives, 2008.
———. *Documents on the Foreign Policy of Israel.* Vol. 13, 1958–1959. Jerusalem: Israel State Archives, 2001.
———. *Documents on the Foreign Policy of Israel.* Vol. 14, 1960. Jerusalem: Israel State Archives, 1997.
Lammfromm, Arnon, ed. *Chaim Herzog: Ha-nasi ha-shishi; Mivhar te'udot me-pirkei hayav.* Jerusalem: Israel State Archives, 2009.
Lammfromm, Arnon, and Haggai Tsoref, eds. *Levi Eshkol, rosh ha-memshalah ha-shlishi: Mivhar te'udot me-pirkei hayav.* Jerusalem: Israel State Archives, 2002.
Oren, Elhanan, and Gershon Rivlin, eds. *David Ben-Gurion: Yoman ha-milhamah.* Vol. 3. Tel Aviv: Misrad ha-bitahon, 1982.
Rosenthal, Yemima, ed. *Yitzhak Rabin, rosh memshalat yisrael, 1974–1977, 1992–1995: Mivhar te'udot me-pirkei hayav.* Jerusalem: Israel State Archives, 2005.
Shaltiel, Eli, ed. *David Ben-Gurion, rosh ha memshalah ha-rishon: Mivhar te'udot.* Jerusalem: Israel State Archives, 1996.

Jordan

al-Watha'iq al-urduniyya, 1967. Amman: Wizarat al-Thaqafa wa al-A'alam, 1967.
al-Watha'iq al-urduniyya, 1968. Amman: Wizarat al-Thaqafa wa al-A'alam, 1973.
al-Watha'iq al-urduniyya, 1972. Amman: Da'irat al-Matbu'at wa al-Nashir, 1984.

Palestine Liberation Organization

Hamid, Rashid, ed. *Muqararat al-majlis al-watani al-filastini, 1964–1974.* Beirut: Munathamat al-Tahrir al-Filastiniyya—Markaz al-Abhath, 1975.

Soviet Union

Naumkin, Vitaly, ed. *Blizhni vostochni konflikt, 1957–1967.* Moscow: Materik, 2003.

United States

US Department of State. *Foreign Relations of the United States. 1955–1957.* Vol. 13, *Jordan and Yemen.* Washington, DC: Government Publishing Office, 1989.
———. *Foreign Relations of the United States. 1955–1957.* Vol. 17, *Arab-Israeli Dispute, 1957.* Washington, DC: Government Publishing Office, 1990.
———. *Foreign Relations of the United States. 1958–1960.* Vol. 11, *Lebanon and Jordan.* Washington, DC: Government Publishing Office, 1992.

———. *Foreign Relations of the United States*. 1958–1960. Vol. 12, *Middle East Region; Iraq; Iran; Yemen*. Washington, DC: Government Publishing Office, 1993.
———. *Foreign Relations of the United States*. 1958–1960. Vol. 13, *Arab-Israeli Dispute; United Arab Republic; North Africa*. Washington, DC: Government Publishing Office, 1992.
———. *Foreign Relations of the United States*. 1961–1963. Vol. 17, *Near East, 1961–62*. Washington, DC: Government Publishing Office, 1995.
———. *Foreign Relations of the United States*. 1961–1963. Vol. 18, *Near East, 1962–63*. Washington, DC: Government Publishing Office, 1995.
———. *Foreign Relations of the United States*. 1964–1968. Vol. 15, *Berlin; Germany*. Washington, DC: Government Publishing Office, 1999.
———. *Foreign Relations of the United States*. 1964–1968. Vol. 18, *Arab-Israeli Dispute, 1964–1967*. Washington, DC: Government Publishing Office, 2000.
———. *Foreign Relations of the United States*. 1964–1968. Vol. 19, *Arab-Israeli Crisis and War, 1967*. Washington, DC: Government Publishing Office, 2004.
———. *Foreign Relations of the United States*. 1964–1968. Vol. 20, *Arab-Israeli Dispute, 1967–1968*. Washington, DC: Government Publishing Office, 2002.
———. *Foreign Relations of the United States*. 1964–1968. Vol. 21, *Near East Region; Arabian Peninsula*. Washington, DC: Government Publishing Office, 2000.
———. *Foreign Relations of the United States*. 1969–1976. Vol. 23, *Arab-Israeli Dispute, 1969–1972*. Washington, DC: Government Publishing Office, 2015.
———. *Foreign Relations of the United States*. 1969–1976. Vol. 24, *Middle East Region and Arabian Peninsula, 1969–1972; Jordan, September 1970*. Washington, DC: Government Publishing Office, 2008.

ELECTRONIC SOURCES AND WEBSITES

The American Presidency Project	http://www.presidency.ucsb.edu
CIA Freedom of Information Act Electronic Reading Room	http://www.foia.cia.gov
Digital National Security Archive	(DNSA) (via university subscription)
Declassified Documents Reference System	(DDRS) (via university subscription)
Foreign Relations of the United States, electronic volumes	http://www.state.gov/r/pa/ho/frus
Gale Group, "The Middle East Online, Series One: Arab-Israeli Relations, 1917–1970"	(via university subscription)
Gerald R. Ford Presidential Library and Museum	http://www.fordlibrarymuseum.gov
Israeli Foreign Ministry	http://www.mfa.gov.il
National Security Archive	http://www.gwu.edu/~nsarchiv
United Nations Information System on the Question of Palestine	http://domino.un.org/unispal.nsf

NEWSPAPERS AND PERIODICALS

al-Ahram
al-Ba'th
al-Difa'
Filastin
al-Gumhurriyya
Ha'aretz
Middle East Record
The New York Times
The Times (London)
Yedi'ot Ahronot

BOOKS, ARTICLES, AND UNPUBLISHED WORKS

Abu Gharbiyya, Bahjat. *Min mudhakirrat al-munadil Bahjat Abu Gharbiyya: Min al-nakba ila al-intifada, 1949–2000*. Beirut: al-Mu'assisa al-'Arabiyya li al-Dirasa wa al-Nashir, 2004.
Abu Iyad [Salah Khalaf]. *My Home, My Land: A Narrative of the Palestinian Struggle*. With Eric Rouleau. New York: Times Books, 1981.
Abu Nuwar, 'Ali. *Hina talashat al-'arab: Mudhakirrat fi al-siyasa al-'arabiyya, 1948–1964*. London: Dar al-Saqi, 1990.
Abu-Nuwar, Ma'an. *The Jordanian-Israeli War, 1948–51: A History of the Hashemite Kingdom of Jordan*. Reading: Ithaca Press, 2002.
Abu-Odeh, Adnan. *Jordanians, Palestinians, and the Hashemite Kingdom in the Middle East Peace Process*. Washington, DC: US Institute of Peace, 1999.
Adamsky, Dima. "How American and Israeli Intelligence Failed to Predict Soviet Intervention in the War of Attrition." In *The Cold War and the Middle East: Regional Conflict and the Superpowers, 1967–73*, edited by Nigel Ashton, 113–135. New York: Routledge, 2007.
Almog, Orna. *Britain, Israel, and the United States, 1955–1958: Beyond Suez*. London: Frank Cass, 2003.
Alon, Yoav. "The Tribal System in the Face of the State-Formation Process: Mandatory Transjordan, 1921–46." *International Journal of Middle East Studies* 37, no. 2 (2005): 213–240.
Amit, Meir. *Rosh be-rosh: Mabat ishi 'al iru'im gedolim u-parshiot 'alumot*. Or Yehudah: Hed Artsi, 1999.
Anderson, Betty. *Nationalist Voices in Jordan: The Street and the State*. Austin: University of Texas Press, 2005.
Ashton, Nigel. *King Hussein of Jordan: A Political Life*. New Haven, CT: Yale University Press, 2008.
Barak, Oren. "Caught in the Middle: The United Nations Emergency Force, Israel, and the 1960 'Rotem Crisis.'" *Diplomacy and Statecraft* 17, no. 2 (2006): 393–414.
Bar-Joseph, Uri. *The Best of Enemies: Israel and Transjordan in the War of 1948*. London: Frank Cass, 1987.

———. "Rotem: The Forgotten Crisis on the Road to the 1967 War." *Journal of Contemporary History* 31, no. 3 (1996): 547–566.
Bar-On, Mordechai. *The Gates of Gaza: Israel's Road to Sinai and Back.* New York: St. Martin's, 1994.
———. *Gevulot 'ashenim: 'Iyunim be-toldot medinat yisrael, 1948–1967.* Jerusalem: Yad Ben-Tsvi, 2001.
———. *Moshe Dayan: Israel's Controversial Hero.* New Haven, CT: Yale University Press, 2012.
Bar-Zohar, Michael. *Yaacov Herzog: A Biography.* London: Halban, 2005.
Bass, Warren. *Support Any Friend: Kennedy's Middle East and the Making of the US-Israel Alliance.* New York: Oxford University Press, 2003.
Bligh, Alexander. *The Political Legacy of King Hussein.* Brighton: Sussex Academic, 2002.
Braun, Arieh. *Hotem ishi: Moshe Dayan be-milhemet sheshet ha-yamim ve-aharehah.* Tel Aviv: Yedi'ot Ahronot, 1997.
Brown, L. Carl. *International Politics and the Middle East: Old Rules, Dangerous Game.* Princeton, NJ: Princeton University Press, 1984.
Bundy, William. *A Tangled Web: The Making of Foreign Policy in the Nixon Presidency.* New York: Hill and Wang, 1998.
Caplan, Neil. "Oom Shmoom Revisited: Israeli Attitudes toward the UN and the Great Powers, 1948–1960." In *Global Politics: Essays in Honor of David Vital*, edited by David Vital, Abraham Ben-Zvi, and Aaron Kleiman, 167–200. London: Frank Cass, 2001.
Chamberlin, Paul. *The Global Offensive: The United States, the Palestine Liberation Organization, and the Making of the Post-Cold War Order.* New York: Oxford University Press, 2012.
Cohen, Amnon. *Political Parties in the West Bank under the Jordanian Regime, 1949–1967.* Ithaca, NY: Cornell University Press, 1982.
Cohen, Avner. "Crossing the Threshold: The Untold Nuclear Dimension of the 1967 Arab-Israeli War and Its Contemporary Lessons." *Arms Control Today,* June 2007. http://www.armscontrol.org/act/2007_06/Cohen.
———. *Israel and the Bomb.* New York: Columbia University Press, 1998.
Cohen, Avner, and William Burr. "Israel Crosses the Threshold." *Bulletin of the Atomic Scientists* 62, no. 3 (2006): 23–30.
Daigle, Craig. *The Limits of Détente: The United States, the Soviet Union, and the Arab-Israeli Conflict, 1969–1973.* New Haven, CT: Yale University Press, 2012.
Dallek, Robert. *Nixon and Kissinger: Partners in Power.* New York: HarperCollins, 2007.
Dann, Uriel. *King Hussein and the Challenge of Arab Radicalism: Jordan, 1955–1967.* New York: Oxford University Press, 1989.
De Atkine, Norvell. "Amman 1970, A Memoir." *Middle East Review of International Affairs* 6, no. 4 (2002): 75–82.
Dishon, Daniel, ed. *Middle East Record, 1967.* Jerusalem: Israel Universities Press, 1971.
———. *Middle East Record, 1968.* Jerusalem: Israel Universities Press, 1973.
———. *Middle East Record, 1969–1970.* Tel Aviv: Israel Universities Press, 1977.
Drory, Zeev. *Esh ba-kavim: Milhemet ha-hatashah ba-hazit ha-mizrahit, 1967–1970.* Modan: Ma'arakhot, 2012.
Farid, Abdel Magid. *Nasser: The Final Years.* Reading: Ithaca Press, 1994.
Fawzi, Muhammad. *Harb al-thalath sanawat, 1967–1970.* Cairo: Dar al-Mustaqbal al-' 'Arabi, 1983.

Feiler, Gil. "Jordan's Economy, 1970–1990: The Primacy of Exogenous Factors." In *Jordan in the Middle East, 1948–1988: The Making of a Pivotal State*, edited by Joseph Nevo and Ilan Pappé, 45–60. Essex: Frank Cass, 1994.
Ferris, Jesse. *Nasser's Gamble: How Intervention in Yemen Caused the Six-Day War and the Decline of Egyptian Power*. Princeton, NJ: Princeton University Press, 2013.
Fursenko, Alexander, and Timothy Naftali. *Khrushchev's Cold War: The Inside Story of an American Adversary*. New York: W. W. Norton, 2006.
Gai, Karmit. *Bar-Lev: Biyografiah*. Tel Aviv: 'Am 'Oved, 1998.
Garfinkle, Adam. *Israel and Jordan in the Shadow of War: Functional Ties and Futile Diplomacy in a Small Place*. New York: St. Martin's, 1992.
Gat, Moshe. "Let Someone Else Do the Job: American Policy on the Eve of the Six Day War." *Diplomacy and Statecraft* 14, no. 1 (2003): 131–158.
Gazit, Shlomo. *The Carrot and the Stick: Israel's Policy in Judaea and Samaria, 1967–68*. Washington, DC: B'nai B'rith Books, 1995.
Gelber, Yoav. *Israeli-Jordanian Dialogue, 1948–1953: Cooperation, Conspiracy, or Collusion?* Brighton: Sussex Academic, 2005.
Gerlini, Matteo. "Waiting for Dimona: The United States and Israel's Development of Nuclear Capability." *Cold War History* 10, no. 2 (2010): 143–161.
Ginor, Isabella, and Gideon Remez. *Foxbats over Dimona: The Soviets' Nuclear Gamble in the Six Day War*. New Haven, CT: Yale University Press, 2007.
Glubb, John Bagot. *A Soldier with the Arabs*. London: Hodder and Stoughton, 1957.
Gluska, Ami. *Eshkol, ten pekudah!* Tel Aviv: Ma'arakhot, 2004.
Golan, Shimon. *Gevul ham, milhamah karah: Hitgavshut mediniyut ha-bitahon shel yisrael, 1949–1953*. Tel Aviv: Ma'arakhot, 2000.
———. *Milhamah be-shalosh hazitot: Kabalat ha-hahlatot be-pikud ha-'elyon be-milhemet sheshet ha-yamim*. Tel Aviv: Ma'arakhot, 2007.
Golani, Motti. *Tihiyeh milhamah ba-kayits: Yisrael be-derekh le-milhemet sinai, 1955–1956*. Tel Aviv: Ma'arakhot, 1997.
Goldstein, Yossi. *Eshkol: Biografiyah*. Jerusalem: Keter, 2004.
Goren, David. *Ha-Gevul she-lo hutash*. Tel Aviv: Ha-Kibuts ha-Me'uhad, 1986.
Gorenberg, Gershom. *The Accidental Empire: Israel and the Birth of the Settlements, 1967–1977*. New York: Times Books, 2006.
Govrin, Yosef. *Israeli-Soviet Relations, 1953–1967: From Confrontation to Disruption*. London: Frank Cass, 1998.
Gubser, Peter. *Jordan: Crossroads of Middle Eastern Events*. Boulder: Westview, 1983.
Haber, Eitan, ed. *Ha-Yom tifrots milhamah: Zikhronotav shel tat-aluf Yisrael Lior, ha-mazkir ha-tsva'i shel rashei ha-memshalah Levi Eshkol ve-Golda Meir*. Tel Aviv: 'Edanim, 1987.
Hahn, Peter L. *Caught in the Middle East: U.S. Policy toward the Arab-Israeli Conflict, 1945–1961*. Chapel Hill: University of North Carolina Press, 2004.
———. "The Cold War and the Six Day War: US Policy towards the Arab-Israeli Crisis of June 1967." In *The Cold War and the Middle East: Regional Conflict and the Superpowers, 1967–73*, edited by Nigel Ashton, 16–34. New York: Routledge, 2007.
———. *The United States, Great Britain, and Egypt, 1945–1956: Strategy and Diplomacy in the Early Cold War*. Chapel Hill: University of North Carolina Press, 1991.
Harik, Iliya. "The Origins of the Arab State System." In *The Foundations of the Arab State*, edited by Ghassan Salame, 19–46. New York: Croom Helm, 1987.

Haykal, Muhammad Hasanayn. *al-Infijar: 1967.* Cairo: Markaz al-Ahram, 1990.
———. *Sanawat al-ghalayan.* Cairo: Markaz al-Ahram, 1988.
Heller, Yosef. *Yisrael veha-milhamah ha-karah: Memilhemet ha-'atsma'ut le-milhemet sheshet ha-yamim.* Be'ersheva: Ben-Gurion University Press, 2010.
Herzog, Chaim. *Derekh hayim: Sipuro shel lohem, diplomat, ve-nasi.* Tel Aviv: Yedi'ot Ahronot, 1999.
Inbar, Efraim. *Rabin and Israel's National Security.* Washington, DC: Woodrow Wilson Center Press, 1999.
Jackson, Robert. *Quasi-States: Sovereignty, International Relations and the Third World.* New York: Cambridge University Press, 1990.
Jones, Clive. *Britain and the Yemen Civil War, 1962–1965.* Brighton: Sussex Academic, 2004.
Jum'a, Sa'd. *al-Mu'amara wa-ma'rakat al-masir.* Beirut: Dar al-Katib al-'Arabi, 1968.
Kafkafi, Eyal. *Milhemet brerah: Ha-derekh le-sinai ve-hazarah, 1956–1957.* Ramat Efal: Yad Tabenkin, 1994.
Karsh, Efraim. "The Collusion That Never Was: King Abdallah, the Jewish Agency and the Partition of Palestine." *Journal of Contemporary History* 34, no. 4 (1999): 569–585.
Kerr, Malcolm. *The Arab Cold War: Gamal 'Abd al-Nasir and his Rivals, 1958–1970.* New York: Oxford University Press, 1971.
Kingston, Paul. "Rationalizing Patrimonialism: Wasfi al-Tal and Economic Reform in Jordan, 1962–1967." In *The Resilience of the Hashemite Rule: Politics and the State in Jordan,* edited by Tariq Tell, 115–144. Beirut: Cermoc, 2001.
Korn, David. *Stalemate: The War of Attrition and Great Power Diplomacy in the Middle East, 1967–1970.* Boulder, CO: Westview, 1992.
Kuperman, Ranan D. "The Impact of Internal Politics on Israel's Reprisal Policy during the 1950s." *Journal of Strategic Studies* 24, no. 1 (2001): 1–28.
Lafeber, Walter. *The Deadly Bet: LBJ, Vietnam, and the 1968 Election.* Lanham, MD: Rowman and Littlefield, 2005.
Lahav, Pnina. "A Small Nation Goes to War: Israel's Cabinet Authorization of the 1956 War." *Israel Studies* 15, no. 3 (2010): 61–86.
Laron, Guy. "The Domestic Sources of Israel's Decision to Launch the 1956 Sinai Campaign." *British Journal of Middle East Studies* 42, no. 2 (2015): 200–218.
———. "'Logic dictates that they will attack us when they think they can win': The 1955 Czech-Egyptian Arms Deal, the Egyptian Army, and Israeli Intelligence." *Middle East Journal* 63, no. 1 (2009): 69–84.
———. "Playing with Fire: The Soviet-Israeli-Syrian Triangle, 1965–1967." *Cold War History* 10, no. 2 (2010): 163–184.
Laskier, Michael. *Israel and the Maghreb: From Statehood to Oslo.* Gainesville: University Press of Florida, 2004.
Lauer, Pierre, and Vick Vance, eds. *Hussein of Jordan: My "War" with Israel.* New York: William Morrow, 1969.
Levey, Zach. *Israel and the Western Powers, 1952–1960.* Chapel Hill: University of North Carolina Press, 1997.
———. "The United States' Skyhawk Sale to Israel, 1966: Strategic Exigencies of an Arms Deal." *Diplomatic History* 28, no. 2 (2004): 255–276.
Little, Douglas. "The Making of a Special Relationship: The United States and Israel, 1957–68." *International Journal of Middle East Studies* 25, no. 4 (1993): 563–585.

Logevall, Fredrik. *Choosing War: The Lost Chance for Peace and the Escalation of War in Vietnam.* Berkeley: University of California Press, 1999.
Louis, William Roger. *The British Empire in the Middle East, 1945–1951: Arab Nationalism, the United States, and Postwar Imperialism.* Oxford: Clarendon, 1984.
Louis, William Roger, and Avi Shlaim, eds. *The 1967 Arab-Israeli War: Origins and Consequences.* New York: Cambridge University Press, 2013.
Lucas, W. Scott. "Redefining the Suez 'Collusion.'" *Middle Eastern Studies* 26, no. 1 (1990): 88–112.
Luft, Gal. "All Quiet on the Eastern Front? Israel's National Security Doctrine after the Fall of Saddam." Saban Center for Middle East Policy, Analysis Paper No. 2. Washington, DC: Brookings Institution, 2004.
Lustick, Ian S. "The Absence of Middle Eastern Great Powers: Political 'Backwardness' in Historical Perspective." *International Organization* 51, no. 4 (1997): 653–683.
Maddy-Weizmann, Bruce. *The Crystallization of the Arab State System, 1945–1954.* Syracuse, NY: Syracuse University Press, 1993.
Mahgoub, Mohamed. *Democracy on Trial: Reflections on Arab and African Politics.* London: Andre Deutsch, 1974.
Medzini, Meron, ed. *Israel's Foreign Relations: Selected Documents, 1977–1979.* Vol. 5. Jerusalem: Ministry of Foreign Affairs, 1981.
Meir, Golda. *My Life.* London: Weidenfeld and Nicholson, 1975.
Monte, Christopher. "Fateful Alliance: Lyndon Johnson and American Policy toward the Arab-Israeli Conflict, 1963–1969." PhD diss., University of Pennsylvania, 2012.
Morris, Benny. *The Birth of the Palestinian Refugee Problem Revisited.* Cambridge: Cambridge University Press, 2004.
———. *Israel's Border Wars, 1949–1956: Arab Infiltration, Israeli Retaliation, and the Countdown to the Suez War.* Oxford: Clarendon, 1993.
———. *1948: A History of the First Arab-Israeli War.* New Haven, CT: Yale University Press, 2008.
———. *The Road to Jerusalem: Glubb Pasha, Palestine, and the Jews.* New York: I. B. Tauris, 2003.
Mufti, Malik. *Sovereign Creations: Pan-Arabism and Political Order in Syria and Iraq.* Ithaca, NY: Cornell University Press, 1996.
Musa, Sulayman. *Tarikh al-urdun fi al-qarn al-'ishrin, 1958–1995: al-Joz al-thani.* Amman: Maktabat al-Muhtasib, 1996.
Mutawi, Samir A. *Jordan in the 1967 War.* Cambridge: Cambridge University Press, 1987.
Nakdimon, Shlomo. *Tikvah She-karsah: Ha-kesher ha-yisraeli-kurdi.* Tel Aviv: Yedi'ot Ahronot, 1996.
Oren, Amiram. "'Seder ha-kohot ha-milhamti—ha'arakhat matsav 1953–1960': Likrat harhavat tsahal be-shenot ha-hamishim." *Iyunim be-tekumat yisrael* 12 (2002): 123–146.
Oren, Michael B. "Did Israel Want the Six Day War?" *Azure* 7 (1999): 47–86.
———. "Levi Eshkol: Forgotten Hero." *Azure* 14 (Winter 2003): 25–72.
———. *The Origins of the Second Arab-Israeli War: Egypt, Israel and the Great Powers, 1952–56.* London: Frank Cass, 1992.
———. *Six Days of War: June 1967 and the Making of the Modern Middle East.* New York: Oxford University Press, 2002.
———. "The Test of Suez: Israel and the Middle East Crisis of 1958." *Studies in Zionism* 12, no. 1 (1991): 55–83.

———. "A Winter of Discontent: Britain's Crisis in Jordan, December 1955-March 1956." *International Journal of Middle East Studies* 22, no. 2 (1990): 171–184.

Pedatzur, Reuven. *Nitsahon ha-mevukhah: Mediniut memshelet Eshkol ba-shetahim le-ahar milhemet sheshet ha-yamim.* Tel Aviv: Bitan, 1996.

Peres, Shimon. *Battling for Peace: Memoirs.* London: Weidenfeld and Nicholson, 1995.

Pinkus, Binyamin. "Atomic Power to Israel's Rescue: French-Israeli Nuclear Cooperation, 1949–1957." *Israel Studies* 7, no. 1 (2002): 104–138.

Podeh, Elie. *The Decline of Arab Unity: The Rise and Fall of the United Arab Republic.* Brighton: Sussex Academic, 1999.

———. "Demonizatsiyah shel ha-oyev: Natser veha-natserism be-'einei mekablei ha-hahlatot be-yisrael (1952–1970)." *Ha-Mizrah ha-hadash* 45 (2005): 151–214.

———. "The Struggle over Arab Hegemony after the Suez Crisis." *Middle Eastern Studies* 29, no. 1 (1993): 91–110.

———. "'Suez in Reverse': The Arab Response to the Iraqi Bid for Kuwait, 1961–63." *Diplomacy and Statecraft* 14, no. 1 (2003): 103–130.

———. "To Unite or Not to Unite—That is *Not* the Question: The 1963 Tripartite Unity Talks Reassessed." *Middle Eastern Studies* 39, no. 1 (2003): 150–185.

Popp, Roland. "Stumbling Decidedly into the Six-Day War." *Middle East Journal* 60 (2006): 281–309.

Quandt, William B. "Lyndon Johnson and the June 1967 War: What Color Was the Light?" *Middle East Journal* 46, no. 2 (1992): 198–228.

Rabin, Yitzhak. *Pinkas sherut.* Tel Aviv: Ma'ariv, 1979.

Rafael, Gideon. *Destination Peace: Three Decades of Israeli Foreign Policy.* New York: Stein and Day, 1981.

Rakove, Robert B. *Kennedy, Johnson, and the Nonaligned World.* New York: Cambridge University Press, 2012.

Rashid, Nathir. *Hisab al-saraya wa-hisab al-qaraya.* Beirut: Dar al-Saqi, 2006.

Raz, Avi. *The Bride and the Dowry: Israel, Jordan, and the Palestinians in the Aftermath of the June 1967 War.* New Haven, CT: Yale University Press, 2012.

Riyadh, Mahmud. *Mudhakirrat Mahmud Riyadh, al-joz al-thani: al-Aman al-qawmi al-'arabi ... bayn al-injaz wa al-fashal.* Cairo: Dar al-Mustaqbal al-'Arabi, 1993.

———. *Mudhakirrat Mahmud Riyadh, 1948–1978.* Cairo: Dar al-Mustaqbal al-'Arabi, 1993.

Robins, Philip. *A History of Jordan.* New York: Cambridge University Press, 2004.

Ro'i, Yaacov. "Soviet Policy toward the Six Day War through the Prism of Moscow's Relations with Egypt and Syria." In *The Soviet Union and the June 1967 Six Day War*, edited by Yaacov Ro'i and Boris Morozov, 1–42. Stanford, CA: Stanford University Press, 2008.

Ro'i, Yaacov, and Boris Morozov, eds. *The Soviet Union and the June 1967 Six Day War.* Stanford, CA: Stanford University Press, 2008.

Ronen, David. *Shanat shabak: Ha-hi'arkhut be-yehudah ve-shomron, shanah rishonah.* Tel Aviv: Misrad ha-Bitahon, 1989.

Rosenak, Michael. "Religious Reactions: Testimony and Theology." In *The Impact of the Six Day War*, edited by Stephen Roth, 209–231. New York: St. Martin's, 1988.

Rubin, Avshalom. "The Limits of the Land: Israel, Jordan, the United States, and the Fate of the West Bank, 1949–1970." PhD diss., University of Chicago, 2010.

Rubinovitz, Ziv. "Blue and White 'Black September': An Israeli Perspective of the Jordan 1970 Crisis." Paper presented at the Annual Conference of the Association for Israel Studies, Be'ersheva, June 1–3, 2009.
Satloff, Robert. *From Abdullah to Hussein: Jordan in Transition*. New York: Oxford University Press, 1994.
———. "The Jekyll and Hyde Origins of the US-Jordanian Strategic Relationship." In *The Middle East and the United States: A Historical and Political Reassessment*, edited by David Lesch, 117–130. Boulder, CO: Westview, 1996.
Sayigh, Yezid. *Armed Struggle and the Search for a State: The Palestinian National Movement, 1949–1993*. New York: Oxford University Press, 1997.
Schueftan, Dan. *Optsiyah yardenit: Ha-yishuv ha-yehudi u-medinat yisrael mul ha-mimshal ha-hashemi veha-tenu'ah ha-leumit ha-falastinit*. Ramat Efal: Yad Tabenkin, 1986.
Seale, Patrick. *Asad: The Struggle for the Middle East*. Berkeley: University of California Press, 1988.
Segev, Tom. *1949: The First Israelis*. New York: Henry Holt, 1986.
———. *1967: Israel, the War, and the Year That Transformed the Middle East*. New York: Metropolitan Books, 2005.
———. *1967: Veha-arets shintah et panehah*. Jerusalem: Keter, 2005.
Sela, Avraham. *The Decline of the Arab-Israeli Conflict: Middle East Politics and the Quest for Regional Order*. Albany: SUNY Press, 1998.
———. "Transjordan, Israel and the 1948 War: Myth, Historiography, and Reality." *Middle Eastern Studies* 28 (1992): 623–689.
Shai, Sha'ul. "Ha-me'oravut ha-iraqit be-milhemet sheshet ha-yamim u-le-aharehah." In *Ha-'Imut ha-iraqi-yisraeli, 1948–2000*, edited by Sha'ul Shai, 56–71. Tel Aviv: Ma'arakhot, 2002.
Shalev, Aryeh. *The West Bank: Line of Defense*. New York: Praeger, 1985.
Shalom, Zaki. *Bein dimona le-washington: Ha-ma'avak 'al pituah ha-optsiyah ha-garinit shel yisrael, 1960–1968*. Sedeh Boker: Ben-Gurion University of the Negev Press, 2004.
———. *David Ben-Gurion, the State of Israel, and the Arab World, 1949–1956*. Brighton: Sussex Academic, 2002.
———. *Diplomatiyah be-tsel milhamah*. Tel Aviv: INSS, 2007.
———. "'Emdot be-hanhagat ha-medinah be-sugiyat ha-status quo ha-territoriyali be-shanim ha-rishonot she-le-ahar milhemet ha-'atsma'ut—behinah mehudeshet." *Iyunim be-tekumat yisrael* 8 (1998): 110–149.
———. *Israel's Nuclear Option: Behind the Scenes Diplomacy between Dimona and Washington*. Brighton: Sussex Academic, 2005.
———. *Ke-esh be-'atsmotav: David Ben-Gurion u-ma'avakav 'al demut ha-medinah vehanhagatah, 1963–1967*. Sedeh Boqer: Ben-Gurion University Press, 2004.
———. *The Superpowers, Israel, and the Future of Jordan, 1960–1963*. Brighton: Sussex Academic, 1999.
Shapira, Anita. *Yigal Allon, Native Son*. Philadelphia: University of Pennsylvania Press, 2008.
Sharon, Ariel. *Warrior*. New York: Simon and Schuster, 2001.
Sheffer, Gabriel. *Moshe Sharett: Biography of a Political Moderate*. Oxford: Clarendon, 1996.
Sheffy, Yigal. *Hatra'ah be-mivhan: Parashat rotem ve-tefisat ha-bitahon shel yisrael, 1957–1960*. Tel Aviv: Ma'arakhot, 2008.

Shemesh, Moshe. *Arab Politics, Palestinian Nationalism and the Six Day War*. Brighton: Sussex Academic, 2007.

———. "The IDF Raid on Samu': The Turning-Point in Jordan's Relations with Israel and the West Bank Palestinians." *Israel Studies* 7, no. 1 (2002): 139–167.

———. *Meha-nakbah la-naksa: Ha-siksukh ha-'aravi-yisraeli veha-ba'ayah ha-leumit ha-falastinit, 1957–1967*. Sedeh Boqer: Ben-Gurion University of the Negev Press, 2004.

———. *The Palestinian Entity, 1959–1974: Arab Politics and the PLO*. London: Frank Cass, 1988.

———. "Prelude to the Six-Day War: The Arab-Israeli Struggle over Water Resources." *Israel Studies* 9, no. 3 (2004): 1–45.

Shilon, Avi. *Begin, 1913–1992*. Tel Aviv: 'Am Oved, 2007.

Shlaim, Avi. *Collusion across the Jordan: King Abdullah, the Zionist Movement and the Partition of Palestine*. New York: Columbia University Press, 1988.

———. "Israel: Poor Little Samson." In *The 1967 Arab-Israeli War: Origins and Consequences*, edited by William Roger Louis and Avi Shlaim, 22–55. New York: Cambridge University Press, 2013.

———. "Israel, the Great Powers, and the Middle East Crisis of 1958." *Journal of Imperial and Commonwealth History* 21, no. 2 (1999): 177–192.

———. *Lion of Jordan: The Life of King Hussein in War and Peace*. London: Penguin, 2007.

Shuqayri, Ahmad al-. *'Ala tariq al-hazima: Ma'a al-muluk wa al-ru'asa*. Beirut: Markaz Dirasat al-Wahda al-'Arabiyya, 2006.

———. *al-Hazima al-kubra: Ma'a al-muluk wa al-ru'asa*. 2 vols. Beirut: Markaz Dirasat al-Wahda al-'Arabiyya, 2006.

———. *Min al-qima ila al-hazima: Ma'a al-muluk wa al-ru'asa*. Beirut: Markaz Dirasat al-Wahda al-'Arabiyya, 2006.

Siniver, Asaf. *Abba Eban: A Biography*. New York: Overlook, 2015.

Sosland, Jeffrey. *Cooperating Rivals: The Riparian Politics of the Jordan River Basin*. Albany: SUNY Press, 2007.

Susser, Asher. *On Both Banks of the Jordan: A Political Biography of Wasfi al-Tall*. London: Frank Cass, 1994.

Tal, David. "Seizing Opportunities: Israel and the 1958 Crisis in the Middle East." *Middle Eastern Studies* 37, no. 1 (2001): 142–158.

Tal, Lawrence. *Politics, the Military, and National Security in Jordan, 1955–1967*. New York: Palgrave Macmillan, 2002.

Tal, Wasfi al-. *Kitabat fi al-qadaya al-'arabiyya*. Amman: Dar al-Liwa li al-Sahafa wa al-Nashir, 1980.

Tarawna, Ahmad. *Rihlati ma'a al-urdun*. Amman: Jaridat al-Dustur, 1997.

Tell, Tariq. *The Social and Economic Origins of Monarchy in Jordan*. New York: Palgrave Macmillan, 2013.

Teveth, Shabtai. *Ben-Gurion: The Burning Ground, 1881–1948*. Boston: Houghton Mifflin, 1987.

Trachtenberg, Marc. *A Constructed Peace: The Making of the European Settlement, 1945–1963*. Princeton, NJ: Princeton University Press, 1999.

Troen, Selwyn Ilan, and Zaki Shalom. "Ben-Gurion's Diary for the 1967 Six-Day War: An Introduction." *Israel Studies* 4, no. 2 (1999): 195–220.

Troen, Selwyn Ilan, and Moshe Shemesh, eds. *The Suez-Sinai Crisis, 1956: Retrospective and Reappraisal*. New York: Columbia University Press, 1990.

Wasserstein, Bernard. *Divided Jerusalem: The Struggle for the Holy City.* New Haven, CT: Yale University Press, 2001.
Weizman, Ezer. *Lekha shama'im, lekha arets.* Tel Aviv: Ma'ariv, 1975.
Westad, Odd Arne. *The Global Cold War: Third World Interventions and the Making of Our Times.* Cambridge: Cambridge University Press, 2005.
Wilson, Mary. *King Abdullah, Britain and the Making of Jordan.* Cambridge: Cambridge University Press, 1987.
Wishart, David M. "The Breakdown of the Johnston Negotiations over the Jordan Waters." *Middle Eastern Studies* 26, no. 4 (1990): 536–546.
Yaqub, Salim. *Containing Arab Nationalism: The Eisenhower Doctrine and the Middle East.* Chapel Hill: University of North Carolina Press, 2004.
———. "The Weight of Conquest: Henry Kissinger and the Arab-Israeli Conflict." In *Nixon in the World: American Foreign Relations, 1969–1977,* edited by Fredrik Logevall and Andrew Preston, 227–248. New York: Oxford University Press, 2008.
Zak, Moshe. *Hussein 'oseh shalom: Sheloshim shanah ve-'od shanah 'al ha-derekh el ha-shalom.* Ramat Gan: Begin-Sadat Center for Strategic Studies, 1996.

INDEX

Note: Numbers in italics refer to figures.

Abbas, Mahmud, 110
'Abduh, Muhammad Abu al-Mu'ati, 143
Abdullah, King, 10–15
Abtal al-'Awda (Heroes of the Return), 138n125
Abu al-Huda, Tawfiq, 15
Abu Gharbiyya, Bahjat, 77, 100n14
Abu Nuwar, 'Ali, 23, 27
Abu-Nuwar, Ma'an, 222
Adha, 'Id al-, 249
'Aflaq, Michel, 117
Ahdut ha-'Avodah party, 19, 30, 42, 90–91, 215
Ahram, al- 67, 123, 225
Alexandria summit, 75–77, 79, 107
Algeria: Arab League and, 253; Jordan and, 63–64, 253, 262, 279; parallels to, 24–25, 29, 109, 117–118, 225; Soviet Union and, 118
Allon Plan, 195, 215, 232, 237, 238–240, 245n112, 275–276
Allon, Yigal, 6, 13, 16, 18; on Jordan, 53–54, 168, 270–271; on nuclear weapons, 42; political rivalries, 19, 42, 231; on the West Bank, 53–54, 168–169, 187–189, 194–195 (*see also* Allon Plan)

AMAN, 35; on Arab summitry, 96–97; on arms race, 38; on Egypt, 37–38, 151, 154; on Egypt-Syria mutual defense pact, 128; on Fatah, 111, 113, 134n28, 223; on Jordan, 76, 89, 108, 166, 269; on Syria, 138n119; on the PLO, 108; on the Soviet Union, 172n62, 206n20; on Tunisian peace advocacy, 97–98; on the Unified Arab Command (UAC), 76–77; on US-Jordanian arms deal, 89
'Amir, 'Abd al-Hakim, 93, 160, 167
'Amir, 'Ali 'Ali, 67, 77, 93, 174n126
Amit, Meir, 53, 68, 98–99, 150–151, 164–165, 191
Anglo-Egyptian Treaty, 20
anti-Semitism, 15–16
April 27 coup scare, 54, 56–57
Arab-Israeli conflict, 3–6; archival revelations, xiii–xv, 289; arms race, 38–40; balance of power, 3–5; détente and, 62, 81, 98, 62, 81, 98; missed opportunity in, 278; Pan-Arabism, 4–5, 11, 27–28, 290; postcolonialism and, 3–4, 32–33, 109
Arab League, 75–77; Alexandria summit, 75; Cairo summit, 77; Fatah vs. 110; Hussein in the, 76, 120, 201–202, 219, 253, 264, 272; Khartoum summit, 201–202; Nasser in the, 37; Palestinians

307

and, 106–107, 120, 278, 280; Tunisia's expulsion from, 97; on water issues, 67, 75. *See also* Unified Arab Command (UAC)
Arab Legion, 11–12, 21–22. *See also* Jordan Arab Army (JAA)
Arab Nationalists Movement, 21, 120, 133
Arab Solidarity Agreement, 27
Arab summitry: Alexandria summit, 75–77, 79, 107; Cairo emergency summit, 264, 272–275, 273; Cairo summit of 1964, 67, 106–107; Casablanca summit, 77, 93–94; Khartoum summit, 201–203; Palestinians and, 106–107, 117
Arad incident, 128–130
Arafat, Yasir, 110; al-Asad and, 275; Cairo summit, 272, 273; on the fida'iyyun, 262; founding of Fatah, 110; Karameh, battle of, 220–221; Meir on, 257, 269; Palestine Liberation Organization (PLO) and, 241
Aranne, Zalman, 186–187
Asad, Hafiz al-, 272, 274–275
'Asali, Talal Abu, 123
Atasi, Nur al-Din al-, 117

Badeau, John, 57
"Baghdad Pact," 20–22, 132
Ball, George, 54–56, 77, 83, 232–233
Bani Sakhr tribe, 250–251
Barbour, Walworth, 60, 83, 126, 169, 193, 213, 220, 224
Bar-Hayim, Shaul, 195–196, 207n58
Bar-Lavi, Ze'ev, 69
Bar-Lev, Hayim, 115, 214–215, 223–228, 255, 270
Barnes, Robert, 75, 83, 89, 114, 121
Barzilai, Yehuda, 146
Barzilai, Yisrael, 215
Ba'thism: Fatah and, 111; in Iraq, 33, 51, 67; Israeli views, 63–64, 128, 130–131, 138n119; in Jordan, 21, 23, 65–66, 126, 143; Nasser and, 51, 65; neo-Ba'thism, 117–126, 130–131, 138n119, 233; in Syria, 63–64, 67, 111, 117–123
Battalions of Victory (Kata'ib al-Nasir), 241

Begin, Menachem, 2; Ben-Gurion vs. 12; expansionism, 2, 91, 168; Gahal party, 163; Herut party, 12, 91; Israeli nuclear program and, 163; Likud party, 277; on the West Bank, 168, 186, 215, 231, 242n11
Ben Bella, Ahmad, 63
Ben-Gurion, David, 9–10, 12–13, 18–20, 25; 1949 armistice, 9–15; on arms race, 38–40; Begin vs. 12; British overflights, 29–30; on great-power involvement, 20, 26, 29, 72n75; Iraq and, 29; on Israel's territorial borders, 9, 19, 56; Jordan and, 27–32, 35–37, 53–57; nuclear program, 26, 40–43, 58–59, 85; Rafi party, 146, 163; retirement of, 20; Suez crisis, 9–10, 20–25, 25; on US-Soviet relations, 37–38, 40, 60, 71n50; US views of, 85–86; West German arms deal, 102n73; Zionism and, 19
Berlin, 3, 37, 40, 59
"Big Lie, The," 182
Bitar, Salah al-Din al-, 117
Black, Eugene, 218
Bourguiba, Habib, 97–98, 264
Brown, George, 149
Brown, L. Dean, 263–264, 272
Bull, Odd, 167
Bundy, McGeorge, 57, 60, 86, 183, 189–194, 232–233
Burns, E. L. M., 25
Burns, Findley, 122, 129, 141–142, 156–157, 182

Cairo emergency summit, 264, 272–275, 273
Cairo summit of 1964, 67, 106–107
Caradon, Lord, 204–205
Carmon, David, 223
Casablanca summit, 77, 93–94
Centurion tanks, 131, 225
Chamoun, Camille, 29
Churchill, Winston, 19, 44n45
Chuvakhin, Dmitri, 98, 127
Circassians, 15
Cohen, Avner, 155

Cold War, 3–4, 96, 278; détente and Arab-Israeli conflict, 62, 81, 98. *See also* Soviet Union; United States
Comay, Michael, 127
covert action, 18, 64
cross-border attacks, 5, 61, 116–117, 152–153
Crown Prince Hassan. *See* Hassan, Crown Prince
Cuban missile crisis, 59, 94

Dablan, Tahir, 241
Danin, Ezra, 109
Dawson's Field, 262–263
Dayan, Moshe, 1, 16–17, 216; fida'iyyun policy, 223–224; Israeli cabinet crisis, 231–232; Israeli-occupied West Bank, 215, 226–227, 230–236, 290–291; on Israel's borders, 90–91, 168; Jordanian civil war, 257–259; Jordanian crisis of 1963, 53–54; Meir and, 254; nuclear program, 62, 163, 277; Six-Day War, 163, 168, 177–178, 184–187, 198–201; Suez, 20–21
de Gaulle, Charles, 64
Democratic Front for the Liberation of Palestine (PDFLP), 262
Desert Forces, 234, 251
détente, 62, 81, 98
Dimona nuclear reactor, 26, 42; as bargaining chip, 150; Peres and, 40, 42; as strategic target, 128, 130, 152, 154; US view of, 60–63, 84. *See also* Israeli nuclear program; nuclear nonproliferation
Dubcek, Alexander, 235
Dulles, John Foster, 26–34

East Bank, 6, 30, 195–198; economy of the, 124–125, 148, 181, 124; Jordanian civil war, 256–258, 265, 270–271, 279–281; Palestinian guerillas in, 189, 221–226, 250–252; Palestinian representation and, 68, 107; refugees in, 178–181, 189; strategic place of, 86, 88–89, 188. *See also* Palestine and Palestinians; West Bank
East Ghor Canal, 75, 124, 221, 250
Eban, Abba, 18; on great power involvement, 30–31; on Israel's borders, 90; on Israeli-occupied West Bank, 201, 203, 212, 217–220, 223–233, 236–241, 255–256; meeting with Hussein, 229; before the Knesset, 97, 127; meeting with LBJ, 154–155; on Palestinian terrorism, 109, 122, 220, 249; Six-Day War, 181–183, 185–186, 189, 193–194; Soviet Union and, 82, 98, 172n61; UN and, 127; US and, 30–31, 98, 105, 154–155, 185, 189–190, 218, 239–241, 255
Eden, Anthony, 21
Egypt: Anglo-Egyptian Treaty, 20; anti-Hashemite propaganda, 52; Arab Solidarity Agreement, 27; decline of, 94–96; Egypt-Syria mutual defense pact, 128; Eisenhower's policy on, 20, 28; Eshkol on, 98–99, 154, 161–164; Iraq and, 29, 51–52; Israeli-Jordanian relations and, 34–38, 65–66, 87–89, 92–93; Israeli intelligence on, 4, 37–38, 98, 150–151, 154, 190–191, 207n58; regional mutual defense treaties, 23; Jordan and, 49–50, 65–68 (*see also* Nasser, Gamal Abdul); Jordanian independence and, 27–29, 35–37, 46n123, 52–57, 65–69; nuclear weapons and, 150–151; Palestinians and, 106–109, 110–112, 120–121, 201–202; Rotem crisis, 38–40, 58; Samu' raid and after, 105, 140–147; Saudi Arabia and, 50, 94, 201; Six-Day War and after, 1, 153–154, 156–169, 161, 180–183, 201–202, 217–223, 227–228, 233; Soviet Union and, 31, 38, 77–78, 94–95, 98–99, 172n62; Suez crisis and after, 20–23, 24; Syria and, 40, 127–130, 138n119; US and, 20, 27–28, 30–34, 37–38, 57–63, 81–84, 94, 217–223, 227–228, 233; USSR and, 94–95, 98; Yemen, 58, 65, 67–68, 76, 93–94, 120, 143–144, 201. *See also* Arab summitry; Nasser, Gamal Abdul
Eilat incident, 223
Eisenhower, Dwight, 20–21, 24, 27–29, 31–33; Egypt and, 20, 28; Iraq and, 29; Jordan and, 27–28; Suez and, 20–21, 24; water issues and, 75
Elath, Eliyahu, 22, 36
Elazar, David "Dado," 166

Erhard, Ludwig, 82
Eshkol, Levi, 61–65, 66, 92, 216, 254; Arab world outreach, 63–64; Ba'thism, 63–64, 130–131; battle of Karameh and after, 220–226; covert operations under, 64; domestic politics during, 178; Egypt and, 98–99, 154, 161–164; Eliat incident and after, 223–224; Israeli nuclear program, 62–63, 80, 85–86, 89–90, 103n82, 150, 163; Jordan and, 68–69, 87–90, 99, 101n39, 112–113, 130–131, 140, 142, 145–146, 149–150; Jordanian arms deal, 81–84, 85–87, 87–90, 101n39, 102n73; Knesset Foreign Affairs and Defense Committee (KFADC), 151; Samu' raid and after, 128–133, 146, 149–156; Six-Day War and after, 177–178, 184–191, 193–196, 198, 200–204; Soviet Union and, 81–82, 98, 101n42, 127, 150, 161–162; Syria and, 117–120, 125–128, 146; UN and, 127, 167–169; US and, 62–63, 72n75, 79–92, 101n39, 101n42, 154–155, 164, 182 (*see also* Jarring mission; Kennedy, John F.; Johnson, Lyndon B.); West Bank Palestinian guerillas, 106, 112–120, 125–133, 184–191, 211–217, 225–239

Fadhil, Sa'id Muhammad 'Ali al-, 143
Faris, 'Abd al-Ra'uf al-, 125
Fatah (Palestinian National Liberation Movement), 110–120, 125–126, 134n28, 134n41, 138n125; battle of Karameh, 220–226; Jordanian civil war, 249–252, 262–263
Fawzi, Ahmad, 252
Fawzi, Mahmud, 1, 153
Faysal of Saudi Arabia, 203–204
Faysal of Syria, 11
Feldman, Mike, 79
fida'iyyun, 106, 132–133, 211–212, 221–226, 233–234, 241–242; Jordanian civil war, 249–253, 255–256, 260–267, 272–275, 282n25; Syrian sponsorship of, 128
Ford, Gerald, 278
Four Power talks, 254
France, 19, 23–24, 29, 64, 212
Gahal party, 91, 163, 187

Galili, Yisrael, 42, 215, 242n11
Gardiner, Toni, 46n123
Gaza Strip, 179, 185; as bargaining chip, 192, 249, 275; Palestinian state in, 185; refugee camps of, 24–25; Suez crisis and after, 5, 24–25, 178, 276
Gazit, Mordechai: on arms race, 81–82, 86, 114, 147–149; on Jordan, 55, 39n101
Gazit, Shlomo, 148–149, 185
general strikes, 199, 263
Geva, Yosef, 115
Ghana, 4, 118
Glubb, John Bagot, 11, 21–22
Goldberg, Arthur, 204–205, 218
Gromyko, Andrei, 82, 172n61
al-Gumhurriya, 51
Gush 'Etsiyon, 200–203, 236

Hadow, Michael, 153, 257
Hafiz, Amin al-, 117
Hammarskjold, Dag, 34
Hammuda, Yahya, 225
Hanun, Hilmi, 279
Harel, Isser, 98
Harman, Avraham, 55–56, 80–81, 146, 185
Harriman, Averell, 85–87, 101n44, 103n82; Harriman-Komer Mission, 84, 85–87
Hasan, Khalid and Hani al-, 110
Hassan, Crown Prince, 111, 122
Hashemite monarchy. *See* Jordan; Hussein, King
Hatum, Salim, 122–123, 125, 143, 161
Hawker Hunter aircraft, 50, 131, 167
Haykal, Muhammad Hasanayn, 67, 145
Heath, Edward, 266
Hebron: anti-Hussein demonstrations in, 51–52, 132–133; "district-first" approach, 234–236; Israeli views of, 13, 29, 166, 188–190; Khirbat Rafat attack, 117–118; Palestinian guerillas in, 130–131; Park Hotel incident, 231
Helms, Richard, 164–165, 233
Herbert, Emmanuel, 36, 64, 130, 190, 229
Heroes of the Return (Abtal al-'Awda), 138n125
Herut party, 12, 19, 91

Herzog, Ya'akov, 35, 64–65, 66; Eshkol and, 193; meeting with al-Rifa'i, 233; meetings with Hussein, 64–65, 76–77, 86, 99, 108, 126, 190–191, 205, 228–229, 238–242; Six-Day War and after, 215–217, 228–229, 233, 236, 238–242, 249, 255; Syria, 99; view of Israel's victory, 190
Husayni, Haj Amin al-, 11, 18, 109
Hussein, King, 15, 273; Arab League, 76, 120, 201–202, 219, 253, 264, 272; Eban and, 229, 238–239; Fatah, 111–113, 115–117; France and, 64; Greater Syria, 11, 33–34; Herzog and, 64–65, 76–77, 86, 99, 108, 126, 190–191, 205, 228–229, 238–242; Johnson and, 77–78, 191–192; Jordanian Red Crescent and, 198; LBJ and, 77–78; marriage of, 46n123; Meir secret meeting, 114; Nasser and, 27–28, 49–52, 65–68, 120, 159–162, 159–169, 161, 227–228; overture to US after Iraqi coup, 32–34; Palestinian representation at Cairo summit, 106–107; al-Shuqayri and, 106–110, 113, 120–125, 160–162; United Arab Kingdom plan, 275–276, 279; visit to France, 64; visit to Moscow, 202; visit to the US, 204–205. *See also* Jordan

IDF. *See* Israel Defense Forces (IDF)
Imam al-Badr, 50
Indo-Pakistani peace talks at Tashkent, 98
Indonesia, 4, 118
inter-Arab relations, 4–6. *See also* Arab summitry; Jordanian foreign policy
Iran, 20, 27, 34, 65, 191
Iraq, 4–5, 9–11, 13; Ba'thists in, 33, 51–56, 67; "Baghdad Pact" alliance, 20; chemical weapons, 278; fall of the monarchy, 29–34, 51–56, 67; Hashemite, 13; Iraqi troops in Jordan, 160–163, 165–167, 223–224, 250–251, 275; Israeli covert operations in, 64; Israeli-Jordanian relations and, 34–36; Jordanian independence and, 9–10, 18–19, 22, 28–31, 257, 259–260, 265–267, 270–271; Kurds, 64, 93, 151; Kuwait, 50; Nasser and, 51–52; Qasim, 'Abd al-Karim, 29, 31, 33; UK and, 22

irredentism, 10, 41, 90–91, 214
Israel: cabinet crisis, 231–232; elections of 1965, 86, 90–91; Knesset, 39, 76, 97, 109, 151–152, 188–189, 191, 195, 256. *See also* Israeli foreign policy; Israeli-Jordanian relations; Israeli nuclear program; *individual political parties and politicians*
Israel Defense Forces (IDF), 11–15, 17–20, 34–42; Arad incident, 130; Jordanian crisis of 1963, 52–59; Jordanian independence and, 24–25; Karameh, battle of, 220–229, 225–226; LAVI war plan, 17; MACCABBI, 151; MATTITYAHU war plan, 41; nuclear program, 48n166, 80, 90; PLO, 108; preemptive vs preventative war, 6, 20–21, 39–41, 91–93; retaliation against Palestinian guerillas, 111–117, 129 (*see also* Samu' raid); Rotem episode, 38–40, 58; Sayeret Matkal, 163; Six-Day War and after, 151–156, 165–169, 211–215; strategic depth, 3–4, 6, 90–93, 277; Suez crisis, 22–25; Syrian water diversion, 76; war plans, 17, 41, 71n39, 151; West Bank occupation, 184–185, 191, 196, 200, 211–215, 221, 223–224
Israeli foreign policy: after the Samu' raid, 145–154; Arab "pluralism" vs. Arab "realism," 97; Ba'thist coup in Syria, 118–119; before the Six-Day War, 162–166; covert operations in Iraq and Yemen, 64; decline of Nasserism, 96–99; Egypt and, 20–23; Fatah and Jordan, 111–117; fear of *mikreh ha-kol* (an all-Arab attack), 94; influence on US, 30; interest in independent Jordan: Jordan and, 3–6, 9–20, 26–29, 99; Jordanian arms deals, 79–87; Khartoum summit, 202; maps of, *8, 189*; National Water Carrier, 67, 75 (see also water issues); occupied territories, 7n5, *179*; on the PLO, 108–109, 111; "open bridges" policy, 198; outreach to USSR, 81–82; Samu' raid and after, 105, 128–133, 140, 141–153; support for an independent Palestine, 289; US and, 79–82 (*see also* United States; *individual presidents*); West German arms deal, 81–82, 88, 102n73. *See also* AMAN;

Israel Defense Forces (IDF); Mossad; *individual politicians and policymakers*
Israeli-Jordanian relations, 9–15; entente, 5, 34–43, 74–104, 140–176; Jordanian crisis of 1963, 52–57, 63–69; Jordanian-Egyptian relations, 65–68
Israeli nuclear program: Allon on, 42; Begin on, 163; Ben-Gurion on, 26, 40–43, 58–59, 85; Dayan on, 62, 163, 277; Eshkol, 62–63, 80, 85–86, 89–90, 103n82, 150, 163; Jordanian crisis of 1963, 58–63; Kennedy on, 42, 57, 59–63; Meir on, 42, 62, 63; Mossad on, 150, 172n63; nonproliferation and, 277; nuclear nonproliferation, 6, 59, 277, 287n177; Shimon Peres and, 26, 40–42, 150–151, 163; start of, 26; support for, 41–42; US and, 58–63, 84, 90; Yom Kippur war and, 277. *See also* Dimona nuclear reactor; nuclear nonproliferation
Israel Workers' List. *See* Rafi party

JAA. *See* Jordan Arab Army (JAA)
Ja'bari, Muhammad'Ali al-, 234
Jadid, Salah, 117
Jarring, Gunnar, 217–220, 224, 227–234, 238–240, 254
Jerusalem: anti-Hussein demonstrations in, 51–52; Jewish Quarter of the Old City, 29–31; Mount Scopus, 29, 31, 54, 71n39, 103n97, 167–168; Romema bombing, 126
Johnson, Lyndon B., 77–90; Eshkol and, 80–81, 87–90, 101n39, 102n73, 155, 216; "five principles" for Arab-Israeli peace, 183; food aid to Egypt, 83; Harriman-Komer mission, 85–87; Hussein and, 77–78, 191–192; Israel and, 84–87; Israeli arms deals, 89–90, 212–213, 216–217; Israeli views of, 80–82; Jordan and, 85–87; Jordan-first approach, 13, 159, 253–255, 291–292; Jordanian arms, 77–79, 84; nonaligned leaders and, 94; Saudi Arabia and, 203–204
Johnston, Charles, 34
Johnston, Eric, 75
Johnston Plan, 75–76, 98–99

Joint Chiefs of Staff, 78, 266, 268
Jordan: Abdullah, 10–15; after civil war, 178–179; after the Samu' raid, 141–145; Ba'thism in, 21, 23, 65–66, 126, 143; economy of, 35, 96, 280; Six-Day War and after, 177–181, 190–192, 196–201, 219–220; Talal, 15; tourism, 96, 124–125, 249. *See also* Israeli-Jordanian relations; Jordan Arab Army (JAA); Jordanian foreign policy; King Hussein
Jordan Arab Army (JAA), 21–23; Jordanian civil war, 249–253, 262–265, 272, 274; opposition to Hussein's marriage, 46n123; Palestine Liberation Army (PLA), 107–108; Samu' raid and after, 131–132; Unified Arab Command (UAC), 77–78; US-Jordanian arms deal and, 86–89
Jordanian Communist Party, 21
Jordanian domestic politics, 21–22, 123–124; 1958 crisis, 26–32; 1963 crisis, 49–73; April 27 coup scare, 54, 56–57; Ba'thist crackdowns, 66, 120; Baghdad pact riots, 21; demonstrations in, 51, 105, 132; economic inequality in, 124–125; impact of Suez, 26; Jordanian civil war, 261–288; parliamentary elections, 22–23
Jordanian foreign policy: Arab League, 76, 120, 201–202, 219, 253, 264, 272; arms deals, 78–79, 81–87; Czechoslovakia and, 64; Egypt and, 49–50, 65–68 (*see also* Nasser, Gamal Abdul); Hatum plot in Syria, 122–123; Palestine, 5, 10, 15, 123–124, 132, 215 (*see also* Palestine and Palestinians; Palestine Liberation Organization [PLO]; West Bank); Palestinian refugees, 10, 14, 132, 214, 219; Poland and, 64; proxy war against Syria, 161; regional mutual defense treaties, 23; retaliatory raids by Israel, 111, 112—115 (*see also* Samu' raid); Samu' raid and after, 105, 128–133, 140, 141–153; US and, 142, 249–250, 252–254; Yemen, 49–50. *See also* Egypt; Israeli-Jordanian relations; Palestine and Palestinians
Jordanian Red Crescent, 198
Jum'a, Sa'd, 145, 156–157, 180, 196–197

Karameh, battle of, 220–229, 225–226
Kata'ib al-Nasir (Battalions of Victory), 241
Katzenbach, Nicholas, 191–192, 218
Kayid, Hasan al-, 222–223
Kaylani, Muhammad Rasul al-, 113, 123, 222, 250–251, 281n11
Kennedy, John F.: Eshkol and, 62–63; Iraq and, 53, 67; Israeli nuclear program, 42, 57, 59–63; Israeli views of, 38, 40, 42, 53; Jordanian crisis of 1963, 54–55, 57; Jordanian views of, 64, 67; nonalignment and, 34, 94; Yemen and, 50, 53
KFADC. See Knesset Foreign Affairs and Defense Committee (KFADC)
Kfar Ruppin kibbutz, 221
Khalaf, Salah, 110
Khammash, 'Amir, 78–79, 83, 142–143, 157, 162, 250–251
Khartoum summit, 201–203
Khatib, Ruhi al-, 125, 197–198
Khayri, 'Abd al-Maksud al-, 125
Khirbat Rafat, Israeli attack on, 117
Khrushchev, Nikita, 24, 31, 40–41, 81–82, 94; calling for Arab-Israeli settlement, 41; visit to Cairo, 77–78
Kimche, David, 207n58
King Hussein. See Hussein, King
King Sa'ud. See Sa'ud, King
Kirkbride, Alec, 13
Kissinger, Henry, 253–255, 259–260, 266–271, 276–278
Knesset, 188–189, 191
Knesset Foreign Affairs and Defense Committee (KFADC), 39, 76, 97, 109, 151–152, 195, 256
Komer, Robert, 60–61, 78–81, 84, 85–87, 146
Kurds, 64, 93, 151
Kuwait, 50, 110, 116
Kuzbari, Ma'amun al-, 50
Ladgham, Bahi, 272, 274
Laos, 96
Laskov, Chaim, 29, 37
LAVI war plan, 17
Lavon, Pinhas, 20

Lebanon, 7, 22, 30, 65, 260, 284n70; Fatah in, 110, 116; military power of, 58, 76–77; Syria and, 50; water diversion and, 67, 75–76
Levinger, Rabbi Moshe, 231
Liberal Party, 91
Liberation Party (Jordan), 21, 23
Libya, 97, 191, 253, 279
Likud party, 277
Lior, Col. Yisrael, 126, 156

MACCABBI, 151
Macmillan, Harold, 29, 40
Macomber, William, 3, 52, 64, 142
Majali, Hazza' al-, 33, 35–36
Makhus, Ibrahim, 117–118
Maki party, 98
MAP. See US Military Assistance Program (MAP) funds
Mapai party, 18–19, 85–86, 90–91, 186, 215
Mapam party, 12–13, 30, 215
Masri, Hikmat al-, 67, 125
Masri, Ma'zuz al-, 279
Masri, Tahir al-, 280
MATTITYAHU war plan, 41
McCloy, John, 61–63, 82
McNamara, Robert, 54, 78, 164–165, 183
Meir, Golda, 25, 28, 254–255; Arafat, views on, 257, 269; British overflights, 30–31; Dayan and, 254; Fatah, 114–115; Hussein, secret meeting with, 114; Israeli nuclear program, 42, 62, 63; Israeli-occupied West Bank, 194, 275–278; Jordanian arms deals, 81, 88, 101n39; Jordanian independence and, 35, 39n101, 52–53, 101n39, 68–69, 83–84, 248, 284n70; Knesset Foreign Affairs and Defense Committee (KFADC) statements, 76, 109; Nixon and, 267–271; PLO, 109; United Arab Kingdom plan, 275–276; United Arab Republic (UAR), 28; United States and, 35, 88, 115, 254–261, 267–271, 284n70; US support for Persian Gulf monarchies, 284n70; water issues, 76; Yemen, 53; Zionism, 28, 68
Meron, Theodore, 200

Middle East. *See* Arab-Israeli conflict
mikreh ha-kol (an all-Arab attack), 94
"mini-PARGOL" plan, 168. *See also* Operation PARGOL
Mollet, Guy, 22
Moorer, Thomas, 266
Morocco, 97, 191, 284n70
moshavim (cooperative agricultural communities), 221
Mossad, 146–147; Egypt and, 4, 98, 150–151, 190–191, 207n58; on nuclear weapons, 150, 172n63. *See also* Amit, Meir
Mount Scopus (Jerusalem), 29, 31, 54, 71n39, 103n97, 167–168
Mukhayba Dam, 75–76
Muslim Brotherhood, 21, 45n63, 110, 120

Nablus, 13, 41, 124, 185, 219, 279; anti-Hussein demonstrations in, 51–52, 132–133; Israeli occupation of, 184, 199
Nabulsi, Sulayman al-, 23, 26–27, 67, 132, 222–223
"NAHAL outpost" at Gush 'Etsiyon, 200
Narkiss, Uzi, 42, 165, 167–168, 184, 195
Nasir, Sharif, 234, 250–251, 253, 281n11
Nasser, Gamal Abdul, 1, 4, 20–24, 93–99, 95, 161, 290–291; Arab League, 37; "Baghdad Pact" vs., 20–21; Ba'thism, 51, 65; Cairo summit of 1964, 67, 106–107; Hussein and, 27–28, 49–52, 65–68, 120, 159–162, 159–169, 161, 192–194, 227–228, 263; Nasserism, 4, 27–28, 52–57, 96–99, 105; Iraq and, 29; mutual defense pact with Jordan, 161; rise of, 20; Sharif Nasir, 234, 250–251, 253, 281n11; Six-Day War and after, 1, 153–153, 156–169, 161, 180–183, 201–202, 217–223, 227–228, 233; Suez crisis and after, 20–23, 24. *See also* Arab summitry; Egypt
National Religious Party, 187, 231, 277
National Security Action Memorandum, 231, 60
National Security Council (NSC), 28, 32, 142; Robert Komer, 60–61, 78–81, 84, 85–87, 146; Washington Special Actions Group (WSAG), 260–261, 266–268
National Socialist Party, 23, 67
National Water Carrier, 67, 75

Negev, 21, 67, 110, 163. *See also* Dimona nuclear reactor
neo-Ba'thism, 117–126, 130–131, 138n119, 233
Nixon, Richard, 253–255, 291–292; Israel and the NPT, 277, 287n177; Jordanian civil war, 258–261, 265–271. *See also* Kissinger, Henry
Nkrumah, Kwame, 4
nonaligned movement, 4, 21, 37–38, 64, 94–95, 191
Non-Proliferation Treaty (NPT), 277, 287n177
NSC. *See* National Security Council (NSC)
nuclear nonproliferation, 6, 59, 277, 287n177
Numayri, Ja'far al-, 272
Nusayba, Anwar, 51, 219–220, 244n58
Nusayba, Hazim, 160, 181
Nusayrat tribe, 221

O'Connell, Jack, 141
oil, 50, 67, 158
"open bridges" policy, 198
Operation FAJIR, 161
Operation PARGOL, 165–166, 168
"Operation Refugee," 180
Oslo Accords, 278

Pakistan, 20, 98, 141
Palestine and Palestinians, 105–109; idea of an "entity," 106; Jordan and, 5, 10, 15, 123–124, 132, 215, 249–253; Oslo Accords, 278; refugees in Jordan, 10, 14, 132, 214, 219; Six-Day War and after, 185, 195–205, 224–292. *See also* Fatah; fida'iyyun; Palestine Liberation Organization (PLO); West Bank
Palestine Liberation Organization (PLO), 107–110, 241; Arab summitry and, 77, 100n14, 106–107; Jordan and, 107–109, 120, 123–125, 129, 132, 143–144, 226; Jordanian civil war, 262–266, 272–274, 279–281, 292; Oslo Accords, 278; Palestine Liberation Army (PLA), 107–108, 112–113, 132, 162; rivals of, 109 (*see also* Fatah)

Palestine National Congress, 110
Palestine National Council, 225
Palestinian guerillas: Abtal al- 'Awda (Heroes of the Return), 138n125; Democratic Front for the Liberation of Palestine (PDFLP), 262; Popular Front for the Liberation of Palestine (PFLP), 249, 251–253, 262. *See also* Fatah; fida'iyyun; Palestine Liberation Organization (PLO)
Palestinian National Council, 262
Palestinian National Liberation Movement. *See* Fatah
Palmah, 13, 16, 18, 42
Pan-Arabism, 4–5, 11, 27–28, 290. *See also* Nasserism *under* Nasser, Gamal Abdul
Parkes, Roderick, 67
PDFLP. *See* Democratic Front for the Liberation of Palestine (PDFLP)
peacekeepers, 34, 57–58, 148–149, 153, 184; West Bank, 34, 57–58, 148–149, 184
Peres, Shimon, 26; on Jordan, 53, 86–87, 270; Kennedy and, 53; nuclear program, 26, 40–42, 150–151, 163; rivalry with Rabin, 42
PFLP. *See* Popular Front for the Liberation of Palestine (PFLP)
Phantom aircraft, 212–213, 216–218, 224, 239–241
Phillips, J. F. S., 263–264
PLA. *See* Palestine Liberation Army (PLA) *under* Palestine Liberation Organization (PLO)
Plan SHAHAM ("Granite"), 56
Plan X, UAC contingency plan, 122
PLO. *See* Palestine Liberation Organization (PLO)
Popular Front for the Liberation of Palestine (PFLP), 249, 251–253, 262
porshim movement, 231
Protocol of Sevres, 22–23
psychological warfare, 149

Qalqiliya, Israeli raid on, 114
Qasim, 'Abd al-Karim, 29, 31, 33
Queen Zayn. *See* Zayn, Queen

Rabat summit, 219, 278, 280
Rabin, Yitzhak, 37–38, 40–42, 59, 92; Fatah and, 111–120; Israeli nuclear program, 48n166, 80, 85; Jordanian arms sales, 81, 85, 87; Jordanian civil war, 258–259, 261, 268–269, 271; military doctrine, 91–93; Nixon administration and, 254–255; Samu' raid and after, 145–146, 150–156; Six-Day War and after, 162–166, 168, 171n46, 214–215, 227–228; Syria and, 127–131; Unified Arab Command (UAC), 76–77; United States, 79–81; US-Soviet relations, 235–236; water issues and, 93–94; Yom Kippur War, 276–279
Radio Amman, 145, 197
Rafael, Gideon, 7n1, 223–224, 271
Rafi party, 85–86, 91, 146, 163, 215
refugees, 10, 14; Gaza Strip, 24, 186; Israeli policy towards, 24–25, 164, 178; resettlement of, 186, 189, 198, 258
Resolution 242, 177, 201–205, 217–219, 228–235, 238–242
Rifa'i, 'Abd al-Mun'im al-, 33, 160, 249
Rifa'i, Samir al-, 32–33
Rifa'i, Zayd al-, 167, 229, 233, 238–239, 249–250, 252, 254–255
Riyadh, 'Abd al-Mun'im, 145, 157, 160–161, 167
Riyadh, Mahmud, 218, 239–240
Rogers Plan, 255
Rogers, William, 254–255
Rostow, Walt: on arms sales to Israel, 218; on Israeli ambitions, 164, 240; on Jordan, 142, 158, 233; Six-Day War and after, 182–183, 204, 228, 230
Rotem crisis, 38–40, 58
Rusk, Dean: arms control and, 61, 63, 172n61; arms sales to Israel, 82, 216–217; arms sales to Jordan, 78; meeting with Meir, 115; Six-Day War and after, 183, 189, 193, 204, 218, 239–240

Salt, Barbara, 29
Samu' raid, 105, 128–133, 140, 141–153
Sapir, Pinhas, 186, 200

Sapir, Yosef, 187
Sasson, Eliyahu, 186, 215
Sasson, Moshe, 126, 185, 195, 207n58, 219–220, 226, 248
Sa'ud, King, 50
Saudi Arabia: Egypt and, 50, 94, 201; Eisenhower and, 28; inter-Arab mutual defense, 23, 27; Johnson and, 203–204; Jordan and, 23, 50, 120, 143, 280; Kennedy and, 50; Khartoum summit, 201, 203–204; Syria and, 50, 120–121; West Germany and, 97; Yemen and, 50, 94
Saunders, Harold, 164, 260
Sayeret Matkal, 163
Sha'ar ha-Golan mine incident, 126–127
Shapira, Ya'akov Shimshon, 186–187
Sharaf, Sami, 57
Sharett, Moshe, 16–18, 20–22
Sharif Nasir. *See* Nasir, Sharif
Sharm al-Shaykh, 87, 236, 240
shema prayer, 146, 171n44
Sherman M-51 tanks, 131, 225
Shiloah, Reuven, 14, 24
Shuqayri, Ahmad al-: Alexandria summit, 107; Khartoum summit, 201–202; King Hussein and, 106–110, 113, 120–125, 160–162; on the Arab League Council, 68
Sisco, Joseph, 249, 255, 258–262, 266–268, 271, 282n25
Six-Day War, 1–8, 167–169; Arab views of, 1; settlement, 177–210, 211–247; start of, 153–156
Skyhawk aircraft, 89–90, 212–213, 216–217
Sneh, Moshe, 98, 174n124
South Korea, 96
South Vietnam, 96
Soviet Union, 5–6, 20–21, 26–29, 81–82, 290; on arms race, 172n61; Cyprus and, 98; Czechoslovakia, invasion of, 235; Egypt and, 31, 38, 94–95, 98–99, 172n62; Geneva talks, 82; Israel and, 101n42, 150, 181; Jordan and, 77–79, 83–84, 88, 226–227; Jordanian civil war, 253–262, 267, 269–271, 276–277; Samu' raid and after, 141–142; Six-Day War and after, 153, 155, 161–162, 181, 192–194, 202–204, 206n20, 235–236; Syria and, 118–120, 127, 128, 138n119; Tashkent Indo-Pakistani peace talks, 98

"Steve," 98
Stevenson, Adlai, 75
Stewart, Michael, 256–257
Straits of Tiran, 1; closure of, 39, 153–155, 158, 163, 186; Israeli navigation rights in, 103n97
Sudan, 253, 272
Suez Canal: incidents along, 235, 249; Israeli navigation through, 40, 98–99, 185–186, 240; strategic weaknesses, 59, 235, 267, 270
Suez crisis, 9, 20–23, 24–26, 181–182; Israel, impact on, 29, 39–41, 53, 57, 91–92; Jordan, impact on, 26, 182, 191
Sukarno, 4
Symmes, Harold, 252, 259–260, 281n11, 282n25
Syria, 4–5; anti-Hashemite propaganda, 52; Arab Solidarity Agreement, 27; Arad incident, 129; Ba'thism in, 63–64, 67, 111, 117–123; Egypt and, 40, 127–130, 138n119; Fatah targets in, 134n28; Hussein's Greater Syria, 11, 33–34; Israeli retaliation in, 111, 127–128; Jordan-Syrian relations, 26–27, 168, 270, 279; Lebanon and, 50; Saudi Arabia and, 50, 120–121; United Arab Republic (UAR), 28

Tal, Wasfi al-, 36–37, 49–50, 70n2, 144–145, 275; on Egypt, 96, 143; opponents of, 159–160; on Palestinians, 113–116, 123–124; on Syria, 121–123, 143; Samu' raid, 128–129
Tal al-Arba'in, Israeli attack on, 117–118
Talbot, Phillips, 83
Talhuni, Bahjat al-, 68, 96, 143–145, 180, 222–224, 234, 249
Tashkent peace talks, 98
Tel-Aviv–Jerusalem railway, 152
Thant, U, 52, 153
Tiberias, 119, 152
tourism, 96, 124–125, 249
Transjordan, 11, 13–14, 37, 180
Tsur, Tsvi, 36–37, 39–42, 52–54, 58–59
Tunisia, 97–98, 191, 264, 272, 284n70
Tuqan, Ahmad, 159–160, 280
Tuqan, Qadri, 125
Turkey, 20, 27, 65
Two Power talks, 254–255

UAC. See Unified Arab Command (UAC)
UAR. See United Arab Republic (UAR)
UNEF. See United Nations Emergency Force (UNEF)
Unified Arab Command (UAC), 67, 76–79, 109, 117; arms sales to Jordan, 77–79, 83, 88; Jordan Arab Army (JAA) and, 77–78
United Arab Kingdom Plan, 275–276, 279
United Arab Republic (UAR), 28, 33, 35–37, 40
United Kingdom, 9, 11–15, 19; Aden protectorate, 94; Cyprus, 24–25; Dawson's Field, 262–263; Jordanian civil war and, 256–257, 266–268; overflights in Jordan, 29–31; Suez crisis, 20–24
USSR. See Soviet Union
United Nations: Jordanian-Egyptian relations and, 52; peacekeepers, 34, 57–58, 148–149, 153, 184; Security Council Resolution 242, 177, 201–205, 217–219, 228–235, 238–242; Security Council Resolution, 248, 227; after the Six-Day War, 192–205; after Suez, 24; Syrian counterattack on Israel, 178; West Bank peacekeepers, 34, 57–58, 148–149, 184
United Nations Emergency Force (UNEF), 58, 144, 153–154, 184
United Nations Relief and Work Agency (UNRWA), 124, 143
United Nations Truce Supervision Organization (UNTSO), 25, 167
United States: American Jewish community, 79–80; Dimona reactor, 60–63, 84; Egypt and, 20, 27–28, 30–34, 37–38, 57–63, 81–84, 94, 217–223, 227–228, 233; Harriman-Komer Mission, 84, 85–87; Israeli and Jordanian MOUs, 87–89, 92–93; Israeli arms deals, 89–90, 212–213, 216–217; Israeli nuclear program, 58–63, 84, 90; Jordan River diversion plans, 75–76; Jordanian arms deals, 79–87, 101n39; Jordanian civil war and, 253–255, 258–261, 266–271; Jordanian crisis of 1963, 53–57; Jordanian relations, 32–34, 37, 87–89; Khartoum summit, 203; Palestinian guerillas, 114–115; Pan-Arabism and, 27–28; Six-Day War and after, 181–184, 189–190, 191–192; West German arms deal, 81–82, 88, 102n73
UNRWA. See United Nations Relief and Work Agency (UNRWA)
US Military Assistance Program (MAP) funds, 80

Vietnam War, 96, 232, 253; guerilla warfare and, 117–119, 147, 225, 256

Wadi 'Ara area, 12
Wahdat refugee camp, 252, 264
Warhaftig, Zerah, 59, 155, 231
Washington Special Actions Group (WSAG), 260–261, 266–268
water issues: Arab water diversion plans, 67–68, 75–76, 85–86, 93–94, 111; East Ghor Canal, 75, 124; Israeli's National Water Carrier, 67, 75; Mukhayba Dam, 75–76
Wazir, Khalil al-, 110
Weizman, Ezer, 41, 156
West Bank: Allon on, 53–54, 168–169, 187–189, 194–195 (see also Allon Plan); Begin on, 168, 186, 215, 231, 242n11; "civil rebellion" in, 198–199; Dayan on, 215, 226–227, 230–236, 290–291; Eban on, 201, 203, 212, 217–220, 223–233, 236–241, 255–256; general strike, 199; Hussein and, 278–281, 292; Israeli occupation after the Six-Day War, 177–178, 184–191, 233–235; Israeli settlements in, 190, 200–201, 221; King Abdullah and, 10–14; leadership of, 195–196; Plan SHAHAM ("Granite"), 56; "state of Ishmael," 185; UN peacekeepers, 34, 57–58, 148–149, 184. See also East Bank; Palestine and Palestinians
West Germany, 59, 81–82, 88, 97, 102n73
WSAG. See Washington Special Actions Group (WSAG)

Yafeh, Aviad, 114, 193, 215
Yahil, Hayim, 56–57
Yariv, Aharon: on Egypt, 128, 151, 171n46; on Jordan, 153, 146, 171n46, 180, 182, 213–214, 222–224; on Palestinian at-

tacks, 108, 111, 182, 256; on Syria, 128; on the battle of Karameh, 225; on the Samu' raid, 146; on the Soviet Union, 172n62, 206n20
Yemen, 50–51; Jordan's involvement in, 50–51; Meir on, 53; Nasser's involvement in, 58, 65, 67–68, 76, 93–94, 120, 143–144, 201; US involvement in, 53
Yom Kippur War, 276
Yost, Charles, 269

Zayd bin Shakir, 253
Zayn, Queen, 15, 22, 34, 64

Zamir, Tsvi, 115, 119
Ze'evi, Rehavam, 185
Zionism, 10–13; Arab anti-Zionism, 15–16, 190; Ben-Gurion and, 19; Eban and, 18; Eshkol on, 231–232; expansionism and, 90; General Zionists, 19; Gush 'Etsiyon, 200–203, 236; Meir and, 28, 68; Palmah, 13, 16, 18, 42; partition of Palestine, 10–11; United States and, 80
Zorea, Meir, 39
Zu'ayyin, Yusuf, 117
Zurhellen, Owen, 269

AVSHALOM RUBIN is a Middle East analyst at the US Department of State. He received his PhD in Middle Eastern history from the University of Chicago in 2010. He lives in Maryland with his family.

www.ingramcontent.com/pod-product-compliance
Lightning Source LLC
Chambersburg PA
CBHW070259240426
43661CB00057B/2593